Evan Morrison Woodward

History of the third Pennsylvania Reserve

Being a complete Record of the Regiment

Evan Morrison Woodward

History of the third Pennsylvania Reserve
Being a complete Record of the Regiment

ISBN/EAN: 9783337176273

Printed in Europe, USA, Canada, Australia, Japan

Cover: Foto ©ninafisch / pixelio.de

More available books at **www.hansebooks.com**

The History of The 3d Regiment, Pennsylvania Reserve.

By MAJ. E. M. WOODWARD,

Author of The Citizen Soldiery; Our Campaigns; Bonaparte's Park and The Murats; History of Burlington County, N. J.; Old Families of Burlington County, N. J.; etc., etc.

Embellished with four finely-executed Steel Portraits.

327 pages, large type, heavy tinted paper, substantially bound in board and cloth. Full index. Price, $2.50. *Now ready for delivery.*

It contains the only full account ever published of the expedition of General George Crook, ("the Grey Fox" of the Indians,) in West Virginia.

The History of The 198th Regiment, Pennsylvania Volunteers, (Sixth Union League, Phila.)

By MAJ. E. M. WOODWARD.

Embellished with four finely-executed Steel Portraits.

About 200 pages, large type, heavy tinted paper, substantially bound in board and cloth. Full index. Price, $2.00. Will be ready for delivery in November next.

These Regiments were organized by Major General H. G. Sickel, and composed part of his command. Their services jointly covered the period of the existence of the Army of the Potomac, from Drainesville to Appomatox Court House. A correct and vivid description is given of their camps, marches, bivouacs, skirmishes and battles, and of the hardships, joys and glories of the tented field. Also, the personal record of every officer and man during his term of service. Many amusing incidents and anecdotes, illustrative of the life and feelings of a soldier, are also given.

The Journal of General Sickel, the regimental books, the reports of battles and campaigns, the evidence elicited by the Congressional Committee on the Conduct of the War, the maps of the Engineer Bureau, war books, numerous letters from officers and men, the author's journal and knowledge of facts, furnished the material for these histories. The whole manuscript was submitted to the inspection of a number of the officers and men of the Regiments; no statement has been made that did not seem to rest upon authentic information, and the end and aim of the author has been to give clear, truthful and impartial histories of the Regiments and the scenes they participated in. Minor omissions doubtlessly have been made, and errors have crept in—perfection is not claimed.

The History of The 3d Pennsylvania Reserve will be sent to any address, post paid, upon the receipt of the price, $2.50. Postals Notes on Bordentown, N. J., or Bank Checks preferred.

Orders for the History of the 198th Regiment, Pennsylvania Volunteers, received, and book mailed to subscribers in November next.

Address,

E. M. WOODWARD,
ELLISDALE, MONMOUTH CO., NEW JERSEY.

Third Pennsylvania Reserve

HISTORY

OF THE

THIRD PENNSYLVANIA RESERVE

BEING A

COMPLETE RECORD OF THE REGIMENT,

WITH

INCIDENTS OF THE CAMP, MARCHES, BIVOUACS, SKIRMISHES
AND BATTLES; TOGETHER WITH THE PERSONAL
RECORD OF EVERY OFFICER AND MAN
DURING HIS TERM OF SERVICE.

BY

MAJOR E. M. WOODWARD,

AUTHOR OF

*The Citizen Soldiery; Our Campaigns; History of the One Hundred
and Ninety-eighth Pennsylvania Volunteers; Bonaparte's Park
and the Murats; History of Burlington County, N. J.;
Old Families of Burlington County, N. J.*, etc.

EMBELLISHED WITH FOUR STEEL-PLATE PORTRAITS.

TRENTON, N. J.:
MacCrellish & Quigley, Book and Job Printers, 16 E. State St.

1883.

Entered according to Act of Congress, in the year 1883, by
E. M. WOODWARD,
In the Office of the Librarian of Congress, at Washington.

TO THE MEMORY OF

GEORGE GORDON MEADE,

THE HERO OF GETTYSBURG, THE SUCCESSFUL COMMANDER OF THE
ARMY OF THE POTOMAC, AND OF THE RESERVES,

WITH THE

HIGHEST ADMIRATION

OF HIS

DISTINGUISHED ABILITY, UNSELFISH PATRIOTISM
AND CHRISTIAN VIRTUES,

THIS RECORD

OF THE SCENES HE PARTICIPATED IN
IS RESPECTFULLY INSCRIBED BY

THE AUTHOR.

CONTENTS.

CHAPTER I.

DIFFERENCE IN THOUGHTS AND SENTIMENTS — THE THREATS OF THE SOUTH — STATES SECEDE — THE CONFEDERATE STATES — PRESIDENTS DAVIS AND LINCOLN — FALL OF SUMTER — CHARLESTON IN ECSTASY — SEVENTY-FIVE THOUSAND TROOPS CALLED FOR — PENNSYLVANIA'S RESPONSE — ORGANIZATION OF THE RESERVE CORPS — CAMP WASHINGTON — MOTTOES — ORGANIZATION OF THE THIRD — ROSTER OF THE REGIMENT.

CHAPTER II.

BATTLE OF BULL RUN, 1861 — LEAVE CAMP WASHINGTON — CAMP CURTIN — BALTIMORE — WASHINGTON — MUSTERED INTO THE U. S. SERVICE — EXCHANGE OF ARMS — TO TENALLYTOWN — GENERAL M'CALL — SCHOOL OF INSTRUCTION — LIQUOR AND CARDS PROHIBITED — REVIEW OF THE DIVISION — CAPTURE BY PICKETS — REVIEW BY THE PRESIDENT — ALARM — PRESENTATION OF FLAGS — ORGANIZATION OF BRIGADES AND DIVISIONS — THE STAFFS — THE POTOMAC LODGE — STATE ELECTION.

CHAPTER III.

INTO VIRGINIA — CAMP PIERPONT — THE LONG ROLL — DEATH OF PRIVATE SEIFERT — RECONNOISSANCE TO DRAINESVILLE — BALLS BLUFF — REVIEW — MOVE CAMP — RESIGNATIONS AND PROMOTIONS — REVIEW AT MUNSON'S HILL — WINTER QUARTERS — THE COLONEL AND THE DELINQUENTS — BAYARD'S SKIRMISH — FORAGING EXPEDITION — BATTLE OF DRAINESVILLE — GALLANTRY OF LIEUTENANT-COLONEL KANE — CHRISTMAS AND PISTOLS — WINTER — VIRGINIA FAMILY — A BRAVE GIRL — PICKETING — "TAKING FRENCH" — DEATHS AND PROMOTIONS.

CHAPTER IV.

1862 — WAITING FOR THE ADVANCE — JOHNSTON SUPERCEDES BEAUREGARD — ARMY CORPS — OPENING OF THE CAMPAIGN OF 1862 — MARCH OF THE RESERVES — HUNTER'S MILLS — ACTIVE MINDS vs. BODILY

Strength — Patriots Aroused — To Alexandria — Review of the First Corps — Department of the Rappahannock — General M'Dowell — To Manassas Junction — Insurgent Debris — Confederate Eagle — Naughty Boys — Catlett Station — White Ridge — Slaves — The Concealed Flag — A Financial Transaction — Review and Inspection — The President — Fredericksburg — Destruction of the Bridges — In Search of her Husband.

CHAPTER V.

Embarkation for the Peninsula — By Steam to the White House — "For the Embalming the Dead" — Brief Sketch of the Siege of Yorktown — Extracts from "The Lost Cause" — Magruder's Report, and Colonel Fremantle — Generals Barnard, Sumner and Keyes; W. H. Hurlbert and Rev. Mr. Minnigerode, on Fair Oaks — To Dispatch Station — To the Chickahominy — The Third Shelled Out — Courtesy of the Picket Line — A Gallant Dash — Battle of Mechanicsville — Insurgents' Account of the Battle — Meade's Colored Man.

CHAPTER VI.

The Retreat Commenced — Battle of Gaines' Mills — Strength of the Armies — Desperate Fighting — Capture of the Eleventh Reserves and the Fourth N. J. — Re-enforcements Called for — Form for the Last Struggle — Succor Arrives — The Enemy at Bay — The Field Hospital — General Reynolds Captured — The French Princes — An Insurgent's Account of the Reserves — The Loss of the Armies and the Reserves — M'Clellan's Report — Magruder's Report — Crossing the Chickahominy — Trent's Hill — M'Clellan and Lee Deceived — The Retreat Continued — Night March — Savage Station — The Wounded — Movements of the Armies — Battles of Allen's Farm and Savage Station — Stragglers and Camp Followers — A Night on Picket.

CHAPTER VII.

The Battle of Glendale — Simmons' Desperate Charges — Death of Simmons and Biddle — Cooper's and Kerns' Batteries Charged — Glorious Charge of the Ninth — Randall's Battery Charged — The Last Struggle of the Day — Desperate Conflict — Bravery of Captain Tapper — The Battery Demolished — Meade Wounded — M'Call Wounded and Prisoner, His Staff and Escort Killed or Wounded — What M'Call, Lee, Pryor, an Officer of the Confederate Army, M'Clellan, Porter, Meade and Beatty Say About It — To Malvern Hill.

CHAPTER VIII.

The Battle of Malvern Hill — The Field — Feeling our Line — Ominous Stillness — The Three O'clock Assault — The Six O'clock Assault — Fearful Carnage — Utter Repulse and Confusion of the Enemy — General Trimble's Account — Heavy Loss of the Enemy — The Loss of Both Armies in the Seven Days' Battle — Both Armies Retreat — Indignation — Porter's and Hooker's Opinion — Kearny's Protest — Harrison's Landing — Remarks — Libby Prison — Kindness of the Insurgent Privates.

CHAPTER IX.

Putting the Army into Fighting Order — As Bright as New Dollars — Nice Predicament — Visit of the President — Gambling Lieutenant — Resignations and Promotions — Midnight Shelling — The Coles House — Ruffin Fires the First and Last Shot — The Young Spy — Hooker's Fight at Malvern Hill — The Ambulance Corps — M'Call — Reynolds' Sword — Withdrawal of the Army — Abandonment of the Campaign — Cause of its Failure.

CHAPTER X.

The Reserves to the Relief of Pope — Embarkation of the Third — Acquia Creek — Falmouth — Banks at Cedar Mountain — Pope's Movements — Arrival of General Meade — To Rappahannock Station — The First to Join Pope — Warrenton — March — Skirmish — Second Bull Run — Fighting of the 28th — King's Battle — Ricketts' Combat — Topography of Manassas Plains — Fighting of the 29th — Jackson's and Longstreet's Position — The Joint Order — Pope's Mistake — M'Dowell and Porter — Manœuvre — Hard Fighting — Charge a Battery — The 30th — Two Days without Food — The Position of the Armies — Reserves Skirmishing — Discovery of the Thunderbolt — Pope's Plan of Battle — Pope's Fatal Blunder — The Reserves Seize Henry's Hill — Glorious Charge — Incessant Assaults — The Bridge Saved — Orderly Withdrawal — Strength of the Armies — Cause of the Loss of the Battle — General Porter's Case — Centreville — Picket — Battle of Chantilly — Runaway School-Girls.

CHAPTER XI.

POPE SUPERSEDED BY M'CLELLAN — CROSS THE POTOMAC — THE MARCH THROUGH MARYLAND — FREDERICK, EARLY IN THE MORNING — THE BOUQUET OF FLOWERS — WANTED HIS TOOTH PULLED — BATTLE OF SOUTH MOUNTAIN — PLEASANTON ATTACKS — BURNSIDE COMES UP — LONGSTREET SUPERSEDES HILL — FALL OF RENO — HOOKER FLANKS — LAUGHABLE SCENE — RESERVES SCALE THE MOUNTAINS — FREE FIGHT — VICTORY — MARCH — BOONSBORO — PRISONERS.

CHAPTER XII.

BATTLE OF ANTIETAM — STRENGTH OF THE ARMIES — THE RESERVES OPEN THE BATTLE — THE 17TH — ATTACK BEFORE DAYLIGHT — DESPERATE FIGHTING — FALL OF MANSFIELD — "BULL" SUMNER GOES IN — HOOKER WOUNDED — GALLANTRY OF BARLOW — RICHARDSON KILLED — BURNSIDE ON THE LEFT — BRILLIANT CHARGE OF HARTRANFT — LOSS OF THE THIRD — LOSS OF THE TWO ARMIES — TROPHIES — FIELD HOSPITAL — A SURGEON'S DUTY — REBELS RECROSS THE POTOMAC — THE FIELD AFTER THE BATTLE — BURYING THE DEAD — GRIFFIN CAPTURES A BATTERY — STUART REPULSED.

CHAPTER XIII.

THE PRESIDENT'S VISIT — STUART RAIDS TO CHAMBERSBURG — RESIGNATIONS AND PROMOTIONS — THE DOCTOR'S BIRTHDAY — EFFORT TO REORGANIZE THE RESERVES — ONE HUNDRED AND TWENTY-FIRST AND ONE HUNDRED AND FORTY-SECOND REGIMENTS, PENNSYLVANIA VOLUNTEERS — PROMOTION OF REYNOLDS — MEADE COMMANDS THE RESERVES — MARCH TO BERLIN — CROSS THE POTOMAC — SNICKER'S GAP — MIDDLEBURG — PAROLED REBS — WHITE PLAINS — WARRENTON — THE GENEROUS CORPORAL — BURNSIDE SUPERSEDES M'CLELLAN — FITZ JOHN PORTER RELIEVED — PLANS OF CAMPAIGN — THE GRAND DIVISION — TO FAYETTEVILLE — DEPARTURE OF SEYMOUR — BEALTON — HARTWOOD — BROOKE'S STATION — THE PICKET — COOL POLITENESS — MARCH.

CHAPTER XIV.

SUMNER SUMMONS FREDERICKSBURG — BOMBARDMENT — LAYING PONTOONS — BATTLE OF FREDERICKSBURG — THE FIELD, AND STRENGTH OF THE ARMIES — GLORIOUS CHARGE OF THE RESERVES — THE HEIGHTS CARRIED — SUPPORT FAILS — FRANKLIN'S TESTIMONY — MEADE'S REPORT

— LEE'S REPORT — EXTRACT — JACKSON'S LOSS EXCEEDS THE RESERVES' STRENGTH — BACK OF THE CITY, ON THE RIGHT — MARYE'S HEIGHTS — DESPERATE CHARGES — HUMPHREY'S GALLANT BUT FATAL CHARGE — THE LOSS OF THE TWO ARMIES — UNWORTHY OF LEE — JACKSON'S REPORT — DIVINE SERVICE ON THE FIELD — FLAG OF TRUCE — OUR DEAD AND WOUNDED — RE-CROSS THE RIVER — BURNSIDE'S NOBLE QUALITIES.

CHAPTER XV.

MARCH TO WHITE OAK CHURCH — WINTER QUARTERS — GENERAL MEADE PROMOTED — SICKEL SUCCEEDS HIM — BURNSIDE'S MUD EXPEDITION — HOOKER SUPERSEDES BURNSIDE — BELL PLAIN — ALEXANDRIA — SICKEL IN COMMAND OF THE DEFENCES — THE FIRST AND THIRD BRIGADES TO GETTYSBURG — DETAILS — CAPTAIN FISHER'S ESCAPE FROM LIBBY — TWENTY-ONE PATRIOTS — NEW FLAGS — RESIGNATIONS AND PROMOTIONS.

CHAPTER XVI.

1863–64 — MOVE TO MARTINSBURG — NEW CREEK — AFTER ROSSER — BACK TO MARTINSBURG — AFTER GILMORE — TO VANCLEVESVILLE — HARPERS FERRY — TO GRAFTON — WEBSTER — FENCE RAILS — ACCIDENT TO MAJOR BRINER — ARRIVAL OF SICKEL — TO PARKERSBURG — DOWN THE OHIO AND UP THE KANAWHA — BROWNSTOWN.

CHAPTER XVII.

1864 — GENERAL CROOK'S EXPEDITION — ITS STRENGTH — SICKEL COMMANDS THE THIRD BRIGADE — HIS STAFF — THE MARCH — EX-PRESIDENT HAYES — GREAT FALLS — COTTON MOUNTAIN — FAYETTE COURT HOUSE — AVERILL DETACHED — WILD AND RUGGED COUNTRY — THE MOUNTAINEERS — RALEIGH COURT HOUSE — ROSECRANS' TRAIN — THE MOUNTAINS FIRED — SKIRMISH AT PRINCETON COURT HOUSE — INSURGENTS' WORKS — SKIRMISH — WOOLF CREEK — SKIRMISH — CAPTAIN HARMER KILLED — VERY THOUGHTFUL — SHANNON'S BRIDGE — BATTLE OF CLOYD MOUNTAIN — POSTING THE TROOPS — POSITION OF THE ENEMY — CLIMBING THE MOUNTAIN — WOOLWORTH KILLED AND LENHART WOUNDED — SICKEL LAYS LOW AND FLANKS — SWINGING FROM BUSH TO BUSH — STORMING THE WORKS — VICTORY — ON TO DUBLIN — THE WOUNDED AND TROPHIES — THE LOSSES — TELEGRAPHING TO THE INSURGENTS — BRECKENRIDGE DECEIVED — DESTRUCTION OF DEPOTS — TEARING UP THE RAILROAD — BATTLE OF NEW RIVER BRIDGE — DEFEAT OF M'CAUSLAND — DESTRUCTION OF THE BRIDGE.

CHAPTER XVIII.

AVERILL'S FIGHT AT WYTHEVILLE — ATTACKING THE REAR GUARD — THE RETURN MARCH — BLACKSBURG — LA RUE'S SKIRMISH — NINETEENTH VIRGINIA CAVALRY — UNION COURT HOUSE — CROSSING THE GREENBRIER — HARD MARCHES — POOR FORAGING — MEADOW BLUFF — SUFFERING OF THE WOUNDED — LEWISBURG — THE RESERVES' THREE YEARS EXPIRE — THE BATTALION — ITS OFFICERS — FAREWELL TO COMRADES — FACES HOMEWARD — CROSS THE SEWELL — REACH CAMP PIATT — BY STEAMER TO PITTSBURG — BY RAIL TO PHILADELPHIA — THE BAND — THE WELCOME.

ILLUSTRATIONS.

The Author,	Frontispiece.
Major-General H. G. Sickel,	Page 17
Lieutenant Colonel John C. Clark,	Page 202
"Tom,"	Page 118

PREFACE.

SO LONG as the sword is to be the arbitrator of the differences among nations, the only safety that remains to a government is in the courage of its soldiery. In the late struggle the national unity was preserved, the principles of self-government perpetuated, and every man's right to himself established, through the blessing of God and the bravery of the men who carried the musket, and who led in the deadly conflict. It is a pleasing task to record their deeds of valor, their privations, hardships and sufferings, their fidelity and constancy.

While the regiment preserved its identity in battle and throughout the campaign, it also sustained intimate relations to the brigade, division, corps and army. Therefore, in giving its history, so much of the operations of the higher organizations has been given as to show its relations with them and preserve the thread of the general narrative.

The journal of General Sickel, kept on the field, the regimental books, the reports of battles and campaigns made by general officers, the evidence elicited by the Congressional Committee on the Conduct of the War, the maps of the Engineer Bureau, war books, numerous letters from officers and men, the author's journal, and knowledge of facts, furnish the material for this history.

The rolls have been so prepared as to show the main items of the record of each individual soldier, and the lists of the killed, wounded and missing of each battle taken from the company reports. The whole manuscript was submitted to the inspection of a number of officers and men of the regiment, before printing; no statement has been made that did not seem to rest upon authentic information, and the end and aim of the author has been to give a clear, truthful and just history of the regiment and the scenes it participated in. Minor omissions doubtlessly have been made, and errors have crept in—perfection is not claimed.

If the perusal of this volume should interest the reader, or revive in the memory of the participants the happy days of the glorious Reserve, or recall the names of comrades or the loved dead, it will be a high source of gratification to the author.

E. M. W.

ELLISDALE, MONMOUTH CO., N. J.,
May 30th, 1883.

THE THIRD RESERVE.

CHAPTER I.

DIFFERENCE IN THOUGHTS AND SENTIMENTS — THE THREATS OF THE SOUTH — STATES SECEDE — THE CONFEDERATE STATES — PRESIDENTS DAVIS AND LINCOLN — FALL OF SUMTER — CHARLESTON IN ECSTASY — SEVENTY-FIVE THOUSAND TROOPS CALLED FOR — PENNSYLVANIA'S RESPONSE — ORGANIZATION OF THE RESERVE CORPS — CAMP WASHINGTON — MOTTOES — ORGANIZATION OF THE THIRD — ROSTER OF THE REGIMENT.

WHEN the Northern war-drum tapped in response to Sumter's guns, it awoke in the loyal heart a sad but firm resolve to sustain the government at any sacrifice, and the world witnessed such an uprising of the masses as history never recorded. In the North, slavery had long been looked upon as a great wrong, and a violation of the rights of man. Still, under the compact of the Constitution, they deemed themselves bound to respect its existence in its locality, but were firmly resolved not to submit to its extension into the territories. The declaration of the leading men and newspapers of the South, that the election of Abraham Lincoln, which the division of their party had made evitable, would be followed by the dissolution of the Union, and the measures taken by the Legislature of South Carolina in case of his election, clearly indicated their determination to destroy the government they could no longer control.

On the 20th of December, 1860, a few days after the result of the election was known, the State of South Carolina formally seceded from the Union. Other States followed her lead in rapid succession, and on the 9th of February, a Southern Convention elected Jefferson Davis President of the "Confederate States of America." They adopted a Constitution, and proceeded to organize their new government by the creation of Departments of State, Judiciary, War, Navy, etc.; to raise, arm, equip and drill a large army, seize the forts, arsenals, barracks, vessels, navy yards and public buildings of the United States, and accredit agents abroad to foreign governments; and upon the inauguration of Mr. Lincoln, he found a hostile government within the limits of the United States.

He had but one duty to perform, and God gave him the light to see it, and the firm resolution to keep steady to his purpose until it was accomplished—the Union saved. And how trifling was the precious blood the warm hearts poured out, and the treasures spent, in comparison with the rich birth-right secured to the living and to the millions unborn.

When Mr. Lincoln assumed charge of the government, he found the army scattered and disintegrated; the navy sent to distant quarters of the globe; the Northern arsenals depleted of arms; the treasury bankrupt; the credit of the United States seriously injured by forced sales of Government securities; the public service demoralized; the various Departments of the Government filled with unfaithful clerks and officers, whose sympathies were with the South, who had been placed in their positions for the purpose of paralyzing his administration. But he drew around him trusty and wise counselors, and proceeded quietly to mature his plans and prepare for the coming storm.

Five months had nearly elapsed since the secession movement was formally inaugurated, and its plotters and upholders were reduced to the choice of either attacking the Union, and thus provoking a war, or sinking gradually but surely out of existence beneath a general appreciation of their own weakness, insecurity, and the stagnation of business. On the 14th of April, the starry flag of freedom was lowered and that of treason and slavery hoisted in its stead, over Sumter's walls. Charleston was drunk with excitement and joyous exultation. Seven thousand men had overcome seventy! Her white population and her gay crowds of visitors thronged her streets and quays. The houses of her wealthy citizens were thrown open, and all were welcomed to enter and partake. Champagne flowed on every hand like water; thousands quaffed and feasted on the richest viands, and, amid the chiming of bells, the firing of cannon and cheers of the citizens, South Carolina took her position as the first nation on the planet. Beauregard at once rose to the altitude of the world's greatest captain, and his achievement ranked with the most memorable deeds of Alexander or Napoleon. Already, in their imagination, the Confederacy had established its independence beyond dispute, and its chivalry was about to start upon its triumphal march, to conquer and despoil the rich cities of the cowardly shop-keepers and mechanics of the North.

On the 15th of April, 1861, President Lincoln issued a proclamation, calling out 75,000 three-months volunteers, to maintain the laws of the United States, and admonishing the insurgents to lay down their arms and quietly submit to the laws within twenty days. It was received with the wildest enthusiasm throughout the North, and in Philadelphia business was suspended, rendezvous opened, and the enrollment and drilling of volunteers commenced. Recruiting parties traversed the city in every direction, the armories of the volunteer companies were crowded to overflowing with men constantly drilling, the public parks were used for the same purpose, and the quietude of the Sabbath was forgotten amidst the preparation for war.

The quota of Pennsylvania was fourteen regiments, and in three days after the call, six hundred men—the first to arrive for its defence—were placed in the national capitol at Washington, and ten days later twenty-five regiments were organized and put in the field, eleven more than the State quota. In addition to this, the Governor was forced to refuse the services of thirty more regiments. The second call was made upon the State in May, for ten regiments; which was simply credited to her, as she had already furnished more than her two quotas.

An extra session of the Legislature of Pennsylvania convened on the 30th of April, and, fully appreciating the magnitude of the war, wisely resolved, in accordance with Governor Curtin's recommendation, to organize, arm, and equip a division, to be called, "The Reserve Volunteer Corps of the Commonwealth," and to be composed of thirteen regiments of infantry, one of cavalry, and one of light artillery, to be held in readiness to obey any requisition of the President on the State for troops. In organizing this division, the conception of which originated with the Governor, the greatest difficulty he experienced was, not in finding officers and men to fill it, but to select from the numerous applicants who beset him at all hours of the night and day in every place he could be found. His Excellency having resolved that the division should be a true type of Pennsylvania, proportioned it among the different counties, so that every township should be represented in it.

Among the regiments organized in Philadelphia at that time, were those of Mann's,* March's and De Korponay's,† from the first of which eight companies were accepted, from the second, seven, and from the last, five. All were mustered into the State service the latter part of May, by Captain Henry J. Biddle, Assistant Adjutant-General of the Division, at the Girard House, where the men were subjected to the most severe examination by the surgeons, who required every one to strip, and rejected all who had the least blemish or defect. The Surgeon-General of the State

---

* William B. Mann, District Attorney of Philadelphia.

† Lieutenant Colonel, Colonel Twenty-eighth Pennsylvania Volunteers.

afterwards pronounced them the finest formed and hardiest body of men he had ever seen collected in one division.

About the same time, Captain H. G. Sickel organized the Ontario Guards, and Captains J. O. Finnie, P. I. Smith, and G. A. and E. M. Woodward, of the DeKorponay regiment, received orders to report to him, and with their companies to proceed to Easton, Pa. Accordingly, on the morning of the 30th of May, they marched to Broad and Green streets, where they found the guards formed, and the battalion, under the command of Captain Sickel, proceeded to Master and America streets, where they took a special train on the North Pennsylvania Railroad to near Easton, where they arrived during the afternoon, and, crossing the Lehigh, marched through the city and out to Camp Washington, where quarters were assigned them to the right of Colonel Mann's regiment.

The camp was on the Fair Grounds, which covered about thirty-five acres, situated on an elevated plateau near the Lehigh river. On the east and north sides of the enclosure were long rows of bunk-rooms, three of which were assigned to each company, and in front of which were the kitchens, facing inwards; and outside of these were the officers' quarters, facing outwards. To the west, occupying about two-thirds of the enclosure, was the race-course, and in the centre was the large fair-building, from whose roof rose a stately dome, from the balcony of which was presented a magnificent view of the surrounding country.

Soon after arriving in camp, the men were furnished with a day's ration, fuel, knives, forks, spoons, tin cups and plates, and plenty of straw to sleep upon. Colonel Mann, commanding camp, the next day issued the following calls:

Reveille, 4 A.M.	Fatigue, 7:45 A.M.	Dress Parade, 6 P.M.
Drill, 4:30 A.M.	Sick Call, 8 A.M.	Recall, 7 P.M.
Recall, 6 A.M.	Drill, 9 A.M.	Supper, 7:30 P.M.
Breakfast, 7 A.M.	Recall, 10 A.M.	Tattoo, 9 P.M.
Guard Mounting, 7:30 A.M.	Orderlies' Call, 12 M.	Taps, 9:30 P.M.
	Dinner, 12:30 P.M.	

Four roll-calls were had each day, and in a little time everything worked smoothly.

A few days later, Colonel March arrived, with his seven companies. Other companies soon followed, and by the middle of June there were twenty-five present. As no clothing or blankets were yet furnished by the State, and as the men had nothing but what they stood in, they soon presented a rather dilapidated appearance, which circumstance, however, did not in the least affect the buoyancy of the spirits of the young patriots, who seemed rather to enjoy the novely of their tattered garments. The good citizens of Easton, with a noble generosity, took the matter in hand; and a Ladies' Aid Society was formed, which supplied abundance of clothing, blankets, quilts, jellies, etc., for the hospital, and pantaloons, shirts, etc., for the needy of the camp.

The rations furnished us was abundant, and of the best quality, consisting of fresh beef, bacon, bread, potatoes, beans, rice, coffee, sugar and small stores, and all were satisfied with them, except those who had not been used to as good at home. The health of the troops was very good, and, as a precaution against small-pox, the whole camp was vaccinated; and to promote the general health, the men were taken to the Lehigh every other day, where they enjoyed themselves hugely in swimming, diving, splashing and paddling around in general.

Among the first things that agitated the brains of the boys, was to devise quaint names and mottoes to place over their quarters, and many of them were typical of those who adopted them. Commencing at the main entrance was Captain McDonough's company, with "Fourth Ward," "Fort Mann," "Fort McCandless." On the right was, "Quaker City Headquarters," "Quaker Bridal Chamber," "Live and Let Live." Next, "Hibernia Engine Company," "Bird-in-Hand." Next, "Rose Cottage," "Dart's Heads," "The Old House at Home," "Gay Roosters," "Don't Tread on Me," "Old Lebanon Garden, Captain Tim Mealey." Next, "Happy Home," "Punch Bowl," "Black Horse," "The Government Keeps Us, and We will Keep the Government." Next, "Bristol Boys, Captain Thompson," "Bower of Love," "Happy Crew," "The Old School-House," "The Old Spring-House." Next, "Ontario Guards, Captain Sickel," "Bill Pool Club," "We Respect All and Fear None." Next, "Never Sink," "Live Oak," "Kensington Boys," "Hike Out and Simmer Down." Next, "Balmoral Castle," "Scotch Rifles," "Wallace's Cave, Captain Finnie." Next, "Penn Rifles, Captain G. A. Woodward," "The Flag Wyoming." Next, "Sunday Mercury, Captain E. M. Woodward," "Green Shirts." Next, "Consolidation Guards, Captain Smith," "Gay and Happy." Next, "Free and Easy," "Happy Family, Captain Kimbell." Next, "Wide Awake, Captain Curtis." Next, "Long Island of Reading, Captain Briner," "Keystone Hook and Ladder Company." Next, "Elephant Guards, Captain Richards." Next, "The Star of North Birdsborough, Captain Lenhart," "Fort Sumter," "The Plow Boys," "Japanese Hotel," "Arctic Circle," "Death to Traitors," "Jeff. Davis at the Sheriff's Ball," "The Blue-Eyed Stranger," "Mount Vernon," "Washington and Lincoln," "White Hall, Newtown, Captain Feaster;" "Traitor Hunters," "Love and Glory," "Game Chickens," "Ellsworth's Heart," "Never Surrender," "The Wheat Field," "The Red Curtain," "Susquehanna Tigers," "Gloria Dei," etc.

It was not to be supposed that so many young men collected together, many of whom were unused to being free from the restraints of home, would all behave with the strictest decorum. A good many of them looked upon it as a grand frolic or excursion, and were bound to enjoy themselves, the principal obstacle to which was the guard, which they soon showed remarkable adroitness in dodging. Four men from each company were given a day's absence from camp at a time, but many more managed to get out without passes. Almost every bunk had its "rat hole," through which the boys made their exit past the conveniently blind guard, who had not been soldiers long enough to know how to perform their duty. A few of these patriots were caught upon their return, and put in the guard-house; but it soon being discovered it afforded a most easy means of egress, a new one was built inside the enclosure, which was christened "Fort Mann."

The boys in camp managed occasionally to get a little whiskey, but the orders prohibiting its introduction into the guard-house were so strict, that it was thought impossible to get any to the prisoners. And it would have, had it not been for the naughty guard, who exchanged arms with those at the gate, and treated the prisoners from their musket barrels.

On pleasant afternoons the camp was the fashionable resort of the neighboring farmers, their wives and daughters and the good citizens of Easton, and it often presented a gay and animated appearance, particularly on Sundays, when, in addition to the dress parade, the troops passed in review before the commander and staff.

On the 14th of June, General M'Call visited camp, to organize the regiments, supposing the independent companies had associated with one or the other of the three colonels who had parts of regiments quartered there. Not finding such to be the case, he issued an order in which he stated, if the regiments were not organized by voluntary association of companies by the 19th inst., he would proceed to organize them in the following manner: "The ten companies which first arrived in camp, and in the order they are now quartered, will constitute the Second Regiment; the next ten will form the Third Regiment; and the next ten, the Fourth Regiment of the Pennsylvania Reserve Volunteer Corps. Each regiment, so formed, will proceed, without delay, to elect their field officers." The companies so quartered were: First, eight of Colonel Mann's and two independent; next, five of Colonel DeKorponay's and five independent; next, seven of Colonel March's and three independent.

Upon a careful canvass of the camp, it was ascertained there were not independent companies enough who were willing to join either of the proposed colonels, to complete their regimental organization. One, by reason of the office he held in civil life, was unjustly very unpopular with an active minority of the men. Another had ruined his prospects by promising the field offices to almost every captain in camp, and being followed to camp by several civilians to whom he had promised the Quartermastership, and of whom he had borrowed money. Under these circumstances three officers agreed to organize an independent regiment, and selected seven companies, whose officers gave the greatest promise of efficiency, and whose character and bearing were congenial, and, upon sounding them, they readily acquiesced. For the purpose of consultation, those interested obtained passes in the evenings, and went down to the Lehigh, where a boat was in readiness to convey them across the river, whence they proceeded to the parlor of Mr. Young's hotel, at South Easton. The only agreement entered into was secrecy, the entire ignoring of the question of field offices until after the organization of the regiment, and then the choice of candidates for said offices by the vote of the officers, and the submission of the same to the men. Each officer pledged his honor to this, and cheerfully, in spirit and letter, they carried it out.

On the 20th, General M'Call again visited camp, and in the evening convened the officers at the commissary's building, and proceeded to organize the regiments. The order was read, when Lieutenant Beatty arose and stated that as Captain Thompson's company did not arrive until several days after some of the companies of the second division had, he should not be thrown in the first division. Against this the officers interested earnestly protested. After all got through who wished to speak, the **General** announced that the names of Captains Thompson, **Sickel** and four of the second division be placed in a hat, and the question of which two companies should go into the first division be decided by lot. Lieutenant Scheetz, Aid-de-camp to General M'Call, drew the slips, and the first two names drawn were Captains G. A. and E. M. Woodward, which completed the Second Regiment.

The companies constituting the Third Regiment, Pennsylvania Reserve Volunteer Corps (the Thirty-second Regiment, Infantry, of the Line, Pennsylvania Volunteers), were:

Company A—"The Second Reading Artillery," of Berks county. Captain, Jacob Lenhart, Jr.; First Lieutenant, Jacob Lehman; Second Lieutenant, Jeremiah A. Clouse.

Company B—"The Salem Independents," of Wayne county. Captain, William D. Curtis; First Lieutenant, George C. Davenport; Second Lieutenant, J. M. Buckingham.

Company C—"The Union Rifles," of Bucks county. Captain David V. Feaster; First Lieutenant, Strickland Yardley; Second Lieutenant, Joseph B. Roberts.

Company D—"The Mechanic Infantry," of Berks county. Captain, William Briner; First Lieutenant, Frank S. Bickley; Second Lieutenant, Florentine H. Straub.

Company E—"The De Silver Greys," of Philadelphia. Captain, John Clark; First Lieutenant, Robert Johnston; Second Lieutenant, George H. Lindsey.

Company F—"The Washington Guards," of Berks county. Captain, Washington Richards; First Lieutenant, Albert P. Moulton; Second Lieutenant, Albert H. Jameson.

Company G—"The Germantown Guards," of Philadelphia. Captain, Richard H. Woolworth; First Lieutenant, John Stanton; Second Lieutenant, John Connally.

Company H—"The Applebachville Guards," of Bucks county. Captain, Joseph Thomas; First Lieutenant, Benjamin F. Fisher; Second Lieutenant, Nelson Applebach.

Company I—"The Montgomery Guards," of Bucks county. Captain, William S. Thomson; First Lieutenant, H. Clay Beatty; Second Lieutenant, Samuel J. La Rue.

Company K—"The Ontario Guards," of Philadelphia. Captain, Horatio Gates Sickel; First Lieutenant, David W. Donaghy; Second Lieutenant, David Wonderly.

The officers, the same night, unanimously chose Captains Sickel as their candidate for Colonel, Thompson for Lieutenant Colonel, and Woolworth for Major; and the next day the men confirmed them without a single dissenting vote. Lieutenant Albert H. Janieson was appointed Adjutant; Lieutenant Franklin S. Bickley, Quartermaster; Dr. James Collins, of Philadelphia, Surgeon; Dr. George L. Pancoast, of the same city, Assistant Surgeon; and the Reverend William H. Leake, of Wayne county, Chaplain.

The vacancy in Company K was filled by the election of William Brian, of Philadelphia, Captain; in Company I, by that of First Lieutenant H. C. Beatty, Captain; Second Lieutenant Samuel J. La Rue, First Lieutenant, and Samuel Beatty, Second Lieutenant; and in Company G that of Hugh Harkins, of Philadelphia, Captain. Soon after, arms, accoutrements and clothing were received from the State and issued to the men.

On the 14th of July, His Excellency Andrew G. Curtin and staff arrived in camp, and a review of the troops was ordered. The men were dressed in light blue pants, dark blue blouses and fatigue caps, and as they marched in review in column of companies past the Governor they presented a very creditable appearance.

The next day Major H. D. Maxwell, the Paymaster General of the State, arrived and payed off the Fourth Regiment, which, on the 16th, left camp for Harrisburg, and the same day the Second and Third were paid off.

CHAPTER II.

BATTLE OF BULL RUN, 1861 — LEAVE CAMP WASHINGTON — CAMP CURTIN — BALTIMORE — WASHINGTON — MUSTERED INTO THE U. S. SERVICE — EXCHANGE OF ARMS — TO TENALLYTOWN — GENERAL M'CALL — SCHOOL OF INSTRUCTION — LIQUOR AND CARDS PROHIBITED — REVIEW OF THE DIVISION — CAPTURE BY PICKETS — REVIEW BY THE PRESIDENT — ALARM — PRESENTATION OF FLAGS — ORGANIZATION OF BRIGADES AND DIVISIONS — THE STAFFS — THE POTOMAC LODGE — STATE ELECTION.

IT WAS on this same day that General McDowell advanced from the Potomac at the head of 35,000 men, to meet the enemy at Bull Run. The battle was fought on the 21st. The enemy were entrenched beyond the creek. The plan of battle was to make a heavy feint, and occupy his attention on his right, while the main body of our troops was to turn his left. It succeeded, and they were doubled up and thrown back upon themselves for over a mile and a half. While being thus driven, General Joseph E. Johnston* arrived with 15,000 fresh troops from the Valley of the Shenandoah to the aid of Beauregard, and M'Dowell was overwhelmed.†

---

*Subsequently a member of the 46th Congress of the United States.

†The effect of this unfortunate **victory on** the Southern mind was most singular and delusive. President Davis considered the recognition of the Confederate States **by the** European powers as certain. The newspapers declared that the question of manhood between the North and South was settled forever; and the phrase of "one Southerner equal to five Yankees," was adopted in all speeches about the war. "DeBow's Review" considered it one of the decisive battles of the world. So certain was **the** establishment of the Confederacy considered, that politicians commenced plotting for the Presidential succession more than six years distant. Mr. **Hunter**, of Virginia, left the Cabinet, being unwilling, by any identification with it, to damage his chances as Mr. Davis' successor. General Beauregard, who was **designated** in some quarters as the next Confederate President, wrote a weak and theatrical letter to the newspapers, dated "Within Hearing of the Enemy's Guns," declining to be a candidate for the office. There was actually a controversy between different States as to the permanent location of the Confederate capital; and the city council of Nashville, Tennessee, appropriated $750,000 for a residence for the President of the Southern Confederacy, as an inducement to remove the capital there.—*Extracted from page* 153 *of "The Lost Cause."*

The defeat of our army and the expiration of the term of service of most of the three-months men endangered the capital, and the authorities at Washington were unprepared for the emergency. Instantaneous relief must be had, and Pennsylvania alone, through the foresight of its Governor, was prepared to give it; and the 15,000 Reserves, whose services had been a few days before offered and declined, were now gladly accepted. If accepted at first, and they had participated in the battle, if the result had not been altered, the army would have been saved from disgraceful retreat. The Governor, prompted by that generous patriotism that always actuated him, hurried forward all the available troops that could be raised, and the whole resources of the State were exerted for that purpose.

On the day of the battle of Bull Run, July 21st, 1861, Colonel Sickel received orders to move his regiment to Washington. About nine o'clock the next morning, the Third bid farewell to their old camp, and crossed the Lehigh to the depot. As they marched through Easton, headed by a fine band, the bells were rung, the citizens cheered and the ladies waved their handkerchiefs. Embarking, the train moved off amidst the cheers of the vast crowd and shrieks of steam signals. The day was exceedingly warm, and the box-cars in which they were transported having no ventilation, the boys produced it by knocking the sides out with the butt of their muskets. Along the route, flags were displayed from every house, and at the villages the populace turned out *en masse* to welcome their passage, and brought offerings of flowers, fruits, cake and milk. About five o'clock in the afternoon, they arrived at Harrisburg and marched out to Camp Curtin, where, that night, they made their first bivouac. The next day they received the balance of their arms and equipments and forty rounds of ammunition, and, towards sunset, entered the cars and moved towards Baltimore, where they arrived about daybreak the following morning.

As this city was not particularly noted for its loyalty, the colonel thought best to halt the train before entering it, and distribute ammunition, being aware of the tranquilizing effect of loaded muskets. Resting in a field near the depot for a few hours, and receiving the necessary orders from General Dix,* they formed and moved to the depot of the Baltimore and Washington Railroad, where they embarked. They numbered nine hundred and seventy-two officers and men, perfectly armed, equipped and well drilled; and as they marched through the streets to the soul-inspiring strains of their band, they were received with a becoming silence and respect.

Leaving Baltimore at noon, they arrived in Washington near sunset, on the 24th, and marched to the Mount Vernon Cane Factory, where they were informally visited by His Excellency President Lincoln, who addressed a few words of welcome and thanks.

At this time the city would have been in great danger if the enemy had possessed the requisite dash. Its streets were filled with three-months men, stragglers and fugitives from Bull Run, who were more intent upon getting their hair dressed and boots blacked than upon finding their regiments. Men with and without arms lined the steps and curb-stones and filled the saloons, and such was the crowded state of the hotels that some of the soldiers could not obtain comfortable board and single rooms. Many of the veterans were surrounded with eager groups of idlers, listening to their recital of the carnage on the field—their hair-breadth escapes—or their hardships in not having butter for their bread or cream for their coffee. These strange scenes impressed sad forebodings upon the minds of officers who had a proper appreciation of the seriousness of the work before them.

After dinner the next day, the Third was formed and marched out Seventh street some distance and encamped,

---

* Subsequently Minister to France and Governor of New York.

where they were mustered into the United States service on the 27th of July, by Lieutenant John Ellwood, Fifth U. S. Infantry. Early on the 30th, the regiment was marched by companies to the United States Arsenal, where they exchanged their smooth-bore Harpers Ferry muskets for rifled ones, and received a complete outfit of accoutrements and non-commission swords.

At one o'clock on the morning of August 1st, 1861, the reveille sounded, and soon bright fires were burning, and the men engaged in cooking two days' rations. Breakfast was eaten, tents struck, the regiment formed, arms stacked, and the men laid down near by to wait for the wagons which they were to receive from the quartermaster's department. Teamsters, generally speaking, are in no hurry to start when they have no one particularly interested in hurrying them off, but they learned wonderful promptness in the Reserves in a remarkably short time. This day, however, they did not arrive until eight o'clock, when the Third took up its march through Washington and Georgetown to Tenallytown, some six miles northwest of the capital, where it arrived in the afternoon. On the road they met the Eighth Reserve for the first time, and little did they think, as they gazed on each other, of the love they would form, the strong love, that grew so warm between all the regiments of the Reserve, and so unselfishly showed itself upon many fields when one went in to save the other. They marched together to the camp, and pitched their tents in a fine woods.

Tenallytown is situated at the junction of the Rockille and Poolsville roads with the Georgetown road, three miles from the latter town, and one and a half from the Chain Bridge. Here was erected Fort Pennsylvania, a most important and formidable earthwork, with a broad and deep ditch, heavy abatis, and guns mounted *en-barbette*, and, near by, two lunettes, named Gaines and Bayard. They were built by the Reserve, details being made from all the regiments for that purpose.

Here, George Archibald M'Call, a graduate of West Point, subsequently an officer in, and Inspector-General of, the United States Army, and a distinguished soldier in the war with Mexico, who had been appointed by Governor Curtin a Major-General to command the Reserve, had, after much difficulty and opposition, succeeded in collecting and consolidating them into one division. This was the earnest desire of the Governor, and of every officer and soldier of the Reserve.

The next evening, the Third was ordered on picket about a mile from camp, and the boys, for the first time, experienced the pleasant excitement of watching for the enemy. But all passed quietly, and towards dark the next afternoon they were relieved by the Sixth Reserve, and returned to camp.

Here General M'Call laid the foundation of the Reserve's future efficiency by his indefatigable exertions to instruct the officers, and through them the men, in their duties in the field. For this purpose, the colonels were directed to organize the officers into classes for mutual instruction in military tactics and army regulations, and the captains to form classes of non-commission officers for instruction in company drill, and the non-commissions to instruct the men. Weekly reports of the progress made by the officers were required, so that those who were incapable or unwilling to learn, could be known and got rid of. Battalion and company drill was commenced with spirit, the manual of arms taught and target firing practiced. The articles of war were frequently read to the companies and inspections held.

Although the introduction of liquor was prohibited by Division orders, still there was plenty of it brought into camp; but the Colonel being one who was disposed to have orders obeyed—by mildness if possible, and force if necessary—issued orders to permit neither citizen nor soldier to enter camp without being searched. He also, for the welfare of the men and to prevent unkind feelings occurring among them, as much as was in his power, positively prohibited card playing for money, and all species of gambling. While many of the men did not like these orders, and knew they would be strictly enforced, the kind words spoken by the Colonel caused a ready acquiescence. Divine service was held—and well attended every Sunday morning—by Chaplain Leake, who was one of the foremost to volunteer as a private in company B. Forty rounds of ammunition were kept in the boxes of each man; the sentinels were ordered to report all signal rockets, fire or smoke, and musket firing was strictly forbidden.

On the afternoon of the 14th, the division was reviewed by General M'Call on a neighboring hill, Colonel Sickel commanding a temporary brigade. The next afternoon, by orders, the division was reviewed by Colonel Sickel. On the 20th, the Reserves were temporarily organized into two brigades; the First consisting of the First, Third, Fourth, Sixth and Eighth Regiments and Batteries A, B, D and F. The Second, of the Fifth, Seventh, Ninth, Tenth, Eleventh and Twelfth Regiments and Batteries C, E, G and H. The regiment of Reserve cavalry was unattached. The "Bucktails" and Second were with General Banks. These two regiments joined the division on the 25th of September.

About this time the pickets of the Third captured some enterprising drovers, who were about sending cattle over the river into Virginia. They and their herd were taken to division headquarters for investigation. Their expressions of loyalty and willingness to take the oath of allegiance to the United States did not, however, save their cattle from confiscation and themselves from imprisonment.

On the morning of the 21st of August, the Reserve passed in review before His Excellency the President, attended by his cabinet and Major-General George B. M'Clellan,* who had a short time before been appointed Commander-in-Chief

---

* Afterwards Governor of New Jersey.

of the armies of the United States. In the afternoon the Third was marched to the reviewing ground and exercised in battalion drill and firing.

The next day the following address was read on dress parade:

"HEADQUARTERS
"PENNSYLVANIA RESERVE VOLUNTEER CORPS,
"CAMP TENALLY, August 21st, 1861.

"*Soldiers of the Pennsylvania Reserve:* This day must be recognized as a propitious inauguration of your future military history. You have this day passed under the scrutinizing inspection of the Commanding General of the Army of the Potomac, in whose ability to successfully prosecute this war the confidence of the country is reposed; you have passed in review before the President of the United States and his Cabinet; and both the General and the President have expressed to me their unqualified approval of your soldier-like appearance on review, and of the discipline thus manifestly shown to exist in the corps.

"It now rests with you, officers of the Pennsylvania Reserve, to carry out to perfection the work so well begun. Upon you devolves the care of your men; let that be unremitting; let every attention to their wants temper the rigid discipline necessary to the formation of the soldier, and with one heart we will uphold the flag of our State, and place her name among the foremost in the cause of our common country. "GEO. A. M'CALL,

"Brigadier-General Commanding."

On the 27th, the enemy fired on the Reserve pickets at Great Falls, consisting of a detachment of cavalry and a battery of artillery; and that evening the drums were heard, and fires seen, of what appeared to be a considerable encampment. A colored man also called across that "the Rebels had a sight of men a half-mile from the river," which was proved to be true by our scouts. The Reserves were ordered to prepare two days' rations for the haversacks, and be in readiness to move at a moment's notice; but the enemy failed to make further demonstration.

On the 29th, Lieutenants Benjamin F. Fisher, of Company H, and David Wonderly, of Company K, having successfully passed their examination, were detailed for duty in the Signal Corps. These officers rose to distinction in the service, and were attached to the headquarters of the Army of the Potomac, the first being subsequently promoted Chief Signal Officer and Colonel U. S. A., and the latter a Captain. Corporal Samuel Cartledge, Company E, privates George Worthington, Company H, James A. Todd, Company K, and Thomas D. Boone, Company D, were also transferred to the same corps.

About this time the enemy across the river showed considerable activity on our right, and, upon one occasion, opened upon the Reserve picket at Great Falls with no less than nine guns, to which the section of Cooper's battery made no reply, being smooth-bores of short range. Upon another occasion, on information received from General Smith, General M'Clellan ordered the Reserves to be held in readiness to fight, the dispatch stating, "he would certainly be attacked within forty-eight hours;" which being read at dress parade, produced the most joyous excitement among the officers and men. Colonel Sickel was ordered to the command of the reserve, consisting of five regiments, and General M'Call put the rest of the troops in motion for the Chain Bridge, but had not proceeded far when the orders were countermanded. These pleasant little excitements were very acceptable to the men, for they, like all new troops, were exceedingly anxious to have a fight.

The camp of the Third, in a fine woods of majestic trees, was put into most excellent order, the lower branches being cut off, stumps extracted, underbrush cleared, barrels sunk at the springs, sinks surrounded with bushes, and all thoroughly cleaned up. Upon dress parade one day the Third was visited by General M'Call and staff, accompanied by Hon. William D. Kelly,* of Philadelphia, who, at the invitation of the Colonel, delivered a short but most impressive and eloquent address, which was responded to by hearty cheers.

The Society of Cincinnati of Pennsylvania, having presented to the State five hundred dollars, to be used towards arming and equipping the volunteers, and the Legislature having directed the same to be expended in the purchase of regimental flags for the Reserves, on the 10th of September, 1861, the presentation took place. The day was a clear and beautiful one, and at nine o'clock in the morning the nine regiments then with the command were drawn up in a large field near the river road, about a half mile from camp. The scene is thus described in Prof. Bates' History of the Pennsylvania Volunteers:

"The color companies were formed in line in front, with the colonel of each regiment at the head of the company. The parade ground was surrounded by a line of guards, to exclude the vast multitude of soldiers and civilians that had collected to witness the presentation. At eleven o'clock, President Lincoln, accompanied by Hon. Simon Cameron,† Secretary of War, drove into the enclosure; a few minutes later, General M'Clellan arrived, escorted by the M'Clellan Rifle Guards, of Chicago, and accompanied by Adjutant-General Lorenzo Thomas, General Butler and General Mansfield.‡ Half an hour later, the sound of artillery, firing the appropriate salute, announced the arrival of His Excellency the Governor of Pennsylvania. Governor Curtin,§ accompanied by the members of his staff, Surgeon-General Henry H. Smith, Judge Maxwell, Paymaster-General, and many distinguished citizens, soon appeared on the

---

* A member of the Congress of the United States for twenty-five years.
† Subsequently U. S. Minister to Russia and U. S. Senator.
‡ Gen. J. K. F. Mansfield, killed at Antietam.
§ Twice Governor of Pennsylvania, subsequently Minister to Russia.

parade ground. Colonel Simmons, Fifth Reserve, which had marched to Washington to escort the Governor to Tenallytown, moved into position at the right of the line, and General M'Call reported his command in readiness to receive the colors. After receiving most cordial greetings from the President, the Secretary of War, the General-in-Chief and the General commanding, His Excellency the Governor proceeded to formally present the colors to the colonels of the several regiments, at the head of their color companies.

"Attended by his staff and General M'Call, he commenced at the right of the line and placed in the hands of each colonel the beautiful flag provided by the State of Pennsylvania, saying, at the same time, 'that he had been delegated by the Legislature of the State to present these colors to them, and he hoped their glory would never be tarnished in their keeping.'"

After receiving the colors, the companies wheeled by platoons and marched around the right and left of the line to the rear, and took their places in the line with their new colors unfurled to the breeze.

The flags were made of silk, fringed with yellow; in the blue field was the coat-of-arms of the State, surrounded by thirty-four golden stars. Having delivered the flags, the Governor returned, and, mounting the seat of his carriage, thus addressed the soldiers:

"*General M'Call and Men of Pennsylvania:* Were it not for the surroundings, one might be struck by the novelty of the scene. Large assemblages of the people of Pennsylvania, on any occasion which calls them together for deliberation on subjects touching the general welfare and the public good, are always attended with a charm that fascinates. But when I look over the thousands of Pennsylvanians away from the soil of their State, in arms, there is inspiration in the occasion.

"I came here to-day on a duty enjoined by the Legislature of Pennsylvania. The remnant of the descendants of the heroes and sages of the Revolution in the Keystone State, known as the Cincinnati Society, presented me with a sum of money, to arm and equip the volunteers of Pennsylvania who might go into public service in the present exigency. I referred the subject to the Legislature. They instructed me to make these flags and pay for them with the money of the Cincinnati Society. I have placed in the centre of the azure field the coat-of-arms of your great and glorious State, and around it a bright galaxy of stars. I give these flags to you to-day, and I know you will carry them, wherever you appear, in honor, and that the credit of your State will never suffer in your hands.

"Our peaceful pursuits in Pennsylvania have been broken. Many of our people have abandoned those arts of industry which lead to development and progress, and have been forced to bear arms. They have responded to the call of the National Government, and while you are here in obedience to that call, your fellow-citizens at home are occupying the camps you have lately vacated. All our material wealth, and the life of every man in Pennsylvania, stands pledged to vindicate the right, to sustain the Government, and to restore the ascendancy of law and order. You are here for that purpose, with no hope of acquisition or vengeance, nor from any desire to be enriched by the shedding of blood. God forbid! Our people are for peace. But if men lay violent hands on the sacred fabric of the Government, unjustly spill the blood of their brethren, and tear the sacred Constitution to pieces, Pennsylvania is for war—war to the death!

"How is it, my friends, that we, of Pennsylvania, are interrupted in our progress and development? How is it that workshops are closed, and that our mechanical and agricultural pursuits do not secure their merited reward? It is because folly, fanaticism, rebellion, murder, piracy and treason prevail over a portion of this land; and we are here to-day to vindicate the right, to sustain the Government, to defend the Constitution, and to shed the blood of Pennsylvanians, if it need be, to produce this result. It will do no harm to repeat here, in the presence of so many Pennsylvanians in arms, that in our State the true principles of human liberty were first promulgated to the world; and there, also, the convention met that framed the Constitution; and Pennsylvania, loyal in the Revolution, now stands solidly and defiantly to arrest the treason and rebellion that would tear into pieces the sacred instrument of our Union of States.

"My friends, one might regret to see so many men of Pennsylvania here in arms to-day. But there is a pleasure in the recollection that you have been willing to volunteer your services in the defence of the great principle of human liberty. Should the wrong prevail, should treason and rebellion succeed, we have no government. Progress is stopped, civilization stands still, and Christianity in the world, for the time, must cease—cease forever. Liberty, civilization and Christianity hang upon the result of this great contest.

"God is for the truth and the right. Stand by your colors, my friends, this day delivered to you, and the right will prevail. I present to you to-day, as the representative of the people of Pennsylvania, these beautiful colors. I place in your hands the honor of your State. Thousands of your fellow-citizens at home look to you to vindicate the honor of your great State. If you fail, hearts and homes will be made desolate. If you succeed, thousands of Pennsylvanians will rejoice over your success; and, on your return, you will be hailed as heroes who have gone forth to battle for the right.

"They follow you with their prayers. They look to you to vindicate a great government, to sustain legitimate power, and to crush out rebellion. Thousands of your friends in Pennsylvania know of the presentation of these flags to-day;

and I am sure that I am authorized to say that their blessing is upon you.

"May the God of battles, in His wisdom, protect your lives, and may right, truth and justice prevail."

General M'Call responded:

"*General Curtin:* Permit me, in the name of the Pennsylvania Reserve Corps, to return, through your Excellency, to the State of our birth, the thanks with which we receive the splendid banners that, in accordance with an act of the State Legislature, you have this day presented.

"The bestowal of these noble banners devolves upon the regiments of this division a responsibility they cheerfully accept; and they trust, with the aid of the God of battles, to bear these stars and stripes proudly in the conflict, and to place the banner of our State amongst the foremost in the cause of the Constitution and the Union of our common country."

The presentation over, the regiments passed in review before the Governor. The distinguished visitors then partook of a collation in picnic style in the grove fronting General M'Call's headquarters. There were a number of ladies in the party, whose presence added greatly to the pleasure of the occasion. The greatest sociability prevailed, and wit and sentiment ruled the hour, without any stiff formality. President Lincoln was in his happiest mood, and was the life of the company, and all present seemed to enjoy themselves much.

After supper on the 11th, the Third, Seventh, Eighth and Eleventh Regiments marched to the Chain Bridge, to support General Smith, who was skirmishing on the other side of the river, and returned to camp about midnight.

On the 16th, the regiments of the Reserve were organized into three brigades, and the brigades into a division, to be officially known as "M'Call's Division," but popularly in the army, and throughout the world where the record of our warfare was read, as the "Pennsylvania Reserve."

THE THIRD RESERVE.

The First Brigade was composed of the Fifth Regiment, Colonel Seneca G. Simmons; the First Regiment, Colonel R. B. Roberts; the Second, Colonel Wm. B. Mann; and the Eighth Regiment, Colonel Geo. S. Hayes—commanded by Brigadier-General John F. Reynolds, Lieutenant-Colonel Fourteenth Infantry, U. S. A. General Reynolds appointed on his staff, Captain Charles Kingsbury, Assistant Adjutant-General; Lieutenants Charles B. Lamborne and Henry S. Spear, Aids-de-camp; Captain Chandler Hall, Quartermaster, and Captain James B. Clow, Commissary of Subsistence, and Dr. Jas. B. King, Brigade Surgeon.

The Second Brigade was composed of the Third Regiment, Colonel Horatio G. Sickel; the Fourth Regiment, Colonel R. G. March; the Seventh Regiment, Colonel E. B. Harvey, and the Eleventh Regiment, Colonel Thomas F. Gallagher—commanded by Brigadier-General George Gordon Meade, Captain U. S. Topographical Engineers. General Meade appointed Captain Edward C. Baird, Assistant Adjutant-General; and Lieutenants J. Hamilton Kuhn and William W. Watmough, Aids-de-camp; Captain Samuel Ringwalt, Quartermaster; Captain James P. Fredericks, Commissary of Subsistence; and Dr. Anthony E. Stocker, Brigade Surgeon.

The Third Brigade was composed of the Tenth Regiment, Colonel John S. M'Calmont; the Sixth Regiment, Colonel W. W. Ricketts; the Ninth Regiment, Colonel Conrad F. Jackson; and the Twelfth Regiment, Colonel John H. Taggart—commanded by Brigadier-General E. O. C. Ord, Captain Third U. S. Artillery. General Ord appointed on his staff Captain Placidus Ord, Assistant Adjutant-General; Lieutenants Samuel S. Steward and A. Brady Sharp, Aids-de-camp; Captain Wm. Painter, Quartermaster; Captain Jas. M. Tillapaugh, Commissary of Subsistence; and Dr. W. G. Lowman, Brigade Surgeon.

The First Rifles, popularly known as the "Bucktails," Colonel Charles J. Biddle, were temporarily attached to the

Second Brigade, and then, for a short time, made independent; but on the opening of the campaign, in 1862, were permanently assigned to the First Brigade.

The First Reserve Cavalry, Colonel Geo. D. Bayard, Lieutenant Fourth Regiment U. S. Cavalry, was not brigaded, its commander reporting direct to division headquarters.

Of the First Reserve Artillery, Colonel Charles T. Campbell; Battery A, Captain Hezekiah Easton; Battery B, Captain James H. Cooper; and Battery G, Captain Mark Kern, were retained with the division, and the rest of the batteries distributed through the Army of the Potomac.

General M'Call, having previously appointed Captain Henry J. Biddle Assistant Adjutant-General, and Lieutenants Henry A. Scheetz and Eldridge Maconkey Aids-de-camp, completed the organization of the departments of his division by appointing Captain Chandler Hall Quartermaster; Captain Jas. B. Clow, Commissary of Subsistence; Lieutenant Estruries Beatty, Ordnance Officer; and Dr. Anthony E. Stocker, Surgeon at division headquarters. Subsequently, Professor Henry Coppeé was attached to the staff as Inspector-General, and the Hon. Edward M'Pherson, having resigned his commission as Captain in the First Regiment on account of having been chosen a representative in Congress from the Seventeenth Congressional District of Pennsylvania, was accepted as a volunteer aid on the staff of General M'Call during the recesses of Congress.

While at Camp Tenally, September 24th, A. L. 5861, A. D. 1861, upon application of Colonel Sickel, Captain Feaster, Lieutenant-Colonel Thompson, H. L. Strong, Captains Beatty and Briner, Hospital Steward F. M. Niblo, Captain Curtis, Sergeant H. C. Tripp, Sergeant-Major Duvall Doran and Captain Richards, the R. W. G. M. George C. Whiting, of the Grand Lodge of Free and Accepted York Masons of the District of Columbia, granted a warrant for the establishment of a Lodge in the Third

Reserve, to be known and recognized as "The Potomac Lodge." The warrant appointed Colonel Sickel Worshipful Master, Lieutenant-Colonel Thompson Senior Warden, and Captain Curtis Junior Warden, and authorized and empowered them to hold communications thereof, for social intercourse and Masonic instruction. The Lodge was organized four days afterwards, and continued to hold camp-meetings as circumstances permitted, taking in a number of new members, and entered, passed and raised to the sublime degree of Master Masons others. This Lodge was the only one of Masons in the Army of the Potomac, although the Most Worshipful Grand Lodge of the District of Columbia, as early as May 2d, 1861, advised that the M. W. G. M. grant special dispensations to such regiments or corps of volunteers of the several States in the service of the United States in their jurisdiction.

On the morning of the 7th of October, Lieutenant-Colonel Thompson, in command of four companies, with wagons to convey the tents, etc., marched to the Great Falls, for a week's picket duty. Late in the afternoon a violent hail storm, accompanied by high winds and thunder, occurred. Some of the stones were of the size of bullets, cutting through the tents, and almost driving the horses wild. It lasted about a half hour, leaving the atmosphere quite cool.

The next day, the fall election in our State taking place, the Reserves exercised the right of casting their vote, each company voting at its captain's quarters. Tickets of both the political parties were supplied in abundance from home, and the men were free from any restraint or improper influence of officers or politicians.

CHAPTER III.

INTO VIRGINIA — CAMP PIERPONT — THE LONG ROLL — DEATH OF PRIVATE SEIFERT — RECONNOISSANCE TO DRAINESVILLE — BALLS BLUFF — REVIEW — MOVE CAMP — RESIGNATIONS AND PROMOTIONS — REVIEW AT MUNSON'S HILL — WINTER QUARTERS — THE COLONEL AND THE DELINQUENTS — BAYARD'S SKIRMISH — FORAGING EXPEDITION — BATTLE OF DRAINESVILLE — GALLANTRY OF LIEUTENANT-COLONEL KANE — CHRISTMAS AND PISTOLS — WINTER — VIRGINIA FAMILY — A BRAVE GIRL — PICKETING — "TAKING FRENCH" — DEATHS AND PROMOTIONS.

EARLY on the morning of the 9th of October, General Smith advanced his division from the neighborhood of the Chain Bridge to Langley, where, deploying his skirmishers, he pushed forward a brigade on the Drainesville pike, and took possession of Prospect Hill. With his main body, he diverged from the pike at Langley to the left, advancing towards Lewinsville, which village he entered and occupied without opposition, leaving the main portion of his troops at Smoot's Hill, and pushing on a detachment to hold Miner's Hill.

To occupy this extention of the lines, the same day orders were issued for the Reserves to march. The two days' rations of the Third were just being put on the fires, when the long roll beat, and the men fell in with their knapsacks slung, eager for the move. No one can conceive what a scene of animation it was without having felt the joy of young, thoughtless soldiers, as they prepare for what they suppose is their first battle. Every heart is light and happy, every eye is bright and sparkling, every bosom heaves with emotions of love and tenderness for those at home, and the manly thought flashes through that they are about to prove themselves worthy of the name of Americans. The drums beat, the bands peal forth martial strains, the bugles sound, the cavalry tramp by with rattling sabres, the artillery rumbles over the ground, the masses of infantry, with their bright flashing muskets and nodding ensigns, unravel themselves and move in long columns of blue, fringed with bright bayonets, followed by the ammunition wagons and ambulances, and all wind down to the banks of the Potomac towards the Chain Bridge. And what a happy moment. They tread the planks, the bands burst forth with "Dixie's Land," and the loud and prolonged cheers of brave hearts echo from shore to shore of the rock-bound river, and their feet press for the first time the " sacred soil of Virginia."

It was three o'clock in the afternoon when the Third left their camp in charge of the sick, under Lieutenant Lehman, for the guards had deserted their posts and mingled in the ranks; and, preceded by the cavalry and the "Bucktails," deployed as skirmishers, crossed the bridge, and moving on the Drainesville pike past Fort Marcy, they bivouacked at dark in a field a little beyond Langley. Pickets were at once thrown out to connect with General Smith's line on the left, and to extend to the Potomac on the right. The night was dark, cloudy and cold, and the men were without tents for the first time, and thus gradually, and to them not unpleasantly, they were becoming inured to the field-life of a soldier, and the next morning at reveille they were as happy and light-hearted as health and youth could make them.

That afternoon the wagons arrived, the tents were pitched and Camp Pierpont established, named in honor of Francis H. Pierpont, the loyal Governor of Virginia. The position assigned to the Reserves was the extreme right of the Army of the Potomac, their picket line extending from the river past Prospect Hill, towards Lewinsville.

The camp of the Third was in a basin surrounded by high hills, with field batteries in front. Near dark on the 11th, Lieutenant-Colonel Thompson, with the picket from the Great Falls, and the balance of the wagons, arrived in camp and pitched his tents.

On the night of the 11th, Smith's pickets, in the neighborhood of Lewinsville, were driven in, and the next day the enemy, consisting of at least three regiments of infantry, some cavalry and a battery of six guns, were discovered near Miner's Hill, concealed in the woods, which led to the supposition that an attack was meditated the next morning. At noon the drums beat, and the men got into fighting order. General M'Clellan and staff, including the Comte de Paris and the Duc de Chartres, rode over and remained during the night at Smoot's house; and at midnight the drums again beat and every preparation was made for an attack.

It was a clear and beautiful night; the moon shone forth in its mild beauty; the stars twinkled with resplendent glory, and not a cloud glided through the sky. The drums beat the long roll, the trumpets of the cavalry and artillery sounded their shrill blasts, and the bands of the infantry pealed forth their inspiring strains. The camp-fires burned brightly, the glittering bayonets and sabres flashed in the light, and every heart beat high with hope. At two A.M., various columns of troops on the Maryland side were put in motion, and moved across the river to a position, to be easily thrown to any point of the line the emergency might require. But alas! after remaining in position until daylight, chilled with the falling dews, the troops were doomed to disappointment. Beauregard had only been on a reconnaissance in force, to ascertain our position since the recent extension of our front.

At dress parade on the 14th, at the command "ground arms," a musket of Company E was discharged, a buckshot from which passed through the heart of Fred'k B. Seifert, and the ball through the arm of Alfred Phillips, privates of Battery B, Captain Cooper. Upon investigation, it was ascertained that the musket was not capped, showing the caps were without the proper metallic covering, which admitted of the charge adhering to the nipple. Seifert's body was sent home the next day, Companies E and D, with the Third's band, accompanying it to Langley.

At midnight on the 18th of October, orders were issued for the Reserve to prepare to move early the next morning, with three days' cooked rations in haversacks; and, accordingly, there was a busy time the balance of the night around the camp-fires. Early in the morning, the regiments were in line, and at seven o'clock they moved up the pike towards Drainesville. The First Brigade, General Reynolds, took the lead, with a squadron of Reserve Cavalry, Colonel Bayard,* in the van, followed by two batteries of the Reserve Artillery, Colonel Campbell,† the "Bucktails," Colonel Biddle,‡ and infantry, with the the ambulances, bringing up the rear. Crossing Difficult creek, they continued on through Drainesville, and halted to bivouac three miles beyond. Soon General M'Call rode up, and ordered them to fall back about four miles, to Thornton's house, at the forks of the Chain Bridge and Leesburg and Alexandria pikes. The artillery was posted to sweep the roads, pickets were thrown out, and the men put in a heavy woods, where they slept peacefully.

The Third Reserves fell into line with the Second Brigade, General Meade, about seven A.M., and following the First Brigade, advanced to within three miles of Drainesville, and halting in an open field, bivouacked for the night, the pickets surrounding the brigade. The Third Brigade, General Ord, moved to Difficult creek, and halted for the night, and General Smith moved a division out the Alexandria and Leesburg pike to cover that road.

The next morning, by daylight the boys were up and hard at work cutting down the chestnut trees, to get the nuts, and capturing the enemy's supply of pigs, turkeys and

---

* George D. Bayard, promoted Major-General. Killed at Fredericksburg, December 13th, 1862.
† Charles T. Campbell, promoted Brigadier-General.
‡ Charles J. Biddle, a soldier of the Mexican War, a distinguished lawyer, and, subsequently, a member of Congress, and editor of the *Philadelphia Age*.

chickens, which interesting operations, however, were interrupted by the commanding officers, and the boys confined to the limits of the camp.

On the march up they found **a number of** houses abandoned by their occupants, **who fled upon their** approach, under the impression, created by their newspapers, that they would carry on the war with rapine and murder. At some houses they found the furniture carried out, **ready for moving.** They also found houses that had been abandoned **for some** time, the inmates having been driven away **by their neighbors on account of their** Union sentiments.

During the day detachments were sent out to reconnoitre **the** neighboring **roads and country, and** make a plane-table **survey of a portion of it, and along the** London and Hampshire **railroad in several places they** encountered the enemy's **scouts,** killing **two and wounding four of them.** Two of the detachments **pushed forward to Goose creek, four** miles from Leesburg. **The next morning, the 21st,** General M'Call, having accomplished the object **of his** advance, in obedience to orders received that **morning from** General M'Clellan, returned to camp, **where** he arrived at 1 P.M., **just three hours** before **the** overwhelming attack **of the enemy on Colonel** Baker's* command at Balls Bluff was **commenced. If the** Reserves had been ordered **to remain at Drainesville on** Monday, they would have been within striking distance of the enemy's rear, and could have, very probably, captured or destroyed them.

Upon M'Call's return **to** Langley, he received **an order from General M'Clellan** instructing him, **if he had not yet** moved his command, to remain at Drainesville **until further orders.** M'Call telegraphed **his** position, **and** asked for instructions, and was ordered **to** rest and hold **his** men ready to move at short notice.

---

* E. D. Baker, Colonel Seventy-first Pennsylvania Volunteers and U. S. Senator from California. Formerly in Congress from Illinois, and a Colonel in the Mexican War. Killed at Balls Bluff.

Arms were stacked, artillery horses re-harnessed, three days' rations cooked, and the men held in readiness until late the next afternoon.

On the morning of the 26th, General M'Call reviewed the Reserves in front of Johnson's Hill. They consisted of the thirteen regiments of infantry of Generals Reynold's, **Meade's** and M'Calmont's brigades, the First Cavalry and the First Artillery. As the field contained but about forty **acres, the regiments were formed in** divisions **closed in** mass, which wheeled into column in mass, **and moved** forward to where General **M'Call and staff were** stationed; but before reaching him, **the divisions broke into** companies at wheeling distance, and passed in review. When **the** line began thus to uncoil itself, it reached a great distance, and presented a splendid appearance.

In the afternoon the camp of the Third was moved about a quarter of a mile nearer Langley, to the right of the pike and the west side of a fine sloping hill, terminating abruptly towards the village. On the crest was located the field and staff, and on the slope the company tents, with a fine parade ground between them.

On the 7th of November, the regiment was paid off by Major **John M. Pomeroy.** On the 10th, Quartermaster Frank S. Bickley resigned, and First Lieutenant **Strickland Yardley, Company C, was** appointed in his place. The next day, **Second Lieutenant** Florentine **H. Straub,** Company D, was elected **First** Lieutenant, **vice Bickley, resigned, and** Sergeant Andrew **J. Stetson was** elected Second **Lieutenant,** vice Straub, promoted. On the 14th, Second Lieutenant J. M. Buckingham, **Company** B, resigned, and Sergeant L. W. Hamlin was elected **Second** Lieutenant in **his place.**

On account of **the distance from Washington, and the difficulty of** getting there, **but few officers cared about taking the** trouble to procure **a pass, and drilling became the favorite** pastime with them. **The regiments being all encamped within** sight **of one another, quite a rivalry sprang** up as to which would become the most perfect. The effect was a marked improvement in battalion drill. About the same time, the colonel established a school of instruction among the officers, which was continued as long as they remained at Camp Pierpont.

On the 20th of November, a grand review of a portion of the Army of the Potomac took place near Munson's Hill, in a valley, or rather plain, two miles long by one broad. About seventy-five thousand troops were formed into three sides of a square. Upon the right were cavalry and artillery, and on the left the Pennsylvania Reserves. Around this immense plain thousands of people and vehicles were gathered.

At noon, the President and wife, in an open barouche, followed by Secretaries Seward and Cameron, a host of distinguished civilians and Foreign Ministers, arrived, and took post in the centre and front of the square. Soon after, General M'Clellan arrived, and took post to the left of the President, surrounded by his generals and staff. A salute of artillery was fired, and the President and Secretaries mounted horses and started on the review. Commencing on the left, they passed down by the Reserve, and as the party, consisting of some three hundred officers, generals and their staffs, rode by, the troops commenced cheering and the bands playing. After passing around, a position was taken, and orders given for the column to pass in review. First came the Reserves, which, after passing, filed to the right and marched at once to their camp, some ten miles off. Then followed General Heintzleman's Division, which passed to the left, and marched some fifteen miles to their post. The divisions of Generals Smith, Franklin, Blenker, Porter and M'Dowell, followed after, and each was dismissed, and marched directly to its camp.

About this time the men commenced preparing winter quarters. These consisted of walls of from four to six logs high, with wedge-tents placed over them. Floors of boards or logs were put down, shelves put up, and small sheet-iron stoves put in. From four to six soldiers generally bunked together, according to their liking.

Some of the men having fallen into the habit of absenting themselves from roll-call, drill, etc., the colonel one morning had the delinquents paraded in front of his quarters, and then marched them out to drill. The men understood the arrangement, and nothing was said to them about it, but the kind manner in which the colonel exercised them not only effectually checked the repetition of the offence but added to their love for him whom they looked upon not only as their commander but as their considerate friend, who at first always used gentle means to induce them to act right.

On the evening of the 26th of November, Colonel Bayard was ordered to scout the country beyond Difficult creek, a small stream crossing the pike about six miles from camp, and make a descent on Drainesville, seven miles further on, with five hundred men of the Reserve cavalry. The village was surrounded just before daylight, and several houses searched for guerrillas reported to harbor there. Four sleeping pickets, Charles Coleman, Philip Carper, Dr. Day and son, and three other citizens, were captured. After a half hour's halt the cavalry took up their march for camp. Two miles from the village, the head of the column was fired on by guerrillas concealed in the pine thickets by the roadside, and Assistant Surgeon Samuel Alexander and Private Joseph Hughling were killed, and two men severely wounded. Colonel Bayard was slightly wounded, and he and Surgeon David Stanton had their horses killed under them. Detachments along the line were immediately dismounted and pushed into the woods, and in a few minutes they killed or captured the whole party.

Among the killed was Thomas Coleman, the proprietor of the hotel in the village, and among the prisoners were Captian W. Farley, of General Bonham's staff, and Lieutenant T. de Caradene, of South Carolina, who were on a courting expedition to the Misses G——, who lived in the neighborhood. Cupid has no business outside the picket lines.

On the 27th, Private Peter W. Wittee, Company C, who died in the regimental hospital, was buried at Langley, with military honors, and the body of Private Joseph R. Barr, Company K, was sent to Philadelphia in charge of Lieutenant Donaghy. About the same time, Private Adam Martz, Company G, was buried at Langley, and the body of Lieutenant John Connally, Company G, was sent to Germantown in charge of Lieutenant Roberts. Orderly Sergeant Francis C. Harrison was elected Second Lieutenant, to fill the vacancy occasioned by the death of Lieutenant Connally.

On the 28th, Company E, Captain John Clark, was permanently detailed as provost guard at Langley, and encamped in the rear of General M'Call's headquarters.

On the 3d of December, the First Brigade started on a foraging expedition, and proceeded about nine miles up the pike to Mr. Thomas' house, where they captured a large number of wagon-loads of corn, etc., that had just been collected for the enemy. Mr. Thomas was an agent of the Confederate Government, whose business it was to scour the country, and collect from the unwilling inhabitants bedding, blankets, clothing, etc., for the use of the army. The Third Regiment returned to camp about six o'clock in the afternoon, much pleased with their trip.

Early on the morning of the 6th, General Meade marched with his brigade, Kern's battery, and a squadron of Reserve cavalry, under Major Jones,* towards Drainesville to Gunnell's farm, lying between the village and the Potomac, with instructions to capture the two nephews of Mr. Gunnell's, who, though not in the army, were in the habit of firing across the river at the Union pickets on the north side. These young gentlemen, with three of their associates and

---

* Owen Jones, of Montgomery county. Promoted Colonel May 5th, 1862.

two colored men, who sought our lines, were sent to General M'Clellan's headquarters, and fifty-five wagon-loads of grain, ten horses, a fine drove of hogs, several oxen, several shot-guns and rifles were brought to camp. Ord's Brigade followed Meade's in supporting distance. The Third arrived back in camp about dark, pretty well tired out.

These continued trespasses of the Reserve upon the enemy's territory brought on the battle of Drainesville. For when Ord's Brigade went out a few days later for a similar purpose, he was met by the enemy, prepared to contest the ground.

THE BATTLE OF DRAINESVILLE, DECEMBER 20TH, 1861.

General M'Call, having learned through his scouts on the evening of the 19th, that the enemy would be at Draines-ville the next day with a strong foraging party and a wagon train, for the purpose of carrying away all the forage and grain from the front of the Reserves, determined to dispute the right of property with them.

Accordingly, early the next morning, General Ord with his brigade, consisting of the Sixth, Captain W. G. Ent;[*] the Ninth, Colonel Conrad F. Jackson;[†] the Tenth, Colonel John S. M'Calmont; and the Twelfth, Colonel John H. Taggart;[‡] the "Bucktails," Lieutenant-Colonel Thomas L. Kane;[§] Easton's Battery of two twenty-four-pound howitzers and two twelve-pound smooth-bores, and four companies of cavalry under Lieutenant-Colonel Jacob Higgins, marched up the pike and through Drainesville, and halted some distance west of it. The enemy were soon discovered advancing north from the direction of Centreville, on the pike near where it joins the Chain Bridge and Leesburg pike, with

---

[*] Promoted Colonel and Brevet Brigadier-General.
[†] Promoted Brigadier-General July 17th, 1862. Killed at Fredericksburg.
[‡] Subsequently chief of Military School for Instruction of officers, Collector of Internal Revenue, and editor of the *Sunday Mercury* and of the *Sunday Times*, Philadelphia.
[§] Promoted Brigadier-General September 7th, 1862. Son of Judge Kane, U. S. Supreme Court, and brother of Dr. Kane, the celebrated Arctic explorer.

the evident intention of seizing the intersection, and cutting the communication of the brigade with camp Pierpont. Ord immediately double-quicked his command, and, galloping down the pike at the head of the artillery, overturned one of the guns as he wheeled into position, and seized the point.

The cavalry was posted on the extreme right, next the Ninth, then the Bucktails, then four companies of the Tenth, then the Sixth, and then the Twelfth; the six companies of the Tenth being with the train. The artillery was then pushed forward to an eminence near the Centreville road, supported by the Bucktails, a portion of whom posted themselves in a brick house near by.

Brigadier-General Stuart,* commanding the enemy, being frustrated in his design, posted Captain Cutt's Georgia battery of six guns on the Centreville road, with the Tenth Alabama, Colonel John H. Forney, and the Eleventh Virginia, Colonel Garland,† on his right; and the Sixth South Carolina, Lieutenant-Colonel Secrest, and the First Kentucky Rifles, Colonel Taylor, on the left, with Stuart's (his own) Virginia regiment of cavalry covering his flanks.

The enemy opened the battle with their artillery, which was at once responded to by Easton's guns, the first shot from which elicited loud cheers from our line, who rose to their feet, and then lay down again. This work, with a steady fire of infantry, lasted nearly a half-hour, when one of the enemy's caissons was exploded, and their guns driven from their position, when General Ord ordered the whole line to charge, which was done with loud cheers. Colonel Taggart, who held the left, valiantly advanced on foot through a dense woods and underbrush; Kane, at the head

---

* Major-General J. E. B. Stuart, late a Lieutenant U. S. Army. Participated as an aid to Lieutenant-Colonel (General) R. E. Lee in the capture of John Brown at Harpers Ferry Killed at Yellow Tavern, May 10th, 1864. Though ever ready for a "fight or a frolic," he espoused the Southern cause through conscientious motives, and was a sincere Christian.

† Promoted Brigadier-General. Killed at South Mountain, September 14th, 1862.

of the Bucktails, received a painful wound in the roof of his mouth, but still continued to lead, though he could not speak; and M'Calmont and Jackson cheered their men on. The enemy, in precipitous retreat, was driven from the field, and the first cheer of victory of the Army of the Potomac was there given.

Our loss was seven killed and forty-eight wounded.* The enemy, who reported the engagement to have been very severe, acknowledged the loss of forty-three killed, one hundred and forty-three wounded, and forty-four missing, the latter probably being mostly wounded or deserters. Colonel Forney was wounded, and Lieutenant-Colonel Martin killed. The Sixth South Carolina lost sixty-five men— partly by the fire of the First Kentucky, who mistook them for Unionists. They left twenty-five horses dead upon the field and two caissons.

General M'Call, by rapid riding, arrived upon the battle-field soon after the action commenced, and assumed command. After the battle, with the Reserves' dead, the wounded of both armies, the prisoners, trophies and forage, they returned to Camp Pierpont.

Early in the day the First Brigade, General Reynolds, moved beyond Difficult creek to within a short distance of Drainesville, and was followed by the Second Brigade, General Meade, but neither participated in the battle, and the whole command arrived in camp about eight o'clock in the evening.

A few days after the battle, Governor Curtin visited the Reserves, to congratulate them and care for the wounded, and he caused the flags of the regiments that participated in the engagement to be sent to Washington, where "Drainesville, December 20th, 1861," was inscribed on each, after which they were returned to them in the presence of the division and an assemblage of distinguished personages.

---

* Counted by the author.

Christmas is always a season of happiness to those who have loved ones at home, no matter how uncomfortable the wanderer may be, for he knows his loved ones are happy, and that he shares a portion of their thoughts and love that day. And the boys were not forgotten by those they held dear, for many were the Christmas boxes received, filled with roast fowls, cake and sweetmeats, and many happy hearts there were in camp that day. Innumerable little dinners were given by comrades of boyhood days, and if the turkey or chicken was not so hot, the cakes and other delicacies not so fresh and nice as at home, the repast was sweetened by the thought they came from dear home.

The usual dress parade was held that day, and when the officers had marched to the front, to salute the colonel, and the parade about to dismiss, Adjutant Jamieson moved the left wing in rear of the right. This unusual movement took the colonel and the men somewhat by surprise, but, supposing the adjutant was about to execute some brilliant military movements that would astonish even Hardie, he was not interrupted. But greater was the surprise when Captain Washington Richards stepped forward and produced a pair of holsters containing a magnificent pair of naval revolvers, which, in a neat and appropriate speech, he presented to the colonel in behalf of his brother officers. The colonel replied in a few neat and eloquent remarks, which were received with great enthusiasm by the officers and men.

The officers, in disposition and taste, very happily agreed, and it was their particular aim to promote kindly and good feelings. There was never any jarring, strife or jealousy among them, all the favors being conferred by mutual consent, and not by the arbitrary will of the colonel, except for the good of the service. In his tent they collected in the evenings around the cheerful fire, and passed the time in pleasant and instructive conversation, and if the discussions were shaping to extremes, they were happily turned into another direction, and they obtained the sobriquet of the "Happy Family." There was considerable religious element in the regiment, and this was duly encouraged, and proper respect was always shown to the chaplain, in whose tent and in some of the company officers' there were frequent prayer meetings, attended by earnest and sincere listeners. The beneficial effect of one kind and well-organized mind in a regiment has far more influence than is generally supposed in promoting the real happiness and welfare of the whole command, and is the surest guarantee of good discipline and faithful discharge of duty.

On the 1st of January, 1862, Orderly Sergeant J. B. Bartholomew was elected Second Lieutenant, Company H, to fill the vacancy caused by the resignation of Lieutenant Nelson Applebach on the 4th ult.

Winter now set in in earnest, and the "sacred soil of Virginia" began to assume very much the appearance of a vast mud-puddle. Almost every day it drizzled, rained and snowed alternately; the sun not blessing us with its genial rays, nor Jack Frost coming to our relief, to extricate us from the mud. Shoe and clothes brushes were at a discount. Nice young men, who formerly prided themselves on their kid gloves and patent-leather boots, began to realize the stern necessities of the case, and officers, sergeants, corporals and privates wandered about in a promiscuous mass, floundering and splashing in the mire, as happy as young ducks in a mud-puddle. Nature, happily, has formed man to be contented with circumstances, and what seems the height of misery to the imagination, in reality loses much of its unpleasantness. The boys ate their rations, thought of their sweethearts, slept warmly in their bunks, stood in the mud on guard, and shivered on picket, making the best of their situation, occasionaly wishing the war was over, and having slight hopes of furloughs in the future.

The reveille rattles, and up springs the soldier—"Fall in, Company A!" rings down the street, and, with variations in the letter, is repeated over the camp. Out stumble the sleepy boys and range themselves in line in front of their tents. Roll-call is soon over, and down they run to the neighboring creek, where their toilet is performed. Back to their tents, and tumbling in, they soon have a glowing fire burning. Then comes breakfast, which fascinating summons is always obeyed, and, with tin plates and cups, to the music of the "tin-plate march," they proceed to the cook's quarters of their company. The milkless coffee is dipped from a huge kettle, and the salt junk from a pile, and, with a few wafers of hard-tack, the patriots march back to their tents, and enjoy a hearty meal.

At eight comes guard mounting—quite an imposing ceremony in clear weather. Then the boys cut their wood and fill their canteens, clean their muskets, sew on buttons, write home, read, cut wooden chains and bone rings, play cards, smoke and talk over old times, and brag about their sweethearts. At noon the dinner call is sounded, and out turns the redoubtable tin-plate band, who waddle through the mud to the kitchen, where it is only by their redoubled energies with the more uproarious rattling of merry voices, that the words of discontent and grumbling are drowned. The beef generally turns out to be an article known to the soldiers as "salt horse," which sometimes gives way to its fresh kindred or bean soup, but is usually only varied with salt pork. The afternoon glides away like the morning, and then comes the unchangeable "hard-tack and coffee." At nine tattoo beats, and the regimental bands, commencing on the right of each brigade, begin playing, and by the time they have ceased, the half hour has expired for taps to sound, when all lights are extinguished and sounds cease. This is the routine of camp in bad weather, but when the ground will permit, drilling and bayonet exercise take place in the morning and afternoon, besides the "dress parade" of the evening.

On the 3d, the regiment was ordered to Difficult creek, to furnish details for and protect Brigade Quartermaster Ringwalt in repairing the bridge at that point. The pickets were ordered to let the column pass, but to prevent all stragglers from following. Upon arrival, pickets were thrown out, and the men went to work with great zeal. It being a fine day, they had a very pleasant time of it—it seeming more like a picnic than work. They returned to camp in time to hold dress parade.

On the 9th, the regiment was paid off by Paymaster Pomeroy, in treasury notes, he allowing one hundred dollars in gold to each captain to make change with for the men. The colonel having requested an expression of opinion by the officers, as to whom should be sent on recruiting service, and Lieutenants Davenport and Roberts being indicated by the ballot, they were accordingly detailed, and left for Pennsylvania on the 18th.

About this time target practice became quite popular, and the crack of muskets was heard daily in the direction of the Potomac. Fourteen rounds per man was allowed; the targets were 10x15 inches, and the distance one and two hundred yards. The firing was very good, and some of the men proved themselves most excellent shots.

Captain Richards, being sick, received permission to move to the house of Mr. Walters, a wealthy farmer, who resided near Langley. Mr. W. was a staunch Unionist, and having strenuously opposed the secession of his State, incurred the bitter hatred of his life-long neighbors, who favored it. They not being able to drive him and his family from their home, the aid of rebel cavalry was invoked, who made several descents upon his house at night, in hopes of capturing him. Mr. W., however, having no idea of going to Richmond, sometimes concealed himself in tree-tops, and at others under the floor of the out buildings, and succeeded in eluding them. At last he was forced to take to the woods, where he remained concealed for over a month, eluding their constant search. During this time food was brought by his daughter, Marietta, a brave, handsome, young girl, who, at night, with cat-like stillness, passed their guards, and deposited it at certain places in the woods, without ever awakening their suspicion. At last the Reserves came, and the rebels, chagrined at missing their prize, fired a number of cannon shot at the house and left.

Mrs. W., though exceedingly inconvenient, freely entertained all who came to her house; and with Captain Richards, an officer of the Second, Captains Scheetz and Beatty, of the staff, Colonel Campbell, of the artillery, General Bayard and Adjutant Buffington, of the cavalry, and several of their wives, there was an agreeable and social company. Miss Marietta, of course, was the great favorite, and her noble and artless heart won the admiration of all, and long after, in distant camps, when these officers met, was her name mentioned in respectful and warm remembrance.

Details for pickets were constantly made, and upon these occasions the two companies upon whom it fell were up bright and early, and, with a day's cooked rations, marched up the pike, where they were inspected by one of the general's aids, who verified the detail. Then they proceeded to Prospect Hill, where they were divided into three reliefs, and relieved the old picket. Shelters of boughs were built for the reserve to lie in, and a considerable portion of the day was spent in cutting wood for the night. Our line was near the Ball house, which, until it disappeared, was the headquarters. Mr. Ball was a violent secessionist, and, like most of his clan, had abandoned his home, and, with his family, gone south upon the approach of our army. The consequence was, everything soon went to ruin—the trees were cut down, fences burnt up, and one board after another disappeared from the house, until the chimney alone marked where it once stood.

This was the case all the way down to the Chain Bridge, and to Alexandria, the only exceptions being of those who had sense enough to remain at home, and those who had returned from the exile into which they had been driven by their secession neighbors. When the rebellion first broke out, the secessionists, although in the minority, with the aid of Confederate cavalry, drove the Union citizens from their houses, impressing the young men, and plundering and robbing the old and helpless.

An old slave and his wife were all that remained on the farm, and their cabin and little garden were undisturbed. They obtained their daily food from the haversacks of the soldiers, for which they appeared grateful. They had great faith in the efficacy of prayer, and when "old Uncle Ben" discoursed upon the war, he was wont to observe: "Massa Linkum has a power of men, and they am mighty fond of chickens. I 'spects Massa Government must be powerful rich to own all dem wagons and hosses." Uncle Ben truly loved the aforesaid gentlemen, and frequently inquired if they "had eber 'sperience' religion."

Picketing, in pleasant weather, was much preferable to the camp; but on the bleak hills near the Potomac, during the bitter cold nights, the wind came rustling down the valley, penetrating to the very bones. Sometimes it was so intensely cold that the men were relieved every hour. The reserve, by huddling up together near the fires, could manage to sleep pretty warm, and many a blessing arose from their hearts to the man who invented sleeping "spoon fashion."

Beyond the picket line was the cavalry patrol, who moved to and fro on the pike, as far as Difficult creek. Sometimes, on cold nights, the patrol would induce one of the infantry, who was off duty, to ride a round for him, while he warmed himself. This, however, it was necessary for them to keep to themselves.

The men had now been a long while from home, and, of course, longed to see those they loved and left behind; but as furloughs could not be granted to all, many were doomed to disappointment. Considerable numbers, however, took a run for a week or so without authority. Many of these, however, were detected in spite of their citizen's clothes, for soldiers have a peculiar look and style about them that is easily recognized by a practiced eye. When the Potomac froze over, this evil became prevalent, in spite of the sure punishment that awaited their return; but the men were willing to stand it for the pleasure of seeing those they loved. Pickets were stationed on the river with orders to shoot down any who attempted to cross. Soldiers on duty are very apt to obey orders, and several men were killed or wounded on the ice. But home, no matter how humble, is the palace of the heart, and surely it was right to deal leniently, upon their return, with those who run the gauntlet.

On the 22d of January, Privates Thomas C. Stone, of Company C; Adam Gilbert, of Company F; and James Rodine, of Company I, were detailed to the battery, and, about the same time, five volunteers from each regiment of the Reserve were called for the western flotilla; and the seventy-five men thus obtained formed the crew of the celebrated gunboat, Carondolet, that run such a glorious career upon the Mississippi.

On the 3d of February, Private James Rose, Company C, died in camp, and his comrades sent his body home. On the 27th, Orderly Sergeant Sebastian Eckle, Company A, was elected Second Lieutenant in place of Lieutenant J. A. Clous, who resigned on account of ill health. On the 28th, Private George W. Morris, Company C, died, and Chaplain William H. Leake resigned on account of failing health, and the Reverend George H. Frear, of Reading, was appointed in his place.

Early in March, orders were issued for three days' rations to be kept in the haversacks, and from the 4th to the 8th the Reserves were each day marched to the Chain Bridge or Difficult creek, to inure them for the coming campaign.

CHAPTER IV.

1862—WAITING FOR THE ADVANCE— JOHNSTON SUPERCEDES BEAUREGARD
— ARMY CORPS — OPENING OF THE CAMPAIGN OF 1862 — MARCH OF
THE RESERVES — HUNTER'S MILLS — ACTIVE MINDS vs. BODILY
STRENGTH — PATRIOTS AROUSED — TO ALEXANDRIA — REVIEW OF THE
FIRST CORPS — DEPARTMENT OF THE RAPPAHANNOCK — GENERAL
M'DOWELL — TO MANASSAS JUNCTION — INSURGENT DEBRIS — CON-
FEDERATE EAGLE — NAUGHTY BOYS — CATLETT STATION — WHITE
RIDGE — SLAVES — THE CONCEALED FLAG — A FINANCIAL TRANSAC-
TION — REVIEW AND INSPECTION — THE PRESIDENT — FREDERICKS-
BURG — DESTRUCTION OF THE BRIDGES — IN SEARCH OF HER HUS-
BAND.

THE nation had waited a long while for the Army of the Potomac to advance, and had now become impatient at its inactivity in front of Washington, with the Baltimore and Ohio Railroad obstructed and broken up on its right, and the navigation of the Potomac stopped by rebel batteries on its left. President Lincoln, late in January, issued a war order commanding a general advance upon the enemy from every quarter on the 22d of February, and a special war order to General M'Clellan to advance upon and seize Manassas Junction, on or before that date. General M'Clellan preferred a movement up the Peninsula, which the President objected to on account of the great delay and expenditure of money it would involve.

On the 30th of January, General Beauregard was succeeded in the command of the insurgent "Army of Virginia," by General Johnston,* who, at once, quietly and gradually commenced the removal of the vast stores at

---

* General Joseph E. Johnston, of Virginia; his father was an officer of Lee's Legion; his mother, a niece of Patrick Henry; was educated at West Point, and served in the United States Army in the grades from Second Lieutenant to Brigadier-General; and in the Confederate Army as General; was wounded at Fair Oaks; surrendered his army to General Sherman, in North Carolina, April 26th, 1865. Is a member of the Forty-sixth Congress of the United States.

Manassas, and completed the evacuation on the 8th of March, the smoke of their burning huts conveying the first intimation of the movement to our scouts.*

The next day, General M'Clellan ordered our army to advance on Manassas, to offer them "an opportunity to gain some experience on the march and bivouac, preparatory to the campaign, and to get rid of the superfluous baggage and other impediments." The cavalry, under Colonel Averill, at noon entered Centreville unmolested, and on the 14th discovered the enemy near Warrenton Junction. On the 13th, at a council of corps commanders at Fairfax Court House, the Peninsula campaign was decided on, providing, among other things, that "a total of 40,000 men be left for the defence of Washington." This was acquiesced in by the President, on condition that General M'Clellan should, "at all events, move such remainder of the army at once in pursuit of the enemy, by some route."†

On the 8th of March the President directed the army of the Potomac to be divided into four army corps, to be commanded by Generals Irwin M'Dowell, E. V. Sumner, S. P. Heintzleman and E. D. Keyes. On the 11th, General M'Clellan was relieved from the command of all military departments except that of the Potomac.

At one o'clock on the afternoon of the 10th of March, the Third Regiment got into line, and, bidding farewell to their happy home at Pierpont, moved on to the pike and took up its line of march towards Drainesville. Through the night and during the morning it had rained, making the roads muddy, and the heavy knapsacks bore hard upon the men's shoulders. But all were in excellent spirits, not knowing the object of the movement, and supposing they would soon meet the foe. The march bore pretty hard upon some of the weaker ones, but sooner than fall out to rest, they threw away their extra clothing, strewing the road with

---

* Pollard.
† The Secretary of War to General M'Clellan, March 13th, 1862.

coats, blouses, blankets, etc. Continuing up the pike, across Difficult creek to Spring Vale, they turned to the left, following a bridle path through the woods and over the hills until near ten o'clock at night, when they halted and bivouacked near Hunter's Mills. The night was cold and rainy, and no fires were lighted, but the boys, wearied with their fifteen miles' march, rolled themselves in their blankets and slept soundly.

The next morning the regiment moved across the road and encamped near Hawkhurst's Mills, which had been burned by the insurgent soldiers on account of the Union sentiment of the owner. The position was about two miles from Fairfax Court House, and was christened by the men "Smoky Hollow." Here they received the "shelter tents," which experience taught them were the best in use for an army in the field, as each man carrying his section, by joining with one or two comrades, could have a comfortable tent in a few moments. In fact, these sheets, with one or two small articles twisted up in them, and worn across the body from the shoulders to the waist, formed the entire kit of the Reserves throughout the war, after they threw away their knapsacks on the peninsula, and nothing could induce them to accept of more than an overcoat or blanket afterwards. Picket duty, company and battalion drill and dress parade served to occupy the time of the men and to keep up the proper discipline.

On the evening of the 14th, during a light fall of rain, they took up their march through the woods, passing, on every side, bivouacs and burning bough huts or arbors, the glare from which lighted them on their way for miles. Reaching the Alexandria and Leesburg pike, they turned to the right, and, passing along it to Powell's Mill, near Difficult creek, they, about midnight, filed into a dense woods, where their fires were soon burning brightly, and they lay down to sleep, despite the falling rain.

Early the next morning, during a heavy rain, the column was put in motion, and moving across the country, struck the Drainesville pike, and, turning down it, crossed Difficult creek and entered a wood, moving back again towards the Alexandria and Leesburg pike by a private road. During the whole day the rain was falling in torrents, flooding the swampy ground and making the march most fatiguing. It was impossible to keep the line closed up, and the men scattered and plunged through the mud, toiling under their heavy knapsacks. Upon reaching the pike a long halt was ordered, for the stragglers to catch up, and ambulances were sent back for those who had given out. Recommencing the march, about three o'clock they filed into the woods and stacked arms. Here was strikingly illustrated the superiority of an active and energetic mind over mere bodily strength to endure hardships. Some of the men set themselves down at the foot of trees, and covering their heads with their rubber blankets, remained all night in that position, feeling the next morning stiff, lame and miserable, while those who stirred about and kept up their spirits and took a little nap in the mud and rain, and then dried themselves by the fires, felt pretty well.

After much patient labor, they succeeded in getting the fires started, and towards night hot coffee was served out. But such was the violence of the storm, that it was impossible to put up the tents, and most of the men spent the night in cutting wood and standing around the fires. At one time, the heavens appeared to outdo themselves, opening their flood-gates and pouring down a torrent of water, stifling the wind, and flooding all below. The fires were almost instantly extinguished, and then the patriots were aroused to a full appreciation of their position. Not to be thus conquered and subdued by the raging elements, they set up their wild shouts and huzzahs, making the woods and hills, for miles around, echo with their noise, until, by indomitable perseverance, they actually got themselves into a good humor. All that was wanted, after they got fully started, to complete their happiness, was a fiddle and "straight four," and then they would have made a full night of it. But morning came, and with it a bright, warm sun, nature appearing to have exhausted herself in the mad rage of the night.

At ten o'clock the next morning the Reserves renewed their march. The day was tolerably fair, but the roads were heavy, and the boys felt hardly rested by their sleepless night from the fatigues of the preceding day. The knapsacks had scarcely grown lighter than when laid down the night before, yet they were full of life and spirit when they passed other troops, greeting them with good-humored and playful remarks. Near Falls Church, they found the old flag waving on a portico, surrounded by several ladies, who welcomed them with smiles of gladness. Passing Munson's Hill, and a long line of field-works erected at different times by the Union and insurgent troops, they arrived near Alexandria, and encamped before sunset on a hill overlooking the city, the Capital, and the Potomac. While they lay here the weather was cold, rainy and disagreeable, rendering the ground mostly unfit for drilling, but every favorable opportunity was taken advantage of for the purpose. They received their full rations and a ration of whiskey every rainy night. On the 25th, a grand review of the First Army Corps was had by General M'Dowell. On the 31st, Private Thomas Leonard, Company K, died from the effect of an amputation, found necessary in consequence of a gunshot wound accidentally received some time before. On the 3d of April, Sergeant James W. Carrier, Company B; Privates Frank Weighter, Company I; Samuel Duckworth, Company G; and Henry D. Boger, Company K, were detailed to the Fifth U. S. Battery, serving with the Reserves. Nearly the whole army was now concentrated around Alexandria, and the transportation of it to the Peninsula commenced, many regiments marching through the city and embarking each day.

For the defence of Washington, with its enormous depots of arms, munitions and provisions, M'Call's and King's divisions of the First Corps were detached from the Army of the Potomac, and the Department of the Rappahannock established, under the command of General Irwin M'Dowell. Reynolds' Brigade moved by rail, on the 9th, to Manassas Junction, during a severe snow storm. Early on the 11th, Meade's and Ord's Brigades commenced their march for the same place, moving along the pike through Fairfax Court House, and bivouacking three miles beyond. The next day they passed through Centreville and halted at Bull Run for dinner, and then, moving on, arrived at their destination in time to prepare their encampment. From Centreville all was a scene of desolation, the farms being stripped of their outbuildings and fences, and most of the wood being cut down by the enemy, who had occupied the country. At Manassas were the vast ruins of the depot, hospital, and other buildings destroyed upon the evacuation. In every direction were seen wrecked cars and machinery; vast piles of flour, pork, beef, tallow, hides and bones; broken wagons, ambulances and caissons; scattered clothing, trunks, bottles, demijohns, tents, barrels and boxes; deserted huts and fieldworks, all mixed up together in inextricable confusion. The only thing left to welcome us was that pet of the South, a Confederate eagle, commonly called in the North a turkey buzzard, whose wings had been clipped by our departed friends, to prevent its escape. Not liking, however, the sanitary condition of our encampment, he left in search of better fare. Soon after our arrival, quite a number of sutler and other "shebangs" were opened in the neighborhood, which furnished us an abundant supply of the various articles so necessary for the soldier's comfort. One individual was doing a thriving business, he having succeeded in smuggling through a barrel of cider, which delightful beverage he dispensed to his thirsty patrons at ten cents a glass. Some of the boys, however, conceived the idea of running opposition to him, and having succeeded, through false pretense, in borrowing an auger and faucet from him, cut a hole in the back of his tent, tapped his barrel, and commenced operations. As they charged but half-price, and gave twice as much, they were liberally patronized, and after selling out in an incredibly short time they decamped, when he was invited around to view the operation.

Early on the 18th, the Third moved off with the brigade, in a southerly direction, soon striking the Orange and Alexandria railroad, on which they crossed Broad and Kettle runs on the new bridges built to replace those destroyed by the enemy. Towards night they arrived near Catlett's Station, where they encamped. The distance made was about twelve miles, and the day being very warm, many of the men threw away their overcoats to lighten their burdens.

Here Dr. Thomas B. Reed was promoted Brigade Surgeon, but, much against his will, was detached from the division, and was ordered to Yorktown. It was his earnest wish to remain with the Reserves during the war. His departure was much regretted, on account of the sincere attachment of the officers and men of his regiment.

On the 21st, Colonel Sickel was detailed as division field officer of the picket line, Lieutenant-Colonel Thompson as brigade field officer, and Companies A, I and F as picket on the heights beyond Cedar creek. It had rained hard for several days, which swelled the creek so much that during the night the railroad bridge was swept away, and the picket was detained until the flood subsided sufficiently to permit them to ford. Here they found, for the first time, honest people, they acknowledging frankly they were secessionists. They did not anticipate war as the result of their movement, but believed if one did occur it would be on northern soil. They regretted the state of affairs now existing, and, when closely questioned, expressed their belief in their ultimate success. On the 26th and 27th, Captain Feaster was detailed, with fifty men, to rebuild the bridge. The next day was clear, pleasant and cool, and in the morning the brigade moved off, over hills and dales, and through the woods and fields, in a southeasterly direction. They passed several churches, a Methodist and a Baptist, but in neither of them had divine service been held for eight months, the war having unsettled society so much, even before our advent. Many slaves were found on the route, who told us they had been for a long while discussing the subject of moving North. They all longed for liberty, excepting the feeble and the old, who had spent a life of unrequited toil, and who did not feel they could care for themselves. Passing through the small village of White Ridge, near sunset they bivouacked in a pine woods, having marched twelve miles. The next morning, the 29th, they moved off early, marching on the fields alongside of the roads. The country became more diversified, and timber heavier. In passing a stately mansion, the men's hearts were gladdened by the sight of the stars and stripes flying from a tree in the lawn, and their loud cheers rolled down the line and through the woods. This flag had been concealed for many months in an artificial hollow in the tree, neatly covered by a piece of bark. At noon, near Hartwood, a long halt was called for dinner, and then they moved on, passing the spot where Colonel Bayard, of the Reserve cavalry, had whipped the enemy on the 18th, and had driven them beyond the Rappahannock. A short ways on they entered Falmouth, through which they passed with banners unfurled and bands playing. The women and children flocked to the doors and windows, and a motley crowd of colored folks followed, the men enraptured with the music, and the women in ecstacy over the flags, declaring them "rale silk." About two miles beyond, they encamped in a fine woods near the Acquia railroad, where they found abundance of fuel and water, articles so necessary for the comfort of soldiers. The march was twenty miles, and the men came in in fine order, with but few stragglers. The ground where we lay was once owned by Washington, he having inherited it from his father. Near here he spent his youth, from the age of ten to sixteen, during which time he obtained the principal portion of his school education.

Falmouth is situated on the Rappahannock, nearly opposite Fredericksburg, with which it was connected by two bridges, which, with several steamboats and sailing crafts, were burnt upon our approach. A church, a factory, a mill, and several stores, and about eighty dilapidated frame houses, constituted its extent. What few articles the inhabitants offered for sale they asked exorbitant prices for, but soon the town was filled with our sutlers, store-keepers and photographers, who gave new life to it.

Some of the Bucktails, who had a large supply of imitation Confederate notes, such as were sold as curiosities in all the Northern cities at a cent apiece, tried one of them on the miller, and with such success that they went back and bought him out, paying nearly eleven hundred dollars for his stock of flour. When he discovered the character of the notes, instead of giving way to vain regrets, he repaired to General M'Call's headquarters, and asked for a pass to cross to Fredericksburg, basing his application on this transaction, he thinking it but right he should have an opportunity to pass them off and reimburse himself before it was known over there. Captain Beatty, of the staff, was detailed to quote Scripture to him bearing upon the subject, but he left in disgust.

Here a division bakery was established, which was capable of turning out 2,160 loaves of bread per day. On the 10th of May, Captain Feaster, with sixty-four men, was detailed to rebuild the Acquia and Fredericksburg railroad bridge, and on the 19th the cars passed over the river. It was partly built of timber which the enemy had dressed for the purpose of constructing gun-boats. On the morning of the 19th the regiment marched to a large open field, where the brigade was reviewed and inspected by Colonel Van Rensselaer, Inspector-General U. S. Army, assisted by Prince, Colonel Felix Salm Salm, Sixty-eighth New York Volunteers. At the review, the bands of the brigade, numbering some sixty instruments, were united, producing a very loud noise.

On the afternoon of the 23d, His Excellency Abraham Lincoln, accompanied by the Hon. Edwin M. Stanton, Secretary of War, and Hon. William H. Seward, Secretary of State, Major-General M'Dowell and staff, and General Shields, who, on account of his wounds, rode in a carriage, reviewed our corps about three miles from camp. As the President rode down the line on a fine, spirited black horse, the troops presented arms, the colors drooped, officers saluted, drums beat, trumpets sounded, and a salute of twenty-one guns fired. Long and loud cheers for the steadfast helmsman broke forth from the men as he passed along.

General M'Dowell had been instructed on the 17th, as soon as General Shields should arrive with his division from the valley, to advance on Richmond overland, and join General M'Clellan. Shields' Division arrived on the 22d, after long and fatiguing marches, and it was decided, at a consultation between the President and the generals, that the movement should commence on the 26th. Hardly had the President departed, than dispatches were received by General M'Dowell informing him of the raid of the enemy, under General Jackson, down the Shenandoah Valley. This wholly changed the plans, and three divisions, under Generals Ord, Shields and King, were sent, with General Bayard's Brigade of Cavalry and four companies of Bucktails under Lieutenant-Colonel Kane, to General Banks' relief. The departure of these troops left the Reserves to hold Fredericksburg, and on the 26th the division moved towards Falmouth, and encamped opposite the city, near the abandoned camps of some New York troops.

The First Brigade the same day crossed the river, and marching through the city, encamped on Marye's Heights in the rear. Six months afterwards some of the hardest fighting of the war occurred on this identical spot. General Reynolds was appointed Military Governor, and, being a soldier and a just man, was vigorous and equitable in his administration. So highly was he respected by the citizens that, upon his being taken prisoner at Gaines' Mills, they sent a deputation to Richmond to intercede for his parole. Fredericksburg is an ancient city of about 5,000 inhabitants, and before the war its exports amounted to considerable. Captain John Smith, of Pocohontas fame, ascended the river in 1608, and fought the Indians on its site. On the outskirts of the city, on the edge of a pretty bluff, is the grave of Mary, the mother of Washington.

On the 31st, Reynolds' Brigade was withdrawn from the city, and rejoined the division. The same day the Third was paid off by Paymaster Pomeroy, and white duck leggins were issued to the men. On the 4th of June the river became so much swollen from the effect of continued rain, that fears were entertained for the safety of the bridges. General M'Call, therefore, ordered the pontoon-bridge to be taken up. In the afternoon the trestle-bridge, not being able to resist the pressure, gave way, and was swept down the river, the wreck coming in contact with the railroad bridge and carrying it away. The timbers of these two being swept against the canal-boat bridge, destroyed it also. The destruction of the bridges occasioned much joy among the inhabitants of the city, who had collected on the bank to witness the scene, and who could not refrain from manifesting it by loud cheers and the waving of handkerchiefs. Certainly we could not expect them to grieve at their enemy's discomfitures.

While here, Colonel John H. Shelmire and Major James Hart, of Pennsylvania, serving in the First New Jersey Cavalry, visited the Third, and dined with the officers. The former was killed at Brandy Station in 1863, and the latter at Dinwiddie Court House in 1865. One afternoon, a buxom widow, apparently of great simplicity of mind, came into camp in search of her husband, to whom she had been married two days before, and who had left early the next morning to breakfast with General Meade. She had not procured a marriage certificate, but knew it was all right, as the ceremony had been performed by the chaplain, who wore two stripes upon his arm. The corporal who officiated upon the occasion was not known to the author, but the young scamp of a husband flourished through the war.

CHAPTER V.

EMBARKATION FOR THE PENINSULA — BY STEAM TO THE WHITE HOUSE — "FOR THE EMBALMING THE DEAD" — BRIEF SKETCH OF THE SIEGE OF YORKTOWN — EXTRACTS FROM "THE LOST CAUSE" — MAGRUDER'S REPORT, AND COLONEL FREMANTLE — GENERALS BARNARD, SUMNER AND KEYES; W. H. HURLBERT AND REV. MR. MINNIGERODE, ON FAIR OAKS — TO DISPATCH STATION — TO THE CHICKAHOMINY — THE THIRD SHELLED OUT — COURTESY OF THE PICKET LINE — A GALLANT DASH — BATTLE OF MECHANICSVILLE — INSURGENTS' ACCOUNT OF THE BATTLE — MEADE'S COLORED MAN.

ON SUNDAY afternoon, June 8th, orders were received for the Reserve to join M'Clellan. Great was the joy of the men, and long and loud their cheers, and the bands pealed forth their inspiring strains. Three days' rations were issued and cooked, and Reynolds' Brigade started at sundown. Early the next morning, tents were struck, knapsacks packed, and Meade's Brigade got into line. It was a cool and pleasant morning, and light was the step of the men as they marched through the woods and over the hills to the banks of the Rappahannock, down which they proceeded to Gray's Landing, where a fleet of steamboats lay to receive them. It was nearly sundown before Reynolds' Brigade was aboard and moved off, and that night the Third bivouacked on a hill near the landing. Early the next morning, all was astir, and, after breakfast, the regiment embarked on the Kent and Hugh Jenkins, and steamed down the river, as happy a set of blue-coats as ever trod this planet. Passing the towns of Port Royal and Tappahannock, they came to anchor about dark, off the mouth of Carter's creek. The next morning, the 11th, the transports weighed anchor at three o'clock, and proceeding down the river into the Chesapeake bay, and heading nearly south, entered the York river about seven o'clock, passing the fortifications and batteries at Yorktown and Gloucester City.

Continuing on, they entered the **Pamunkey** river at its confluence with the **Mattapony**, where West Point is situated, and winding their way up that crooked stream through fleets of transports of all kinds and descriptions, they arrived at White House in the middle of the afternoon, where they disembarked and stacked arms, giving the boys time to wash themselves and replenish their stock of tobacco.

Soon they fell in and marched about a mile inland, passing an establishment with a conspicuous sign—"For the Embalming the Dead"—whose proprietors' faces brightened up at the sight of their anticipated customers. The boys received their handbills with much interest, and made particular inquiries as to the *modus operandi*, some proposing to go through the operation at once, if it would not interfere with their eating hard-tack, and others simply giving their orders with instructions not to spoil their countenances.

Let us briefly allude to the operations of the Army of the Potomac on the Peninsula up to this time. On the 2d of April, 1862, General M'Clellan arrived at Fortress Monroe, the greater portion of his army* having preceded him. On the 5th of April, he commenced the siege of Yorktown, and intended to assault it on the 6th of May, but, on the 4th, discovered the enemy had abandoned the works during the night.†

---

* The official return of General M'Clellan, made April 30th, gives the strength of his army as: aggregate, 130,378; fit for duty, 112,392.

† Pollard says:

"General Magruder, the hero of Bethel, and a commander who was capable of much greater achievements, was left to confront the growing forces on the Peninsula, which daily menaced him, with an army of 7,500 men, while the great bulk of the Confederate forces was still in motion in the neighborhood of the Rappahannock and the Rapidan, and he had no assurance of re-enforcements. The force of the enemy was ten times his own; they had commenced a daily cannonading upon his lines; and a council of general officers was convened, to consider whether the little army of 7,500 men should maintain its position in the face of ten-fold odds, or retire before the enemy. The opinion of the council was unanimous for the latter alternative, with the exception of one officer, who declared that every man should die in the intrenchments before the little army should fall back—' By G—, it shall be so!' was the sudden exclamation of General Magruder, in sympathy with the gallant suggestion. The resolution demonstrated a remarkable heroism and spirit. Our little force was adroitly extended over a distance of several miles, reaching from Mulberry Island to Gloucester Point, a regiment being posted here and there in every gap, plainly open

The pursuit of the enemy was prompt and energetic, and the battle of Williamsburg was fought and won. The divisions of Franklin, Richardson and Porter were transported up the York river, and on the 7th the enemy were defeated at West Point. On the 17th, a fleet of gun-boats had ascended the James to Drewry's Bluff. The battle of Hanover Court House was fought on the 27th, and the enemy defeated. On the 31st of May and the 1st of June, the battle of Fair Oaks* was won.

On the night of the Reserves' landing at White House, two days' rations were cooked, and the next morning, the 13th, the Third moved out under Lieutenant-Colonel Thompson, and the brigade under the command of Colonel Sickel. They marched on the railroad; the country through which they passed was mostly low, heavily wooded, and interspersed with numerous swamps. In the cuts of the railroad there were seen considerable deposits of marine shells and coral, indicating, at some remote period, this portion of the Peninsula had been the bed of the ocean. Coral was particularly noticeable on the surface at the field of Glendale. The day was excessively warm, and many of the men lightened their load by throwing away their overcoats and

---

to observation, and on other portions of the line the men being posted at long intervals, to give the appearance of numbers to the enemy. Had the weakness of General Magruder at this time been known to the enemy, he might have suffered the consequences of his devoted and self-sacrificing courage; but as it was, he held his lines on the Peninsula until they were re-enforced by the most considerable portion of General Johnston's forces, and made the situation of a contest upon which the attention of the public was unanimously fixed as the most decisive of the war."

Colonel Fremantle, of the British Coldstream Guards, in his "Three Months in the Southern States," says:

"He (Magruder) told me the different dodges he resorted to to blind and deceive M'Clellan as to his strength, and he spoke of the intense relief and amusement with which he, at length, saw that General, with his magnificent army, begin to break ground before miserble earthworks, defended only by 8,000 men."

* General J. G. Barnard, chief engineer, and General W. F. Barry, chief of artillery, in their report of the campaign say:

"The repulse of the rebels at Fair Oaks should have been taken advantage of. It was one of those occasions which, if not seized, do not repeat themselves. We now know the state of disorganization and dismay in which the rebel army retreated. We now know that it could have been followed into Richmond. Had it been so, there would have been no resistance to overcome to bring over our right wing. Although we did not then know all that we now do, it was obvious at that time that, when the

blankets. About five o'clock they reached **Dispatch Station**, and moved into the fields, to the right of the road, and encamped near the Chickahominy river. That night, news came that the enemy's cavalry had attacked a train at Tunstall's Station, and **threatened** White **House.** Reynolds' Brigade marched down the railroad in **pursuit** of them.

Orders were issued forbidding the sounding of calls, and ordering the tying to trees of all who fired muskets. Through the day, the sound of artillery was heard continually.

At five o'clock on the morning of the 18th, the Reserves marched for the extreme right of the line of the army, the position assigned to them at the request of General M'Dowell when we parted from him. About noon, we bivouacked near Gaines' house, some three hundred yards from the river. This ground had just been vacated by Franklin's division, and was separated from the river by a heavy woods, from the edge of which we could see the enemy on the other side, busy at work. In the afternoon, they opened with their artillery on some of our workmen, to which a Reserve battery replied. On our side, one man was wounded, and a gun dismounted.

---

rebels struck the blow at **our left wing**, they did not leave any means in their hands unused to secure success. It was obvious enough that they struck with their whole force; and yet we repulsed them in disorder with three-fifths of ours. We should have followed them up at the same time that we brought over the other two-fifths."

General Sumner testified before the committee on the conduct of the war:

"If we had attacked with our whole force, we should have swept everything before us; and I think the majority of **the officers who** were there think so."

General Keyes testified:

"**After the battle of** Seven Pines * * * * If the army had **pressed on after the enemy with** great vigor, we should have gone to Richmond."

William Henry Hurlbert (rebel) says:

"The roads into Richmond were literally crowded with **stragglers, some throwing away their guns**, some breaking them on the trees—all with **the same story, that their** regiment had been 'cut to pieces,' that the 'Yanks were swarming the Chickahominy like bees, and fighting like devils.' In two days of the succeeding week the provost marshal's guards collected between 4,000 and 5,000 stragglers, and sent them into camp."

The Rev. Mr. Minnigerode, Rector of St. Paul's **Church**, Richmond, in regard to Fair Oaks, says:

"**Fears** were **entertained in** Richmond, by the citizens, that M'Clellan would get in. Large numbers left the place; some ran off and left their houses vacant, while others sold out at a great sacrifice."

The next day, Reynolds' and Seymour's* brigades moved about a mile and a half to the right, near Nunally's and Ellison's mills, on the roads leading to Mechanicsville over Beaver Dam creek. Eight companies of the Third were detailed for picket, near the banks of the Chickahominy, on W. B. Sydney's farm. On the 20th, the enemy taking a fancy to the Third's encampment, shelled it out, tearing a number of tents and splintering the trees, but doing no other damage. After they got through, the camp was moved a half mile to the rear, where it was beyond the polite attention of their misguided brethern aross the river. It was evident some of the Confederate officers opposite to us were gentlemen, for one morning when our field officer of the picket line, Lieutenant-Colonel M'Intire, of the First, was visiting the posts, he found the enemy relieving their guard on the breastworks, and upon their perceiving him, they presented arms, which compliment he returned.

On the 22d, orders were issued for the Reserves to form line of battle every morning at three o'clock, to stack arms at sunrise, and remain in camp, with accoutrements on, ready for any sudden emergency. There being an alarm on the picket line during the night of the 23d, Lieutenant Stetson and nine men were sent at daylight to ascertain the cause. Some men are always full of enterprise, and ready to engage in dare-devil exploits, and Sergeant Edward L. Lennon, Corporal James E. Masters and Private Elwood Trimer, Company C, being of that stamp, crossed the Chickahominy and attacked the enemy's picket line, killing one man and creating considerable commotion among them. They succeeded in getting back safely, but had a lively time of it while in the river, the balls splashing around them in every direction.

Affairs were now approaching a crisis in front of Richmond. General M'Clellan, on the 20th of June, five days

---

*General Ord having been promoted a Major-General in May, and ordered to the West, he was succeeded by Brigadier-General Truman Seymour.

before the opening of the Seven Days' battle, reported his army to number: present for duty, 115,102; special duty, sick and in arrest, 12,225; absent, 29,511; total, 156,838. On the 26th of June, his chief of the "Secret Service Corps," reports the enemy to number 180,000 present for duty. Their official reports since published, establishes the fact that they numbered but 70,000 men fit for duty.

General M'Clellan having at last completed his bridges and entrenchments, on the 25th ordered an advance of our picket line on the left, preparatory to a general movement on the city the next day. General Hooker's division of Heintzelman's Corps was pushed forward, which resulted in the battle of "Oak Grove."

General Robert E. Lee, who had assumed the command of the insurgent army upon General Joseph E. Johnston being wounded at Fair Oaks, also resolved at the same time upon assuming the offensive, and with this view, had rapidly and secretly moved Jackson from the valley in front of Banks to Ashland, facing our extreme right. The whole of the insurgent army was to connect with him, and advance upon our right, with the exception of Huger's and Magruder's* divisions, left in front of our left and center, for the defence of Richmond. This plan of battle, of striking an army on one flank and doubling it up upon itself, was identically the same as that adopted by General M'Dowell at the first Bull Run.

The force of the enemy on our right wing was not less than 50,000 men, and to oppose this was Fitz John Porter's Fifth Corps of but 27,000, to which the Reserves were attached.

THE BATTLE OF MECHANICSVILLE, JUNE 26TH, 1862.

As early as the 24th, General M'Clellan began to suspect this movement, and on the morning of the 26th, all the

---

* Major-General J. Bankhead Magruder. When a Lieutenant-Colonel United States Artillery, he called upon the President and said: "Mr. Lincoln, every one else may desert you, but I never will." Two days afterwards he joined the rebels.

wagons of the Reserve except the ammunition were ordered to be sent to his headquarters. On that day the Fifth Reserve, Colonel Simmons, and the six companies of the Bucktails under Major Roy Stone,* were on picket from Mechanicsville to above Meadow Bridge. At noon the Second, Colonel M'Candless,† marched past Mechanicsville to Shady Grove Church, where they met the Eighth Illinois Cavalry, Colonel Farnsworth,‡ who were being driven in by General Branch's§ advance. M'Candless, throwing out skirmishers and deploying his regiment to delay their advance, gradually fell back. The Bucktails on the left also retired, but Captain Irvin's‖ company, which was posted on the Grenshaw road, was cut off and captured. The Third, Colonel Sickel, left camp at one o'clock with muskets and cartridge-boxes, and moved to Mechanicsville, where a line of battle was formed, but soon afterwards all withdrew to Beaver Dam creek, where it was determined to give battle.

This position was naturally a strong one, the left resting on the Chickahominy, and the right extending to a dense woods beyond the upper road, which were occupied. The passage of the creek was difficult through the greater part of the front, and with the exception of the roads crossing at Ellison's Mill, near the left, and that near the right, above mentioned, impracticable for artillery. On the right of the last-named road, on an elevation, an epaulement for four fieldpieces was thrown up, and rifle-pits for a regiment each were constructed in front of each brigade on the left of the road.

---

* To Colonel One Hundred and Forty ninth Pennsylvania Volunteers. Appointed Brevet Brigadier-General September 7th, 1864.

† Appointed Brigadier-General. A prominent lawyer of Philadelphia; State Senator and Secretary of the Interior of Pennsylvania, 1875.

‡ Colonel E. J. Farnsworth. Appointed Brigadier-General.

§ General L. O'B. Branch, of North Carolina. Killed at Antietam.

‖ Captain Edwin A. Irvin. Promoted Lieutenant-Colonel. Disabled at Fredericksburg December 13th, 1862.

The line of battle was formed in the following order: On the extreme right were six companies of the Second Regiment, Lieutenant Colonel M'Candless; then the six companies of the Bucktails, Major Stone; the Fifth Regiment, Colonel Simmons; the First Regiment, Colonel Roberts; and the Eighth Regiment, Colonel Hayes; composing Reynolds' Brigade. Then the Tenth Regiment, Colonel Kirk; the Ninth Regiment, Colonel Jackson; and the Twelfth Regiment, Colonel Taggart; which occupied the extreme left, and belonged to Seymour's Brigade. Meade's Brigade in reserve, consisted of the Third Regiment, Colonel Sickel; the Fourth Regiment, Colonel Magilton; and the Seventh Regiment, Colonel Harvey. Easton's battery of four twelve-pounder Napoleon guns, and Kerns' battery of six twelve-pounder howitzers, were also held in reserve. Four of Cooper's battery of ten-pound Parrot guns, were placed in the epaulement, and two outside of it, near the Bucktails. Smead's regular battery of four twelve-pounder Napoleons, was placed on the left of the road commanding it. De Hart's regular battery of six twelve-pounder Napoleons, was stationed near the front and center, commanding a more distant view of the same road, and also the lower road direct to the village by Ellison's Mills. The Fourth Pennsylvania Cavalry, Colonel Childs,* attached to the Reserves, were held in readiness, but were not called into action. It should be mentioned that the Sixth Regiment, Lieutenant-Colonel M'Kean, having been detached some days before, was at Tunstall's Station, on the railroad, while the Eleventh Regiment, Colonel Gallagher, was on picket on the Chickahominy.

About three o'clock in the afternoon the insurgents' lines were formed in our front, and their skirmishers were rapidly advanced, delivering their fire as they came forward. They were speedily driven back by the infantry and artillery. In

---

* Colonel James H. Childs, of Allegheny county. Killed at Antietam.

a short time the enemy, who were commanded by General Lee in person, consisting of the divisions of A. P. Hill,* D. H. Hill and Longstreet,† under cover of a heavy artillery fire, boldly and rapidly advanced in force, and attacked the whole position from right to left, in the face of a destructive fire they could not effectively return. It was not long, however, before it was apparent that his main attack was directed upon the extreme right, and General M'Call ordered the Third, Colonel Sickel, that had been stationed near the left center, and Kerns'‡ battery of howitzers thither to the support of the Second, who were hotly engaged. On this point was concentrated a heavy fire of artillery, and regiment after regiment of Georgians were hurled headlong against the Second, whose left wing was repeatedly bent back by them, but never broken. For three hours the most desperate contest was maintained, when at last the Second swung its left to the rear, to give play to Kerns' guns, which opened a most destructive fire of shell upon the broken and confused masses of the enemy, on the opposite side of the swamp.

After this, the enemy retired for a time from the close contest on the right, but, from the right center to the extreme left, kept up a heavy discharge of artillery and musketry, which was rapidly replied to by the Reserves. Somewhat later in the day, a heavy column came down the road to Ellison's Mill, where another most determined attack was made. Here, for hours, the battle was hotly contested, the Twelfth, Colonel Taggart, maintaining their position with desperate determination. General M'Call, fearing the enemy would turn the extreme left, sent the Seventh, Colonel Harvey, below the Mill, to hold the creek, and dispatched Easton's battery to Taggart's assistance. The fire of the artillery and infantry was incessantly dealing

---

* Killed at Petersburg, Va., April 2d, 1865.
† Since Collector of the Port of New Orleans.
‡ Captain Mark Kerns, of Franklin county. Killed at second battle of Bull Run.

destruction to the determined enemy, who, from their greatly superior numbers, were enabled to precipitate column after column of fresh troops upon our hard-pressed left and center.

Although the attack was not renewed on the center and right in force, there was a sharp contest going on there all the while, particularly at a ford on the extreme right, where Major Woodward, with two companies of the Second, was stationed, and took fifteen prisoners.

About dark, Griffin's Brigade, together with Edwards' battery arrived, and were sent to the weakest point, the extreme right, but only one regiment, the Fourth Michigan, Colonel Woodberry, was brought into action, they relieving the Fifth Regiment, who had completely exhausted their ammunition. About nine o'clock at night, after a battle of six hours, the enemy withdrew, and the contest ceased.

General M'Call's greatest anxiety was for our right, and there is no doubt, if Lee had detached a portion of his vastly superior force to turn it, or had Jackson arrived in time, we would have been swept from the field with fearful slaughter. The attack should have commenced earlier in the day. Near the close of the battle, fresh re-enforcements came to our relief, but the officers and men refused to give place, and, replenishing their ammunition, lay down upon their arms. All night long was heard the most pitying moans of the enemy's wounded, that lay in the swamp and woods beyond.

The strength of the Reserve upon the field was about 7,000. Their loss was but thirty-three killed and one hundred and fifty wounded.* The strength of the enemy was admitted to be 20,000, and General M'Call says: "I learned from official authority, while a prisoner in Richmond, that General Lee's loss in killed and wounded at Mechanicsville did not fall short of 2,000." In official returns published, it was admitted that the First North Carolina lost one-half

---

* For the loss in the Third, see Appendix A.

its effective force, and the Forty-fourth Georgia nearly two-thirds.

Generals M'Clellan and Fitz John Porter arrived upon the field at ten o'clock at night, and, learning of Jackson's advance to turn our right, at three o'clock the next morning sent orders to General M'Call to withdraw the Reserves and fall back to the rear of Gaines' Mills. During the consultation, General Porter hesitated, and expressed fears that M'Call would be cut to pieces in withdrawing.

Before the movement was commenced, the enemy renewed the attack, mostly on the left. Under these circumstances, and in broad daylight, the execution was most delicate and difficult, yet it was successfully accomplished, great caution and deliberation being used to screen the movement, and the troops being withdrawn slowly and at intervals. Meade's Brigade and batteries were the first to move; then came Griffin's Brigade and battery; next, Reynolds', under cover of the Bucktails and Cooper's guns; and last, Seymour's, from the extreme left; the Twelfth, Colonel Taggart, being the last to leave the field. All this was done under fire, and so well and deliberately that the regiments filed past General M'Call as steadily as if from the parade ground. Not a man, gun, or musket was left upon the field, and our dead were all buried.

Mr. Pollard, in "The Lost Cause," pages 284-5, speaks of this battle as two separate engagements, the "Battles of Mechanicsville and Beaver Dam." After stating that Mechanicsville was strongly fortified, he says: "A deafening cannonade of half an hour disturbed the last hours of evening. The flash of guns and long lines of musketry fire could be seen in bright relief against the blue and cloudless sky. As night drew on, a grander scene was presented to the eye. Barns, houses and stacks of hay and straw were in a blaze; and by their light our men were plainly visible, rushing across the open space through infernal showers of grape. A few moments more, and the

Federal guns were silenced; a loud noise of many voices was heard; and then a long, wild, piercing yell, and the place was ours.

"The enemy was now forced to take refuge in his works, on the left bank of Beaver Dam creek, about a mile distant." * * *

After this statement, not one word of which is true, as there was not a shot fired at Mechanicsville that day, he passes over the real battle as an insignificant affair, and then describes a "terrible and critical action" as taking place the next morning, the 27th, in which Jackson flanked us, and we retired rapidly down the river. As Mr. Pollard was the editor of the *Richmond Examiner* during the war, and probably visited the field soon after the battle, it would be supposed he would have been more correctly informed as to the location of the conflict and the facts of it.

We fell back slowly and in good order, but in anything but a good humor, the boys not having sufficient military acuteness to appreciate the difference between a "change of base" and a retreat. General Meade's colored man, however, who was looked upon, not only as a profound scholar, but high authority on all subjects of military strategy, clearly elucidated the matter to them: "A retreat am de going whar one dunt wanto by force of de fisical 'bility of de rebels, and a change of base, am de going to de same place by de moral swason of de instinct."

CHAPTER VI.

The Retreat Commenced — Battle of Gaines' Mills — Strength of the Armies — Desperate Fighting — Capture of the Eleventh Reserves and the Fourth N. J.— Re-enforcements Called for — Form for the Last Struggle — Succor Arrives — The Enemy at Bay — The Field Hospital — General Reynolds Captured — The French Princes — An Insurgent's Account of the Reserves — The Loss of the Armies and the Reserves — M'Clellan's Report — Magruder's Report — Crossing the Chickahominy — Trent's Hill — M'Clellan and Lee Deceived — The Retreat Continued — Night March — Savage Station — The Wounded — Movements of the Armies — Battles of Allen's Farm and Savage Station — Stragglers and Camp Followers — A Night on Picket.

ABOUT ten o'clock that morning we arrived at Gaines' Mills, and were lain down in a field. Already orders had been issued to evacuate White House, and to destroy all stores and munitions that could not be removed, and the "change of base" from the Pamunkey to the James river was commenced. The troops of General Fitz John Porter, on the left bank of the Chickahominy, were drawn into position around the bridge-heads, and all the heavy guns, wagons and stores were removed to the Richmond side of the river.

The Battle of Gaines' Mills, June 27th, 1862.

Our position was a strong one, on ground rising gradually from the ravine of a small stream, screened in part by trees and underbrush. The line of battle was about an arc of a circle, formed on the interior edge of the woods bounding a plain of clear land, stretching some 1,200 or 1,500 yards back from the river. Morrell's division held the left of the line, in a strip of woods on the left bank of the stream, resting its left flank on the descent to the Chickahominy, which was swept by our artillery on both sides of the river, and extended into open ground on the right, where it joined Sykes' division, which, partly in woods and partly in open ground, extended in the rear of New Coal Harbor.* Each brigade had in reserve two of its regiments.

The Reserves formed the second line of battle; and it was Porter's intention not to put them into the heavy fighting if he could avoid it, as they had been engaged until late the previous night, and suffered from want of sleep, and had been under fire in the morning. Meade's Brigade was posted on the left, near the river; Reynolds on the right, covering the approaches from Coal Harbor and Despatch Station to Sumner's Bridge; and Seymour's in reserve to the second line. The Reserve's artillery occupied the space between the lines, and the cavalry of the division, the Fourth Pennsylvania, was placed under cover of a slope in the rear. General P. St. George Cooke,† with part of the First and Fifth United States and the Sixth Pennsylvania Cavalry, was posted in the rear, to aid in watching that direction.

The troops were all in position by noon, with the artillery on the commanding ground and in the intervals between the divisions and brigades. About two o'clock, A. P. Hill commenced the attack on our right, followed by Longstreet on our left. In the meantime, Jackson, D. H. Hill and Ewell brought their troops into action, and Lee, under a terrific fire of artillery and infantry, ordered a charge upon the whole line. At this time the enemy numbered 50,000 men, and Porter but 27,000. Upon several points of the line they advanced with their infantry six and eight lines deep, the first delivering their fire and lying down, were followed by the others in rapid succession, producing a storm of lead against which it seemed impossible any troops could stand. The sound of this fire resembled one long, loud explosion of artillery, lasting for several minutes, without any perceptible break or variation, and many, for

---
* New Cool Arbor.—*U. S. Engineer's map*, 1865.
† His son, a General in the rebel army, was wounded at **Centreville, Va., Oct., 1861.**

some time, were unable to comprehend what produced it. The Reserves, forming the second line, were ordered to close upon the first, some of the regiments going into the line at once, and filling up the gaps, while others, lying down immediately in the rear, were ready to spring upon their feet at an instant. In the meantime all the batteries of the Reserves were vomiting forth their fire, and the enemy were pounding against our infantry. The Fourth Michigan having suffered terribly, Sickels moved the Third into their position—they shifting to the left—and at once engaged the enemy, and for two hours continued the combat, he having his horse killed under him. The battle at this point was most severe, the enemy, in succesive ranks, pouring in their deafening roars of musketry, and charging with desperate fury. But the steady and low fire of the Third was doing more execution, and hurled them back repeatedly. The muskets of the Third were now becoming so heated and choked with powder as to render many of them unserviceable, and their fire perceptibly diminished. At last, the Eleventh Reserves, and Fourth New Jersey, Colonel James H. Simpson, Major U. S. A., came to their relief, and, under the terrible fire, took their place, but even their united strength could not withstand the crushing assaults. Enveloped in the smoke, they were finally borne down and captured. Upon the Third coming out, they were met by General Meade, who most heartily congratulated them upon their "cool valor," and ordered them to the support of a Rhode Island battery.

The din of battle was still rolling on, and the assaults of the enemy continued with unabated fury. Porter continually asked for relief, but M'Clellan, on the other side of the river with his 60,000 good and true men, was deceived by the vigorous fusillade of Magruder's and Huger's 25,000. Near four o'clock, Slocum's division came to our aid, raising our force to 35,000 men. They, like the Reserves, were mostly broken up and sent in by regiments along the line, whereever the pressure was most severe. For hours the battle raged on, charge after charge being repulsed along the line, to be immediately renewed by fresh troops, led on with desperate courage, until near sunset, when they, massing their forces on our right and left, charged the whole line with reckless valor, and drove us back in good order, but with mutual carnage. At this time, General Cooke, in command of our cavalry, without orders, charged the enemy's infantry on our left, but was instantly repulsed, and his horses, becoming unmanageable, rushed upon our batteries, leading the gunners to suppose they were charged upon by the enemy. Several of the guns were thus deserted and lost.

Every officer and man upon the field knew our position was a most desperate one, that retreat over a few narrow bridges was impossible, that we must maintain our position or be driven into the Chickahominy with frightful slaughter; therefore, the struggle became one of life or glorious death for the army. A second line of battle was formed, steady and solid as the rocks of the mountains. The guns were placed in position, and resolute and silent, without a tremble in the heart, stood the men, ready to receive the shock of the last desperate struggle. At this moment, the rays of the setting sun lit up the west behind the enemy, who halted to dress their lines upon the crest of the hill. Loud cheers were heard in the distance, and French's and Meagher's brigades dashed upon the field and deployed on our center front. Then arose the defiant cheers of the whole army. The enemy perceiving that succor had at last reached us, and not knowing the meagreness of it, halted and lay down upon their arms for the night. About eight o'clock the battle ceased, and we were moved some distance towards the rear, near a field hospital, where the wounded were being continually brought in for surgical treatment, after which they were lain upon the grass, a blanket thrown over them, and a canteen of water put by their side, where some slept and others died. The poor fellows displayed great fortitude, and though many of them were horribly mangled and suffered intense pain, only suppressed murmurs escaped their lips. All of the Third were collected and lain together, and were cared for by their comrades until the regiment moved. While the surgeons were at work by the flickering light of candles, the insurgents opened fire upon them with shell, but they continued, hiding the lights as best they could with their caps and bodies. At the time the Eleventh Reserve and the Fourth New Jersey were captured, General Reynolds, his Assistant Adjutant-General, Captain Charles Kingsberry, and his orderly, were cut off also. They concealed themselves in the woods during the night, but early the next morning, while endeavoring to make their escape, were captured by a rebel patrolling party. The command of the Second Brigade, therefore, devolved upon Colonel Seneca G. Simmons, of the Fifth Reserve. Among those present upon the field, and who appeared to know not what fear was, were the French Princes, the Comte de Paris and the Duc de Chartres, officially known in our army as Captain Louis Philippe and Captain Robert E. Orleans, U. S. Volunteer Aids-de-camp to General M'Clellan.

An officer of the Confederate army thus describes the battle. It was the Reserves, however, and not Meagher's troops, that he alludes to, as Meagher did not arrive upon the field until sunset:

"The attack was opened by the columns of Hill (First), Anderson,* and Pickett. These gallant masses rushed forward, with thundering hurrahs, upon the musketry of the foe, as though it were joy to them. Whole ranks went down under that terrible hail, but nothing could restrain their courage. The billows of battle raged fiercely onward; the struggle was man to man, eye to eye, bayonet to bayonet. The hostile Meagher's Brigade" (Reserves), "composed chiefly of Irishmen, offered heroic resistance. After

---

* Brigadier-General G. B. Anderson. Killed at Antietam.

a fierce struggle, our people began to give way, and at length all orders and encouragements were vain; they were falling back in the greatest disorder. Infuriated, foaming at the mouth, bare-headed, sabre in hand, at this critical moment General Cobb* appeared upon the field, at the head of his legion, and with him the Nineteenth North Carolina and the Fourteenth Virginia regiments. At once these troops renewed the attack, but all their devotion and self-sacrifice were in vain. The Irish" (Reserves) "held their position with a determination and ferocity that called forth the admiration of our own officers. Broken to pieces, and disorganized, the fragments of that fine legion came rolling back from the charge. The Nineteenth North Carolina lost eight standard-bearers, and most of their staff-officers were either killed or wounded. Again, Generals Hill (First) and Anderson led their troops to the attack, and some regiments covered themselves with immortal glory. Our troops exhibited a contempt of death that made them the equals of old, experienced veterans; for, notwithstanding the bloody harvest the destroyer reaped in our ranks that day, no disorder, no timid bearing revealed that many of the regiments were under fire and smelt gun-powder then for the first time. But the enemy, nevertheless, quietly and coolly held out against every attack we made, one after the other. Notwithstanding the fact that solitary brigades had to stand their ground from four until eight o'clock P.M., they performed feats of incredible valor; and it was only when the news came that Jackson was upon them in the rear that, about eight, they retired before our advance. Despite the dreadful carnage in their ranks, they marched on, with streaming banners and rolling drums, and carried with them all their wounded and all their baggage; and when the cavalry regiments of Davis and Wickham went in pursuit, repelled their assault also with perfect coolness.

---

* Brigadier-General T. R. R. Cobb, of Georgia, brother of Howell Cobb. Killed at Fredericksburg, Va.

"By this time night had come on and overspread the field of death with darkness, compassionately shuttting out from the eyes of the living the horrid spectacle of slaughter. Quiet gradually returned; only a feeble cannonade could be heard upon our furthest left, and that, too, little by little, died away. The soldiers were so fearfully exhausted by the day's struggle that many of them sank down from their places in the ranks upon the ground. Although I, too, could scarcely keep in the saddle, so great was my fatigue, I hastened, with one of my aids, to that quarter of the field where the struggle had raged the most fiercely. The scene of ruin was horrible; whole ranks of the enemy lay prone where they had stood at the beginning of the battle. The number of wounded was fearful, too, and the groans and imploring cries for help that rose on all sides had, in the obscurity of the night, a ghastly effect, that froze the blood in one's veins. Although I had been upon so many battle-fields in Italy and Hungary, never had my vision beheld such a spectacle of human destruction."

Our loss in this battle, though not specifically reported, probably was not far from 4,500. Greeley, in his "American Conflict," places it at 8,000, but in this he is evidently mistaken.* Among the wounded of the Third was Captain Geo. C. Davenport.† The loss in the Reserves was 1,217 killed, wounded and missing. Nineteen guns were also lost upon the field. The loss of the enemy was never officially reported, but probably was not as heavy as our own. The wearied and exhausted men, who had fought for two days, and many of them without a mouthful to eat, threw them-

---

* General M'Clelian, in his official returns of the killed, wounded and missing of the Seven Days' Battle, gives M'Call's loss as 3,074, Porter's as 4,278, making a total of 7,352. The Reserves lost 183 at Mechanicsville, and 1,674 at Glendale, a total of 1,857. This, deducted from the 7,352, leaves 5,495. Porter lost very heavily at Malvern Hill and, putting it at 1,500, certainly a very low estimate, 3,995 remains for the loss of the Reserves and Fifth Corps at Gaines' Mill, to which add 500 for Slocum's loss, thus making the total 4,495. The Reserves numbered one-fifth of the troops present, and their loss was very far the heaviest of any division engaged.

† For the loss in the Third, see Appendix A.

selves upon the ground, and sank to sleep with their cartridge-boxes strapped upon them and their muskets in their hands. But their slumbers were of short duration, as soon orders came to wake them up and get into line without noise. It was hard work to arouse the sleepy boys, it being necessary to roll some of them over, shake them, pound them, and even to lift them upon their feet. Having got the men in line, the Reserves waited here until near morning, to cover the withdrawal of the army from the left bank of the Chickahominy, and then crossing the bridge opposite Trent's Hill about seven o'clock, they blew it up, and moving on about a mile and a half, halted and lay on the hill during the day.

While the battle of Gaines' Mill was progressing, the enemy were not idle on the Richmond side of the Chickahominy, where, with 25,000 men, they were keeping up a succession of imposing but hollow feints and alarms, impressing M'Clellan that a vastly superior force to his own menaced him on that wing of his army.* General Lee supposing, from the stubborn resistance he received on the left, and the absence of any serious demonstration on the right bank of the river, that M'Clellan was retreating on his base at York river, immediately pushed General Stuart's cavalry and Ewell's infantry in that direction, they occupying White House early on the 29th, which had been abandoned by our

---

* General Magruder, in his official report of his participation in the Seven Days' Battle, says:

"From the time at which the enemy withdrew his forces to this side of the Chickahominy, and destroyed the bridges, to the moment of his evacuation—that is, from Friday night (27th) until Sunday morning—I considered the situation of our army as extremely critical and perilous. The larger portion of it was on the opposite side of the Chickahominy; the bridges had all been destroyed, but one was rebuilt—the New Bridge—which was commanded fully by the enemy's guns from Golding's; and there were but 25,000 men between his army of 100,000 and Richmond.

"Had M'Clellan massed his whole force in column, and advanced it against any point of our line of battle, as was done at Austerlitz, under similar circumstances, by the greatest Captain of any age, though the head of his column would have suffered greatly, its momentum would have insured him success, and the occupation of our works about Richmond, and, consequently, the city, might have been his reward. His failure to do so is the best evidence that our wise commander fully understood the character of his opponent."

troops, who, not being able to remove all the munitions and provisions, destroyed a vast amount. In the meanwhile the enemy had concentrated our army in a strong position, between the Chickahominy on one side and its extensive works fronting Richmond on the other, and, having destroyed the communication with our base, the march for the James river was commenced. General Keyes' Corps was ordered to move at once across White Oak Swamp and seize and hold the *débouchés* of the roads on the James river side, and the rest of the army followed with as little delay as possible.

During the day, rations were received and issued, the men being greatly in need of them, as some had been forty-eight hours without food. But they were without haversacks to put them in, as they had marched to the field of Mechanicsville with muskets and cartridge-boxes only; and General M'Call subsequently ordered their camp to be burnt.* However, as soldiers are never at a loss for ways and means, they substituted the extremities of their shirts, which answered most admirably. We remained on an open field, under a broiling sun, during the 28th, which really afforded but little rest. About ten o'clock that night, we got into line, and stood in the rain until about one, when we moved off towards the James river. With the Reserves was Hunt's reserve artillery, consisting of thirteen batteries, which, with our own, and our trains, extended the column many miles, and as our flanks were exposed to attack, Seymour's Brigade was placed, by regiments, between the batteries. Our movement, owing to narrow and bad roads, was necessarily slow, and in the darkness of the night we toiled through the woods and swamps, unable to see but a few feet on either side. While thus moving, one of the wagon-guard of the Fourth, stepped into the woods a little way, and his musket being accidentally discharged, he was mistaken for a foe,

---

* All the division wagons had been sent, by order of General Porter, to M'Clellan's headquarters, early on the 26th.

and a number of shots fired at him. This, frightening some of the teams, they dashed in among us, which, with the unexplained firing, for a time created considerable excitement, during which a soldier of the Second had his leg broken. About day-break, on Sunday morning, we reached General M'Clellan's headquarters, at Savage Station, on the York River and Richmond railroad, where we found the greatest confusion and disorder prevailing. Hundreds of wagons and ambulances covered the fields, in every direction. Nearly three thousand wounded and sick soldiers were lying in the tents, houses and woods. Here they found the wounded of the Third, and moved them together, and did all they could for them, filling their canteens, and giving them money. These may seem but little acts of kindness, but to the wounded soldier, who has lain upon the field for days, helpless, weak and famishing, the little canteen of water is more highly prized than any earthly gift. The money they received they were ruthlessly plundered of, and their canteens and blankets were taken from them by the heartless officials at Richmond, but the warm words of kindness spoken by their comrades long remained to cheer them.

For such as could hobble off, they provided crutches and canes.* They were all cheerful, and bore their sufferings with composure until later in the day, when they found they were to be left to fall into the hands of the enemy. Happy

---

*"I think I have never seen examples of greater endurance than exhibited upon the part of the wounded in this retreat. Saturday they were lying all day at the hospital, with little or no attention. The weather was exceedingly warm. Sunday they marched all day through a sweltering sun, resting perhaps two hours in the middle of the day. The garments of many of them were stiff with blood. They had no nourishing food. Their wounds had simply been bound up, without further attention, and they were already much annoyed with worms. * * * Still there was not a murmur. All endured cheerfully. Toward evening the wounded men passed through a field in which were a number of sheep, when Sergeant Hollister, notwithstanding his arm was so shattered as afterwards to require amputation, took his revolver, and, in company with others, after a hard chase, succeeded in bringing one of them down. Having detailed one of my men to help them along, he made them a good kettle of mutton broth, of which they all partook, and were much invigorated."—*Extract from Colonel Ayers' (Tenth Regiment, P. R. V. C.) Account.*

were those who, being seriously wounded, died before they reached the insurgent hospitals, where amputations were performed for slight wounds, or the poor sufferers left to die of neglect, filth and abuse.

Here, also, were vast quantities of commissary and quartermaster's stores and ammunition. The latter were loaded into a train of cars, and, with a locomotive, run into the Chickahominy—a fuse being attached and so well-timed that at the instant of the plunge the explosion took place. The halt here was not long, but moving on from the station, we met a large number of prisoners captured during our battles, and about noon crossed White Oak creek bridge, some distance beyond which we entered a pine woods and lay down in line of battle, ready to resist any attack from the direction of Richmond. Here we rested for a couple of hours, and delivered up the precious charge of General Hunt's reserve artillery, it being now considered safe.

Before proceeding further, we will detail the general movements of the hostile armies and the events of the day. The essential operation was the passage of our trains and the reserve artillery across the swamp, and their protection against attack from the direction of Richmond, and the establishment of our communication with the gun-boats on James river. For this purpose, Sumner and Heintzleman's Corps and Smith's division were directed to take up a line of advance covering, with their right resting near Savage Station, and to hold the same until dark on Sunday the 29th. Lee having discovered our line of retreat on the afternoon of the 28th, ordered Longstreet and A. P. Hill to recross the Chickahominy near Gaines' Mill, and pursue and attack our rear; and Jackson to move between us and the Chickahominy on our left, while Magruder and Huger were to advance from toward Richmond, and strike us on our right flank.

At Allen's Farm, on the railroad, about nine o'clock in the morning, the enemy made a spirited attack on Sumner's front, but were gallantly repulsed.

About noon General Magruder, on the Williamsburg road near Savage Station, came in sight, but, not liking appearances, sent to Huger for re-enforcements, and at four in the afternoon attacked in full force. A stubborn little battle was fought, and at nine o'clock in the evening they were forced to withdraw. Our troops then, by order, fell back upon White Oak Swamp, General French's Brigade forming the rear guard, crossing and destroying White Oak Swamp bridge, at five A.M. on the 30th. These two engagements were the first that any of the troops of the Army of the Potomac, that remained on the Richmond side of the river, had been in since the commencement of the Seven Days' battle.

Our division remained in this position, on high, open ground, in the hot sun, until five o'clock P.M., when General M'Call received orders to move to the crossing of the Quaker and New Market roads, and take a position to repel any attack from Richmond. The object of this movement was to cover the Turkey Bridge—Quaker or Willis Church road, leading from White Oak Swamp to Malvern Hill, along which our trains moved all night. On our march, we found the road nearly blocked up with innumerable wagon-trains, ambulances and artillery, besides a drove of 2,500 head of cattle. Many, slightly wounded, were limping along, and thousands of stragglers and camp followers swarmed around. Through these we wound our way, disheartened at the demoralizing sight, retreating as we were from a foe to whom our hearts bid defiance. We halted at Nelson's farm, the battle-field of the next day, where a skirmish had taken place between the cavalry in the morning. General M'Call made his headquarters at the farm-house during the night. Leaving Meade's and Seymour's brigades in reserve in line of battle, at dark,* Reynolds' (now Simmons') Brigade and a battery of artillery moved off to the front about a

---

* General M'Call, in his official report, states we reached this position about midnight. With all due respect to such high authority, the author is satisfied he was mistaken, as he conversed with Captain Scheetz, of his staff, and the General, upon their dismounting at Nelson's house, and the sun was then setting.

mile, crossing a small run, and turning to the left through a deep woods, where they lay on picket on a by-road. The night was intensely dark, and they were unable to see but a short distance from them. The men were lain down on the edge of the road, with orders for no one to speak or sleep, but to be ready to spring into line at an instant's notice. In front of them, at the distance of fifty paces, pickets were posted. The countersign was—to bare the right arm, and raise and lower it twice.

When all was the stillness of death, a rapid fire of musketry opened a few hundred yards in our rear, and we were unable to tell whether it was an attack of the foe or our friends firing upon one another. We afterwards ascertained it was some of Porter's corps, who had got on the wrong road, and, countermarching, had mistook their friends.

About the middle of the night a number of the battery horses got loose, and dashed down the rear of the line like a charge of cavalry, and several shots were fired into them in rapid succession. One of the horses being wounded, kept up a most unearthly moaning through the night, making the most distressing noise possible to imagine; and the farm dogs, far and near, were continually barking, indicating the proximity of the foe. In fact, and we strongly suspected it at the time, we were surrounded on all sides by the enemy, who knew our exact position, and had it in their power to cut in pieces or capture us, but they wished to bag the whole division, and were waiting for the arrival of Huger's division in the position assigned to it. Fortunately it was delayed on its march, for which the General was severely censured by his government. Thus passed this night of silent excitement, that did more to unnerve the body than the severest shock of battle.

The Reserves were attached to the Fifth Corps, and General Porter directed General M'Call on Sunday night to bivouac upon the field. During the night Porter, with Sykes' and Morrell's divisions of his corps, marched by, and neglected either to notify General M'Call of the movement, withdraw his troops, or send him any orders for their disposition. A large portion of the army and its vast trains had yet to pass this point, and the enemy were pounding away at Franklin, in the rear. M'Call at once saw the importance of his holding this position, to save the army from being cut in two, though he felt, as every officer and man of the Reserves felt, that they had done more fighting and marching, and lost more sleep and men, and suffered more for want of food, than any other division in the army. They well knew that thousands of troops had not been brought into battle during the hard struggle, and were comparatively fresh. Yet, as the neglect of their corps commander[*] had left them alone to fight another desperate and hard battle against overwhelming odds, they calmly awaited the contest.

---

[*] General Fitz John Porter has since explained this, saying, "he no longer considered M'Call's troops as attached to his command." No orders had been issued detaching them from his corps, and he continued to issue orders to them as long as they remained on the Peninsula.

CHAPTER VII.

THE BATTLE OF GLENDALE—SIMMONS' DESPERATE CHARGES—DEATH OF SIMMONS AND BIDDLE—COOPER'S AND KERNS' BATTERIES CHARGED—GLORIOUS CHARGE OF THE NINTH—RANDALL'S BATTERY CHARGED—THE LAST STRUGGLE OF THE DAY—DESPERATE CONFLICT—BRAVERY OF CAPTAIN TAPPER—THE BATTERY DEMOLISHED—MEADE WOUNDED—M'CALL WOUNDED AND PRISONER, HIS STAFF AND ESCORT KILLED OR WOUNDED—WHAT M'CALL, LEE, PRYOR, AN OFFICER OF THE CONFEDERATE ARMY, M'CLELLAN, PORTER, MEADE AND BEATTY SAY ABOUT IT—TO MALVERN HILL.

BATTLE OF NEW MARKET CROSS-ROADS, OR GLENDALE,* JUNE 30TH, 1862.

IT BEING the last day of the month, the Reserves were mustered in line of battle for pay, and while this was in progress the pickets commenced exchanging shots, and so close were they, that several men were wounded before it was finished. Having got that matter off their minds, and not having any rations to bother with, they lay down upon the ground to rest. The position occupied by the division was on both sides of the New Market, or Long Bridge road, near its crossing with the Charles City road, in front of the Quaker or Willis Church road, leading to Malvern Hill and Turkey Bridge. The field was a large, open plain, with a front of about eight hundred yards, and a depth of one thousand yards, intersected towards the right by the New Market road and a narrow strip of timber, parallel to it, and on the left, near the center, with a marshy woods, near which was a small farm-house. In the rear of the plain was a steep, wooded hill, running to a broad plateau, or table-land, across which ran the Quaker road, leading to the river.

---

* This battle has been variously called New Market Cross-Roads, Charles City Cross-Roads, Glendale, and by the rebels, Nelson's Farm. Glendale is the name by which it is most familiarly known.

It was a beautiful battle-field for a fair fight, without any advantage of ground to either party, but too large for the Reserves, the lands on either flank being open.

General Meade's Brigade was posted on the right, across the New Market road; General Seymour's on the left, extending to the marshy woods; and General Reynolds', now Simmons', was held in reserve near the center of the line, on the plateau in rear of the woods. The artillery was placed in front of the line; Randall's battery on the right, supported by the Fourth and Seventh Reserves; Cooper's and Kerns' batteries opposite the center, supported by the First, Colonel Roberts, and the Ninth, Colonel Jackson; and Deitrich and Kennerhein's German batteries, accidently left by Porter, on the left, supported by the Tenth, Colonel Kirk, and the Twelfth, Colonel Taggart. The Fourth Pennsylvania Cavalry, Colonel Childs, was drawn up on the left and rear, but, not being called into action, was subsequently ordered to fall back.

Some distance to the right and rear of the Reserves was posted Kearney's division, and on the plateau, to the left and rear, was Sumner's, and further to the left and rear, Hooker's. These troops could have been effectively brought into action, but the General-in-chief was not present upon the field, and his only instructions to the generals of his army were to occupy certain positions, and to resist the enemy until the trains moving towards the river should pass all the cross-roads. Of these disjointed and independent commands, M'Call held the center, resting on the principal road from Richmond, with both his flanks exposed. Early in the day, Jackson's artillery was heard pounding away at Franklin, at White Oak Swamp, to the right and rear, which he continued through the day and into the night.

From daylight our pickets had been exchanging occasional shots with the enemy, who were in the vicinity in considerable force, awaiting re-enforcements. Near eleven o'clock a squadron of cavalry was thrown forward on the Charles

City and New Market roads, and the First and Third Regiments were ordered to support them. Colonel Sickel moved out with his regiment, and resting his right on the New Market road, dropped out the companies at intervals, extending his line for a mile south of the road, and stationed the out-post pickets. About half past two o'clock the enemy appeared in force, covering his whole front with heavy columns of infantry, and driving in the cavalry. A skirmish immediately commenced, but with such little spirit by the enemy that Sickel threw out flanking parties to observe them, when he soon ascertained they were pushing troops to cut off and capture him. He at once concentrated his regiment, when a sharp encounter ensued, which checked their advance, when, receiving orders to fall back, he took his position in line of battle. The enemy, who were commanded by General Lee in person, accompanied by Jefferson Davis, consisted of Longstreet's and A. P. Hill's divisions, estimated among the strongest and best of the Confederate army, and numbering between 18,000 and 20,000 men.* Having waited several hours for the arrival of Huger or Jackson, he opened with his batteries along the entire line, and, under cover of their fire, sent forward two regiments on the left and right center, to feel for a weak point. The first fell upon the Seventh, Colonel Harvey, and was handsomely repulsed;* and the last, upon the Third, who received it at fifty paces with a withering fire of musketry.† Still this gallant regiment, the Ninth Virginia, continued to advance, but finally broke and fled, leaving two-thirds of its number upon the field.†

The enemy were soon discovered massing their troops on the left, with the object of turning that flank. General M'Call immediately rode forward at the head of the Bucktails, Major Stone, and posted them in the marshy woods. He then ordered the left wing to change front on that flank,

---

*General M'Call's official report.
†Prof. Bates' History Pennsylvania Volunteers, Vol. I, page 612.

and sent Colonel Simmons with the Fifth and Eighth Reserves to re-enforce them. The cannoneers of the two German batteries, after firing a few random rounds, were panic stricken, and, cutting their harness, dashed to the rear with their horses, breaking through, tramping down, and disorganizing four companies of the Twelfth, that formed their support.* The enemy, in the meantime, had concentrated the fire of his artillery upon this point, and seized this favorable opportunity to charge with his infantry. With loud yells they rushed upon our lines, breaking down and crushing out Colonel Taggart's six companies of the Twelfth, that held the extreme left. Their dense masses dashed onward with loud screams and yells, confident of overpowering and sweeping from the field the Reserves, whom they believed they at last had in their power. But the gallant Simmons was there with the Fifth and the Eighth, the Ninth and the Tenth, and, facing his line to the left, led a counter-charge with such desperate fury that the exultant foe was broken and hurled back to the forest. Here followed the first of those desperate hand-to-hand struggles that signalized this day. Had Simmons been left alone with the enemy, who thrice outnumbered him, they never could have formed their lines again, but, fresh troops coming to their support, he was driven back. In this encounter the Seventh and the Seventeenth Virginia Regiments were nearly annihilated, the greater portion being either killed, wounded, or taken prisoners.† In the meantime, the last regiment of the reserve, the Second, Colonel M'Candless, had advanced to a position to the right of the marshy woods, where they were joined by a detachment of the Twelfth, rallied by Adjutant Theodore M'Murtrie. Sim-

---

*General M'Call, in person, posted the Twelfth on the extreme left. Soon afterwards, General Seymour rode up and ordered it to be divided, and four companies to erect a breastwork of rails, with two companies in rear for support, and the other four companies to support the Dutch batteries, leaving a gap of two hundred yards between the wings. This unfortunate disposition of the regiment rendered it impossible to fight it advantageously.

† Bates' History Pennsylvania Volunteers, Vol. I, page 668.

mons' command was borne by them to the right, but the gallant Simmons and Seymour rallied a few men of the Fifth and Eighth, and had time to lay them down beside the Second. Now for the dash of a handful against a vast mass, to gain a few moments' time to rally the brigade. On came the exultant foe, again rushing in triumph over the field. But, when within fifty yards of us, the little line arose, and delivering a volley, rushed upon them with the bayonet. Then followed another of those desperate struggles so seldom witnessed in war. The firing instantly ceased. The maddening yells and curses of the men, amidst the crashing steel, alone was heard. The hostile banners were wrenched again and again from their bearers' hands, and trampled to the earth, to be instantly rescued by a desperate rally. Friend and foe went down in each others embrace, and the fury of hell pervaded the mass. But the long lines of the enemy nearly closed around the little handful. The object had been gained—a few moments' time—and, overpowered, with their glorious banners still flaunting, they were swept from the field.* Here fell the heroic Simmons. "A soldier by profession and a man of the strictest honor; a patriot from principle and brave to a fault; the Reserves Corps lost no more trusted leader nor loved companion in arms." Here fell, too, the fearless Biddle, the Adjutant-General of the Reserves, and a host of gallant officers and brave men. Nearly one-half of those engaged were either killed or wounded. Colonel Hays had his horse shot under him. Driven across the field, the men rallied on the brigade, which had by this time re-formed; the wild charge of the enemy was checked, and their desperate and determined attempt to force the line, cut off the right wing, and capture the immense trains then moving to the left, completely frustrated. Meanwhile, four companies of the Twelfth, that had formed the support of the German batteries, and which had been broken and trampled down by

---

* Half-past five o'clock.

the artillerymen dashing through them with their limbers and horses, and detachments from the Fifth, Eighth and Tenth, with wounded and prisoners, retired to the left and rear upon Hooker's division. Here Colonel Taggart rallied his regiment and these detached men, and, leading them forward, formed to the right of the Sixteenth Massachusetts, which position he maintained until the Reserves withdrew, sustaining a loss of four officers and over one hundred men.

While these sanguinary struggles were progressing on the left, the center and right were sharing in the glory and death of the field. On the center, at the same instant that Simmons led his last charge, the enemy precipitated heavy columns on Kerns' and Cooper's batteries, determined to carry them at any sacrifice of life. These dense masses, emerging from the woods, dashed over the field for eight hundred yards with yells and screeches, perfectly reckless of life. Though the batteries swept their fronts clean, yet onward the columns dashed to within twenty, thirty or forty yards, when the infantry, pouring volleys of musketry into them, dashed upon them with the bayonet. Three times the enemy's columns were driven back with great slaughter. Kerns' caissons having been sent to the rear by General Seymour, and the last round in the limbers being expended, he withdrew his guns, seeing which, the enemy precipitated their united force upon Cooper's battery, bayoneting and shooting the gunners, and, after a desperate encounter, carrying it.* The Ninth Reserves, which had been temporarily withdrawn from its support to succor another battery, at this instant returned, and hearing of its loss, demanded to be led to its recapture; and the gallant Colonel Jackson,† with what other parts of regiments and men he could rally, led them to the seemingly hopeless charge. Dashing across the field, with arms trailed, they sprung upon the foe at the

---

* Seven o'clock.—*M'Call's Testimony.*

† Colonel Conrad Feger Jackson, Allegheny county. Appointed Brigadier-General, July 17th, 1862. Killed at Fredericksburg, Va.

moment the guns were being turned against them. A desperate struggle ensued, in which the bayonet and clubbed musket did the principal work. But the Reserves not only recaptured the battery and the Seventh Reserve's flag, but took the Tenth Alabama's flag, and bore them triumphantly back to their lines.*

The enemy, having been repulsed in his attempts upon the left and center, at last concentrated all his strength for a final desperate effort to crush the right. From the commencement of the battle, he had never ceased his vigorous attacks upon the whole line, but now appeared to abandon the entire field for this one point. Meade was expecting the assault, and M'Call, in anticipation of it, had repaired there, but had not a solitary regiment to bring with him, they all being required on the other parts of the field. The enemy, under cover of a heavy fire of artillery, advanced a brigade in wedge-shape, with a wild recklessness but seldom equalled, to charge Randall's battery. Despite the fearful carnage, they charged almost to the muzzles of the guns, but the fire was too terrible to endure, and, at last, they broke, and scattered like chaff before the wind. Before they were out of range of the infantry, a second brigade, that followed them as a support, dashed boldly forward to the very guns, where they, too, were hurled back by the sheets of flame of the artillery and infantry. Almost instantly came the third suppporting brigade, wild with fury and reckless of life, and now commenced the last desperate struggle of the day. The infantry had stood perfectly cool, delivering their fire of musketry; but now their four regiments were assaulted in overwhelming numbers, the two first attacking brigades having been rallied and led to the charge. In the tumult, the guns were overturned and every horse of the battery killed, and the scene presented was one confused heap of men, horses, carriages and limbers. Three times Sickel rallied his men to the charge, and gallantly they

* Prof. Bates' History Pennsylvania Volunteers, Vol. I, page 788.

held their ground, "until one of those unfortunate mistakes of war occured, which has so often marred the operations of armies. A supporting regiment, in the smoke of battle, mistaking the Third for the enemy, opened fire upon its ranks, throwing them into disorder, and causing them to break,"* they taking with them seven prisoners they had just captured. Sickel had his horse shot under him, and, with the officers, strove to rally the Third, but the fire in the rear and front was too severe. A portion of the men were rallied, and, with the majority of the officers, continued in the contest.† The supporting regiment took the Third's place, but soon after a portion of the Fourth gave way. The balance maintained its ground, and fought with great desperation. In the hand-to-hand conflict that ensued, Captain Tapper saw a powerfully-built officer single him out, and advance with uplifted sword. Tapper, who was of iron nerve, did not hesitate to accept the challenge. A parry of swords ensued, when the Captain discovered another officer rushing upon him. Instantly advancing, he dealt his foe a blow upon the head that brought him to his knees—without moving a step, he half-wheeled to the right, and, with a horizontal blow, cut the other officer across the face, staggering him back—his first antagonist was now upon his feet and prepared to attack, when Tapper, regardless of defense, plunged his sword through his body, and, turning upon the other, buried his blade in his skull. The gallant Captain received only a number of slight wounds.

General M'Call, in his official report, thus graphically describes the scene: "I had ridden into the regiments and endeavored to check them; but, as is seen, with only partial success. It was here, however, my fortune to witness,

---

* Bates' History Pennsylvania Volunteers, Vol. I, page 612.

† EXTRACT FROM GENERAL M'CALL'S REPORT: * * * "My thanks are likewise due to Colonel Roberts, commanding First Regiment; Colonel Sickel, commanding Third Regiment; Colonel Hays, commanding Eighth Regiment; Colonel Jackson and Captain Cuthbertson, of the Ninth Regiment, and other brave officers not commanding regiments, of whom Lieutenant-Colonel M'Intire, Major Woodward and Major Woolworth are among the many wounded.—*Moore's Rebellion Record, page 66*, Docs., Vol., Comp.*

between those of my men who stood their ground and the rebels who advanced, one of the fiercest bayonet fights that, perhaps, ever occurred on this continent. Bayonets were crossed and locked in the struggle; bayonet wounds were freely given and received. I saw skulls crushed by the heavy blow of the butt of the musket, and, in short, the desperate thrusts and parries of a life-and-death encounter, proving, indeed, that Greek had met Greek when the Alabama boys fell upon the sons of Pennyslvania.

"My last reserve regiment I had previously sent to support Cooper, and I had not now a man to bring forward. My men were bodily borne off the ground by superior numbers. A thick wood was immediately in rear, and the Confederates did not follow my men into the thicket. It was at this moment, on witnessing the scene I have described, that I bitterly felt that my division ought to have been re-enforced.

"My force had been reduced, by the battles of the 26th and 27th, to less than six thousand, and on this occasion I had to contend with the divisions of Longstreet and A. P. Hill, estimated among the strongest and best of the Confederate army, and numbering that day from eighteen to twenty thousand.

"The center was, at this time, still engaged, and I could not withdraw any troops from it."

The Reserves were driven back to the woods, but the enemy immediately retired, they being too severely punished to pursue or enfilade the line, or even attempt to hold the battery. They abandoned the field, their wounded and dead, and all they had won, and retired to the wood in their rear. The sun had already set,* and darkness was spreading over the abandoned field, strewed with its thousands of dead and wounded, the wreck of Randall's battery, and the two German batteries, whose guns stood as they were left. In this struggle, General Meade was severely wounded in the arm and hip, Colonel Harvey was crushed by a limber,

---

* The sun set at 7:35.

and Lieutenant Colonel M'Intire received a bone wound in the thigh. Over forty horses were killed around the battery.

General M'Call, in his official report, says: "In a short time, Lieutenant Colonel Thompson, Third Regiment, came up, and reported to me that he had collected about five hundred men, with whom he was then advancing. I rode on with him, at the head of the column, in a direction to bring this force upon Kearny's left.

"On arriving near the ground where Randall's battery stood, I halted Thompson's command, wishing to ascertain whether any of my men were still in front of me. I had left Captain Conrad's company about one hundred yards in advance, but it was now so dark I could scarcely distinguish a man at ten paces. The battle, in fact, was now over; the firing on the left and center had ceased, and there was only a desultory firing between Kearny's men and the enemy, some distance to my right. I rode forward to look for Conrad, and on the ground where I left him I rode into the enemy's picket, the Forty-seventh Virginia, Colonel Mayo, resting under some trees, and, before I knew in whose presence I was, I was taken prisoner. Unfortunately for myself, I had no staff officer with me, or I should have sent him forward to examine the ground instead of going myself; but my adjutant-general, the valiant Captain Henry J. Biddle, had been mortally wounded; Lieutenant Scheetz had his horse killed, and was injured by the fall; my chief-of-ordnance, the gallant Beatty, had been severely wounded at my side, and only left me when I had insisted on his doing so; my excellent orderly, Sergeant Simeon Dunn, Fourth Pennsylvania Cavalry, was also fatally wounded at my side; and out of my escort of a captain and twenty men of the Fourth Cavalry, but one corporal (the brave King) and one private remained with me; these two men were made prisoners with myself. About the time I was taken prisoner, the desultory firing on my right died away."

The Reserves had collected in the woods, about three hundred yards in rear of their first line of battle, and there re-formed. General M'Call was a prisoner, and all his staff and escort either killed or wounded. The gallant Meade, commanding the Second Brigade, had been borne off the field wounded. Simmons, commanding the First Brigade, had been killed, and Seymour, commanding the Third Brigade, could not be found. Hosts of field and company officers had gone down, and the division was without a recognized leader for two hours. The commanding officers of the regiments acted independent of, but in concert with, each other, and formed their line of battle, and remained in the position occupied by Simmons' Brigade at the opening of the battle, until between two and three o'clock the next morning, when, under the command of General Seymour, they withdrew and rejoined M'Clellan at Malvern Hill, after every gun and wagon of the train of the Army of the Potomac, they had fought so desperately to defend, had passed safely to the river.

The loss of the Reserves in this battle was 1,674 killed, wounded and missing, being over thirty per cent. of the 5,600 men present in the battle. In the Third, Captains William Brian, H. Clay Beatty and Joseph Thomas, Lieutenants Jacob Lehman, Joseph B. Roberts and Francis E. Harrison, were wounded.* The loss of the enemy on the left of our line was about equal to our own, and on the center and right, where they recklessly charged the batteries, it certainly far exceeded ours. We lost, also, eighty six horses killed; and the wreck of Randall's and the two German batteries were abondoned for want of 'means to take them off the field.† They lost over two hundred prisoners and three stands of colors. We lost not a flag.

---

* For the loss in the Third, see Appendix A.

† The artillery officers, during the night, sought General Heintzleman, and asked the use of his artillery horses to haul their guns off with, but were refused, he fearing a renewal of the battle.

The object for which this battle was fought—the defence of the immense supply train while passing, and the holding of the enemy in check at this point, where he strove desperately to cut in two the retiring column of the Army of the Potomac—was fully achieved. His design was utterly frustrated, and he signally repulsed.

Thus ended this glorious and bloody battle, which was the hardest contested field upon the Peninsula. That the Reserves fought it alone against thrice their number, and within sight and hearing of three or four times their number of national troops, who did not lose ten men, is an incontestable fact.

Let us see what the enemy had to say about this battle. General Lee, in his official report, says:

"The superiority of numbers and advantage of position were on the side of the enemy. * * *

"Could the other comrades have coöperated in the action, the result would have proved most disastrous to the enemy. After the engagement, Magruder was recalled to relieve the troops of Longstreet and Hill. His men, much fatigued by their long, hot march, arrived during the night."

Brigadier-General Roger A. Pryor, Fifth Brigade, Longstreet's corps, says:

"Arriving on the field, I discovered that the brigade on my right had been repulsed, and that my command were exposed to a destructive fire on the flank as well as in front. Nevertheless, they stood their ground, and sustained the unequal combat until re-enforced by the brigade of General Gregg. We did not return to our original position until the enemy had abandoned the field and surrendered his artillery into our possession. In this engagement, my loss was uncommonly heavy in officers as well as men. The Fourteenth Alabama, bearing the brunt of the struggle, was nearly annihilated. I crossed the Chickahominy on the 26th with 1,400 men. In the fight that followed, I suffered a loss of eight hundred and forty-nine killed and wounded and eleven missing."

An officer in the Confederate army, reporting the battles of the Seven Days' fight, in regard to Glendale, says:

"General M'Clellan had taken his position on the New Market road, which formed his center. This point he had strengthened with nineteen pieces of heavy artillery, and collected his best troops there, and firmly and cooly awaited our attack. We had, at all hazards, to drive the enemy from the neighborhood of our capital, or succumb ourselves. No other choice remained for us. During the four days of massacre that had already passed, our troops had been transformed into wild beasts; and hardly had they caught sight of the enemy, drawn up in order, ere they rushed upon them with horrible yells. Yet calmly, as on the parade ground, the latter delivered their fire. The batteries in the center discharged their murderous volleys on our men, and great disorder ensued among the storming masses. General Lee sent all of his disposable troops to the rescue, but M'Clellan opened upon these newly-formed storming columns so hellish a fire that even the coldest blooded veteran lost his self-possession. Whole ranks of our men were hurled to the ground. The thunder of the cannon, the crackling of the musketry from a hundred thousand combatants, mingled with the screams of the wounded and the dying, were terrific to the ear and the imagination. Thus raged the conflict, within a comparatively narrow space, seven long hours, and yet, not a foot of ground was won. All our reserves had been led into the fight, and the brigade of Wilcox was annihilated. At length the coming of night compelled a truce, and, utterly overcome by fatigue, the soldier sank upon the ground at his post, thoughtless of even the friend torn from his side, and engrossed only with the instinct of self-preservation. But, 'water! water!' was the cry from the parched lips on all sides. The empty flasks contained not a drop, alas! and at length sleep overcame each worn-out warrior, and even thirst and hunger were forgotten. Gloomy and out of humor, General Lee rode through the camping-ground of the decimated regiments, attended by his staff, and then, with a dry, harsh voice, ordered up the divisions of Wise and Magruder to bury the dead."

Surgeon Marsh, of the Fourth Reserves, who remained to take charge of our wounded, fell into the enemy's hands, and the next morning General Longstreet, who would not credit the statement that the Reserves were alone, inquired of him what troops had been engaged. He replied that he had been in the battle, and knew only of the action of M'Call's division, which had fought on the ground they were standing on. "Well," said Longstreet, "M'Call is safe in Richmond, but if his division had not offered the stubborn resistance it did, on this road, we would have captured your whole army. Never mind, we'll do it yet."

General M'Clellan, who was not present at the battle, in his report of it quotes very freely from the reports of Generals Heintzleman and Hooker, in regard to the operations of our division, who, being in our rear, and separated by a strip of pine forest from the battle-ground, could know but little of what took place. In it he says: "General Heintzleman states that, about *five o'clock* P.M., General M'Call's division was attacked in large force, evidently the principal attack; that in *less than an hour the division gave way.* * * * Later in the day, at the call of General Kearny, General Taylor's First New Jersey Brigade, Slocum's division, was sent *to occupy a portion of General M'Call's deserted position*, a battery accompanying the brigade."

There is not an officer or man of the division, who was present at this battle, but knows these statements are absolutely erroneous in every particular. There is abundant testimony to refute them, some of which we annex.

Besides the official report of General M'Call, which is a sufficient refutation of the charge, we have his testimony before the "Joint Committee on the Conduct of the War," in which he states: "I have no desire to treat lightly the reverses on both flanks of my division on this hard-fought field; they were the almost inevitable results of greatly superior numbers, impelled on those points with great impetuosity; but the Pennsylvania Reserves, as a division, although terribly shattered, were never 'routed'; they maintained their ground with these exceptions, for three hours, against thrice their numbers, in, I believe, the hardest-fought and bloodiest battle in which they have ever been engaged, and in this opinion I am sustained by most of those officers, if not all, with whom I have conversed on the subject.

"Had my division been routed, the march of the Federal army would certainly have been seriously interrupted by Lee forcing his masses into the interval. When I was surrounded and taken prisoner, I was conducted at once to Lee's headquarters. Here Longstreet told me they had seventy thousand men bearing on that point, all of whom would arrive before midnight; and, had he succeeded in forcing M'Clellan's column of march, they would have been thrust in between the right and left wings of the Federal army. Now, under this very probable contingency, had I not held my position, the state of affairs in the left wing of M'Clellan's army would have been critical indeed; but Lee was checked, as Longstreet admitted, by my division, and the divisions in the rear, together with the Pennsylvania Reserves and others, moved on during the night, and joined M'Clellan at Malvern Hill before daylight."

General Porter says: "Had not M'Call held his place at New Market road, June 30th, the line of march of the Federal army would have been cut by the enemy."

General Meade says: * * * "It was only the stubborn resistance offered by our division (the Pennsylvania Reserves), prolonging the contest till after dark, and checking till that time the advance of the enemy, that enabled the concentration, during the night, of the whole army on James river, *which saved it.*"

Captain Erkuries Beatty, chief-of-ordnance on General M'Call's staff, says: "The battle of the 30th, which opened about four P.M., was, in my opinion, the most desperate of the three battles in which the 'Reserves' were engaged. Our position was one of great responsibility, in reference to the safety of the whole army. General M'Call fully appreciated it, and the military proportions of the old hero loomed up to the grandeur of the occasion. His whole manner and appearance evinced the determination to triumph or die. As the battle progressed, the whole energy of the veteran soldier was roused. He entered into the thickest and hottest of the conflict with intense earnestness and entirely regardless of peril, although all the time in the midst of a tempest of deadly missiles. The portion of the field to which he gave his personal attention was our center and right, and our troops were cheered by his constant presence with them. He rode from regiment to regiment, and dashed along shouting words of encouragement, to inspirit both officers and men. At times, under the fierce onsets of the desperate rebel foe, our ranks would reel, and stagger, and fall back. But most active of all, in checking the stampede and turning back the fugitives, was their veteran General himself, and his presence and rallying cry was most potent in bringing them again to a stand. Then, regaining their self-possession, and speedily re-forming their line, they would again rush forward with cheers, and drive back the rebel desperadoes. About six o'clock P.M., I received a rifle ball through the thigh of my right leg. The General urged me to go to the rear and find a surgeon at once, but, as I felt no bone was broken, I determined not to leave him while I had strength to remain on my horse.

"The battle continued to rage; the 'Reserves,' worn down by the labor of the two previous battles, long marches and loss of sleep, and feeling that fresh rebel troops were constantly pouring on the field, began to yield to the unequal contest. But the General redoubled his efforts to keep their ranks firm. Again and again they rallied. I am sure he felt proud of their good conduct—the noble 'Reserves,' whom he had organized and given a year's training and discipline, and who, in these last five days, were realizing his highest expectations. But they had fought long and well, and the sun was near the horizon, and the General looked anxiously for the re-enforcements which had been promised him. All at once he turned round to me and said he was struck, and the dull sound of the ball, striking, as I thought, the upper part of his breast-bone, had not escaped my ear. I immediately and earnestly urged his going to the rear to a surgeon, and the horses' heads were turned in that direction. We had not proceeded far, however, before he succeeded in getting his shirt open at the neck, and remarked to me that he could feel no blood. Expressing the opinion that he had only been struck by a spent ball which had done him no injury, he immediately turned his horse, and declared his intention of returning to the battle-field, but enjoining upon me to seek a surgeon and have my wound dressed without delay."

While the battle of Glendale was progressing, General Jackson, who was ordered to gain the right flank and rear of the army, found his progress impeded at White Oak Swamp by General Franklin, who repulsed all his efforts to cross. During the night Franklin withdrew, and early the next morning the enemy crossed and marched to Malvern Hill. About four P.M., the same day, the rebel General, Holmes, moving down the banks of the James, discovered Warren's Brigade of Porter's Corps on the extreme left of our line, and, unlimbering his guns, opened upon him. Being somewhat surprised at the concentrated fire of thirty guns, which suddenly responded, he hastily retired, leaving two of his cannon.

In the meantime all our trains and reserve artillery had passed on to the river, and about midnight Seymour commenced the withdrawal of the Reserves from Glendale, which was gradually and quietly done. The Second Brigade was under the command of Colonel Sickel. As we marched down the Quaker road, we overtook many of our wounded, and at Willis Church we found collected a large number. The boys sought out such as could be helped, and took them along. Just before daybreak we reached the plain in front of Malvern Hill, crossing which we moved to the high ground and laid down our wearied bodies to sleep. Five days and five nights had now passed. Three days of battle, one of rest, and one of marching. Three nights of broken sleep upon the battle-fields, one of wearied marching, one of watching on picket. Three days' scanty rations, uncooked, and is it surprising that on the sixth day the Reserves sank down on Malvern and slept soundly amidst the thunder of battle? Hundreds of them slept peacefully there, with the shell and round-shot falling continually among them.

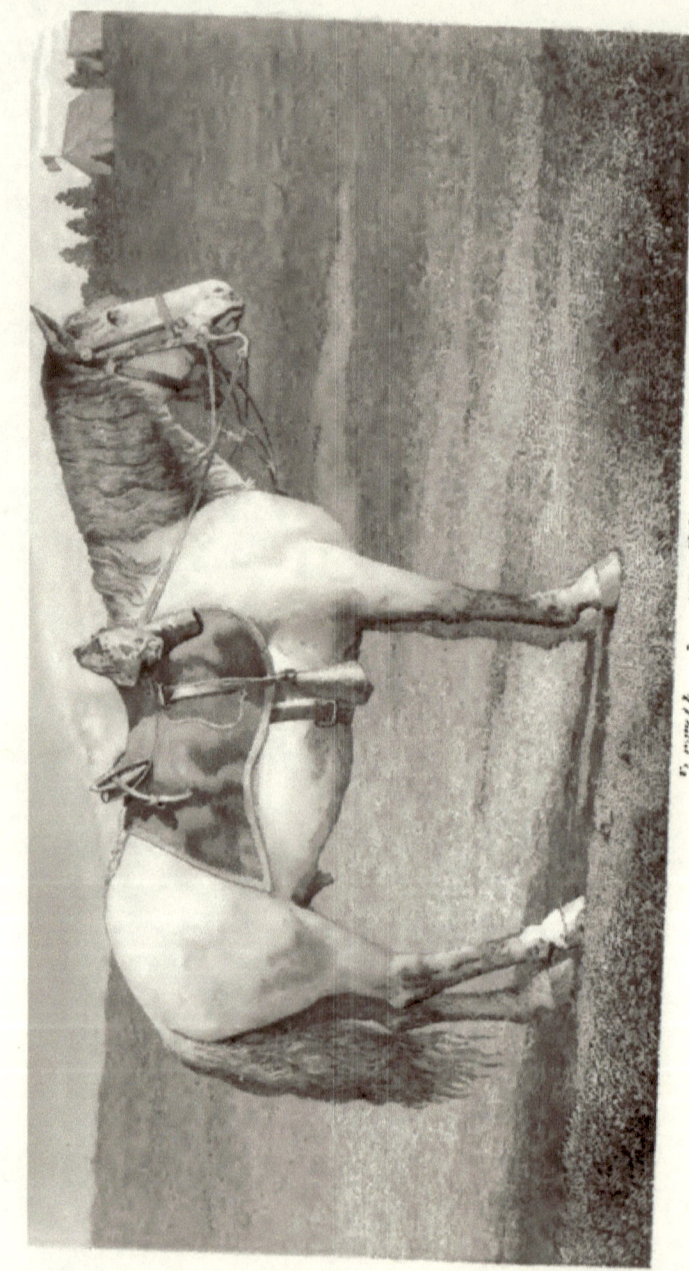

CHAPTER VIII.

THE BATTLE OF MALVERN HILL — THE FIELD — FEELING OUR LINE — OMINOUS STILLNESS — THE THREE O'CLOCK ASSAULT — THE SIX O'CLOCK ASSAULT — FEARFUL CARNAGE — UTTER REPULSE AND CONFUSION OF THE ENEMY — GENERAL TRIMBLE'S ACCOUNT — HEAVY LOSS OF THE ENEMY — THE LOSS OF BOTH ARMIES IN THE SEVEN DAYS' BATTLE — BOTH ARMIES RETREAT — INDIGNATION — PORTER'S AND HOOKER'S OPINION — KEARNY'S PROTEST — HARRISON'S LANDING — REMARKS — LIBBY PRISON — KINDNESS OF THE INSURGENT PRIVATES.

BATTLE OF MALVERN HILL, JULY 1ST, 1862.

GENERAL PORTER, having been misled and delayed in his passage through the swamp, did not reach this position until 9 A.M. on the 30th, when he at once proceeded to post his troops as they arrived. During the day and night, the whole Army of the Potomac was concentrated here, to make the last stand of the campaign. The enemy followed, flushed with the knowledge of our retreat, the sight of our dead and wounded, and the spoils of the fields. Although they had been defeated in every battle but that of Gaines' Mills, they had gained the campaign, and believed it required but one more desperate effort to annihilate or capture us. Jefferson Davis, and all the officials of the Confederate government were there, to witness the closing scene of the last drama.

Malvern Hill is an elevated plateau, about a mile and a half by three-fourths of a mile in area, mostly clear of timber, and with several converging roads crossing it. In front were numerous ravines, and the ground sloped gradually towards the north and east to a heavy woods, giving clear range for artillery in those directions. Towards the northwest, the plateau falls off more abruptly into a ravine, which extends to James river. Upon this hill the left and center of our line rested, while the right curved backwards, through a wooded country, towards a point below Haxall's, on the James river. The left of our line was held by the Fifth Corps, General Porter; next was the Fourth, General Keyes; next, the Third, General Heintzleman; next, the Second, General Sumner; and next, the Sixth, General Franklin; with both flanks resting on the James river. The Reserves were held in reserve, upon the highest ground on the field, behind the right of Porter. The line was very strong along the whole front of the open plateau, but from thence to the extreme right the troops were more deployed. The right wing was rendered as secure as possible by slashing the timber and barricading the roads. Two hundred and fifty pieces of artillery were posted upon different parts of the field, mostly on the left and center, and, in some places, tier above tier. Commodore Rogers,* commanding the flotilla on James river, placed his gun-boats so as to protect the extreme left flank.

The advance of the insurgents, under Jackson, came down the Quaker road, while Magruder's and Huger's divisions advanced on the direct road from Richmond. Longstreet's and A. P. Hill's divisions, having had the heaviest of the fighting thus far, and been badly cut up, were held in reserve in rear of Jackson, and were not brought into action. With their exception, the whole of the "Army of Virginia" were fought against Porter's corps, Couch's division, Sickel's and Meagher's brigades, they being the only troops actively engaged, the attack being confined exclusively to the left wing and left center. Apart from the great strength of our position, we had more men than the enemy upon the *field*, and more and heavier guns; though they were enabled to bring into the *fight* far more men than we could. About ten A.M., the enemy emerged from the woods, and commenced feeling along the whole left wing with his artillery and skirmishers,

---

* John Rogers, who captured the **English insurgent ironclad Atlanta**, near Savannah, Ga., June 17th, 1863.

which was promptly responded to on our side, and, in about an hour, the firing on both sides nearly ceased. An ominous stillness, indicating the maneuvering and placing in position of troops, now followed. About two P.M. a heavy column of the enemy moved to our right, occupying two hours in passing. It disappeared, and was not heard of again, it probably returning by the rear and participating in the attack on the left. At this time General M'Clellan made a tour of the field, and was received with loud cheers along the line. During this long silence, our troops lay quietly upon the field, eating their scanty rations, and enjoying the rest they had not known for so long.

About three P.M., Jackson pushed forward on both sides of the Quaker road, D. H. Hill's and Whiting's divisions on his right and left, with Ewell's in the center; Huger simultaneously advanced on their right, with Magruder's three divisions on his right, the order from Lee being to break our lines by a concentric fire of artillery, and then " charge with a yell," no matter what their loss was, right over our lines, and drive us into the river. The infantry attack, after a brief cannonade, was made with great intrepidity; but, with fearful carnage, they were hurled back. This affair occupied about one hour, when the firing ceased on the whole field, and the enemy evinced neither a disposition to attack nor withdraw. About six o'clock the enemy suddenly opened upon Couch and Porter, on the left center, with the whole strength of his artillery, and at once began pushing forward his columns of attack to carry the hill. Now opened a most desperate and sanguinary struggle. Brigade after brigade, forming under cover of the woods, started at a run across the open space and charged our batteries, but the heavy fire of our guns, with the cool and steady volleys of the infantry, in every case, sent them reeling back to shelter, and covered the ground with their dead and wounded. Fresh lines were immediately hurled forward with utter desperation and recklessness. No troops ever showed more courage than the enemy did upon this occasion. They were driven back, broken and confused, only to unite and return again to the assault. From batteries upon batteries were vomited forth sheets of flame and clouds of smoke, whose storm of grape and canister mowed down the columns of advancing valor, leaving vast gaps, that were filled up by the mad and infuriated masses. To add to the terror of the slaughter, the gun-boats in the river opened with their eleven-inch guns, throwing their shells into the woods, which were filled with the enemy, tearing into splinters the largest trees and creating great havoc.

About seven o'clock, as fresh troops were being pushed in by the enemy, Sickle's and Meagher's brigades were drawn from the right and sent in. Until dark, the enemy persisted in his efforts to take the positions, but, despite his vastly superior numbers and desperate valor, his attacks were all repulsed with fearful loss. The sun went down, but the carnage did not cease, for though the musketry closed, the fiery messengers of death coursed their swift-winged path through the skies, dealing destruction among the enemy, who but feebly replied. About nine o'clock all firing ceased. Never was a repulse more signal, the confused masses of the enemy's infantry, artillery and cavalry, all struggling together, choking the roads and crossing the fields in every direction. So complete was the confusion, that two or three days elapsed before the men of the different regiments and commands could be collected together and put in shape. This is the testimony of Doctors Collins, Donnelly, and other of our surgeons, who remained with our wounded at Willis Church and Glendale.* Thus ended

---

* Brigadier-General J. R. Trimble, [severely wounded at Gettysburg, Pa.,] of Ewell's [severely wounded near Thoroughfare Gap, Va., August 28th, 1862,] division, giving an account of the conduct of his brigade in this battle, says: "The next morning, by dawn, I went off to ask for orders, when I found the whole army in the utmost disorder—thousands of straggling men asking every passer-by for their regiments; ambulances, wagons and artillery obstructing every road; and, altogether, in a drenching rain, presenting a scene of the most woeful and disheartening confusion."

THE THIRD RESERVE. 123

this one-sided carnage. General M'Clellan, who had been to Harrison's Bar, on the Galena, during the day, was present at the last desperate charge of the enemy. The loss of neither army in this battle is known, but, there is little doubt, that of the enemy was treble our own.

As the army, in its retreat, was occupied in marching by night and fighting by day, its generals found no time for collecting data which would enable them to give exact returns of the casualties in each engagement. The aggregate of our entire losses, from the 26th of June to the 1st of July, inclusive, was officially returned by General M'Clellan as follows:

	Killed.	Wounded.	Missing.	Total.
First, M'Call's division	253	1,240	1,581	*3,074
Second, Sumner's corps	187	1,076	848	2,111
Third, Heintzleman's corps	189	1,051	833	2,073
Fourth, Keyes' corps	69	507	201	777
Fifth, Porter's corps	620	2,460	1,198	4,278
Sixth, Franklin's corps	245	1,313	1,179	2,737
Engineers		2	21	23
Cavalry	19	60	97	176
Total	1,582	7,709	5,958	15,249

*General M'Call, in his official report, states the loss of the Reserves to be 3,180.

It will be observed that the division of Reserves lost more than any corps, excepting the Fifth, and more than Sumner's and Keyes' or Heintzleman's and Keyes' combined. They constituted about one-fifteenth of the available army, and their loss was more than one-fifth of the whole loss sustained.

The loss of the enemy in the Seven Days' is not known but from their reckless attacks upon our strong positions at Mechanicsville, Gaines' Mill, Glendale and Malvern, it must have equaled, minus unwounded prisoners, if not exceeded, our own. The official reports of two corps commanders show an aggregate of 9,836 killed, wounded and missing;* while other subordinate reports indicate heavy losses in other divisions.†

It seems strange that Lee should have attempted to assault our position at Malvern Hill, upon the points he did, under any other supposition than that we were cowards, ready to run upon a vigorous attack being made. He evidently, however, did not entertain this opinion, or he would not have feared to weaken his force between us and Richmond, and make a serious demonstration upon our center and right while he attacked our left, or have made the main assaults upon our right, where our position was not near so strong.

As soon as the battle was over our victorious army began to retreat, leaving our dead and most of our wounded upon the field. Up to this moment the majority of the army, at least of the Reserves, hoped and believed this struggle would end in their at least attempting to take Richmond, and never for a moment did it enter their heads they were not able of successfully coping with the enemy. Knowing they were victorious upon every field but one, they could not understand what they had to fear from the foe, and when the order came at night to retreat, their feelings were those of deep indignation and sorrow.

Even Fitz John Porter's devotion to his chief was temporarily shaken, he exclaiming, in deep indignation, "We ought rather to pursue the defeated foe than to be shamefully flying from him." General Philip Kearny, surrounded by a group of general officers, to whom the order was read,

	Killed.	Wounded.	Missing.	Total.
*Jackson's corps	966	4,417	63	5,446
A. P. Hill's corps	619	3,271	...	3,890
Total	1,585	7,688	63	9,336

† Confederate Brigadier-General R. S. Ripley, chief of artillery, reports that his brigade entered into these fights 2,366 strong, including ambulance corps, of whom 889 fell at Malvern, and three out of four colonels were killed. Brigadier-General Garland reports his loss in all the battles at 844. Brigadier-General Howell Cobb reports that his brigade, of Magruder's division, went into battle at Savage Station 2,700 strong, whereof but 1,500 appeared on the battle-field of Malvern, where nearly 500 of them were killed and wounded.

exclaimed: "I, Philip Kearny, an old soldier, enter my solemn protest against this order for retreat. We ought, instead of retreating, to follow up the enemy and take Richmond. And, in full view of all the responsibility of such a declaration, I say to you all, such an order can only be prompted by cowardice or treason."* But it was predetermined to retreat, whether we were victorious or defeated, and on the afternoon of the 30th, when the Reserve were hurling back the assaults of the enemy at Glendale, the advance of the army train reached Harrison's Landing.

About eleven o'clock that night, the sleepy boys were waked up and got into line. Moving on past Haxall's house, with sad hearts we wound our way down the hill to the river road, along which we marched, passing over Turkey bridge. The night was extremely dark, but the road, which for a long distance was exceedingly bad, was lit up by thousands of candles placed in the trees and bright fires burning upon the wayside, which were continually replenished by the guards. At daybreak we entered a field of wheat ready for cutting, where we lay down and rested for an hour, and then moved on. Other troops that followed us rested on portions of the same field, until all was trampled under and destroyed. It soon after commenced raining, turning the deep dust into heavy mud, and in a short time the road was rendered almost impassable. But onward the column moved until it crossed Cimage creek, and debouched into the open plain of Harrison's Landing. The Reserves were moved to the right, and put into a heavy pine woods, where they somewhat sheltered themselves by building bough arbors. During the day and night the rain descended in torrents, making the kindling

---

*General Hooker, before the Committee on the Conduct of the War, testified as follows:

"*Question*—Had the defeat of the enemy at Malvern been followed up by our whole force, what would have been the probable result?

"*Answer*—Richmond would have been ours beyond a doubt.

"*Question*—Instead of that, you fell back to Harrison's Landing?

"*Answer*—Yes, sir. We were ordered to retreat; and it was like the retreat of a whipped army."   *   *   *   *   *   *   *   *   *   *

of fires impossible, but, as the boys had but little to cook, it did not matter much. The withdrawal, under General Keyes, was effected with no loss, except a few wagons that broke down, the rear guard leaving Malvern at ten A.M. on the 2d of July, and coming into the Landing early the next morning. The advance guard of the enemy, who had followed upon our rear, posted a few guns and opened with shell upon us, to which we soon replied. The Reserves were formed about nine A.M. in the open field near the bridge, where they stood in mud up to their knees, with shells bursting and round shot whistling over their heads until three P.M., when they moved to the right, and bivouacked near the banks of Herring creek.

While the "change of base" was being executed, the position at the White House was evacuated. No less than seven hundred vessels were in the river at the time, all of which were removed under cover of the gun-boats and Stoneman's cavalry.

Thus ended the "Seven Days' Battle,"* which, though termed a change of base, was simply a retreat. It was a movement of great delicacy, most successfully executed, under incessant and determined attacks of an enterprising enemy. The forty miles of wagons, the immense artillery train, a drove of 2,500 head of cattle, in fact, the army and its entire material was successfully transferred with an incredible small loss of material. All was conducted with order. There was no fear or haste, no hurrying, or smashing up of wagons; yet there was no moment of repose, no opportunity to properly care for the wounded; and the dead, excepting at Mechanicsville, were left unburied. The enemy had a perfect knowledge of the roads, paths, bridges, and topography of the country, and were well supplied with friendly guides. They closely watched every movement,

---

* Properly, this should be called the Six Days' Battle, for, to make it seven, the advance of M'Clellan's pickets, terminating in the affair at Oak Grove, on the 25th, would have to be included, which had no connection with the movement.

and were enabled to hurl superior numbers on our flank and rear, which they did with remorseless impetuosity. While an advancing army loses nothing in men and material by capture, it is necessarily the reverse with a retreating one, which, though it may be successful in every combat, loses the advantage of following up its victories, which are transferred to the enemy. Though this has a tendency to increase the *morale* of the one, and diminish that of the other, such did not appear to be the case with our army, for the men went into every battle in most excellent spirits, and with full confidence of victory, and, upon our arrival at the Landing, they were proud of their achievements, and in good heart, and had unbounded confidence in General M'Clellan, and would, at any moment during the retreat, or at the Landing, fearlessly assumed the aggressive.

In regard to the positions of the opposing armies until the 28th, both Generals M'Clellan and Lee were deceived. M'Clellan supposed the large mass of the enemy lay between him and Richmond on his left, while, in fact, only Generals Huger's and Magruder's divisions of 25,000 men were south of the Chickahominy, in front of 75,000 men. Lee supposed almost the whole of M'Clellan's army was concentrated on the right of our line north of the river, and that we were retreating on our base at the White House, when, in fact, Porter, at no time, had barely 35,000 men to oppose the desperate efforts of 50,000 rebels. The elaborate and powerful defensive works, that cost our army so much delay and labor to erect, were never used by us. Throughout the whole struggle, the Union and Confederate troops displayed upon every field the most desperate bravery and indomitable courage, and learned, by the manly qualities they discovered, to respect each other. Never upon the field did we see or hear of an act of cruelty; and the testimony of our wounded and the surgeons who remained with them, was to the universal kindness they received from the privates of the enemy. It is to be regretted that the same cannot be said of their officers; and all united in attesting to the bitter animosity and heartlessness shown by the non-combatants and civilians.

After the battle of Glendale, Surgeons James Collins, of the Third, and E. Donnelly, of the Second, among others, volunteered to remain behind, and take charge of our wounded, and from them we subsequently learned many interesting facts in regard to their treatment and condition. Our wounded were collected on the lawn near Nelson's house, by some Confederate privates who volunteered to help. They brought them water and divided their scanty rations among them. They spoke and acted towards them with the greatest kindness, but the sufferings of the poor boys were great. With no medicine or stimulants, with a scanty supply of water, and the clothing of the boys only for bandages, the doctors amputated the limbs and dressed the wounds of hundreds who were sinking from loss of blood and want of food. No medicine, liquor, food or assistance could be obtained from the officials, one of whom, a surgeon of the C. S. A., deliberately stole Dr. Donnelly's case of instruments when he was half through an operation. In two weeks all the wounded who had survived the exposure and neglect they had been subjected to upon the field where they fell, were hauled in army wagons, over corduroy roads, to Richmond, a few miles distance. Upon their arrival, they were huddled into Libby prison, a loathsome hole, foul with the stench of water-closets and the putrifaction of the bodies in the dead-house underneath, which were exposed to their sight through a large open grating in the floor. A little medicine was doled out to them. A pittance of tainted beef and hard-tack was given each day. Without a change of clothing, or blankets to cover themselves with at night, or water to wash with in the morning, they were huddled together by hundreds; and this was the treatment they received from the insurgent government in their capital.

But the treatment they received from the soldiers was universally kind. When we say soldiers, we do not mean the guards around the prison, who had never been upon the field, but the men who had fought them, and had learned to respect a foe. With these, the boys were all right. On the field, when we drove them from positions formerly held by us, we found, in many cases, our wounded had been supplied with water, and sometimes placed behind logs or trees; and at Glendale, when several of the Seventeenth Virginia were taken prisoners, although under a heavy fire, they picked up and carried off some of our wounded. They were cheered for this, a compliment very seldom paid to a foe upon the battle-field. Many other acts of kindness were frequently done upon the field, that showed there was not felt the bitter animosity and vindictiveness displayed by civilians and politicians. At Malvern, the morning after the battle, both armies had strong pickets upon the field; and the enemy were permitted to remove their wounded, but they fired upon our men when they attempted to remove ours. This, however, was an absolute military necessity on their part, as it was of the utmost importance to conceal from us the extent of their disaster, and the demoralization and flight of their troops.

The position we now occupied was a very strong one, and in the broad area were collected the whole army, an immense amount of stores and ammunition, and vast numbers of siege-guns, mortars, etc. At the landing, lay a large fleet of vessels, of every size and description.

CHAPTER IX.

PUTTING THE ARMY INTO FIGHTING ORDER — AS BRIGHT AS NEW DOLLARS — NICE PREDICAMENT — VISIT OF THE PRESIDENT — GAMBLING LIEUTENANT — RESIGNATIONS AND PROMOTIONS — MIDNIGHT SHELLING — THE COLES HOUSE — RUFFIN FIRES THE FIRST AND LAST SHOT — THE YOUNG SPY — HOOKER'S FIGHT AT MALVERN HILL — THE AMBULANCE CORPS — M'CALL — REYNOLDS' SWORD — WITHDRAWAL OF THE ARMY — ABANDONMENT OF THE CAMPAIGN — CAUSE OF ITS FAILURE.

GENERAL SEYMOUR, being the only general officer left in the Reserves, assumed the command. General Meade, being absent, wounded, Colonel Sickels succeeded him in command of the Second Brigade; and Lieutenant-Colonel Thompson took command of the Third Regiment. The Fourth of July, our natal day, was duly celebrated by the firing of salutes and the display of flags, among the most conspicuous of which were those captured from the enemy. General M'Clellan issued a patriotic address to the army, which was read at the head of the regiments, and received with enthusiastic cheers. Steps were taken at once to reorganize, equip, and put the army into fighting order again. The stragglers soon found their regiments. Upon inspecting the arms, it was found that, in the same regiments, were collected every calibre and pattern known in the service: the Springfield, Harper's Ferry, Sharpe's, Burnside, Maynard's, Enfield, Tower, Belgium, French, Richmond, Palmetto, etc.; the men who having lost their own, appropriating their neighbors. When not of the calibre of the regiment, they were turned in, assorted, and re-issued; so that each regiment, brigade and division, if possible, would be armed alike. Accoutrements, ammunition, and clothing, were likewise distributed as fast as received, and, in an incredible short time, the whole army was in as good condition as ever to meet the enemy.

While these matters were occupying the attention of the general officers, the great question that agitated the soldier's mind was the getting rid of the "graybacks," who, there was every reason to suppose, had domiciled themselves upon the person of the patriots, and held them in a ticklish position. As we had destroyed all our clothing except what we stood in, and as soap was an article that could neither be bought nor "appropriated," and as clothing was issued by piece-meal, it was a task more easily undertaken than accomplished. But what can not an American accomplish? By dint of washing, scrubbing, scouring and constant vigilance, the triumph was achieved; and the boys came out in their new uniforms as clean and bright as new dollars. It is a matter of impossibility for an army to pass through what we did in the summer without being overrun with vermin, and a soldier of the Army of the Potomac who declares he never had any, did not belong to the Reserves. Early one morning, some of the boys determined to go up the creek so far that no vermin would be found floating on the water. They had carefully kept their clothes up the trees until they got full suits. Afraid to trust the precious bundles in their hands, they swung them over their shoulders on sticks. Up the levee they marched, and finding a nice place, were soon enjoying a glorious splash. Soon the well-known whistle of the bullet was heard, and they discovered the insurgent pickets on the other side. With the creek before them, a swamp behind, a long embankment their only means of retreat, and their clothes out of reach, they found themselves in a pretty predicament. Lying behind the embankment stripped, with the scorching rays of the sun pouring down upon them, soon became uninteresting; and to save themselves from broiling, they rolled in the mud and tried baking. This operation, renewed as soon as the mud commenced cracking on them, formed the principal feature of their amusement until darkness covered their retreat; but it killed the vermin.

On the 8th, President Lincoln visited the army, and, on account of the hard service we had lately gone through, declined a review, but rode along the lines of the divisions, which were drawn up to receive him. He was most enthusiastically cheered by the troops, honoring the chief who had pledged himself to preserve us a nation, regardless of cost or sacrifice.

On the morning of the 14th, we moved our camp about two miles, near to Evlington Heights, on the right of our line. Here we occupied a broad, open plain, near the creek, where the men could enjoy most excellent bathing. As good water was scarce, every regiment dug a fine, deep well, from which they obtained a bountiful supply of cool water. Sibley tents were issued, and our rations brought up to the full standard, with cabbage, beets, onions, and other vegetables in addition, brought by the Sanitary Commission. Division guard-mounting, company and battalion drills, and dress-parades, were ordered. Several reviews, by Generals M'Clellan and Seymour, took place; the sutlers arrived, and letters and newspapers were received daily.

The morals of an army are never so good in camp as on the march. While here, General Seymour issued stringent orders against gambling, which was indulged in by the unwary for excitement, and by the unprincipled sharps to fleece them. We knew of a young lieutenant, of a neighboring regiment, who, in a few days after the paymaster came, invariably gambled away his two months' pay, and, at the end of three years' hard service, was mustered out in debt to the sutler and all his comrades of whom he could borrow, and with hardly clothes upon his back.

On the 19th, the United States truce steamer Louisiana came down the river from City Point, loaded with paroled Union prisoners from Richmond, among whom were Captain William Brian, and Lieutenants Roberts and Lehman. Also, a large number of the boys, most of whom were sent North to the hospitals. Doctor Collins, the efficient surgeon of the Third, who had remained with the wounded, also came, and was welcomed. All bore testimony of the kindness of the privates and cruelty of the officials of the Confederate Government. While here, some of the officers and men were prostrated from exhaustion, and much sickness of a mild nature prevailed, caused by their systems being overtaxed. Nearly two hundred officers and men, out of five hundred and seventy-one present, were sick or in quarters, at one time, in the Third. Lieutenant-Colonel William S. Thompson, a gallant officer, was forced to resign on account of ill health. He subsequently entered the naval service, and was killed in action, April 19th, 1865. The Rev. George H. Frear, the most excellent and good chaplain, also resigned with much regret, on the same account. Captain William D. Curtis, Company B; First Lieutenant Jacob Lehman, Company A; Second Lieutenants Sebastian Eckle, Company A; George H. Lindsey, Company E; and Edward K. Mull, Company F, all brave, efficient, and faithful officers, were also forced to resign on account of their health. Assistant Surgeon Henry S. Colston, about the same time, was promoted Surgeon of the Eighty-first Regiment, Pennsylvania Volunteers; and Captain Joseph Thomas, Company H, one of the most intelligent officers and disciplinarians in the regiment, resigned, to accept the position of Surgeon in the One Hundred and Eighteenth Pennsylvania Volunteers.

An order having been issued, by General Seymour, discontinuing elections for officers in the Reserve corps, and directing vacancies to be filled from the officers and men who, by faithful and gallant conduct, were deserving of it, Colonel Sickels took great pains to ascertain the opinion of his command upon these points before selecting the names of those to forward to fill the vacancies occasioned by the resignations.

The following promotions were accordingly made, which gave great satisfaction to all:

Captain John Clark, Company E, to be Lieutenant-Colonel.

Captain William Briner, Company D, to be Major.

Company A—Second Lieutenant Michael Walters, to be First Lieutenant; Amos W. Seitzinger, to be Second Lieutenant.

Company B—First Lieutenant George C. Davenport, to be Captain; First Sergeant F. Gilbert Nicholson, to be First Lieutenant.

Company D—First Lieutenant Florentine H. Straub, to be Captain; Second Lieutenant Andrew J. Stetson, to be First Lieutenant; First Sergeant Jacob V. Shilling, to be Second Lieutenant.

Company E—First Lieutenant Robert Johnston, to be Captain; First Sergeant Thomas H. Bamford, to be Second Lieutenant; Sergeant Edwin A. Glenn, to be Second Lieutenant.

Company F—Henry S. Moulton, to be Second Lieutenant.

Company H—First Lieutenant Benjamin F. Fisher, to be Captain; Second Lieutenant J. B. Bartholomew, to be First Lieutenant; First Sergeant William M'Carty, to be Second Lieutenant.

About the same time, Doctors Samuel L. Orr, of Philadelphia, and George J. Rice, of Bucks county, were assigned to the regiment as Assistant Surgeons.

A little after midnight on the 1st of August, the rebel General French, with forty-three guns, approached stealthily to Coggin's Point and Coles House, opposite our encampment, and opened a heavy fire upon us and the shipping. The shells and round shot exploded and flew around camp in the most lively manner, creating great excitement among the "contrabands," who entertained a mortal dread of "them rotten shot." The majority of the boys, taking a philosophical view of the matter, considered themselves about as safe in one place as another, and did not disturb themselves from their blankets, while others, of a more excitable nature, after admiring the pyrotechnical display for a time, lighted their candles and went to playing cards. In about a half-hour our guns silenced their fire, and, before daylight, French decamped, leaving three dead, a disabled caisson, and flag behind. Our loss was ten killed and fifteen wounded. No harm was done to the shipping. The next morning, the Coles House, which had been a rendezvous for the enemy, was destroyed, and our troops took possession of the point. The following day, Colonel Sickel was ordered over with detachments from his own regiment and the Eighth, numbering some eight hundred men. Having established his pickets, he advanced to the house of Hon. Edmun Ruffin, who fired the first and last shot of the war. The first was at Sumter, and the last at his own head. Here were discovered some insurgent cavarly, but they left without firing a shot. Seventeen mules were captured, and a number of important letters, which the command brought over the next day. The boys secured an abundance of fruit, vegetables and chickens. Details were continued daily, entrenchments thrown up, and some heavy guns put in position.

One day our detail brought in a civilian, who attempted to run through the pickets. He was an intelligent young Virginian, who crossed the river with them in the morning, representing himself as being connected with the commissary department, and appeared perfectly at home with the men. When taken, he was on horse-back, and tried hard to escape. He showed considerable bitterness against his captors, appeared indifferent as to what they might do with him, and, although annoyed at his capture, an expression of concealed fun was, in unguarded moments, caught lurking in his bright eyes. He was turned over to the provost-marshal. The next day he crossed again with a squadron of cavalry, from whom he managed to slip, and, despite their efforts, escaped. We afterwards learned he was a Union spy.

Upon information received from Washington, that deserters had reported the enemy moving southward of the James, leaving but a small force in Richmond, General Hooker was ordered with his own division and Pleasanton's cavalry to advance upon Malvern Hill. Through the incompetency of his guides, Hooker's first attempt miscarried, but the next night, with Sedgwick's* division to re-enforce him, he turned the hill, and drove the enemy up the river road towards Richmond. Our loss was three killed and eleven wounded. The enemy's was heavier, beside one hundred prisoners. Colonel Averill, with part of the cavalry, pushed on to White Oak bridge, driving thence the Eighteenth Virginia Cavalry, killing and wounding several, and capturing twenty-eight men and horses. Hooker encamped on Malvern that night, and on the 7th returned to camp. While this movement was being made, the Reserves were held in readiness to support it.

The regimental bands were mustered out on the 6th, a late act of Congress providing for brigade bands only. On the same day, an ambulance corps for each army corps was organized, on the basis of a captain for each army corps; a first lieutenant for each division; a second lieutenant for each brigade, and a sergeant for each regiment. One transport cart, one four-horse and two two-horse ambulances for each regiment, each provided with two stretchers, and having a driver and two men. Sergeant Frederick R. Barth, Company H, was detailed for this service. About this time, Lieutenants Samuel La Rue and John Staunton, Sergeants John F. Bender, John H. T. Christien, Benjamin D. Henning, James E. M'Masters and George W. Unruh, Corporals Charles H. Loper and Franklin Tressel, and Privates Robert Clark, Nathan S. Harkness and John W. Yeich, were detailed to go to Pennsylvania on recruiting service.

On the 7th, "Old Greenback," the paymaster, Major John M. Pomeroy, arrived in camp, and paid off the regiment. On the 8th, Doctors Howard and William Trego, Edward

---

* Major General John Sedgwick, of Conn., was thrice badly wounded at Antietam, and killed at Spottsylvania Court House, May 9th, 1864, while placing some of his guns, and bantering some of his men, who winced at the singing of rebel bullets. He was struck in the head by a rifle ball and instantly killed.

Hutchinson, Jacob A. Cadwallader, and George Worstall, of the Sanitary Commission, visited the Reserves, to look after the health of the soldiers. Steamers laden with vegetables, etc., the generous donations of citizens, were constantly arriving at the landing.

On the 13th, Generals M'Call and Reynolds arrived from Richmond, and the Reserves paraded to receive them. Their reception was most enthusiastic, the bands playing, the boys cheering, and throwing their hats in the air. They addressed a few words to the men, thanking them for the hearty reception, and assuring them they would rejoin the division as soon as their health permitted. But the severity of the campaign, and the close confinement in Libby prison, had so seriously impaired M'Call's health, that he proceeded home to obtain the medical care he so much needed. This separation was final between the general and the division, every officer and man of which respected, honored and loved him. It was he who organized, disciplined and brought to that high state of efficiency the division, which rendered them so efficient in the field, and won for them a proud and glorious name wherever the story of our war was read. In a few weeks he became satisfied he would never again be able to lead us on, and not wishing to obstruct the promotion of others in this hour of the nation's trial, he tendered his resignation. The citizens of Chester county, where he resided, soon after his return home presented him with an elegant sword, in testimony of their appreciation of his services in the field.

General Reynolds succeeded to the command of the Reserves. The night he arrived the sergeants of his brigade met and resolved to raise a subscription among themselves and the men to present him a sword. The money was freely given, and placed in the hands of the author to procure the gift. It coming to the knowledge of the general, he refused to receive it, but being assured that it came from the men only, that there was no axe to grind, and that no officer would attempt to make capital out of it, he consented. The sword was procured; a magnificent and costly one, studded with diamonds and gems of the purest water. It was borne from Fairfax Station to the field of Gettysburg. A note was addressed to the general, requesting him, in the lull of battle, to receive the gift direct from the boys, but ere that hour came Reynolds passed in glory to immortality.

About the same time, orders were received to pack our knapsacks and label each with the owner's name, and send them down to the landing to be shipped in charge of the quartermaster's sergeant to Alexandria. Orders were also received to have three days' cooked rations in haversacks and five in bulk, and be prepared to move. On the 30th of July, Major-General H. W. Halleck, commanding United States army, issued orders for the shipment of all the sick from Harrison's Landing to the north, who at that time numbered about 12,500 men.

It having been determined to withdraw the army from Harrison's Landing to Acquia Creek, orders for the same were received on the 4th of August. The reasons that led to this determination were, that at that time General M'Clellan's army numbered but ninety thousand effective men, and the army of General Pope, charged with covering Washington, numbered but thirty-eight thousand. The former was twenty-five miles from Richmond, and the latter about eighty or ninety miles from Washington, while between them were the enemy, who, according to M'Clellan's estimate, numbered over two hundred thousand men. This would enable the enemy to fall with his superior numbers upon one or the other, as he might elect, without either being able to re-enforce the other in case of attack. It was in the enemy's power at any time to exchange Richmond for Washington, and while the loss of their capital would be seriously felt by them, the loss of Washington to us, in the then state of our foreign relations, would be conclusive, or nearly so, in its results upon the war.

General M'Clellan most earnestly protested against the withdrawal of his army, he contending that the true defence of Washington was on the banks of the James river. He asked for re-enforcements to the extent of 35,000 men, but the Government had but 26,000 east of the Alleghenies, exclusive of those under Pope and at Fortress Monroe. General Halleck, in writing to General M'Clellan, says: * * * "In regard to the demoralizing effect of a withdrawal from the Peninsula to the Rappahannock, I must remark that a large number of your highest officers—indeed, a majority of those whose opinions have been reported to me—are decidedly in favor of the movement." * * * Subsequent events proved the absolute necessity of withdrawing the army from the Peninsula.

It having been ascertained that the enemy were moving North in force, Jackson entering Gordonsville on the 19th of July, General M'Clellan, in obedience to orders from Washington, embarked five batteries for Acquia Creek, where Burnside had landed with infantry only on the 3d of August. On the 13th, the enemy, in anticipation of an advance on Richmond, burnt the wharves at City Point.

General M'Clellan intended to move his entire army by water, from the Landing, but repeated and urgent messages from Washington induced him to move the bulk of his troops by land to Fortress Monroe, and on the 14th, Porter's and Heintzleman's corps, preceded by Averill's cavalry, marched, via Jones' bridge and Barrett's Ferry, down the Peninsula. The other troops followed, and General M'Clellan, with the rear-guard, breaking camp on the 16th, crossed the Chickahominy two days afterwards. The movement was covered by General Pleasanton, with his cavalry and horse artillery, he remaining at Haxall's, near Malvern, until the army had passed Charles City Court House. Porter's corps embarked at Newport News on the 20th. The rest of the army there, at Yorktown and Fortress Monroe: M'Clellan and staff leaving the latter point on the 23d, and arriving at Acquia Creek the next day.

Thus ended the ever-memorable and unfortunate campaign of the magnificent Army of the Potomac on the Peninsula. Ten severely-contested and sanguinary battles had been fought, besides numerous smaller engagements. The men submitted to privations, exposures, sickness, and even death, without a murmur, and never was a government more cheerfully or devotedly served than our own was by this army. Its failure was undoubtedly caused by the fact that the enemy nearly always chose the time and place of battle, and, though uniformly inferior in aggregate numbers, usually managed to bring the larger force into action—fighting two-thirds to three-fourths of his entire strength against one-fourth to one-half of ours. Our chief, though incessantly calling for re-enforcements, never succeeded in bringing nearly all the troops he already had into action at any one time.

CHAPTER X.

The Reserves to the Relief of Pope — Embarkation of the Third — Acquia Creek — Falmouth — Banks at Cedar Mountain — Pope's Movements — Arrival of General Meade — To Rappahannock Station — The First to Join Pope — Warrenton — March — Skirmish — Second Bull Run — Fighting of the 28th — King's Battle — Ricketts' Combat — Topography of Manassas Plains — Fighting of the 29th — Jackson's and Longstreet's Position — The Joint Order — Pope's Mistake — M'Dowell and Porter — Manœuvre — Hard Fighting — Charge a Battery — The 30th — Two Days without Food — The Position of the Armies — Reserves Skirmishing — Discovery of the Thunderbolt — Pope's Plan of Battle — Pope's Fatal Blunder — The Reserves Seize Henry's Hill — Glorious Charge — Incessant Assaults — The Bridge Saved — Orderly Withdrawal — Strength of the Armies — Cause of the Loss of the Battle — General Porter's Case — Centreville — Picket — Battle of Chantilly — Runaway School-Girls.

BUT to return to the movements of the Third. Pope was being overwhelmed by the the entire rebel army under Lee, and urgently called for help. The Reserves were at once put on steamers and pushed to his relief. At four o'clock on the afternoon of the 11th of August, the Third formed and moved to the landing, where they lay until evening, when they embarked aboard the steamers Hero and Secor, and, bidding farewell to the scenes of their glory, passed down the river and came to anchor about midnight. Early the next morning, they again got under way, passing the standing masts of the frigates Cumberland and Congress, that sunk gloriously fighting to the death the ironclad Merrimac.* Rounding Fortress Monroe, they steamed into the bay and headed northward. In the afternoon a violent rain

---

* March 8th, 1862. The Merrimac was commanded by Admiral **Frank Buchanan,** who was wounded, and was destroyed three days afterwards by **order of Commodore Tatnall.**

and hail storm occurred, roughing the bay and cascading some of the men. At nine P.M., they came to anchor near the mouth of the Potomac. Early the next morning (the 13th), they proceeded up the river to Acquia Creek, where they arrived about eight o'clock, and, debarking during the afternoon, were transferred to cars and conveyed opposite Fredericksburg, near their old camping-ground of the preceding May. Here they occupied the tents left standing by M'Dowell's troops.

General John Pope was, on the 26th of June, the day of the battle of Mechanicsville, assigned to the command of the "Army of Virginia," consisting of the corps of Major-Generals M'Dowell, Fremont* and Banks. His command consisted of about 40,000 disposable troops, scattered from Fredericksburg to Winchester, and he was charged with the covering of Washington, the Baltimore and Ohio railroad, and to make a diversion in favor of M'Clellan, by threatening Richmond from the north. On the 16th of July, Ewell, with a division of Lee's army, entered Gordonsville. On the 7th of August, all the infantry and artillery of Pope's army, amounting to 28,000 men, were assembled along the turnpike from Sperryville to Culpepper, excepting King's division, which was opposite Fredericksburg. The cavalry pickets extended on the right from the Blue Ridge on the Rapidan, down the same until they joined King's, at its junction with the Rappahannock.

On the 9th, General Banks† was ordered to move forward to Cedar or Slaughter Mountain, and re-enforce Crawford's‡ brigade in its strong position, and hold the enemy in check. Banks, however, left this position late in the day, and advanced at least a mile, throwing his whole force of, as he

---

* Fremont was relieved at his own request, as he considered Pope his junior; and General Frank Sigel succeeded him.

† Ex-Governor of Massachusetts. Speaker of the XXXIVth Congress.

‡ S. W. Crawford, wounded at Antietam. Subsequently, commander of the Reserves.

supposed, 14,000 men* into action against Jackson's 20,000, strongly posted, and sheltered by woods and ridges. This advance was everywhere swept by the fire of the enemy's artillery and infantry, concealed in the woods and ravines beyond. The battle lasted about an hour and a half, during which our troops did all that troops could do for victory, but the odds was too heavy against them, and they were driven back to their former position with heavy loss. About this time, Ricketts' division came up, and General Pope arrived upon the field, and drew in Banks' too extended lines, and the enemy were driven back. An artillery fight was kept up until midnight. Sigel's corps, in the meantime, arrived, and were pushed in abreast of Ricketts. Both sides suffered severely, our loss being estimated at 1,800, and the enemy acknowledged that of 1,314, including General C. S. Winder, two colonels and one major killed.

In this battle General Geary,† with five Ohio regiments and the Twenty-eighth Pennsylvania, made the most desperate charge of the day, and was himself severely wounded with most of his officers.‡

Before daylight the next morning, Jackson withdrew his forces two miles, and clung to the mountains and woods until the night of the 11th, when he fell back across the Rapidan, in the direction of Gordonsville, leaving many of his dead and wounded on the field. General Pope was subsequently re-enforced by General King's division, from Fredericksbug, and by Reno, with 8,000 of Burnside's army, and advanced again to the Rapidan and Robinson's rivers. His cavalry having captured the adjutant of I. E. B. Stuart,

---

*General Pope, in his official report, says: "The consolidated report of General Banks' corps, received some days previously (to the battle), exhibited an effective force of something over 14,000 men. It appeared subsequently, however, that General Banks' force at that time did not exceed 8,000 men."

†John W. Geary, an officer of the Mexican War, Alcalde of San Francisco, Governor of Kansas, Colonel of the Twenty-eighth Pennsylvania Volunteers, and twice Governor of Pennsylvania.

‡Greeley's American Conflict, Vol. II, page 177.

with a letter from General Lee, dated August 15th, that clearly indicated the whole of the insurgent army was rapidly assembling to overwhelm him, he held fast to his position to the last, so as to afford time for the arrival of M'Clellan's army, and on the 18th commenced retreating across the Rappahannock, which he accomplished without loss early on the 20th. The insurgents followed closely, and after three days' skirmishing at Rappahannock Station and Kelly's Ford, without any prospect of success, commenced moving up the stream, intending to turn our right.

On the morning of the 16th, Colonel Sickel received intelligence that a force of rebel cavalry had crossed the river, during the night, some distance above, and were moving towards Potomac bridge, on the Fredericksburg and Acquia Creek railroad, to cut our communication. He at once dispatched Major Briner, with companies D, H, and K, for its protection. The same day, the Sixth Reserves arrived; and the next, General Meade, who, having sufficiently recovered from his wounds, came into camp. He was received with loud cheers by the men, and the regiments paraded under arms. He assumed command of his brigade, which was now the First. The old First became the Second, under General Seymour, and General Jackson took command of the Third. The Reserves were now transferred to M'Dowell's corps. On the 21st, General Reynolds and staff, and all the Reserves excepting the Second Regiment,* having arrived, they moved forward towards Kelly's Ford. That night, at nine o'clock, with three days' rations in the haversacks, the Third marched through Falmouth, and moved up the river, on the Bealton road. The night was dark and stormy, and after marching five miles they lay down along the road-side and slept. Early the next morning they moved on, halting

---

* The Second was the last of the Reserves to leave Harrison's Landing. On arriving at Falmouth, on the 22d, Colonel M'Candless moved up the river, and by the night of the next day was within four miles of Rappahannock Station. Learning our troops had abandoned that point, he pushed through the enemy's country, and, after a hard and perilous march, rejoined the division, at Warrenton, on the night of the 26th.

for breakfast about eight o'clock. This day the boys, for the first time that season, met with fruit, and although it was green, and they were suffering much from diarrhœa they could not restrain their appetites from enjoying the luxury, and, contrary to all expectation, it proved a most effectual remedy, their systems being disposed to scurvy, and the acid of the fruit acting as an antidote. Passing by Hartwood, they halted at the Grove Churches for dinner. The march was long and wearisome, but the booming of the guns, that came rolling down the river, quickened their steps, and near sundown they reached Barnetts' Ford. It soon set in to rain, and the men suffered much with the wet and cold, being without blankets, as the Reserve had nothing but what they stood in, except muskets and cartridge-boxes. Early the next morning, the 23d, they were again in motion, and near noon reached Rappahannock Station, being the first of the Army of the Potomac to join General Pope. A sharp artillery duel was progressing, and our troops had commenced falling back. Leaving our friends, the light artillery pounding away at the enemy, who were not the least backward in responding, we moved on early in the afternoon, and bivouacked in the rain, after dark, near Warrenton Junction, on the Alexandria railroad. The next morning, the 24th, they moved off early, the day proving oppressively hot and the roads hilly. With but few and short halts for rest and water, they pressed on, and about noon saw the spires of Warrenton, near which they halted for a while, when, moving, passed through the town and about two miles down the Waterloo pike, where they bivouacked in a wood and lay in readiness to support General Sigel, who was flirting with the rebs, some distance beyond. The next day they received rations, which they had done without the day before, and during it and the succeeding day, were kept in readiness to move, the sound of artillery, as usual, being heard in different directions.

General Pope's army about this time, the 24th, occupied Warrenton Sulphur Springs and Waterloo Bridge, on the Rappahannock, and faced west from thence to Warrenton and Manassas Junction. Sigel's corps and Buford's cavalry were at Waterloo Bridge; Banks' corps, behind them; Reno's, near Sulphur Springs; M'Dowell's near Warrenton, and Porter between Kelly's Ford and Falmouth.

While Longstreet attracted Pope's attention in front, Stonewall Jackson, " whose force amounted to something more than 25,000, besides Stuart's cavalry, numbering 6,000 men," [A. H. Guernsey's (rebel) paper, in the New York *World*, July 5th, 1866,] crossed the Rappahannock above Waterloo Bridge, on the 25th, and, moving northeastwardly, passed through Thoroughfare Gap, and, turning to the southeast, before dark the next day, the 26th, struck the Alexandria railroad at Bristoe Station, thus placing himself between Pope and Washington. The same night he dispatched Generals Stuart and Trimble to Manassas Junction, which they surprised. Here they captured a large amount of stores and other property, which they destroyed.

Early the next morning, the 27th, they drove Colonel Scammon across Bull Run creek at Union Mills, and raided along the railroad, burning and capturing unopposed up to Fairfax and Burke's Stations. General Taylor,* with the First, Second, Third and Fourth New Jersey Infantry, of Franklin's corps, hastened by railroad to meet them, but was quickly routed, and himself mortally wounded, by Jackson, who had arrived with his own and A. P. Hill's division, comprising ten brigades and twelve batteries.

Jackson's success so far was complete, but his position was very critical. He was now between Pope and Washington, and, if General Pope could concentrate his superior force before Lee, with the balance of his army arrived, Jackson would be crushed and overwhelmed. General Pope ordered M'Dowell to march and reach Gainesville by

---
*George W. Taylor, New Jersey.

the night of the 27th, and Reno and Heintzleman to move by Greenwich and the railroad and join his right, and Porter to push for Gainesville as soon as Banks arrived at Warrenton Junction.

On the morning of the 27th, the Reserves marched through Warrenton, past New Baltimore, and towards dark bivouacked at Buckland Mills, where Broad Run crossed the Warrenton pike, and lay under arms all night. The insurgent Jackson the day before crossed the pike near here, moving from Thoroughfare Gap to Bristoe Station. In the afternoon we heard Hooker's guns to our right, he encountering Ewell, whom Jackson had left at Bristoe, four miles west of it, and drove him towards Manassas Junction, he leaving his dead, wounded and baggage on the field. The same night General Pope ordered Fitz John Porter to move at one A.M. on the 28th to Manassas Junction, and M'Dowell to press forward at the earliest dawn to the same point.

The Second Bull Run, or Plain of Manassas, August 28th, 29th and 30th, 1862.

At three o'clock on the morning of the 28th we were under arms and commenced our march, with batteries ready to be thrown into position, and a strong line of skirmishers on the left and front. After passing Gainesville, and while on the Warrenton and Alexandria turnpike, about ten o'clock, the head of the column was opened upon by a rebel battery, posted on the hills to our front and left. The column was immediately deployed and Cooper's rifles brought to bear upon them, under cover of which General Meade ordered Sickel to deploy his regiment and feel their support. The Third advanced rapidly up the ascent, and, after a brisk skirmish, drove the enemy from their position. During this affair a shell exploded in the midst of the Eighth, killing two men and wounding six others. Adjutant Swearenger lost a leg and had his horse killed under him. We then resumed our march, striking across the country toward

Manassas Junction, where the enemy was supposed to be, but Jackson, who was not easily caught napping, had evacuated that position early the previous night, marching toward Centreville and Sudley Spring.

General Pope reached the junction at noon. General Kearny, followed by Hooker and later by Reno, moved towards Centreville, the advance of the former, near dark, coming in contact with the rear of some of Jackson's forces, the main body of which had taken a position on the unfinished railroad between Groveton and Sudley Spring, there to await the arrival of Longstreet, who was expected through Thoroughfare Gap. King's division of M'Dowell's corps, moving on the Warrenton pike toward Centreville, where Pope still thought Jackson was, was attacked about 6:30 P.M. by Ewell's division of Jackson's force. Gibbon's Brigade and two regiments of Doubleday's Brigade were engaged, and a sanguinary combat ensued, lasting until after nine o'clock.

When we heard the thunder of this conflict, we were near Bethlehem Church, and turning to the left, took the Sudley Spring road toward the Warrenton pike. We had already marched many long and weary hours, but, tired and exhausted, we pressed on until the musket firing became distinct, the flashes seen and the mingled voices of the combatants heard. Darkness put an end to the fight. After marching eighteen hours and twenty-four miles, many without anything to eat, we stretched our wearied limbs upon the grass to sleep.

At the time this combat was progressing, Ricketts' division and the cavalry, in all about ten thousand strong, which had been sent early in the day, by General M'Dowell without orders, to block Thoroughfare Gap, encountered Longstreet's corps, which had reached the Gap at three o'clock that afternoon. As Longstreet had no time to lose, he paid little attention to his repulse, but hurled his battalions on his opponent. Ricketts did not make the stubborn resist-

THE THIRD RESERVE.   149

ance the circumstances required, but commenced retreating in the dark.

Ricketts moved to Bristoe, and King, with about nine thousand men, withdrew to Manassas Junction, both fearing being crushed between Longstreet and Jackson. Thus the Warrenton pike was left unobstructed and the juncture of these two forces unopposed. This was the critical hour of the battle.

That the reader may more fully understand the operations of the field, we will endeavor to give a general idea of the topography of the region, and of the position of the contending forces. The Bull Run mountains run nearly north and south, and are cloven by two gaps, Thoroughfare and Hopewell, about three miles apart. Jackson had marched up the western side of this range, crossed it at Thoroughfare Gap, and swooped down upon Pope's rear. Longstreet was following upon the same track. From the mountains, the country slopes eastward towards Bull Run river, the distance between the mountains and the river at the Stone Bridge being ten or twelve miles. The intervening plain, known as that of Manassas, is wooded and often rugged. The Warrenton turnpike crosses this plain from northeast to southwest; the Manassas Gap railroad crosses it from southeast to northwest; the railroad and turnpike intersect each other at Gainesville, a village about midway between the mountains and river. Let the letter $\bowtie$ serve to represent these features. The line running downwards from the left to right stands for the railroad; that running upwards from left to right, the turnpike. The upper left-hand corner is Thoroughfare Gap; the upper right-hand corner is the Stone Bridge; the lower right-hand corner is Manassas Junction, five miles distant from the bridge. At the intersection of the two lines is Gainesville. Just below the turnpike, a mile from the Stone Bridge, is the first Bull Run battle-field; just above it, two miles further west, is that of the second Bull Run, more properly called Groveton, from a hamlet there situated. In fact, both battle-fields cross the turnpike, but the first was mainly below, the second mainly above. The distances, as closely as can be measured upon the large government map, are: Thoroughfare Gap to Gainesville, five miles; Gainesville to Groveton, four miles; Groveton to Stone Bridge, three miles; Manassas to Gainesville, seven miles.

On the morning of the 29th, Jackson, with 25,000 men, was drawn up, his right at Groveton, his line extending northward about two miles. Directly in his front was half of Pope's force, under Reynolds, Sigel, Heintzleman and Reno, 25,000 strong. The other half, of nearly equal strength, under M'Dowell and Porter, lay along the Manassas railroad from the Junction part way to Gainesville. General Pope, who was at Centreville, felt he had Jackson sure within his grasp, surrounded by 50,000 men, and that he could crush him before Longstreet's arrival. Pope, however, was greatly deceived, as Longstreet, in a letter dated Coffinville, Mississippi, September 23d, 1866, [papers, etc., furnished by the Committee on Military Affairs of the Senate, p. 471,] states: "My command arrived within supporting distance of Jackson's command about nine A.M., 29th August, near Groveton."

General Pope, at 10:30 that morning, not knowing the positions of either Jackson or Longstreet, sent the following order, No. 26.

"HEADQUARTERS ARMY OF VIRGINIA,
"CENTREVILLE, August 29th, 1862.

"*Generals M'Dowell and Porter:* You will please move forward with your joint commands towards Gainesville. I sent General Porter written orders to that effect an hour and a half ago. Heintzleman, Sigel and Reno are moving on the Warrenton turnpike, and must now be not far from Gainesville. I desire that, as soon as communication is established between this force and your own, the whole command shall halt. It may be necessary to fall back behind

Bull Run, at Centreville, to-night. I presume it will be so, on account of our supplies. I have sent no orders of any description to Ricketts, and none to interfere in any way with the movements of M'Dowell's troops, except what I sent by his aid-de-camp last night, which were to hold his position on the Warrenton pike until the troops from here should fall upon the enemy's flank and rear. I do not even know Ricketts' position, as I have not been able to find out where M'Dowell was until a late hour this morning. General M'Dowell will take immediate steps to communicate with General Ricketts, and instruct him to rejoin the other divisions of his corps as soon as practicable. If any considerable advantages are to be gained by departing from this order, it will not be strictly carried out. One thing must be held in view, that the troops must occupy a position from which they can reach Bull Run to-night, or by morning. The indications are that the whole force of the enemy is moving in this direction at a pace that will bring them here by to-morrow night or next day. My own headquarters will be for the present with Heintzleman's corps, or at this place.

"JOHN POPE,
"Major-General Commanding."

This order, and a subsequent one, dated 4:30 P.M., directing Porter to march on Jackson's right flank, were based upon the erroneous supposition that Longstreet was fully twenty-four hours distant; that Jackson's corps was the only body to be encountered; that the Union force was consequently nearly double that of the Confederates; whereas, the juncture of the enemy had been completed some hours before, "giving them a preponderance of three to two." [A. H. Guernsey's (rebel) paper, *New York World*, July 3d, 1866.] M'Dowell, by virtue of his rank as senior general, took command of the whole force, and in some measure annulled the joint order, by separating the forces. Both he and Porter deviated from the order. M'Dowell, instead of moving west towards Gainesville, withdrew King's division from Porter, and, uniting Ricketts' division with it, marched towards Groveton. The propriety of his doing so does not appear to have been questioned. Porter, being left by M'Dowell with Longstreet in his immediate front, remained in his position, holding the superior force of the enemy in check, and, by inviting attack or by threatening it, kept him from going against General Pope's scattered army. By this action he was rendering the most efficient aid in his power to the Union army. He has been blamed for not attacking Longstreet. If M'Dowell with the joint commands had attacked Longstreet, a general battle would have at once been brought on, and, with Pope's army not in hand, and with the enemy in position to place themselves between the two wings of it, the result, undoubtedly, would have been most disastrous.

Early on the morning of the 29th, the Reserves were formed and moved forward to meet the enemy. They were now separated from M'Dowell and the rest of his command, and were acting under the orders of Sigel. We advanced some distance, and passed through a woods into an open plain, where we were drawn up on the left of a mass of troops and pushed into a woods beyond. Soon we were ordered back, and then commenced a series of movements and evolutions and feints upon the enemy that took us several times over the same ground, often under fire of rebel batteries and with a hot sun pouring down upon us. The day was extraordinarily hard upon the men, who were worn out and weak, they being now completely out of rations, and having no opportunity to fill their canteens. The Third held the extreme right of the division, which was on the left of Schenck's. At one time, Schenck having withdrawn, the enemy pushed in troops on our right and attempted to cut us off, but the movement was detected in time to fall back to a plateau south of the pike.

Sigel, who was nearest the enemy, opened the day by an early attack, and was fully engaged by seven o'clock, gaining ground by hard fighting until half-past ten, when, the enemy receiving large re-enforcements, he was forced to be contented with holding his own. The enemy, under Jackson, were now in position, with their left resting on Sudley Springs, and right a little south of Warrenton pike. His front was covered by an embankment of an abandoned railroad, and his troops sheltered by a dense woods close up to it. Heintzleman's corps occupied the right of our line, resting on Catharpen creek, near its junction with Bull Run; Sigel's, the center; and the Reserves, under Reynold's, the extreme left, south of Warrenton pike. In fact, the two armies confronted each other with the railroad embankment between them. Up to four o'clock, a succession of heavy skirmishes from point to point along the front took place. About half-past four, M'Dowell approached with the balance of his corps. General Pope, who was still in ignorance of the presence of Longstreet in front of Fitz John Porter, had sent, about half-past four P.M., an order to Porter to march upon and attack Jackson's left flank, and, about six o'clock, presuming Porter was upon or near the point designated, directed Heintzleman and Reno to attack the enemy's left front. The assault was made with great gallantry. Kearny, having changed front on the left, led his division to the charge, sweeping back and rolling up the first line on to their center and right. The conflict at this point was maintained with great spirit, and Grover's Brigade broke through two of the enemy's lines, and penetrated to the third before it was checked.* A little before sunset, General M'Dowell, under the impression the enemy were in full retreat down the Warrenton pike, sent King's (now Hatch's) division of his corps in pursuit. On the double-quick, Hatch, at the head of the column, followed by his own, Doubleday's and Patrick's brigades, crossed an arm of the Bull Run close to Groveton, when suddenly his skirmishers encountered those

---

*General Pope's official report. Grover attacked at three o'clock, and was not supported. Pope's report of hour is wrong.

of the enemy. A well-sustained and rapidly-increasing musketry fire from an unyielding line, together with a vigorous cannonade, soon convinced General Hatch that the enemy was not in retreat, but, strongly posted, determinedly resisted his advance. In response to the furious attacks, the Confederates brought up heavy re-enforcements, and finally, with a charge, forced Hatch's division to retire, with a large number of killed and wounded and the loss of one gun. (Captain J. A. Judson, an Assistant Adjutant-General in King's division.) The enemy engaged proved to be Hood's* division, whom Longstreet had ordered to make a forced reconnaissance.

While these movements were being made, General Reynolds was ordered to threaten their right and rear. Pushing on over an open field, a rebel battery was found posted on an elevation about a half-mile to the left of the pike, which opened fire upon them. Reaching the base of the elevation, within a few hundred yards of the battery, it was determined to try it. The Second, under M'Candless, with the First in support, was sent into a wood to the right and front to draw its fire. Generals Seymour and Jackson, at the head of most of their regiments, gallantly led them to the charge up the hill; but they had not only the fire of the battery to encounter, but a heavy supporting force of infantry, and, notwithstanding their steadiness, they were forced to fall back, forming and lying down within three hundred yards of the guns. Unfortunately, in this assault, the guns of Ramson's battery were smooth-bores, and could offer no cover by their fire to the storming party.

After the battle ceased, the Reserve were withdrawn to the position they occupied the night before, and, hungry and wearied, they lay down on their arms to sleep. But, unfortunately for us, some boys belonging to the "Coffee Brigade" kindled small fires to boil their much-coveted

---

*General John B. Hood, whom Jefferson Davis sent to troll Sherman out of Georgia.

beverage, by which the enemy discovered our bivouac, and opened at long range, with solid shot, by which several were killed and wounded. The boys, however, were too tired to pay much attention to this. Regiments from each brigade that night were sent on picket, which, on the battle-field, means to lie down in line of battle within a short distance of the enemy, and be prepared for an attack at any moment.

The next morning, the 30th, at three o'clock, we were again under arms, ready for the coming struggle. The men were now absolutely suffering for food, they having been entirely out of rations for two days.* They were worn down by constant marching, fighting and loss of sleep, and were unfit for the field. Many were so utterly exhausted that it was necessary to send them to the rear, they being unable to continue with us. The boys, who had been without food for two days and had hardly murmured before, now complained to their colonel. Sickel sat upon his horse and listened to their story, which he knew was too true. He told them in a kind voice he could get them no rations, that he had nothing but cartridges to give them. When they looked on his pale face, and saw he was hardly able to keep the saddle, they ceased to complain. The opening gun of the day sounded, the shot whistled over our heads, loud cheers arose from the boys, and the Reserves were satisfied with their cartridges.

Our battle-ground this day was substantially that of yesterday, but extending further to the left. Our army, facing westward, was posted in a form of an inverted V with unequal arms, the opening towards us. The short arm, just south of the Warrenton Pike, was occupied by the Pennsylvania Reserves, who held the extreme left. The long

---

*General Pope, in his report, says: "On the morning of the 30th, as may be supposed, our troops, who had been so continually marching and fighting for so many days, were in a state of great exhaustion. They had had little to eat for two days previous, and the artillery and cavalry horses had been in harness and saddled continually for ten days, and had had no forage for two days previous. It may easily be imagined how little these troops, after such severe labor, and after undergoing such hardship and privation, were in condition for active and efficient service."

arm, north of the pike, stretching off towards Sudley Springs, was held, commencing on the Reserves' right, by Porter, Sigel, Reno and Heintzleman, with Ricketts' and Kings' divisions, under M'Dowell, in reserve. Elevated ground immediately in front and to the left of the Reserves, was covered with dense timber, interspersed with patches of pine and scrub oak. To the right of the Reserves, and in Porter's front, was a narrow but dense forest. Between the forests, one-half mile apart, and skirting the Warrenton pike on Porter's front, was cleared ground, a natural glacis, rising rapidly to an elevated ridge held by the enemy and crowned by numerous artillery. This artillery commanded the pike and the cleared ground, and concentrated a flank and direct fire upon any attacking column. The enemy's skirmishers held the open ground and the forests. His forces and movements were concealed from us, whilst the least of ours, as far back as Centreville, were open to his view. Unsuccessful efforts had been made the day before to gain possession of these forests.

Soon after daybreak, the Reserves, under General Reynolds, took up their position on the extreme left of the line, near the Henry house, they being intended as the pivot in the attack which Porter's corps was to make on the enemy's right, then supposed to be on the pike and in retreat. The Bucktails and Second, supported by the Third,* were deployed as skirmishers, and advanced beyond Young's creek over a rising piece of ground, flanked on either side by heavy woods. Up this they slowly crept, among the dead of the preceding day, and, after feeling for the enemy for some time, discovered them occupying a store and some out-buildings, from which they were soon driven. Taking

---

* General Reynolds, in his official report of the operations of his division that day, states: "The advanced skirmishers were the First Rifles, (Bucktails,) Colonel M'Neil, and the First Infantry, Colonel Roberts, supported by the Seventh Infantry, Lieutenant-Colonel Henderson." This, however, is a mistake. The author was present with his regiment, the Second, Colonel M'Candless, and conversed with both Colonels M'Neil and Sickel, and could not be mistaken in regard to it.

up a position on the extreme edge of the woods, near Groveton, a sharp fire was opened by both sides across a broad clearing, beyond which the enemy were posted in a woods with their sharp-shooters in the trees, from which they were dropped in a lively style by volleys from squads of our men, who marked every tree from which smoke issued.

As it was desirable to ascertain the strength of the enemy in our front, we were ordered to advance, and crossing the clearing, we drove the enemy before us and about four hundred yards into the woods, where we halted. A masked battery was discovered to our right and front, and a large force of infantry on our left and rear, masked by cavalry, about twelve hundred yards distant. Our regiments were about-faced, marched to the edge of the woods, their lines dressed, muskets brought to a shoulder, and then moved across the clearing with deliberation, and when they reached the position they charged from, were fronted and lain down. This was the discovery of the thunderbolt that was about to be hurled upon us, for it was the advance of a heavy mass that had turned our left flank. In retiring, a number of muskets were destroyed, and an attempt made to bring off a brass howitzer that M'Dowell had abandoned the day before, but its spokes were cut and a wheel broke down. Lying down, all was quiet for about an hour, the enemy remaining stationary, to concentrate their forces. In the meantime, Meade's Brigade came up, and the Third rejoined them.

General Pope's plan of battle was to attack the enemy's left, along the Haymarket road, and, with that view, he strengthened our right. Lee's plan was to turn our left, and he had concentrated the mass of his troops towards that point. Pope's plans were based on the erroneous impression that the enemy had been some hours retreating. General M'Dowell, who was the governing spirit upon the field, who had made a reconnaissance on our extreme right, had mistaken the contraction of Lee's lines for a retreat. One paroled prisoner of our own, taken the evening before, came into our lines during the morning and reported the enemy retreating during the night in the direction of Gainesville,* which seemed to confirm M'Dowell's report. That any general should parole prisoners upon a battle-field, and permit them to go direct into an enemy's lines, and carry information of his retreat, if he really was retreating, seems as improbable as it does to suppose any one could be deceived by such information.

So much was General Pope deceived, as to the attitude of the opposing forces, that at noon he issued the following special order:

"The following forces will be immediately thrown forward in pursuit of the enemy, and press him vigorously during the whole day. Major-General M'Dowell is assigned to the command of the pursuit; Major-General Porter's corps will push forward on the Warrenton turnpike, followed by the divisions of Brigadier-Generals King and Reynolds.

"The division of Brigadier-General Ricketts will pursue the Haymarket road, followed by the corps of Major-General Heintzelman." * * *

In an order issued at a later hour, General Pope says: "Major-General M'Dowell, being charged with the advanced forces ordered to pursue the enemy." † * * *

No such movement was ever attempted.

About two o'clock, by order, Porter, supported by King, attacked the enemy, who were still supposed by Pope to be retreating along the pike; and, at the same time, Heintzleman and Reno, supported by Ricketts, were ordered to assail them to his right. The enemy, from his elevated, crescent-shaped position, swept with artillery the ground over which our troops advanced. He opposed them with a heavy musketry fire from behind the railroad embankments, where he

---

* General Pope's official report.
† "Papers, etc., furnished by the Committee on **Military Affairs of the Senate**," p. 357.

was driven, and stood almost unharmed. Butterfield, Sykes and Hatch (with Heintzleman, Ricketts and Reno on the right, not engaged), emerging from the sheltering timber, rapidly advanced, gallantly attacked and desperately contended for victory. The resistance could not be overcome. Let us read Stonewall Jackson's official report of this combat:

"In a few moments our entire line was engaged in a fierce and sanguinary struggle with the enemy. As one line was repulsed another took its place and pressed forward, as if determined, by force of numbers and fury of assault, to drive us from our position. So impetuous and well sustained were these onsets, as to induce me to send to the commanding general for re-enforcements, but the timely and gallant advance of General Longstreet, on the right, relieved my troops from the pressure of overwhelming numbers, and gave to those brave men the chances of a more equal conflict." * * *

Such was was the fury of the Union assault that Jackson supposed he was far outnumbered, whereas, the combatants were nearly equal, with the advantage of the strong position in favor of the enemy.

It was soon after this attack commenced that the Reserve skirmishers fell back over the clearing, and, when General Reynolds saw it, he inquired of Colonel M'Candless why he had withdrawn. Upon being informed, he replied that it was impossible. Putting spurs to his horse, he dashed through our skirmishers to the left, and into the open ground. There he found the enemy's line of skirmishers nearly at right angles to our line, covering our left flank, with cavalry behind, perfectly stationary, masking a column of infantry formed for attack on our left flank, when our line should be sufficiently advanced. The skirmishers fired upon him, but his hour had not yet come, and he run the gauntlet unscarred, but losing an orderly who followed him. Reynolds reported the fact to General M'Dowell, our corps commander, "who came upon the ground, and directed me to form my division to resist this attack, the dispositions for which were rapidly completed. Other troops were to be sent to my support, when the commanding general (M'Dowell) observing the attack of Porter to have been repulsed, ordered me with my division across the field to the rear of Porter, to form a line, behind which the troops might be rallied." [General Reynolds' official report.] Our line fell back over the same ground we advanced on in the morning, and joined the division, which was drawn up on the Bald Hill, in rear of a heavy wood. Our rifles, to the right of us, were soon engaged with a battery, whose range they soon got, and forced it to withdraw.

The Reserves were then ordered to the right and rear of Porter, but before the rear of our column had left the position, the threatened attack by the enemy burst into a furious assault upon our left and along the entire line. The rear brigade, the Third, under Colonel Anderson,* with three batteries, were obliged to form on the ground on which they found themselves to oppose it. Tower's and M'Lean's brigades of Ricketts' division formed with them, but the assault was too severe for them to withstand long, and, after heavy loss, little by little they were forced to yield. Four of Kerns' guns were taken, but not until he was killed and twenty-four of his men lay around him, and twenty-seven horses had been shot down.† Cooper lost his caissons. The brigade sustained itself most gallantly, and, though severely pushed on both front and flank, maintained its position until overwhelmed by numbers, when it fell back, taking up new positions whenever the advantages of ground permitted.

---

* General Jackson ruptured a blood vessel in battle the day before, and the command of the brigade devolved on Colonel Harding, of the Twelfth, who, being severely wounded in the early part of the fight, turned the command over to Colonel Anderson, of the Ninth.

† Prof Bates' History Pennsylvania Volunteers, Vol. I, p. 969.

Reynolds, with Meade's and Seymour's brigades and Ransom's battery, hurried across the field to the right, under a heavy fire of round and shell. Passing by the Robinson house and crossing a road, our course was diverted by the difficult nature of the ground, and the retreating masses of the broken columns among the troops of Heintzleman's corps, already formed, by which much time was lost and confusion created, which allowed the enemy to sweep up with his right, so far as almost to cut us off from the pike There was nothing left but the Third Brigade and the three batteries of Reserve artillery and scattered troops of other commands to resist the advance of the enemy upon our left. Arriving on the brow of a hill, our brigades and battery took up a position near a road, from which we overlooked a large portion of the field, and Porter's troops commenced forming behind us, but on account of the position at Bald Hill being forced, we were ordered to the extreme left, where we took a position on a hill to the right of the Henry house, not far from our first position in the morning. Here we formed in column of brigade, with Ransom's battery in front, which threw its shells at long range upon the heavy masses of the enemy, who were advancing. There we remained under a shower of shells, with the boys being knocked over pretty rapidly, but all in good heart.

At last, we saw division after division of our army give way, and soon all upon the field appeared in utter confusion, except the dense columns of the enemy that were advancing with wild shouts of victory, intent upon seizing the Warrenton pike, to cut off the retreat over Bull Run. The quick eye of Reynolds had perceived this, and he brought the Reserves here to prevent it, it being necessary to maintain the position at any sacrifice. On rushed the exulting insurgents with loud yells, determined to go right over every obstacle to the pike. Silently stood the Reserves at a rest, watching their approach. The gallant Reynolds dashed to the front, and seizing the flag of the Second, waved it aloft, shouting, "Follow me, Reserves." A prolonged yell burst from the brigades as they dashed upon the foe. The columns met on the brow of a declivity, and, for a few moments, the most fearful carnage ensued. The dead and wounded were trampled under foot. The rear ranks pressed on till, faltering and trembling, the fierce foe were crushed down and hurled back upon the denser masses that supported them. Reynolds, with the standard waving above his head, and Meade and Seymour in the thickest of the fight, urging the men on, presented a scene of heroic grandeur.

On pressed the Reserves, wild with their cry of battle, driving the enemy into the woods, on and over their support that lay five or six line deep, who sprung to their feet and met them with a sheet of flame, and dropped to give range to those behind. On both flanks swarmed the enemy, and the flaming missiles from several batteries were bursting in their midst. For an instant they were in the fire of hell, completely enveloped in smoke and flame. The pressure was too much, and they were literally whirled from the ground. But they had not yielded the pike yet, nor did they intend to. Reynolds, Meade and Seymour were in their midst, and they could not leave them. Rallying again on their old position, with Ransom's guns dealing death, the foe came thundering upon them, but the steady and low fire of the line hurled them back until Buchanan, with a division of regulars, came to their succor. Hordes of the enemy were now pouring upon this one point, determined to carry it at any sacrifice; but the Reserves held them at bay until after dark, when they were forced back nearly a mile, but still covering the pike. Porter's forces now came to their relief, and, with their ammunition entirely spent, muskets thoroughly heated, and the men almost exhausted, they were withdrawn to the rear. Nearly the whole army had now been withdrawn from the field,* and with the Third Brigade, in the early part of the night, they marched towards Centreville, and bivouacked with Sykes upon the east bank of Cub Run.

General Reynolds, in his official report, gives the loss of our division as six hundred and fifty-three.† The loss of the contending armies in this battle was never stated by their commanders.‡

Among those killed, in the Third, was Captain H. Clay Beatty, one of the most promising young officers in the division. A lawyer by profession, a gentleman by nature, a soldier through principle, high-minded, honorable and brave, he won the respect and esteem of his fellow officers, and the love of his men. The Reserves, and the Union, never lost a braver and kinder heart than his.

Of our generals, Pope, in his report, said:

"Brigadier General John F. Reynolds, commanding the Pennsylvania Reserves, merits the highest commendation at my hands. Prompt, active, and energetic, he commanded his division with distinguished ability throughout the operations, and performed his duty in all situations with zeal and fidelity. Generals Seymour and Meade, of that division, in

---

* Pope, in his official report, says:

"About eight o'clock at night, therefore, I sent written instructions to the commanders of corps to withdraw leisurely towards Centreville, and stated to them what route each should pursue and where they should take post. General Reno was instructed with his whole corps to cover the movements of the army towards Centreville. The withdrawal was made slowly, quietly, and in good order, no pursuit whatever having been attempted by the enemy. A division of infantry, with its batteries, was posted to cover the crossing of Cub Run."

† For the loss in the Third, see Appendix A.

‡ General Lee, officially, claims to have captured, during his campaign against Pope, from Cedar Mountain to Chantilly, more than 7,000 prisoners, besides 2,000 of our wounded left in his hands, with 30 pieces of artillery, and 20,000 small arms. Our loss of railroad cars, munitions, and camp equipage, must have been immense. The rebel medical director makes their losses, in *two days* of the fighting on Manassas Plains, 1,090 killed, 6,154 wounded—total, 7,244. Longstreet reports his losses, from the 23d to *the 30th* of August, inclusive, at 4,725. A. P. Hill reports the losses in his division, from the 24th to the 31st, at 1,548. Probably the entire rebel loss in the campaign did not fall short of 15,000 men. We must have lost heavily in stragglers, who never rejoined their regiments, and our total loss probably reached 20,000.

like manner performed their duties with ability and gallantry, and in all fidelity to the Government and to the army."

During the night, and part of the morning of the 31st, Sunday, it rained very hard. Soon after daybreak, we marched to Centreville. Everything was in great confusion. The roads, deep with mud, were crowded with soldiers, orderlies, and wagons. Squads of prisoners, and a long train of ambulances, were moving towards Washington. Omnibusses, carriages, and other vehicles, impressed by the Government, covered the fields in every direction. Long lines of horses, tied to ropes, were coming out from Washington. Hundreds of Government officials and citizens arrived, loaded with tobacco, envelopes, postage stamps, etc., which they generously distributed.

Colonel Sickel, who was entirely unfit for the field, was now forced to give up. Sick, unable to eat, suffering from the effect of a *coup de so-leil* a few days before, forced to yield the command of his regiment on the battle-field to Lieutenant Colonel Clark, he was yet unwilling to leave his comrades, and went with them through all the fighting, cheering and encouraging them on the best he could. It was only when he saw them safe at Centreville, with the prospect of rations, that he was willing to part from them.

Towards noon, the division marched to the rear about two miles, and halted. Coffee and crackers were issued, and soon our fires were burning. This was a perfect godsend to us, every mouthful of coffee we drank seeming like so much life passing into us. We remained here a couple of hours, during which time we devoured the best part of our three days' rations, when we marched back to Centreville, where, about dark, we had salt-beef issued to us. Soon after, with light hearts and heavy stomachs, our division marched out to relieve General Reno, who covered the crossings of Cub Run, our artillery shelling the woods as we advanced. We were posted on a range of high, wooded hills, resting on our arms all night, the enemy being about as well used up as we were, and contenting themselves with a little skirmishing while we were moving into position. It rained hard all night, and it was a long and wearied watch. About daybreak an officer was awoke by something pulling at his boots, and looking around, he beheld the most gladdening sight the eyes of a soldier could rest upon: A few inches from the ground, on one side was a cup of coffee, and on the other a bunch of crackers, while between, radiant with joy, was the shining face of a young contraband, looking lovelier than the cherubs of Michael Angelo in their flight to heaven with expanded wings.

Soon we were relieved, and, as we marched back, we passed long lines of ambulances going to the field after the wounded, and army wagons conveying rations to them, a flag of truce being arranged for that purpose. That day, September 1st, the regiments were mustered for pay.

General Lee, though not disposed to try the experiment of Malvern Hill again, was not idle, and the morning after the battle dispatched Jackson's and Ewell's divisions to turn and assail our right, and cut off our communication with Washington. Piatt's and Griffin's brigades of Porter's corps, that had marched from the battle-field on the morning of the last day of our desperate struggle; Franklin's corps, that had been near Centreville, unknown to Pope, the whole of the same sad day, and Sumner's corps, that arrived there afterwards, swelled our army to 60,000 men. On the 1st of September, it lay on the pike from Centreville to Fairfax Court House. Pope suspected Lee's movements, and had ordered Sumner and Hooker to dispose of their forces to resist it.

Chantilly, September 1st, 1862.

About noon, we moved off on the fields along the pike, which was filled with wagons moving both ways. Just before sunset, when opposite Chantilly, Jackson, with a superior force of infantry, but no artillery, commenced an attack on two divisions of Reno's troops. The Reserves were immediately put into position to support them. The battle soon became furious, and continued until after dark. In the midst of it a thunder storm occurred, so furious that the sound of battle was unnoticed at Centreville, but three miles off. Generals Isaac J. Stephens and Philip Kearny, both of New Jersey, were killed, and the command devolved upon General Birney, who finished the contest by a bayonet charge. Birney held the field through the night, burying our dead and removing the wounded. Our loss did not exceed a total of 500 men. This battle was called, by the insurgents, Ox Hill. Jackson's flank movement proved a failure, and our retreat was no further annoyed by the enemy.

The next morning, beeves were shot and issued to the men. Soon afterwards we moved off down the pike, through Fairfax Court House to Anandale, where we turned to the left, and, after an hour's halt, marched on past Ball's Cross Roads to the neigborhood of Arlington Heights. On the road we passed wagons, artillery and fresh troops, moving the other way. The new regiments were easily distinguished by their white faces, new clothes and full knapsacks. We happened to halt a few moments alongside of one of these, when an animated discussion arose among our boys as to where they came from, and who they were. Some contended they were just off of Chestnut street, or out of band-boxes, while others suggested they were runaway school-girls. This latter idea seemed to prevail, and the Miss Nellies, Katies and Sallies, were tempted with crackers and cartridges, in exchange for locks of their hair. One thoughtless youth, who estrayed into our ranks, was surrounded by the boys, but managed to escape, when, with reddened cheeks and flashing eyes, he came to a charge, and swore he would bayonet the first Reserve who attempted to kiss him. Before nine o'clock that night all the army was inside the intrenchments, except three corps on the Vienna and Chain Bridge roads, which arrived the next day.

The next morning, the 3d, we moved about three miles, near the Arlington House, the late residence of General Robert E. Lee, now a National Cemetery, where slumber thousands of our Union dead, where we lay in the woods until the afternoon of the next day, when we marched to Upton Hill. The Reserves were now in a sad plight. The majority of the boys were nearly shoeless, some had lost their caps, and very many had no blouses. What clothes they had were ragged and torn, and there was hardly a blanket among them. New clothing, however, was soon issued, and when the boys got a chance to wash their hands and faces they thought they looked very fine. This operation they had no opportunity to perform for about eight days.

Here terminated our short but arduous campaign in the "Army of Virginia," under General John Pope. The strength of Pope's army at the battle of Bull Run, on paper, was 65,600 men. Of these, Piatt and Griffin's brigades, 5,000 strong, were at Centreville on the 30th; (Pope) Banks', 5,000 strong, were at Bristol on the 29th and 30th, guarding supplies. The strength of Lee's army at the battle was 62,900, all of whom were in action.* Lee's army outnumbered Pope's 7,300.† Doctor A. H. Guernsey's paper (which "is considered quite accurate and just" by the Confederate generals,) put the rebel force in the battle at 71,000 men. The failure of Pope is to be attributed to a number of causes:

That Ricketts, considering the favorable ground east of Thoroughfare Gap, did not offer the stubborn resistance he was capable of, to the march of Longstreet, is evident. Ricketts' march on Bristoe, to a very slight extent,

---

* Proceedings and Report of Board of Army Officers, April 12th, 1878, in the case of Fitz John Porter, part I, page 508.

† *Ibid*, page 462.

justified King's withdrawal from the Warrenton pike. These two movements left Longstreet's march to unite with Jackson unobstructed.

The mistake in supposing, on the morning of the 30th, that Lee's army was in full retreat down the Warrenton pike, when, in fact, the left wing of it was in an almost impregnable fortress—the Independent railroad embankment and cut—and the right wing was being heavily re-enforced, to turn on our left flank.

That the plan of battle originally settled upon—of falling back and concentrating our army behind Bull Run creek, within easier reach of re-enforcements and supplies—was changed to an offensive one.

The exhausted state of our troops, for want of rations.

Of the 91,000 veteran troops of the Army of the Potomac who left Harrison's Landing, but 20,500 re-enforced Pope. Franklin and Sumner, with 19,000 more, marched from Alexandria, and arrived at Centreville after the battle was lost. Alexandria was swarming with troops under General M'Clellan, and was full of supplies. Pope's army was absolutely without food during one, two and three days. There was no enemy between Alexandria and Pope after the night of the 28th. General Pope received a letter on the morning of the 30th, from General M'Clellan, informing him that "rations and forage were at Alexandria, waiting a cavalry escort." Forage and rations, and citizens in private carriages, came to us after our defeat without a "cavalry escort," when there was really more danger than before the battle.

Subsequently charges were preferred by General Pope against Major-General Porter, upon which he was tried and convicted by a court-martial ordered by the President. He was sentenced "to be cashiered, and to be forever disqualified from holding any office of trust or profit under the government of the United States." Severe as this sentence was—worse than death to Fitz John Porter—it appears to have been justified by the weight of evidence. After-discovered evidence convinced General Porter, who had always felt himself wronged by the verdict, that he could establish the correctness of the defence he gave on his trial. Upon his appeal, President Hayes, April 9th, 1878, ordered a Board of Officers to examine the case. The two principal points that seemed to justify the verdict were: The alleged failure to obey the order requiring him to move his command at one A.M. on August 28th; the failure to attack on the 29th. As to the first, the intense darkness of the night and the bad roads, that were blocked by wagon trains, induced him, by the advice of Generals Morell, Sykes and Butterfield, to delay the movement until three o'clock. As to the second, the responsibility for not doing so up to noon, rested with General M'Dowell, as senior officer, vested with the command. As to the advisability of attacking, the only chance of success was with the combined forces early in the day. General Pope based his orders upon the supposition that Longstreet was fully twenty-four hours distant; that Jackson's corps was the only body to be encountered; and that the Union force, consequently, was nearly double that of the insurgents, whereas, what Porter strongly suspected then—in fact knew—that Longstreet was in his immediate front with a superior force, we now have undoubted evidence was the fact. That attacks must sometimes be made under such circumstances as Porter was in is undoubtedly true, for it is sometimes necessary for a portion of an army to sacrifice itself to save the rest of the army. General Porter, by not attacking, by the mere position of his troops, and by his movements that day, rendered a much more important service to the rest of the army, by keeping at least double his numbers in front of him, and paralyzing them so far as any action against our right was concerned, and by delaying the general battle until the next day, when Pope had his army for the first time really in hand. The report of the Board of Officers fully justify Porter's conduct, and says, "that in our opinion, justice requires at his hands (the President's) such action as may be necessary to annul and set aside the findings and sentence of the court-martial."

When a great wrong has been done and the error of it ascertained, all feelings of honor demand a frank acknowledgment of it and restitution. Are we not too great a nation, too magnanimous a people, to suffer the continuation of a wrong? Porter, by this nation, and by history, will have justice done him.

The Porter inquiry case gave our friends, the late Confederates, an opportunity to place on record the gallant deeds of their arms upon that field, and we read them, as Americans, with pride.

But the blood of Bull Run was not shed in vain. The rights of the South, under the Constitution, had strong advocates in the North. "The Union as it was, and the Constitution as it is," was a political watch-word. The restoration of the Union was the prevailing wish, and to accomplish it the large majority in the North would have freely forgiven the past and guaranteed the South in their property in slavery. The Nation did not yet recognize the great issue of the war—slavery. The sacrifice of more blood and treasures was needed to clear our vision and purify our heart. The South was not yet reduced to the helpless condition of submission to the will of God.

CHAPTER XI.

POPE SUPERSEDED BY M'CLELLAN — CROSS THE POTOMAC — THE MARCH THROUGH MARYLAND — FREDERICK, EARLY IN THE MORNING — THE BOUQUET OF FLOWERS — WANTED HIS TOOTH PULLED — BATTLE OF SOUTH MOUNTAIN — PLEASANTON ATTACKS — BURNSIDE COMES UP — LONGSTREET SUPERSEDES HILL — FALL OF RENO — HOOKER FLANKS — LAUGHABLE SCENE — RESERVES SCALE THE MOUNTAINS — FREE FIGHT — VICTORY — MARCH — BOONSBORO — PRISONERS.

GENERAL POPE, having resigned his command, was succeeded by General M'Clellan, on the 2d of September. Pope's original army had been greatly demoralized, but that of M'Clellan was in good heart, and the portion of it that had been in the late campaign only needed a little rest. On the 3d, D. H. Hill, with the van of the insurgent army, crossed the Potomac near Edwards' Ferry, into Maryland; and Lee, soon following with the balance of his army, entered Frederick on the 8th. M'Clellan, early apprised of this movement, put his army in motion to meet him.

About this time the Reserves were transferred from M'Dowell's to the First Corps, commanded by General Hooker. About two o'clock on the morning of the 7th, we fell in, and moved off through the woods to the pike, crossing the Potomac on Long Bridge, and marching through the thronged streets of the Capital with our drums beating. Proceeding out the Leesboro road, we lay down to rest. That afternoon we moved on to Leesboro, about seven miles distant, where we lay in a scrub-oak thicket until the afternoon of the 9th, when we marched through Mechanicsville and bivouacked about sunset near Brookville. About noon the next day, we moved to the head-waters of the Patuxent and bivouacked, and the succeeding day to near Poplar Springs. The insurgent cavalry had left this place the night before. In our march through Maryland, we found some loyal inhabitants, but the majority were passively so only. The insurgent soldiery, in the main, conducted themselves very well, but cattle, horses, and stores of all kinds, that would contribute to the subsistence or efficiency of this army, were seized by wholesale, and crossed over the Potomac. The articles taken were paid for in quartermaster's orders; but who wished to invest in such paper? At the urgent request of Governor Curtin, General Reynolds was detached from the Reserves on the 12th, and sent to Pennsylvania to organize the 75,000 "emergency men" the Governor had called out for the defence of the State. General Meade, thereupon, succeeded to the command of the division. In the absence of Colonel Sickel, the senior officer of the brigade, the command of the same devolved upon Colonel Magilton. On the same day, our troops had a brief skirmish at Monocacy Bridge, and drove the rear guard of the enemy out of Frederick. While in possession of the city, the "Liberators" ordered all the stores to be opened, which they soon emptied of their contents, paying for the same in their worthless trash. They also opened recruiting offices, but the citizens, who had shown no gluttonous appetite to fight for the Union, listened unmoved to the pealing anthems of "My Maryland" and other southern hymns.

General M'Clellan here had the good fortune, on the 13th, to obtain a copy of Lee's general order, dated September 9th, developing his prospective movements. This directed the seizing of Harpers Ferry, and the re-crossing of the Potomac by a large portion of the army, and its return to Maryland. Thus possessed of his adversary's designs, unknown to him, and when it was too late to change them, he was enabled to move with greater promptness and certainty. Our army, which had been slowly moving through Maryland in five columns, covering Washington and Baltimore, was now concentrated near Frederick.

South Mountain, September 14th, 1862.

At three o'clock on Sunday morning, our drums rattled the reveille on the banks of the Monocacy, and, after coffee and crackers, we filed off on the National road, and marched through Frederick. The inhabitants were hardly awake, and those we saw were universally dressed in neat, snowy white. There were many bright eyes peeping through the window-slats, and handkerchiefs mysteriously waving. A good sprinkling of miniature flags were displayed, and, altogether, Frederick presented a novel and interesting sight early in the morning. Moving on, we wound our way up the Catoctin Mountain, on the summit of which an artillery fight had taken place the day before, in which one of the enemy's caissons had been exploded. From here the scenery is magnificent. In our rear lies the valley of the Monocacy, with Frederick resting on its breast; and in front stretches that of the Catoctin, with the South Mountains beyond. Down this beautiful valley winds the broad creek that gives it name, and in which is situated Middletown. Long lines of troops and ammunition wagons were moving across it, towards the mountains, from whose sides issued puffs of white smoke and came the booming of cannon.

About noon we marched through the town, a pretty place, whose inhabitants lined the streets and welcomed us on our way to battle. Bread, cakes, milk, water, and fruit, were freely given by the good people, whose hearty welcome made us feel for the first time we were among friends. A pretty young lady stepped from the side-walk, and handed to the adjutant of the Second a bouquet of flowers. She spoke not a word, but crimsoned when their eyes met. That night young Cross lay dead upon the field, and the flowers were found buttoned inside his coat. Marching on, with happy hearts, we came to the Catoctin, where Pleasanton's cavalry had skirmished and driven Stuart's, the day before, but not until they succeeded in destroying the bridge and burning the mill and surrounding houses. Here we rested for a while, and made coffee. One of the boys had an aching tooth, and asked the surgeon to extract it. "Why, my dear boy, we are going into battle in a little while." "I know that," replied the boy, "but who wants to go to heaven with the tooth-ache."

At this time Jackson's corps and Walker's * division had recrossed the Potomac into Virginia,† and M'Law's corps of about 20,000 was skirmishing at Harpers Ferry.‡ Longstreet had marched toward Hagerstown, and detached six of his brigades, under Anderson, to coöperate with M'Law's against Maryland Heights and Harpers Ferry. This left D. H. Hill's division, of five brigades of 5,000 men,§ and Stuart's cavalry to hold Turner's Gap and the adjacent passes of South Mountain. Lee, to thus divide his army, certainly showed an utter contempt of his adversary's enterprise, or of all rules of warfare.

Turner's Gap, through which the National road passes, is about four hundred feet high, and the crests on either side rise some six hundred feet higher. The old Hagerstown road is half a mile to the north, and the old Sharpsburg road an equal distance to the south, both rising higher than the Gap. Early in the morning Pleasanton's cavalry had been skirmishing with the enemy, and when General Cox's division arrived, about nine A.M., one brigade was sent up the Sharpsburg road to ascertain if they held the crest on that side in force. Such proving to be the case, Cox with his division, supported by General Reno's corps, at once commenced the attack, which was continued with desperate fighting until noon, when the musketry firing ceased until two o'clock, each side awaiting re-enforcements. During this time, and somewhat later, nine of Longstreet's brigades arrived, raising the enemy's force to nearly 30,000 men, and

---

* Major-General W. H. J. Walker, of Georgia. Killed at Decatur, Ga., July 22d, 1864.
† September 11th.
‡ September 12th.
§ General D. H. Hill's official report.

Longstreet coming upon the field, and ranking Hill, took the chief command. In the meantime, Hooker with our corps arrived, and, taking the old Hagerstown road, moved to the right, to turn their left flank. About two P.M. Wilcox's division came up, and General Reno ordered him to move up the Sharpsburg road, and take position to the right of it. Wilcox, at General Cox's request, sent two regiments to his support, and a section of Captain Cook's battery was placed upon the crest near the road, and opened fire across the Gap upon an insurgent battery. As Wilcox was deploying, the enemy suddenly opened with a battery at short range, and drove the cannoneers, with their limbers, from the guns, which were nearly lost, but saved by a determined charge of the Seventy-ninth New York and Seventeenth Michigan. The division was then formed on the right of Cox's, and sheltered as much as possible under the mountain-side, until the whole line advanced.

Shortly before this General Burnside arrived, and directed Reno to move up the divisions of Sturges and Rodman[*] to the crest alongside of Cox and Wilcox, and to attack with his whole force as soon as Hooker was well up the mountain on the right. It was half-past three before these troops were in position, when Clark's battery was sent to assist General Cox. The advantage of the enemy's position was still very great, all our movements being seen by him, while his positions and strength were concealed from us. Besides this, our men had to struggle up the steep mountain-side, while the enemy lay behind the stone walls and rocks, and took advantage of the inequality of the ground. The disproportion between the troops actually engaged was not so very great, probably about one-third more on our side, which left heavy odds against us. About three o'clock, under a heavy fire of artillery, a general advance of the line took place, and was signalized by gallantry on both sides, but our steadiness

---

[*] Brigadier-General Isaac P. Rodman. Killed at Antietam.

prevailed, and they were gradually driven back until the crest was ours. At the head of his troops, about sunset, fell the gallant Major-General Jesse L. Reno.

While the left was thus engaged, the right, under General Hooker, was also climbing up the mountain-side. About two o'clock we moved from the Catoctin along the National road, and turned off to the right on the old Hagerstown road, passing by Mount Tabor Church, then through the woods and over the fields, along the base of the mountain for about a mile and a half, when we halted. The inhabitants, who had never witnessed a battle, took advantage of this opportunity, and accompanied us on our march, keeping between us and the mountains, the better to see all that passed. The enemy, who had been watching our movements, opened from a gun, throwing a shell in close proximity. The effect upon the sightseers was magical, they breaking through our lines with wild screams, and knocking the boys around like toys. The men, with a bound, cleared the fences, and run like deer, but many of the poor women were left hanging on the posts by their petticoats and hoops, while the terrified children lay upon the ground and shrieked. Never did we see a battle opened with such a prelude before, and it did us more good than all the harangues our generals could have delivered.

General Seymour, whose brigade occupied the extreme right, deployed the Bucktails, with the Second as a support, as skirmishers. Advancing up the foot-hills, we soon became engaged, driving the enemy close on to the mountains, where, coming to a stone wall, they rallied and made a desperate resistance; but the flags of the Reserve were forced over it, and then took place the most exciting and spirited fight we ever witnessed. Generally speaking, fighting is too earnest work for the boys to see much fun in it, but the women down the road put the devil into their heads, and the insurgents could not knock it out of them. The ground was of the most difficult character for the movement of troops, the mountain-side being very steep and rocky, and obstructed by stone walls, rocks and timber, from behind which the enemy, in lines and squads, kept up an incessant fire. All order and regularity of our lines was soon destroyed, and the regiments became mixed up, the battle partaking of the nature of a free fight, in which every one went in according to his fancy. From wall to wall, and rock to rock, the enemy were driven, squads of boys outflanking them, and getting outflanked in turn. But higher and higher we went, until at last our banners caught the last gleam of the setting sun, and the cheers of victory rolled down the mountain-side. It was dark before the battle was over, but desultory firing of musketry lasted until nine o'clock. Hooker, fearing we were going too fast for safety during the action, sent Duryea's Brigade to our support, but they did not arrive until after dark, when they loudly cheered the victors. When the Reserves prepared to move up the mountain, General Meade ordered Lieutenant-Colonel Clark, commanding the Third, to move his regiment some distance to the right, and occupy an eminence to protect that flank, and watch any movement of the enemy in that direction. When the action became general, the First Massachusetts Cavalry arrived, and relieved Clark, who moved his command in the direction of the fire, and was ordered by Meade to the support of Ransom's battery, who had a section of guns on a prominent and exposed position. Here they remained until the close of the battle.

The loss in the Reserves was 399, and among the wounded were Colonel Thos. F. Gallagher, commanding the Third Brigade, and Colonel Bolinger, of the Seventh. General M'Clellan reported our total loss at 312 killed, 1,234 wounded, and 22 missing, making a total of 1,568. We took 1,500 prisoners. He says: "The loss of the enemy in killed was much greater than our own, and probably also in wounded." This, however, from the nature of the ground and fighting, could not have been so, but was probably the reverse.

In the ——— Regiment, there was a man who had been through the Mexican war, and in this so far, but who had never been in a battle, he always shirking; and neither the threats of his officers nor the ridicule of his comrades could induce him to go into danger, as he declared he had a presentiment he would be killed in the first fight. At last he refused to do fatigue duty, and, as a soldier who will neither fight nor work is not particularly desirable about a regiment, an officer detailed two men to make him go in and take his chance along with his comrades. Soon after he got under fire he lay down behind a log, where he was reasonably safe; but rising to go to a rock a few feet off, he fell dead, pierced by nine of the enemy's balls.* Shirking, of course, was never allowed, and no man of proper spirit would disgrace himself in the eyes of his comrades by it. Some brave men, at times, from not being well, felt nervous, and went to their officers and asked to be excused from going in, and we never knew of an instance of their being refused.

Ammunition was supplied through the night, and at noon the next day the Reserves left the mountains and moved off on the National road towards Antietam, the Third marching with the battery. At Boonsboro, we found the churches and buildings filled with the enemy's wounded, and a large number of prisoners doing fatigue duty with them. Many of these were our old friends of Longstreet's corps, whom we had met in every battle but one, and a young reb. of the Seventeenth Virginia, who was wounded and taken at

---

* Bravery is born in us, and not acquired. It lies in the blood and is a species of instinct. It is involuntary, and depends not upon ourselves. It is always thoughtlessly impetuous, and is inspired by the impulse of example, the blindness arising from common danger and the heat of battle.

Courage, which is generally confounded with bravery, is not always united with it. It is in the soul, and is a real virtue, a sublime and noble sentiment. It is animated by patriotism, self-respect, and a zeal for the cause engaged in. It is not inaccessible to fear; but it overcomes it. Bravery, in the hour of danger, is sometimes weakened by reflection; courage is always strengthened by it.

Glendale, and who was again slightly in luck, grasped the hand of his captor with the warmth and delight of a schoolboy. Here, early in the day, our cavalry overtook the enemy's, killing and wounding a number, and capturing two hundred and fifty prisoners and two guns. At Boonsboro we turned to the left, and marched to Keedysville. Early the next morning, the 16th, the Third rejoined the division, which laid to the right of the Keedysville and Williamsport road, and were just in time to receive a scanty supply of coffee and crackers to breakfast on.

Before dark, on the 14th, Franklin had driven the enemy from Crampton's Gap several miles southeast of Turner's Gap. The next morning, at eight o'clock, Harpers Ferry, with its 11,500 troops and vast supplies, was causelessly surrendered by Colonel Miles,* of Bull Run dishonor. On the morning of the 16th, Jackson rejoined Lee at Antietam. At noon Walker arrived, and on the 17th M'Laws came up. By the evening of the 15th the whole of M'Clellan's army was concentrated in the same neighborhood, the batteries posted, and the men laid down upon their arms.

---

* Colonel Dixon S. Miles, Second Infantry. Killed while the white flag was flying.

CHAPTER XII.

BATTLE OF ANTIETAM — STRENGTH OF THE ARMIES — THE RESERVES OPEN THE BATTLE — THE 17TH — ATTACK BEFORE DAYLIGHT — DESPERATE FIGHTING — FALL OF MANSFIELD — "BULL" SUMNER GOES IN — HOOKER WOUNDED — GALLANTRY OF BARLOW — RICHARDSON KILLED — BURNSIDE ON THE LEFT — BRILLIANT CHARGE OF HARTRANFT — LOSS OF THE THIRD — LOSS OF THE TWO ARMIES — TROPHIES — FIELD HOSPITAL — A SURGEON'S DUTY — REBELS RECROSS THE POTOMAC — THE FIELD AFTER THE BATTLE — BURYING THE DEAD — GRIFFIN CAPTURES A BATTERY — STUART REPULSED.

ANTIETAM, SEPTEMBER 16TH AND 17TH, 1862.

ANTIETAM creek is crossed by four stone bridges—the upper one, on our right, on the Keedysville and Williamsport road; the second one, about two and a half miles below, on the Keedysville and Sharpsburg pike; the third, about a mile below the second, on the Rohrersville and Sharpsburg road; and the fourth, near the mouth of Antietam creek, on the road leading from Harpers Ferry to Sharpsburg, and some three miles below the third. The stream has a few difficult fords. The enemy's position was a very strong one, on the heavily-wooded heights west of Antietam creek, stretching from it to the Potomac, with both flanks and rear protected by them. They were commanded by General Lee, and consisted of Generals Jackson's, Longstreet's, D. H. Hill's, Ransom's, Jenkin's, Stuart's and other troops, and numbered from 70,000 to 80,000,* though Lee says they were under 40,000 men.

Our forces were composed of Generals Hooker's, Sumner's, Fitz John Porter's, Franklin's, Burnside's and Banks'

---

* Pollard, in his Southern History of the War, says of this battle:
"It was fought for half the day with 45,000 men on the Confederate side; and for the remaining half with no more than an aggregate of 70,000 men."
The *Richmond Enquirer* of September 23d, says it has "authentic particulars" of the battle; and that "the ball was opened on Tuesday evening about six o'clock, by all our available force, 60,000 strong, commanded by General Robert E. Lee in person."

corps, Couch's division and Pleasonton's cavalry, and numbered 87,164 men. This includes, however, 4,320 cavalry, which were of little use; Couch's division of 5,000 men and Humphrey's division of raw recruits, neither of which arrived until the battle was over, and numbered about 15,000 men.

General Lee, to gain time, on the 15th and 16th ostentatiously displayed his infantry to sight, exposing them to our artillery fire, but the next day they were kept well concealed in the woods. On the 16th, the two armies faced each other idly until four o'clock in the afternoon, when "Fighting Joe Hooker" was sent on his old errand of turning the enemy's left flank, backed by Sumner, Franklin and Mansfield, who were to come into action successively nearer the enemy's center.

It was near three o'clock when our division, followed by Ricketts' and Doubleday's, which constituted our corps, crossed the Antietam at a ford and the upper bridge, and advanced to open the battle. A squadron of cavalry preceded us, and after moving about a mile on the Williamsport road we turned sharp to the left, into the fields, with woods in front and on either side. We advanced slowly in columns of division, ready to form to resist cavalry, which hovered on our flanks and front. The Bucktails and eight companies of the Third were thrown out as skirmishers, and Lieutenant-Colonel Clark, with the remaining division of his regiment, advanced with the column. The skirmishers were soon engaged, and the enemy opened with a battery, to which Cooper's replied, and Seymour's Brigade advanced to their support. The Second and Third Brigades were immediately pushed forward by Meade, and delivering heavy volleys, steadily advanced, driving the enemy from the strip of woods over the fields to the woods beyond. In the corn-field in our front was a battery supported by masses of infantry deployed around it, which played upon Seymour's Brigade. General Meade posted Ransom's battery of twelve-pounders on the far edge of the woods just gained, which opened a destructive enfilading fire upon them, soon causing the infantry to seek the shelter of the woods, and the guns to withdraw to its edge, from which they shelled the woods we occupied. Darkness closed the contest, though the artillery continued firing slowly until near ten o'clock. That night we rested on our arms, on ground won from the enemy. Our pickets were so close that several of the enemy's unintentionally got into our lines at different points, and were captured. During the night, the enemy made two attacks upon our pickets, but were repulsed each time without our losing any ground.

Such was the position of the contending forces that the battle must commence the next morning, as soon as it was light enough to distinguish friend from foe. At three o'clock,* our pickets, fearing other troops would get ahead of them, and being determined the Reserves should have the honor of opening this day's battle also, commenced a brisk skirmish, and were at once re-enforced by the Second, and, in a short time, by the balance of Seymour's Brigade, which, by early daylight, was engaged in a desperate struggle in the second line of woods. Ricketts' division was soon after sent, by General Hooker, to re-enforce Seymour's Brigade; and Doubleday's division was advanced to the right, along the woods occupied by the Second and Third Brigades of Reserves. Hood's division, that fought us the afternoon before, and bothered us through the night, was replaced by Ewell's and D. R. Jones' divisions, under General Jackson, who commanded the left wing of the enemy. Against these veterans, Meade hurled the Reserves, backed by the other troops, and drove them into the woods and almost through it, but not until the rebel General Stark was killed, and Jones and Lawton were wounded. Hood's division now returned, backed by the brigades of Ripley, Colquitt, Garland † (now under Colonel M'Rae), and D. R.

---

* September 17th.
† Brigadier-General Garland. Killed at South Mountain.

Jones, and the conflict was renewed with determined energy. Back into the woods we pressed them, until we felt the full weight of the fire of the fresh troops, when our lines showed signs of wavering.

Hooker called on Doubleday, for his "best brigade, instantly." Gallantly they dashed up, led by Hartsuff, and were soon on our right, delivering their volleys. Our lines were steadied, and the woods resounded with the continuous roar of musketry, and the waves of flame and smoke swayed to and fro. By this time the whole of the enemy's re-enforcements were in action, pressing us hard, forcing back our right flank, and curving us into a simi-circle. Seymour was there, cheering us on, and the gallant Hartsuff, whose brigade received the weight of the enemy's shock, and had been driven back, fell wounded in our ranks. In spite of all the exertions of the officers and the determination of the men, who needed no urging on, we were broken down and driven back by the sheer heat of the fire.

The Reserves, we suppose, were very much like other troops, and when they were once thoroughly broken up and scattered, it was merely the waste of lives to attempt to rally them under fire, without a support was near. We have seen the attempt made a number of times, but it always resulted in the same thing. We were broken up this time, and ran as fast as our legs would carry us, for about five hundred yards, when we came to a depression of the ground, where the division all collected. The officers and men waved their flags, and called aloud the number of their respective regiments, and in an incredible short time—a very few moments—our bright lines were re-formed; our bright lines —for we never saw our brigade look so glorious before. Seymour knew by the boys' eyes how their hearts felt, and with loud cheers they followed him, and dashed upon the surprised foe, to whom they appeared to rise from out the earth.

Meade, whose quick eye had discerned our trouble, instantly brought Ransom's guns into battery, which opened upon the advancing column with grape and canister. The Third Brigade, Colonel Anderson, formed behind a fence bordering the blood-soaked corn-field, and poured into the enemy enfilading volleys. The Second Brigade was double-quicked to our rescue, and, with our own and Ricketts', hurled back the enemy from the corn-field far into the woods.

At daybreak, the Third, under Lieutenant-Colonel Clark, having been rejoined by the detached companies of skirmishers, moved with the Second Brigade to the right, with the Third Brigade on the right and Doubleday's division in advance. Moving in columns of battalions in mass, they advanced towards the Hagerstown pike, until reaching a ravine in front of the corn-field. Here the enemy opened upon them, and a warm contest ensued for the possession of the field. The troops in front giving way, Meade deployed both brigades, and formed his line of battle along the fence bordering the corn-field, for the purpose of covering the withdrawal of these troops. At this moment, Seymour's Brigade, some distance to the left, gave way, and Meade ordered the Second Brigade to their rescue. The brigade started on the double-quick, moving to the left flank in line of battle, but, on account of demonstrations on their front, they were halted and faced several times, during which they were exposed to a severe fire of artillery and musketry, from which they suffered severely. Arriving in their position, they fronted and immediately engaged the enemy, and, with Seymour and Ricketts, drove them back into the woods. Anderson, at the same time, with the Third Brigade, gained full possession of the bloody corn-field.

Soon after General Hooker's corps became engaged he ordered up Mansfield's corps, which had crossed the Antietam during the night, and bivouacked about a mile in our rear. General Williams' division was deployed on our right, with the right of its right brigade, under Crawford, resting on the Hagerstown and Sharpsburg pike. General Green's division joined Williams' left. During the deployment the gallant Mansfield fell, mortally wounded, while in front of his troops. The command of the Twelfth Corps now devolved upon General Williams, and it became engaged about seven A.M., the attack being opened by Hampton's Pittsburg, Cothran's New York, and Knapp's Pennsylvania batteries. The enemy, who occupied the woods on the west of the pike in force, pushed a column of troops into the open field, east of the pike. The woods were traversed by outcropping ledges of rock; and several hundred yards to the right and rear was a hill, which commanded the debouche of the woods, and on which their artillery was posted. In the fields between was a long stone wall, continued by breastworks of rails, behind which was placed infantry. The woods formed a screen, behind which all this was concealed. For about two hours the battle raged with varied success, the enemy endeavoring to drive our troops into the second line of woods, and ours, in turn, to get possession of the line in front. Our troops at last succeeded, by desperate fighting, in driving the enemy into the woods beyond the pike, near the Dunker Church. In this conflict, General Crawford, commanding Williams' division, was seriously wounded.

General Sumner's corps, having crossed the Antietam in the morning, about nine o'clock, Sedgwick's division was sent to relieve Crawford's, and, entering the woods west of the pike, they drove the enemy before them. The first line was met by a heavy fire of musketry and shell from the breastworks and batteries, and, at the same time, a heavy column attacked and drove back Green's division, and gained the rear of Sedgwick's. General Howard* immediately faced the third line to the rear, preparatory to a change of front to meet the column advancing on the left, but his line received so severe and destructive a fire in front, while executing this movement, and which it was unable to return,

---

* Major-General O. O. Howard, wounded at Fair Oaks. Subsequently, chief of the Freedman Bureau.

that it gave way towards the right and rear, and was soon followed by the first and second lines. General Gorman's Brigade and a regiment of Dana's soon rallied, and checked the advance of the enemy. The second and third lines now formed on the left of Gorman's Brigade, and poured a destructive fire upon the enemy. General Gordon, whose brigade Sumner had ordered to the support of Sedgwick, arrived after Sedgwick had given way, and, finding himself opposed by a superior force, was compelled to withdraw to the rear of the batteries at the second line of woods. As Gordon's troops unmasked our batteries on the left, they opened with canister, and the enemy, unable to withstand their deadly fire in front, and the musketry from the right, were driven back with great slaughter.

During this assault, Generals Sedgwick and Dana were seriously wounded. About the time of Sedgwick's advance, General Hooker, who had just reconnoitered the ground in front on foot, and had re-mounted amid a shower of bullets, received a severe and intensely painful wound through the foot, and was compelled to leave the field. At his request, General Meade assumed the command of his corps. General Seymour thereupon took command of the Reserves; and Colonel Roberts, of his brigade. Ten o'clock came. The Reserves, who had but little or no sleep during the night, had been fighting from before daybreak. They had been twenty-two hours without food, having neither supper nor breakfast, and many of the men's cartridge-boxes were entirely empty. Hooker had sent for fresh troops, to replace them, and, amidst a hail of musket-balls, they marched to the rear as coolly and steady as on parade. Crossing the blood-soaked corn-field, they entered the first strip of woods, and were lain down to await the issue of an assault upon the right, which being repulsed without their assistance, they moved beyond the woods, on to a ridge, where rations and ammunition awaited them. "By two P.M., the division of the Pennsylvania Reserves now commanded by General

Seymour, were organized on this ridge, supplied with ammunition, and held in readiness to repel an attack, if the enemy should attempt one on our right flank, or assist in any advance he might make."*

While the conflict was so obstinately raging on our front and right, General French's division, of Sumner's corps, was engaged with the enemy further to the left. An attempt to carry the line of heights was met with a counter-charge by the insurgents, but repulsed. Successive attempts to turn their right and left were foiled, and after a bloody combat of four hours, French paused, having gained considerable ground, but not carrying the heights.

On the left of French, General Richardson's division was hotly engaged. They moved steadily forward under a severe fire, and engaged the enemy near Roulette's house. Reaching the crest, they found the enemy posted in a sunken road, and in a corn-field in rear of the road. Here Meagher's Brigade exhausted their ammunition in a hot combat with the enemy, and the gallant General being wounded, they were ordered to give place to Caldwell's Brigade. The battle raged with great fury, when Colonel Barlow† seized the opportunity of turning the enemy's left flank in the sunken road, with the Sixty-first and the Sixty-fourth New York Volunteers. He captured over three hundred prisoners and three flags, and, the other regiments of Caldwell's Brigade advancing, they drove the enemy in confusion through the corn-field beyond. Soon after, the enemy, maneuvering behind a ridge, successively attacked them on the right and left flanks and front, but were signally repulsed each time, and hurled back, our lines advancing and seizing Doctor Piper's house, a defensible building very near the Hagerstown pike, and about the center of the enemy's lines. Here the infantry fighting ceased, the artillery being brought into

---

*General Meade's official report.

†Colonel Francis C. Barlow, of New York. Appointed Brigadier-General September 19th, 1862. Wounded at Gettysburg, Pennsylvania.

play. Near this point fell Major-General Israel B. Richardson, mortally wounded. With the exception of some minor fighting, and the repulse of a heavy line of infantry by General Pleasanton, with sixteen guns, the operations on this portion of the field closed. About noon, Franklin's corps arrived from Crampton's Gap, and was sent to the right, where Sumner's and Meade's corps were hotly engaged.

General Burnside's corps held our extreme left, opposite the bridge on the Rohrersville and Sharpsburg road. This was held by General Toombs,[*] with the Second and Twentieth Georgia Infantry, some sharp-shooters, and the batteries of General D. R. Jones. Burnside was ordered at eight A.M. to carry the bridge and heights beyond, and to advance along the crest upon Sharpsburg and its rear. Several attempts were made to execute this order, but were repulsed until about one P.M., when it was carried by a brilliant charge of the Fifty-first Pennsylvania, Colonel John F. Hartranft,[†] and Fifty-first New York Volunteers. The enemy retreated to the heights, but it was three o'clock before Burnside charged up the heights, carrying them handsomely, some of his troops reaching the outskirts of Sharpsburg. It was a short-lived triumph, however. Lee, who had been too hard pressed on his left to spare any troops, was now re-enforced by A. P. Hill's division, which had just arrived from Harpers Ferry. Hill, under cover of a heavy fire of artillery, charged our extreme left and front, and drove our men back down the heights, and pressed on towards the bridge until checked by the fire of our batteries on the opposite side. Darkness soon after put an end to the combat, and the enemy held the heights. Brigadier-General Isaac P. Rodman, who led our charge, was mortally wounded, and General Branch, of North Carolina, who led the insurgent, was killed.

---

[*] Robert Toombs, of Georgia, this day wounded.
[†] Subsequently twice Governor of Pennsylvania.

General M'Clellan, in his official report, says: "If this important movement had been consummated two hours earlier, a position would have been secured upon the heights from which our batteries might have enfiladed the greater part of the enemy's line, and turned their right and rear; our victory might thus have been much more decisive." Thus terminated, indecisively, one of the bloodiest days of the war, in which, for fourteen hours, over 150,000 men and 500 pieces of artillery * were engaged. That night the enemy withdrew their line far to the rear, beyond the Hagerstown pike; and we slept on the field from which we drove them.

General Meade says: "The Reserves went into action 3,000 strong, and lost in killed and wounded over 570 men," or about one-fifth. Meade received a contusion from a spent grape-shot, and had two horses killed under him. Among those killed was Colonel M'Neal of the Bucktails, a gallant soldier, an accomplished gentleman and a sincere Christian. The loss in the Third was heavy,† and among those killed was Captain Florentine H. Straub, of Company D, a brave and gallant officer, who appeared to know not what fear was. Among the wounded was Captain George D. Davenport, Company B, and Lieutenant F. G. Nicholson, of the same company, both brave and meritorious officers.

M'Clellan puts the loss of our army in this battle at 2,010 killed, 9,416 wounded, and 1,043 missing, making a total of 12,469. Lee, in his official report of this battle, written March 6th, 1863, is silent as to his loss. The "Reports of the operations of the Army of Virginia, from June, 1862, to December 13th, 1862," published by the insurgent government, makes their loss in the Maryland battles only 1,567 killed, and 8,724 wounded, making a total of 10,291; and says nothing of the missing. This is, palpably and purposely, an under-statement. M'Clellan says: "About 2,700

---

* M'Clellan's report.
† For list of the killed and wounded, see appendix A.

of the enemy's dead were, under the direction of Major Davis, assistant inspector-general, counted and buried upon the battle-field of Antietam. A portion of their dead had been previously buried by the enemy. * * * Thirteen guns, thirty-nine colors, upwards of 15,000 stand of small arms, and more than 6,000 prisoners, were the trophies which attest the success of our army in the battles of South Mountain, Crampton's Gap, and Antietam. Not a single gun nor color was lost by our army during these battles."

The reports of Lee's corps or division commanders, gives the following aggregates:

	Killed.	Wounded.	Missing.	Total.
Longstreet's	964	5,234	1,310	7,508
Jackson's	351	2,030	57	2,438
D. H. Hill's	464	1,852	925	3,241
A. P. Hill's	63	283	....	346
Total	1,842	9,399	2,292	13,533

D. H. Hill reports that, out of less than 5,000 men, he had 3,241 disabled. Lawton's Brigade lost 554 men out of 1,150.

By night almost all the wounded were collected in and around the different farm-houses and buildings, where the same attention was shown to the enemy's as to our own.* Rude tables were put up, on which the operations were performed, and from which dripped the blood, while near by were the amputated arms and legs. The wounded lay near by, gazing at the sight, patiently and resignedly waiting their turn to be lifted upon the tables, around which the surgeons stood with their sleeves rolled up, performing the operations with perfect coolness and seeming indifference. A surgeon

---

* This is literally true. After the battle, the author visited the hospitals in search of the wounded of his regiment, and particularly noticed that the wounded were treated in rotation, regardless of the side they fought on. He saw rebel limbs amputated while there were thousands of Unionists waiting their turn. The rebels spoke of the kindness of our stretcher-men in removing them from the field, where they expected to be left for days, as they had left our wounded on the Peninsula and at Bull Run.

understands well that skill and dispatch is what is required, and if he was to permit the sympathy he feels for the poor sufferer to have play, it might prove a great misfortune to the patient. Where there are thousands of cases which require immediate attention, and which will take the limited number of surgeons several days to attend to, the individual is necessarily overlooked for the good of the mass. Where the probabilities are strongly against saving a man, he is not operated upon, but made as easy as circumstances will admit, and the same principle is applied to the saving or losing of a limb. This is an imperative necessity that the exigency of the occasion requires. After the operations were completed, the patients were laid on straw or hay, in the buildings, or on the grass in rows, and over those that were exposed were stretched blankets to protect them from the rays of the sun. Water and food were distributed to them by the nurses, and the stretcher-men removed and buried those that died.

Numerous farmers of Maryland and Pennsylvania visited the hospitals, bringing with them bread, cakes, pies, cooked poultry, milk, etc., which they distributed to the wounded, and all of them appeared anxious to get a soldier to take home to nurse.

General Lee, of course, did not care to renew the battle the next day, and M'Clellan remained quiet. General M'Clellan states it was his intention to renew the battle on the 19th, but, when his cavalry advance reached the river, they discovered the enemy had decamped, leaving us only his dead and some 2,000 badly wounded. The whole army was moved forward towards the river, our division marching early in the morning to the front and right about three miles, crossing the Hagerstown and Sharpsburg pike, and encamping near the Potomac, above Sharpsburg. Our route took us over and along the enemy's line, and we found the fields and woods literally covered with their dead. At one point, where they had crossed the fields and pike obliquely, and where they must have received a terrible fire of musketry, the formation of their line was distinctly marked by their dead, who were stretched in long rows, showing, at the time they received the fire, they were well dressed. The effect of this fire must have been crushing, none of their dead lying in front of their line, though to the rear the ground was covered with them. In one thing their dead differed from ours: large water blisters, in many cases, entirely covered their hands. The Confederates were dragged into rows, by ropes placed around their ankles, and covered with earth. Many of our men were buried by their comrades, and their graves marked with their names and regiments penciled on boards. Where the bodies were not marked with slips of paper, or could not be identified, they were buried in rows, in wide graves, side by side. It impressed one with sad feelings to see such terrible destruction of human life, and caused us to wonder if we were not demons instead of God's creatures.

The enemy having posted eight batteries, supported by six hundred infantry, under Pendleton, to cover his crossing, at dark on the 19th, General Griffin, with his own and Barnes' brigades, of Porter's corps, crossed, and, after a smart action, took four guns, and drove back their support; but the next day a part of the corps, making a reconnaissance in force, was ambushed by A. P. Hill, and badly cut up, with the loss of two hundred prisoners. In this affair, the One Hundred and Eighteenth Pennsylvania Volunteers, Colonel Provost (The Corn Exchange Regiment), suffered severely.

On the 19th, General Stuart recrossed the Potomac, at Williamsport, with 4,000 cavalry and a battery of six guns, backed by 10,000 infantry. General Couch was dispatched with his division, supported by other troops, and attacking, drove him back with considerable loss. On the 20th, General Williams, with the Twelfth Corps, occupied Maryland Heights; and on the 22d, Sumner, with the Second Corps, took possession of Harpers Ferry.

CHAPTER XIII.

THE PRESIDENT'S VISIT — STUART RAIDS TO CHAMBERSBURG — RESIGNATIONS AND PROMOTIONS — THE DOCTOR'S BIRTHDAY — EFFORT TO REORGANIZE THE RESERVES — ONE HUNDRED AND TWENTY-FIRST AND ONE HUNDRED AND FORTY-SECOND REGIMENTS, PENNSYLVANIA VOLUNTEERS — PROMOTION OF REYNOLDS — MEADE COMMANDS THE RESERVES — MARCH TO BERLIN — CROSS THE POTOMAC — SNICKER'S GAP — MIDDLEBURG — PAROLED REBS — WHITE PLAINS — WARRENTON — THE GENEROUS CORPORAL — BURNSIDE SUPERSEDES M'CLELLAN — FITZ JOHN PORTER RELIEVED — PLANS OF CAMPAIGN — THE GRAND DIVISION — TO FAYETTEVILLE — DEPARTURE OF SEYMOUR — BEALTON — HARTWOOD — BROOKE'S STATION — THE PICKET — COOL POLITENESS — MARCH.

ON THE 1st of October, the President, Abraham Lincoln, visited the army, and remained with us several days, during which he rode through the encampments, reviewed the troops, and visited the hospitals. At the latter he made short addresses, and took many of the sufferers by the hand, speaking kindly to them, and showing the same regard and feeling for the Confederate wounded as for our own.

Lee soon retired to the vicinity of Bunker Hill and Winchester, and on the 10th of October sent Stuart, with 1,800 cavalry and a battery of horse-artillery, on a raid into Pennsylvania, and around our army. Crossing the Potomac above Williamsport, Stuart pushed rapidly to Chambersburg, where he burnt a great many buildings, destroyed 5,000 muskets, and paroled 275 sick and wounded soldiers. General M'Clellan made extensive preparations to insure his capture, but his plans were foiled by lack of energy and zeal upon the part of those entrusted with the execution of them. Stuart re-crossed the Potomac, below the Monocacy.

While we lay here, the following changes took place in the regiment: Captain David D. Feaster, Company C, a brave officer, who had rendered good service to his country, was discharged on account of physical disability. Second Lieutenant Joseph B. Roberts, another brave officer of the same company, was discharged on account of wounds received at Glendale. Adjutant Albert H. Jamieson, a gallant and meritorious officer, was honorably discharged on account of ill health. Harry S. Jones, "My sergeant-major, who cannot lie," was promoted Adjutant, vice Jamieson, discharged. Orderly-Sergeant John H. Crothers, was promoted First Lieutenant, Company C, vice Yardley, promoted Captain and Assistant Quartermaster, U. S. Volunteers. Corporal Henry W. Sutton was promoted Second Lieutenant Company C, vice Roberts, discharged. First Lieutenant Andrew J. Stetson was promoted Captain Company D, vice Florentine H. Straub, killed at Antietam. Second Lieutenant Jacob V. Shillings was promoted First Lieutenant Company D, vice Stetson, promoted. Orderly-Sergeant Albert Briner was promoted Second Lieutenant Company D, vice Shillings, promoted. Orderly-Sergeant Henry S. Moulton, promoted Second Lieutenant Company F, vice Jamieson, discharged. First Lieutenant Samuel J. La Rue, promoted Captain Company I, vice H. Clay Beatty, killed at Bull Run. Second Lieutenant Samuel Beatty was promoted First Lieutenant Company I, vice La Rue, promoted. Orderly-Sergeant Jackson Hutchinson was promoted Second Lieutenant Company I, vice Beatty, promoted. About the same time, the Reverend John J. Pomeroy, of Franklin county, was appointed Chaplain, vice the Reverend George H. Frear, resigned.

On the 17th, Colonel Sickel rode into camp, much to the joy of the men, who turned out and received him with loud cheers. The 20th being the birth-day of the most estimable surgeon of the Third, Doctor Collins, he entertained the officers in the large hospital tent. After doing ample justice to the excellent supper, the guests spent the evening in agreeable and social conversation, recalling home and by-gone days.

While we lay here, Governor Curtin was anxious to withdraw the Reserves, for the purpose of recruiting and reorganizing them, and, in a letter to His Excellency the President, said:

* * * * * * *

"The Pennsylvania Reserve Corps, numbering thirteen regiments of infantry, one regiment of cavalry and one of artillery, with a numerical strength of fifteen thousand seven hundred and sixty men, were taken into the service of the United States in July, 1861, immediately after the first battle at Manassas. The thirteen regiments of infantry did not muster four thousand men after the battle of Antietam. All of these regiments are much reduced in number, whilst many of them can scarcely be said to retain regimental organizations. The brilliant history of the Reserve Corps in the war, and the State pride, which has followed them since they entered the service, together with the circumstances surrounding their organization, would, I have no doubt, prove such incentives to enlistment, that the corps could be filled to the maximum in a short space of time.

"I suggest that the corps be returned to the State, and placed in the camp at this capital, and, if I am correct in my impression, the success would affect the minds of our people favorably, and other regiments in the service could be filled in their turn promptly.

"It is proper that, in this connection, I should say that the suggestions reflect the opinion of all the officers of the corps." * * *

The governor, however, was not successful in his endeavor, and renewed efforts were made to fill up our ranks by recruiting parties. It may as well be stated here, the Reserves, during their three years' service, received over 5,000 recruits, making the entire number of men they took into the field over 20,000. Our division had become so reduced in strength that it became necessary to re-enforce it by the addition of other regiments. Therefore, the One Hundred and Twenty-first Pennsylvania Volunteers, Colonel Chapman Biddle, (a Philadelphia regiment,) was assigned to the First Brigade; and the One Hundred and Forty-second Pennsylvania Volunteers, Colonel Robert P. Cummings,* was joined to the Second Brigade. When General Reynolds returned to the army, he was assigned to the command of our corps, the First. General Meade then resumed the command of the division.

On the 6th of October, General M'Clellan received orders to "cross the Potomac and give battle to the enemy, or drive him south." This order was responded to by calling for re-enforcements and supplies. Between the 26th of that month and the 2d of November, the army crossed. The plan of the campaign was to move parallel to the Blue Ridge, seize the passes of the mountains, and head the enemy off somewhere between the Potomac and Richmond.

On Sunday, the 26th, the Reserves broke camp at ten A. M., and marched towards Berlin. A cold rain-storm prevailed all day, rendering the movement tiresome and hard upon the men. That night they bivouacked in Pleasant Valley, near the western base of the South Mountains. Late the next afternoon they reached Berlin. Early on the 30th they crossed the Potomac on the pontoons, and encamped near Lovettsville, Virginia, where, on the 31st, they were inspected and mustered for pay. On the 1st of November they marched through Waterford, and encamped about two miles west of Hamilton. The next day, Captain Washington Richards and Sergeants John M. James and George B. Davis were detailed to proceed to Camp Curtin, Pennsylvania, to bring on recruits. The next morning the division marched, and, towards dark, passed through Philomont, whose inhabitants appeared not to know the name of it, and bivouacked two miles beyond, near Snicker's Gap, where there had been a lively artillery skirmish in the morning for the possession of the pass. Our dismounted

---

* Of Somerset county. Killed at Gettysburg, July 1st, 1863.

cavalry drove the enemy out. Early the next morning, the 4th, we moved a short distance, to Uniontown, and halted until three P.M., when we marched on, passing Franklin's corps and Couch's division at their bivouacs, and lay for the night on a high table-land. Early the next morning we moved off, fording the head-waters of Goose creek, a broad and rapid stream, and passed through Middleburg, and halted beyond to take dinner. Here we found a number of paroled wounded rebs, who appeared quite sociable with the boys. About 4 P.M. we again moved on, and, as there was a long wagon train in advance, and the roads were exceedingly bad, the march was slow and tedious. After dark we passed through White Plains, a deserted village on the Manassas Gap railroad, and, marching two miles beyond, countermarched a mile back, and bivouacked in a heavy woods about ten o'clock. Although it was raining and we had been fourteen hours marching sixteen miles, and the boys were tired, we soon had bright fires burning, and were as contented as soldiers could be.

The next morning, the 6th, we marched at eight o'clock towards Warrenton, the infantry moving on the fields, to leave the road clear for the artillery. Arriving at the gap between the Watery and the Pig-Nut Mountains, the Bucktails and the Second were thrown out as skirmishers, to clean the woods out on either side. They succeeded in scaring up a number of squirrels, but no gray-backs. We then marched on, and, about four P.M., entered Warrenton, and moved through and beyond it about a mile, where we encamped near our old ground of the preceding August. The inhabitants of the town, if they really felt any delight at our arrival, certainly did not manifest it by any outward signs, the female portion keeping in doors, and the men looking on in silence. We passed, however, a number of wounded paroled prisoners, whose countenances were more friendly, they saluting us in an easy matter-of-course style. The town was completely cleaned out of everything in the way of goods, the stores were closed, and business suspended. It now being within our lines, the inhabitants were exceedingly anxious to obtain supplies, and a moderate amount of provisions were allowed to come in. Yet some of them showed no gratitude for the same. A negro shoemaker, who soled a pair of boots for an officer, was ordered by his master to refuse greenbacks, and to demand gold or Confederate money, it being supposed the "Yanks" possessed none of the last named. In this, though, they were sadly mistaken, for an enterprising color-corporal generously offered to pay the bill, he receiving five dollars in corporation currency in exchange for his ten-dollar bill, fresh from the banking establishment of some news-boy in Philadelphia.

While we remained here, the weather was cold and unpleasant, and a violent snow-storm occurred. On the 7th of November, General M'Clellan was relieved of the command of the Army of the Potomac, and supersede by General Ambrose E. Burnside. Whatever verdict history may pass upon General M'Clellan, it cannot be denied he possessed a strong hold upon the affections of the army. No officer or soldier who served under him will attempt to deny this. And there is no better proof of the thorough discipline of the army than the cordial and earnest support it immediately gave to the new commander. About the same time, General Fitz John Porter was relieved of his command.

What General M'Clellan's plan of campaign was, is not fully known. It is certain though, that, at one time, he contemplated advancing on Richmond via Culpepper Court House and Gordonsville. He also issued orders for the rebuilding of the wharves at Acquia landing, and rebuilding the Acquia and Fredericksburg railroad. On the 6th of November, he ordered Captain Drum, his chief engineer, to remove all the pontoons at Berlin to Washington, and hold them in readiness to move. These movements indicated an advance via Fredericksburg. Our movement south had been so slow that it was impossible to bring the enemy to battle north of the Rappahannock. The plan proposed by General Burnside was to make a feint against Culpepper, and then, by a rapid movement, to seize the heights of Fredericksburg, and, establishing his base there, advance on Richmond from the north. This plan had the advantage of covering Washington. The army was divided into three grand divisions. The right, consisting of the Second and Ninth Corps, was commanded by General Sumner; the center, composed of the Third and Fifth Corps, by General Hooker; and the left, of the First and Sixth Corps, commanded by General Franklin. The Eleventh Corps constituted the reserve, and was commanded by General Sigel.

At noon on the 11th, we moved off to the southwest, and, before night, encamped near Fayetteville, about two miles from the Rappahannock. On the 14th, the Third went on picket for twenty-four hours, Colonel Sickel commanding the division line. As it was fine, clear weather, they had a very pleasant time. The next day they were relieved by the One Hundred and Twenty-first, Colonel Biddle. Here, General Seymour was relieved of the command of the First Brigade at his own request, his health not permitting him to go through a Winter campaign. He was succeeded by Colonel William Sinclair, U. S. A., commanding Sixth Reserves. The Third Brigade was now commanded by General Jackson.

The next morning, the 17th, during a drizzling rain, we moved off down the Bealton and Hartwood Church road, passing Bealton Station, Morrisville and the Gold Mines. After dark, when near Rockypen run, by the blunder of an aid-de-camp, we were sent into a woods so thickly overgrown with underbrush that we were forced to about-face and retrace our steps, and seek bivouac-grounds for ourselves near by. The next morning we marched along the fields to Hartwood Churches, where we took the road to

Stafford Court House, and, crossing Potomac creek, we ascended a steep hill that severely tested the strength of the teams to haul the guns and wagons up. It was a very hard day's march through the rain and mud, and towards night we encamped near the banks of Accaheek creek. For the past ten days the booming of cannon had been heard in the direction of the upper fords of the Rappahannock. We remained here four days, during which it rained continually, and heavy details were made to corduroy roads. So particular were our Generals to prevent depredations being committed on private property, that hourly roll-calls were ordered in each regiment, and the absentees were ordered to be put under arrest upon their return.

About eight A.M., on the 22d, we moved along the fields bordering the Telegraph road and passed through Stafford Court House to Brooke's Station, on the Acquia Creek and Fredericksburg railroad, where we arrived about noon, and encamped on an elevated plain overlooking an extensive meadow. Here we found the remains of insurgent huts, which they occupied during the previous Winter. The sutlers, who always precede the paymaster, soon arrived with a supply of goods, and the boys were enabled to replenish their stock of tobacco, which they had been out of for some time.

On the 1st of December, Major Pomeroy arrived and paid the regiments off. An officer asked for two months advance pay, and the Major accommodated him at his own risk. Just before his departure, the officer handed him a sealed envelope. Upon opening it, the Major found a twenty-dollar greenback enclosed, which he returned to the officer, saying, "I cannot receive any compensation for accommodating one who is fighting for our country." While we lay here we received a full supply of clothing, some of the men being almost bare-footed and without blankets, and many of them in need of stockings, under-clothing and great coats. Our rations were made full and liberal, and the men appeared in excellent spirits.

We remained here sixteen days, and had a very pleasant line to picket on, making our headquarters at Mr. Schooler's house. Mr. S. and his family were strong secessionists, but had the good sense and breeding to submit to circumstances with grace. We rode up to the house, ordered our horses to be put into the stables, and the saddles and blankets into the parlor, which we took possession of. A young lady of excellent education and fascinating manners soon appeared, and took a seat by the fire we had built. She informed us they were secessionists at heart, and that her two brothers were in the Confederate army, but, situated as they were, they treated with respect the Union officers whose *duty* placed them there. Such frankness won our hearts, and could she or any one else expect us after that to submit to her cool politeness? Their clock was out of order—a very fortunate affair for us. One of our officers had studied clock-making in his early youth, having dissected his mother's Lepine. He at once overhauled the clock, and, luckily, set it running. The piano was sadly out of tune, and another officer, possessed of a critical ear for music, with a cone-wrench put it in excellent order. In fact, we made ourselves at home and generally useful, and, by showing a proper respect for their feelings and sentiments, and getting the right side of madam, we succeeded in overcoming their cold politeness and gaining their sincere friendship. They played for us "My Maryland," "The Bonny Blue Flag," and other Confederate songs, which they sung with spirit; spoke of the battles past, and of the approaching one. The mother showed us many times the likeness of her darling, "Charley," a handsome boy of sixteen, who belonged to the Forty-seventh Virginia, whom we promised to treat kindly should the fortune of war ever place it in our power to do so. Under the flag of truce to bury the dead after Fredericksburg, we handed to a Confederate officer an unsealed note, from the mother to Charley.

While we lay here, Lieutenant-Colonel John Clark was detailed to report to General Haupe, for duty as railroad constructor, and was ordered to take charge of the Acquia and Fredericksburg railroad. He never again rejoined the regiment, much to the regret of every officer and man.

We remained at Brooke's Station until the 8th of December, when we broke camp early in the morning, and marched. It was very cold, and the roads were frozen hard and covered with sleet, which made it tiresome for the men and horses. At noon we encamped in a meadow near White Oak Church, having marched eight miles. While we lay here, all the detailed men were ordered into the ranks, and sixty rounds of cartridges supplied to each man.

LIEUT. COL. JOHN CLARK.

CHAPTER XIV.

SUMNER SUMMONS FREDERICKSBURG — BOMBARDMENT — LAYING PONTOONS — BATTLE OF FREDERICKSBURG — THE FIELD, AND STRENGTH OF THE ARMIES — GLORIOUS CHARGE OF THE RESERVES — THE HEIGHTS CARRIED — SUPPORT FAILS — FRANKLIN'S TESTIMONY — MEADE'S REPORT — LEE'S REPORT — EXTRACT — JACKSON'S LOSS EXCEEDS THE RESERVES' STRENGTH — BACK OF THE CITY, ON THE RIGHT — MARYE'S HEIGHTS — DESPERATE CHARGES — HUMPHREY'S GALLANT BUT FATAL CHARGE — THE LOSS OF THE TWO ARMIES — UNWORTHY OF LEE — JACKSON'S REPORT — DIVINE SERVICE ON THE FIELD — FLAG OF TRUCE — OUR DEAD AND WOUNDED — RE-CROSS THE RIVER — BURNSIDE'S NOBLE QUALITIES.

GENERAL SUMNER'S advance reached Falmouth November 17th, and on the 21st he summoned Fredericksburg to surrender. The authorities replied that, while it would not be used to assail us, its occupation by our troops would be resisted to the utmost. Most of the inhabitants, thereupon, abandoned the place, which was occupied by General Barksdale's* Mississippi Brigade, who posted themselves as sharp-shooters in the houses along the river. Lee's engineers were busy fortifying the heights in the rear. On the 28th, Wade Hampton dashed across the river above, raiding up to Dumfries, capturing some cavalry and sutlers' wagons. On the 5th of December, General D. H. Hill assailed, with artillery, the gun-boats near Port Royal, and forced them to retire. He then threw up fortifications, to prevent their return.

THE BOMBARDMENT OF FREDERICKSBURG, DECEMBER 11TH.

At two o'clock in the morning, the reveille was sounded, awaking the boys from their slumber on the hard, frozen ground, and soon the valleys and hills were lit up by innu-

---

* William Barksdale, of Mississippi. Killed at Gettysburg, Pa.

merable fires, around which they gathered to prepare their coffee. Soon we took up our march, the bright stars lighting us on our way, and as the columns defiled through the gorges and woods the heavy tramp of men alone was heard. Soon the sound of artillery in front announced the great drama was about to open. Moving on to within a mile of the river, we halted, loaded, and stacked arms in a heavy pine woods, where we lay for the day and night.

The roar of artillery, by this time, became incessant along the river-front, and the men, collecting on the hills, had a fine view of the bombardment, which now commenced in earnest. The engineers had attempted to lay pontoon bridges opposite the city, but the tenacity with which Fredericksburg was held by the sharp-shooters compelled Burnside to dislodge them by bombardment. One hundred and forty-three guns were brought to bear upon the city, a large portion of which opened fire. The sight was a magnificent one, and towards dark it became grand. The city was on fire in several places, the flames and smoke ascending high into the air, while shells were seen bursting in every quarter. Great care was taken by the cannoneers to avoid injuring the churches, but the other prominent buildings received due attention. An officer rode up to a battery, and, saluting the Lieutenant, said: "Lieutenant, do you observe that high building to the right of the white steeple? That is the Shakespeare Hotel, and the proprietor and his ladies are particular friends of mine; do me the favor of sending my compliments to them." A gun was trained upon the building, and soon a shell went crashing through the walls. "Thank you, Lieutenant, for your kindness; you have enabled me to pay a debt of gratitude I have owed them since May last," and off rode the facetious officer. The enemy's sharp-shooters kept up a vigorous fire upon the cannoneers and officers who lined the bank, their bullets at that long range whizzing wickedly by.

The pontoons had been laid half-way over during the night, but at daylight the workmen were driven off. Finding it impossible to dislodge the enemy with artillery, the pontoon boats were filled with troops and run over, and the men, landing, drove the sharp-shoooters from the streets and houses, killing and wounding a number, and taking thirty-five prisoners. Our loss in the whole operation was nearly three hundred men. Among the first to volunteer to cross was the Rev. A. B. Fuller, the beloved Chaplain of the Sixteenth Massachusetts, who was killed by a musket ball. The city, from the bombardment and subsequent firing on during the battle, and the ransacking by the soldiers of both armies and the dishonest of its population, was reduced to a state of great dilapidation.

At midnight, on the 10th, the Third Brigade, with Ransom's and Simpson's batteries, under General Jackson, marched to the river, which they reached before daylight, and the Bucktails and Tenth were deployed as skirmishers along the bank of the stream. The enemy were driven from the opposite shore by the fire of the guns and the unerring aim of the sharp-shooters, and the bridges successfully laid.

Four pontoon bridges were laid opposite the city, and two about three miles below, and the possession of both banks secured.

The Battle of Fredericksburg, December 13th, 1862.

Early on the 12th, we marched to the river bank. Portions of our corps had commenced crossing the pontoons, and, about eleven o'clock, the Reserves moved over, and halted in line of battle on the bottom land on the south bank, near the Burnett home. Here we ate our dinner, after which we moved up on the plateau, and the whole army formed in line of battle, presenting one of the grandest sights we ever witnessed. Some slight skirmishing took place on our front and right, the enemy using artillery. This was continued, to some extent, during the balance of the day, but the night passed quietly, we sleeping on our arms undisturbed.

General Lee's army, fully 80,000* strong, was posted on the heavily wooded heights south of the Rappahannock, from a point on the river about a mile above Fredericksburg, near Dr. Taylor's house, opposite the head of Beck's Island, to Captain Hamilton's, some four or five miles below, with his right resting on the bluffs of Massaponax creek. The right wing of his army was commanded by General Jackson; and the left, by General Longstreet.

In the plain between the bluffs of the river and these heights was the Union army, with the grand division of Sumner in and before Fredericksburg on the right; Hooker's grand division in the center, and Franklin's on the left. Our strength was about 100,000 men. The heights receded gradually from the river, and on our left the plateau was two miles broad. The enemy's three hundred guns were all advantageously posted, and swept the whole field, while all our heavy guns were on the bluff north of the river, where they could not render effective service.

Our corps, the First, under General Reynolds, held the extreme left of the line; and the Reserves, the left of the corps. Early on the 13th, the enemy threw out skirmishers on our left, and the Bucktails and Second were sent to resist them. The division moved forward across the Smithfield ravine, and advanced down the river a half mile, when it turned sharp to the right, and, crossing the Bowling Green road, moved to within a thousand yards of the base of the heights, where we lay down on the crest of the field, behind our batteries. Our division formation was the First Brigade in line of battle facing the heights, with the Sixth Regiment deployed as skirmishers; the Second Brigade in rear of the First three hundred paces; the Third Brigade by the flank, its right flank being a few yards to the rear of the First Brigade, having the Ninth Regiment deployed on its flank as skirmishers and flankers. Simpson's battery was posted on the front and left of the Third Brigade, and Cooper's

---

* Greely's American Conflict, II Vol., page 344.

and Ransom's batteries on a knoll on the left and front of the First Brigade.

Hardly had we got into position before Stuart's horse batteries, near the Bowling Green road, opened a brisk fire upon our left and rear. The Third Brigade was faced to the left, thus forming, with the First, two sides of a square. Simpson's, Cooper's, and Ransom's batteries, were brought to bear upon them, and, in conjunction with some of Doubleday's batteries in our rear, in twenty minutes silenced and compelled their withdrawal.* During this duel, two companies of the Third Brigade drove back a party of the enemy's sharp-shooters, who had advanced under cover of the hedges on the Bowling Green road.

During this time, the heavy fog that hung over the field had lifted, and revealed to the enemy our whole line of battle, while theirs was concealed from our view by the forest and nature of the ground. The Reserves, having been selected by General Reynolds, commanding the First Corps, to storm the heights, Amsden's battery, which had just rejoined from detached duty, was posted on the right of Cooper's; and Ransom's battery was moved to the right and front of the First Brigade. The Third Brigade changed front, and formed in line of battle on the left of the First Brigade, its left extending so as to be nearly opposite to the end of the ridge to be assaulted. The formation was barely executed before the insurgent Lieutenant-Colonel Walker opened fire from fourteen pieces of artillery, posted on their extreme right front. Our three batteries of twelve guns immediately turned upon them, and, after half an hour's firing, blew up two of their limbers or caissons, and drove the men from the guns.

---

* Shortly after nine A.M., the partial rising of the mist disclosed a large force moving in line of battle against Jackson. Dense masses appeared in front of A. P. Hill, stretching far up the river in the direction of Fredericksburg. As they advanced, Major Pelham, of Stuart's horse-artillery, who was stationed near the Port Royal road, with one section, opened a rapid and well-directed enfilading fire, which arrested their progress.—*General Lee's official report*, " *Battle-field of Fredericksburg*," (*Insurgent*), p. 28.

Our men immediately sprang to their feet, and, as they were cheering, **Meade** dashed up, and ordered us to charge. The First Brigade advanced over the field, driving the enemy's skirmishers before them until they reached the woods, out of which they drove them to the railroad and the base of the heights, where they were found strongly posted in rifle-pits and behind temporary defences. Right straight over these we went, and drove the enemy out of them and up the heights. The heaviest firing coming from the right, we obliqued over to that side, flanking Archer on the left and Lane on the right, and breaking up and scattering their brigades.* Pressing on, we drove everything before us, until our flags crowned the crest of the hill, when, crossing the road, we reached the open ground, across which we charged with wild yells, striking Gregg's Brigade, scattering it like chaff, and killing its commander.† So sudden and impetuous was the charge, the enemy were taken by utter surprise.‡ We were now beyond their musket stacks, which they had not time to seize, and nearly up to their ambulances and hospital tents. On we dashed upon Thomas' Brigade, and drove it in flight, and then upon the divisions of Early§ and Taliaferro,|| backed as they were by other

---

* Hill, in forming his division to receive the attack, had placed the brigades of Archer, Lane and Pender from right to left in advance, with Gregg in the rear of the interval between Archer and Lane, and Thomas in the rear of that, between Lane and Pender. While Fields' Brigade, under command of Colonel Brockenbrough, was ordered to support the fourteen guns of Lieutenant-Colonel Walker on his right, Meade, continuing to push forward his line, drove back Lane's right and Archer's left, and, wedging his way through, crossed the railroad, and reached the portion of the New Military road held by Gregg's men, capturing, as he did so, several standards and two hundred prisoners.—*Battle-field of Fredericksburg (Insurgent)*, p. 61.

† Brigadier-General Maxcy Gregg, Governor-elect of South Carolina. "Tell the Governor of South Carolina I cheerfully yield my life for the independence of my State," were the dying words of this mistaken but gallant soldier.

‡ So sudden and unlooked for was Meade's success, that General Gregg, mistaking the advancing Federals for a body of Confederates, did what he could to prevent his men from firing, and fell mortally wounded while doing so.—*Battle-field of Fredericksburg (Insurgent)*, p. 16.

§ Jubal A. Early, whom Sheridan rendered famous in the valley.

| At this moment the second line, composed of Early's and **Taliaferro's** divisions, moved forward at a double-quick and turned the tide. Meade's confused line was compelled to draw back. The enemy was closing in on either flank, and the alternative of a rapid retreat only was left him.—*Battle-field of Fredericksburg (Insurgent)*, p. 17.

troops of Jackson. They met us with a counter-charge, the first shock of which we broke and hurled back, but they instantly rallied and poured into us a deadly fire, and, their artillery, galloping up and wheeling into battery, unlimbered and enfiladed us from the right flank. The division of D. H. Hill came upon our left on the double-quick, and opened upon us terrific volleys of musketry, and, all support failing, we were forced to retreat, but not until a desperate hand-to-hand struggle had taken place, and the crown of victory was snatched from Burnside's brow.

The Second Brigade advanced in rear of the First, and, upon reaching the railroad, received so severe a fire on their right flank that the Fourth Regiment, Lieutenant-Colonel Woolworth, halted and formed, and faced to the right, to repel the attack. The Third and Eighth regiments advanced up the heights; and Sickel, having the left and receiving a severe fire upon that flank, inclined in that direction. Onward they gallantly advanced until the crest was reached, when they encountered a heavy force of the enemy masked behind a thick under-growth of pine, who poured into them a heavy volley. Delivering their fire, the Third charged, with yells, and drove them from their cover.

At this moment the First Brigade commenced falling back, followed by the enemy in overwhelming numbers, line after line succeeding each other, as if the whole strength of Jackson's[*] wing was concentrated upon this point. Sickel opened upon the advancing masses, and maintained a desperate struggle with them as long as possible, losing in that short time fearfully, but at last, overpowered, they were driven down the heights and to the railroad, they being the last regiment to leave the crest. Here a part of the regiment was halted and fronted; and General Meade, who was attempting to form a second line in the rear, rode up. A

---

[*] Lieutenant-General (Stonewall) Thomas Jonathan Jackson; killed at Chancellorsville, on the night of May 2d, 1863, by the fire, they say, of his own men. His loss was the greatest ever sustained by either party, in the fall of a single man.

desperate attempt to rally was made. The flags were waved to the front, and M'Candless, Sickels, Talley and others, collected some men and made a stand. Meade, whom it was supposed nothing could excite, having but a division to command, was in for fight in hot earnest, and broke the point of his sword upon a retreating lieutenant's shoulder-blade. But all was useless. The Reserves had done all that mortal men could do, and they felt if they stood they would be simply wiped-out by the fire of an overwhelming foe, without achieving any good. A heavy infantry fire was concentrated upon them, and the enemy's lines came pouring down the heights. Yet the insurgents halted, to dress their lines. Volleys were poured into us, and every musket was vocal, but the little handful was swept from the field, and reaching our batteries, we lay down behind them, the enemy not following beyond the base of the heights. Here we found Collis' Zouaves (One Hundred and Fourteenth Pennsylvania Volunteers), of Birney's division.

The Third Brigade, which held the extreme left of our line, had not advanced over one hundred yards before the batteries on the heights on its left was re-manned, and poured a destructive fire into its ranks. General C. F. Jackson attempted to out-flank the battery on the right, and succeeded so far that some of the regiments advanced across the railroad, and ascended the heights in their front; but here the gallant Jackson fell, and so severe a fire, both of artillery and infantry, was opened upon them, that they were compelled to withdraw.

When General Gibbons, whose division lay on our right, saw us advance, he sent forward his First Brigade. Seeing they faltered, he ordered up the Second Brigade, but such was the severity of the fire they were subject to, he could not get them to charge. He then formed the Third Brigade in column on the right of his line, and they advanced as far as the railroad, the enemy's outer line, at the base of the heights, but not until we had been driven back there, when we all retired together.

THE THIRD RESERVE.

General Meade stated, prior to the assault, that he could take the heights, but could not hold them without support. He sent three different times to General Birney, whose division had replaced the Reserves at the battery from whence we advanced, twice requesting him, and the third time ordering him, to advance to his support. To the requests he answered, he was under the command of General Reynolds, and could not move without his orders. When he received the order, he sent a brigade, under General Ward, who arrived just as we had retired from the woods.

Franklin's left grand division was composed of Reynolds' and W. F. Smith's corps and Bayard's cavalry, and numbered 40,000 men in all. With these, he had twenty-three field batteries of one hundred and sixteen guns, and sixty-one guns on the north bank of the river. On the night of the 12th, he was re-enforced by two divisions of Hooker's center grand division, Kearny's and Hooker's own, under General Stoneman, which raised his force to 55,000 men, or over one-half our entire army. At seven A.M., on the 13th, he received his order for the attack,* and although not as clear, precise and positive as language will allow, was certainly clear enough for him to have supported the attack. With all the force at his disposal, he picked out the weakest division to make the attack, and supported it with only 5,000 men, who rendered very indifferent aid.

---

* "General Hardie will carry this dispatch to you and remain with you during the day. The General commanding directs that you keep your whole command in position for a rapid movement down the old Richmond road, and you will send out at once a division, at least, to pass below Smithfield, to seize, if possible, the heights near Captain Hamilton's, on this side of the Massaponax, taking care to keep it well supported and its line of retreat open. He has ordered another column, of a division or more, to be moved from General Sumner's command up the plank road to its intersection of the telegraph road, where they will divide, with a view of seizing the heights on both of these roads. Holding these heights, with the heights near Captain Hamilton's, will, I hope, compel the enemy to evacuate the whole ridge between these points. He makes these moves by columns, distant from each other, with a view of avoiding the possibility of a collision of our own forces, which might occur in a general movement during the fog. Two of General Hooker's divisions are in your rear at the bridges, and will remain there as supports. Copies of instructions to Generals Sumner and Hooker will be forwarded to you by an Orderly very soon. You will keep your whole command in readiness to move at once, as soon as the fog lifts. The watch-word, which, if possible, should be given to every company, will be 'Scott.'"

General Franklin, in his testimony before "the Committee on the Conduct of the War," states: "I never dreamed that this was considered as a strong attack at all until since the battle took place. At that time I had no idea that it was the main attack, but supposed it was an armed observation to ascertain where the enemy was. That night, General Burnside sent for me, and I supposed his object in sending for me was to tell me what kind of attack was to come off the next day." What General Franklin's idea of a battle was, we do not exactly know, but, at the time, it struck us very forcibly that this partook somewhat of the nature of one.

General Meade, in his official report, says: "While I deeply regret the inability of the division, after having successfully penetrated the enemy's line, to remain and hold what had been secured, at the same time I deem their withdrawal a matter of necessity. With one brigade commander killed, another wounded, nearly half their number *hors du combat*, with regiments separated from brigades, and companies from regiments, and all the confusion and disaster incidental to the advance of an extended line through woods and other obstructions, assailed by a heavy fire, not only of infantry but of artillery, not only in front but on both flanks, the best troops would be justified in withdrawing without loss of honor."

In his testimony before "the Committee on the Conduct of the War," he says: "If we had been supported, there is every reason to believe we would have held the ground. The effect of this would have been to have produced the evacuation of the other line of the enemy's works in rear of Fredericksburg."

General Lee, in his official report, says: "About one P.M., the attack on the right began by a furious cannonade, under cover of which three compact lines of infantry advanced against Hill's front. They were received as before by our batteries, by whose fire they were momentarily checked, but soon recovering, they pressed forward until, coming within range of our infantry, the contest became fierce and bloody. Archer and Lane repulsed those portions of the line immediately in their front, but before the interval between these commands could be closed, the enemy pressed through in overwhelming numbers and turned the left of Archer and the right of Lane. Attacked in front and flank, two regiments of the former and the brigade of the latter, after a brave and obstinate resistance, gave way. Archer held his line with the First Tennessee and the Fifth Alabama Battalion, assisted by the Forty-second Virginia Regiment and the Twenty-second Virginia Battalion, until the arrival of re-enforcements. Thomas came gallantly to the relief of Lane, and, joined by the Seventh and part of the Eighteenth North Carolina Regiments of that brigade, repulsed the column that had broken Lane, and drove it back to the railroad. *In the meantime a large force had penetrated the wood as far as Hill's reserve, and encountered Gregg's brigade.* The attack was so sudden and unexpected that Orr's rifles, mistaking the enemy for our own troops retiring, were thrown into confusion."

In "Burnside, and the Ninth Army Corps," page 220, we find: "By twelve o'clock, most of the dispositions on our side were made, and General Meade began to advance with earnestness and vigor. His division consisted of three brigades, of which the Third was on the left, the First on the right, closely followed by the Second. General Gibbon's division was ordered to hold itself ready as a support. The troops went forward with great spirit and resolution. In handsome style they charged up the road, regardless of a hot fire from the enemy, crossed the railroad, ascended the heights beyond, broke through the enemy's first line, penetrated very nearly the enemy's second line, under General Taliaferro, and gained a position near Captain Hamilton's house, capturing and sending back three hundred prisoners and more. Nothing could be better than this gallant charge.

It was made in the midst of a destructive fire of musketry in front, and a severe enfilading fire of artillery, and for a time carried everything before it. Finding an interval in the enemy's line, between the brigades of Archer and Lane, General Meade took advantage of it, and wedged his advance in, turning the flanks of both brigades and throwing them into confusion. He next struck Gregg's brigade and broke it to pieces, with the loss of its commanding officer. General A. P. Hill's line was then pierced, and General Meade's next duty was to break the line of General Taliaferro. But this was not so easy. For an hour and a half had the gallant little division pushed forward in its successful career. But it was now bearing the brunt of a contest with the entire corps of General Jackson, which had been ordered to meet the audacious attack, and it could not maintain itself without continued support. * * * General Meade had come within a hair's breadth of achieving a great success. His attack had been so vigorous as to be almost a surprise. His troops had come upon the enemy, in some cases, before he had time to take the muskets from the stacks."

When the Second Brigade reached the railroad, the Fourth Regiment faced to the right, the Third and Eighth pushed up the heights, and the Seventh Regiment obliqued to the left, within a hundred yards of a rifle-pit, and opened fire. The Second Regiment, in charging, struck our right of the pit, and a portion of it half wheeling to the left, gained the rear, and opened a deadly fire upon its occupants, by which they were slaughtered like sheep. Many attempted to escape by running the gauntlet, they becoming perfectly wild and blind with the fire, and heeded not the call to halt. With their arms up to shield their heads, they staggered to and fro up the hill within a few yards of our line, meeting certain death. While our men were frightfully slaughtering them, the largest body of the enemy were lying in the pit making no reply, but we were receiving the heavy fire of the Seventh in front of the pit; and our men, in the excitement of the battle, could not see the position of affairs, supposing the fire came from the enemy. It was, therefore, almost impossible to stop the fire of our men. At length an officer of the Second, sheathing his sword, with cap in hand, advanced between the two lines, and asked the insurgents if they "wished to fight or surrender." "We will surrender if you will allow us," was the reply. The officer not wishing to send any of our men to the rear with them, and to prevent treachery, took several of them with him, and, advancing in front of the pit, succeeded in stopping the fire of the Seventh, upon which he got out the rest, numbering over three hundred, and sent them to the Seventh. No sooner had he got clear of the prisoners than he received thirteen bullet holes through his clothes, from a party who had concealed themselves, two of whom were captured and shot down. The rifle-pit was choked with the dead and wounded, and the rear of it was literally covered with them, the Second killing, wounding and capturing near three times their own number. They were the Nineteenth Georgia Infantry. The Seventh received the credit of taking the rifle-pit and the prisoners, and capturing the standard, although it was wrenched from the hands of its bearer by an officer of the Second.* The flag was given to Charles Upjohn, who, being afterwards wounded, gave it to a corporal of the Seventh, who received a medal from the War Department.

The conflict with the Reserves was the only fighting done by Jackson's troops during the day, except the brief strug-

---

*General Meade, in his official report, gives the Seventh the credit of this affair. He based his report upon those of the brigade commanders, who were dependent on the regimental commanders, who, in turn, made up their reports from those of the company commanders. The General could not intentionally wrong a regiment or man of his command. The author, that justice might be done to his regiment, in Prof. Bates' State History of the Pennsylvania Volunteers, addressed a letter to the General upon the subject. He replied that he believed the statement, substantially the same as the above, to be correct, and expressed his sincere regret that he was misinformed at the time. In justice to the Seventh, it should be stated they probably were not aware the Second had taken the pit or the prisoners, as the Second, upon the surrender, immediately pushed up the heights.

gle with Gibbons, whose loss was heaviest before delivering fire. Jackson officially gives his total loss at 3,415, almost as many as the Reserves took into the action. Our loss was 1,842, or nearly one-half our men.

While these operations were transpiring on the extreme left, the center was quiet, and the right hotly engaged. The enemy's works immediately in the rear of Fredericksburg consisted of three tiers, the first an embankment four feet high, faced with stone, against which our artillery made no impression. Braver men never lived than those who stormed Marye's Heights that day, but all their valor availed naught. With the lifting fog Couch's division moved from the city and pressed up the heights, pierced and plowed through by the enemy's batteries, and when they reached the wall the insurgent infantry rose and mowed them down like grass. It was followed by French's and Hancock's* corps, who dashed themselves against those impregnable heights; and when the remnant of one brigade or division fell back, it was succeeded by others, each in its turn to be exposed to the useless slaughter. At two P.M., General Hooker was ordered to the assault, and after trying to dissuade Burnside from making it, he brought all his batteries to play upon one point, to breach the wall. He continued the fire until sunset, without producing any apparent effect. Humphrey's † division was now formed in column of assault, and with empty muskets they dashed up the heights. The head of the column arrived within fifteen or twenty yards of the wall, when Barksdale's Brigade poured into their faces the deadliest of volleys, and they were hurled back as quickly as they advanced, leaving 1,760 out of 4,000 upon the hill-side, now slippery with gore. The whole movement did not occupy fifteen minutes, and it is doubtful if they killed a man.

---

*In this charge Colonel Dennis Heenan, Lieutenant-Colonel A. St. Clair Mulholland, and Major George H. Bardwell, One Hundred and Sixteenth Pennsylvania Volunteers, were severely wounded.

† Major-General Andrew A. Humphrey, Pa. Chief of Engineers, U. S. A.

In addition to the musket fire the men were exposed to, the crests of the surrounding hills formed almost a semicircle, and these were filled with artillery, and the focus was the assaulting column, and it was within good canister range. Against this impregnable point Burnside insisted upon hurling his columns, in useless slaughter, all day long, and at the sacrifice of 10,000 brave and true men. As if by some strange infatuation, his whole energy and aim appeared to be centered here, when victory was within his grasp on the left.

Thus terminated the fatal day of Fredericksburg. The loss in the Third was heavy,* and among the killed was Lieutenant Jacob V. Shillings, a brave and promising officer; and among the wounded was Captain William Brian, a most valuable officer, whose leg was amputated while in the hands of the enemy; and Lieutenant Michael Walters, who lost a foot. Our loss that day was 1,152 killed, 9,101 wounded, and 3,234 missing, making a total of 13,487. It may possibly have reached, but certainly did not exceed, 15,000. To show the reliance that can be placed in the insurgent statements, it is only necessary to say that Lee reported his loss at the preposterous low number of 1,800 killed and wounded. His actual loss, as embodied in the detailed reports of Jackson and Longstreet, was over 5,000,† and probably reached 7,000.‡

Our division remained behind the batteries until near sunset, when we marched to the ground occupied the night before, where we slept on our arms. Late in the afternoon,

*See Appendix A.

	Killed.	Wounded.	Missing.	Total.
† Jackson's right wing	344	2,545	526	3,415
Longstreet's left wing	251	1,516	127	1,894
Total	595	4,061	653	5,309

‡ General Lee, on the 21st of December, thus congratulates his army: "The immense army of the enemy completed its preparations for the attack without interruption, and gave battle in its own time, and *on ground of its own selection*. It was encountered by *less than twenty thousand* of this brave army; and its columns, crushed and broken, hurled back at every point, with such fearful slaughter that escape from entire destruction became the boast of those who had advanced in full confidence of victory."

the enemy showed some indications of attacking us, but they were soon abandoned.*

Early in this battle Colonel Sinclair, commanding the First Brigade, was severely wounded, and the command devolved upon Colonel M'Candless. Colonel Sickel's coat was perforated by three bullets, and his field-glass shattered. In our retreat an officer saw a quail, so terrified by fright that he knocked it over with his sword.

Incredible as it may appear, after all the useless and horrible carnage, the next morning General Burnside formed a column of attack, to again make the insane attempt to storm Marye's Hill. It was only through the forcible remonstrance of Sumner that he was induced to abandon the idea, and he actually felt himself bound to excuse himself before the Committee on the Conduct of the War, for not making it.

During the day there was considerable artillery and infantry skirmishing, and we were several times called into line to meet the enemy. It being Sunday, about two o'clock the excellent and beloved Chaplain of the Third, the Rev. Mr. Pomeroy, determined to hold religious worship. Surrounded by a few friends, with uncovered heads they raised their voices in a sweet hymn as they advanced in front of the line to a clear space. Soon around them was collected a large concourse of attentive listeners. He spoke of the justness and righteousness of the cause we were engaged in,

---

* Jackson, in his official report, with great candor says: "Repulsed on the right and left, the enemy soon after re-formed his lines, and gave some indications of a purpose to renew the attack. I waited some time to receive it; but he making no forward movement, I determined it prudent to do so myself. The artillery of the enemy was so judiciously posted as to make an advance of our troops across the plain very hazardous, yet it was so promising of good results, if successfully executed, as to induce me to make preparations for the attempt. In order to guard against disaster, the infantry was to be preceded by artillery, and the movement postponed until late in the evening; so that if compelled to retire, it would be under the cover of night. Owing to unexpected delay, the movement could not be got ready till late in the evening. The first gun had hardly moved forward from the woods a hundred yards, when the enemy's artillery re-opened, and so completely swept our front as to satisfy me that the proposed movement should be abandoned." From this, probably, arose Pollard's ridiculous story of Jackson's advising a night attack with his men stripped naked and armed with bowie-knives. Where would they have got the knives from?

of the duty of all citizens to defend their country, as the child defends its mother, of courage in battle, of mercy to the wounded, of fortitude in suffering, of love and kindness to comrades. But he exhorted them, above all precious gifts and treasures, to seek the blood of Jesus for salvation. When he spoke of our fallen comrades, of the gloom it would cast over the cottage homes of Pennsylvania, he moved all hearts to sadness, and when he raised his eyes to heaven in humble prayer, heeding not the exploding shells of the foe, we thought what entire confidence that pure man placed in the protection of our God. While thus engaged in worship, the call to arms was sounded. The men took their place, and the beloved Chaplain walked down the line with cheerful words and looks for all, appearing like a pleasant gentleman with his friends.

Sunday, with its alarms, wore away, and Monday morning came, the two armies confronting each other. During the day a flag of truce was agreed upon, to bring off the wounded and bury the dead. A detail of twenty-five men was made from each regiment for the purpose. We found our dead stripped, and even the wounded were robbed of their clothes. What the poor fellows' sufferings were, during those December nights, God only knows! But few were left alive. The insurgents, ashamed of their cruelty, sought to excuse themselves by stating it was the reiterated order of their officers. The lines were established near the base of the heights, and the enemy brought our men to us. The wounded were sent to the rear, and the dead properly buried. Among the latter was young Lieutenant Dehou, an Aid-de-Camp to General Meade, who fell while carrying an order to General Jackson. As he lay upon the ground, his marble-like form looked like a fine piece of sculpture, and the rich, golden curls clustered around his forehead and partly concealed his handsome features. He was a brave and gallant youth, and noted for his manly virtues.

That night, the 15th, we got under arms soon after dark, and leaving our camp-fires brightly burning, moved slowly and noiselessly towards the river, which we crossed on muffled pontoons, and moved back about a mile. The crossing on the right was soon after commenced, and by morning the whole army was over, without the loss of a man or gun.

After this disaster, it was useless to continue General Burnside in command of the army. But, though he sadly erred in judgment, his subsequent conduct and bearing showed him possessed of noble qualities. Although he felt that Franklin had not done his duty, he excused others and took the blame on himself. Thus he wrote to General Halleck: "The fact that I decided to move from Warrenton on to this line rather against the opinion of the President, Secretary of War, and yourself, and that you have left the whole movement in my hands, without giving me orders, makes me the more responsible."* The chief cause of the failure was the delay of over three weeks in the arrival of the pontoons after Sumner reached Falmouth, enabling the enemy to concentrate his forces there, and resist our seizure of the heights.

---

* Official Report, December 19th.

CHAPTER XV.

MARCH TO WHITE OAK CHURCH — WINTER QUARTERS — GENERAL MEADE PROMOTED — SICKEL SUCCEEDS HIM — BURNSIDE'S MUD EXPEDITION — HOOKER SUPERSEDES BURNSIDE — BELL PLAIN — ALEXANDRIA — SICKEL IN COMMAND OF THE DEFENCES — THE FIRST AND THIRD BRIGADES TO GETTYSBURG — DETAILS — CAPTAIN FISHER'S ESCAPE FROM LIBBY — TWENTY ONE PATRIOTS — NEW FLAGS — RESIGNATIONS AND PROMOTIONS.

WE REMAINED in our position until the 18th, when we marched about five miles, and bivouacked in an open field. The next morning we moved a mile, and formed an encampment in a thick pine forest on a hill-side, near White Oak Church. That night the Third went on picket; and the thermometer indicating seven above zero, they suffered much. Here we made preparations to go into winter quarters. Some of the men dug pits, about two feet deep, which they logged up above ground, and stretched their shelter tents over. Comfortable fire-places and chimneys were built, and, with abundance of dry leaves to sleep upon, they got along quite comfortably. Two or four generally bunked together; and by splicing blankets, and lying spoon-fashion, slept quite warm.

General Meade having been assigned to the command of the Fifth Army Corps, he issued the following farewell to our division:

"HEADQUARTERS THIRD DIVISION,
December 25th, 1862.

"*General Order No. 101.*

"In announcing the above order, which separates the commanding general from the division, he takes occasion to express to the officers and men that, notwithstanding his just pride at being promoted to a higher command, he experiences a deep feeling of regret at parting from them with whom he has so long associated, and to whose services he here acknowledges his indebtedness for whatever of reputation he may have acquired.

"The commanding general will never cease to remember that he belonged to the Reserve Corps; he will watch with eagerness for the deeds of fame which he feels sure they will enact under the command of his successors, and though sadly reduced in numbers from the casualties of battle, yet he knows the Reserves will always be ready and prompt to uphold the honor and glory of their State.

"By command of   MAJOR-GENERAL MEADE.
"(Signed)   EDWARD C. BAIRD, A. A. G."

The command of the Reserves devolved upon Colonel Sickel, in whom General Meade had always shown great confidence. The Colonel retained Captain Baird as Assistant Adjutant-General, and appointed Adjutant Harry S. Jones, Aid-de-Camp. Captain Jacob Lenhart assumed command of the regiment, and Lieutenant George M. Rohne was appointed Acting Adjutant. While we lay here, we experienced constant heavy rain and snow storms, that turned our encampment into a vast mud-puddle, and rendered the roads almost impassable. Almost daily, details were made from the regiments to corduroy the roads; and we passed our time about as disagreeably as possible.

General Burnside was not disposed to give up the campaign yet, and, on the 26th, ordered three days' cooked rations and sixty rounds of cartridges to be issued to each man, and the army held in readiness to move at a moment's notice. The intention was to make a feint above Fredericksburg, and cross some six miles below; while General Pleasanton, with 2,500 cavalry and a battery of horse artillery, was to cross at Kelly's Ford, and to raid across the Virginia Central, the Lynchburg and Weldon railroads, blow up the locks of the James River canal, and to report to General Peck, at Suffolk, from whence they were to be transferred back to Acquia Creek by steamboats. Several other minor expeditions were to be sent out, to distract the enemy's attention. On the 30th, orders were issued for the army to move, but the President arrested it by telegram, as clandestine representations had been made to him by officers, that, in the existing temper of the army, it would inevitably end in disaster.

Orders to hold ourselves in readiness to move were, however, repeatedly renewed up to January 20th, 1863, when, at noon, we broke camp, and marched up the river ten miles, where we halted at dark, and bivouacked in a thick scrub-oak woods. About four o'clock it commenced raining, and continued without intermission all night, and by the next morning the roads and fields were impassable. It was the most severe and trying storm ever experienced in that region by us. About daylight, however, we got under way, and marched about three miles, to Banks' Ford, where we halted. Here the army was brought to a stand, and literally stuck in the mud. The snow, the driving sleet, the pouring rain, and a general breaking up of the roads, hitherto hardly frozen, rendered locomotion impossible. The pontoon trains could not move. The supply trains were in the rear, unable to come up, and twenty-eight horses stalled with a gun. It was next to impossible to get our camp-fires lighted, and the cold rain descended in torrents all day. The enemy, who had been informed of our intended movement, and had seen Sumner's trains moving on the crest of the hills, were on the opposite side of the river, ready to receive us, and offered to send over a brigade to help lay our pontoons.

We remained here hopelessly floundering in the mud until the morning of the 23d, when, seeing the utter impossibility of our undertaking, we were ordered to retrace our steps back to our old camp, which we reached late in the afternoon. Sickel sent out all the ambulances, and brought in twenty loads of prostrated men. During this movement, not a particle of forage was furnished for the field and staff horses.

General Burnside having discovered, as he believed, the officers who had interfered with his plans by disheartening communications to Washington, prepared a general order dismissing Major-General Hooker and Brigadier-Generals W. T. H. Brooks and John Newton, and relieving from duty, with his command, Major-Generals W. B. Franklin and W. F. Smith, and Brigadier-Generals John Cochrane* and Edward Ferrero, and Lieutenant-Colonel J. H. Taylor. He, however, on the advice of a friend, submitted the order to the President, who decided, instead of approving the order, to relieve General Burnside. On the 28th of January, 1863, General Joseph Hooker assumed command of the army. General Sumner,† at his own request, was also relieved of his command.

The Reserves, by this time, had become so much reduced by hard fighting, that earnest efforts were made by Governor Curtin, Generals Meade, Reynolds, and others, to secure their return to Pennsylvania, in a body, with a view to recruiting their ranks. This purpose was not effected; but, about dark on the 5th of February, Colonel Sickel received a telegram from General Doubleday, who, for a short time, commanded the division, stating that in consideration of the arduous and gallant services of the Reserves, they were to be withdrawn to Washington, to rest and recruit. The news was sent to each regiment, and created the liveliest joy. In despite of the cold rain the camp-fires were soon brightly burning, around which the boys gathered and talked of the good times coming until late at night. The next morning, before reveille beat, all were up, and soon after breakfast everything was packed ready to move. About three that afternoon the order to march came. Falling in, and bidding farewell to our old camp, and the gallant One Hundred and Twenty-first and One Hundred and

---

* Brigadier-General John Cochrane. Resigned February 25th, 1863.

† Brevet Major-General Edwin V. Sumner, U. S. A. (Bull Sumner). Died at Syracuse, N. Y., March 21st, 1863.

Forty-second Pennsylvania Volunteers, who had been temporarily attached to our division before the last battle, we took up our march for Bell Plain. Although the distance was not four miles, on account of the bad roads we did not reach there until after dark, but the boys plunged through the mud with light hearts, for in every breast was the secret hope of seeing home for a little while. The First Brigade, Colonel M'Candless, embarked on transports during the night; the Second, Colonel Bolinger, and the Third, Colonel Fisher, embarked the next morning, and all arrived at Alexandria the same day, where Colonel Sickel received orders to encamp the division at Upton's Hill. The Reserves were now in the defences of Washington, and attached to the Twenty-second Army Corps. The presence of Moseby's guerillas on the line of the railroad, and in front of Alexandria, caused the First Brigade, under Colonel M'Candless, to be sent to the neighborhood of Fairfax Court House on the 12th; and soon after, the Second Brigade was moved to Alexandria, and Colonel Sickel placed in command of the defences of the city. The Twenty-third Maine, One Hundred and Fifty-third New York, and the First District Columbia Volunteers, were added to his command. Adjutant Harry S. Jones was appointed Acting Assistant Adjutant-General, until the return of Captain Baird, when he was appointed Aid-de-Camp. Lieutenant Eberhart, of the Eighth Reserves, was appointed Acting Assistant Commissary of Subsistence, and Private Isaac G. Buck, Company K, was detailed as Orderly. Captain Robert Johnston was detailed to the Provost Marshal's office. Lieutenants Edwin A. Glenn, George M. Rohne and Albert P. Moulton served as Acting Adjutants of the Third, at different times, until the return of Adjutant Jones to the regiment. Lieutenant F. G. Nicholson was detailed an Aid-de-Camp to General Slough, Military Governor of Alexandria; and Private Joseph F. Hoover, Company B, as Orderly.

The duties of the men while here were not of the exciting and stirring nature of the field, but much more arduous. The Third was daily required to furnish a picket, grand, reservoir, headquarters and camp guard, of one hundred and twenty-five men, besides officers; and, every other day, two companies to lie behind the batteries.

Soon after the battle of Chancellorsville took place, and Lee showed signs of moving into Pennsylvania, fears were entertained of an insurgent raid on Alexandria; and a new line of earthworks, closely skirting the city, was thrown up, double rows of stockades erected, and the camp of the Third moved to within a mile of it. Colonel Sickel established his headquarters at the Colross House. The signal of alarm by the pickets was four muskets fired in rapid succession, to be repeated by the interior guards, upon which all the roads were to be obstructed with wagons, etc. The troops were under arms a number of times, but no enemy appeared. The Third was detailed, upon several occasions, as a guard to the railroad trains carrying forage to Hooker's army, they going as far as Warrenton Junction.

When it was ascertained the enemy were moving north, strenuous efforts were made to have the Reserves attached to the Army of the Potomac, petitions to that effect being sent to the authorities at Washington and Harrisburg, and a number of officers detailed to urge the matter. Representation was made of the ardent anxiety of the officers and men to march to the defence of the state that sent them forth, and was the home of all they loved and held dear; but the authorities at Washington were loath to spare them from the defence of the Capital. In the meantime, Generals Meade and Reynolds both had applied to the War Department to have us attached to their corps. Reynolds was offered, in lieu, a full division, which he declined. General Meade, however, succeeded in having the First Brigade, Colonel M'Candless, and the Third, Colonel Fisher, assigned to him, under the command of General S. W.

Crawford, but, the day they arrived, he assumed the command of the army, he being its last and successful commander.

This was a great disappointment to the Second Brigade, who, on the 25th of June, with envious hearts, bid farewell to the gallant Third, as it marched to the post of honor.

Soon after, Captain Washington Richards, F; Lieutenants Albert Briner, D, and William M'Carty, H; Sergeants Lewis Griffith, A; Henry C. Tripp, B; and Charles W. Stout, E; Corporals S. C. Moorhead, I, and James Brooke, K; and Private Charles Y. Clark, C, were detailed to proceed to Philadelphia after recruits. Soon after their return, Captain Richards, one of the most loved and respected officers of the regiment, was transferred to the Veteran Reserve Corps, his failing health not permitting him to continue longer in the field. About the same time, Captains William Brian and George C. Davenport, and Lieutenant Michael Walters, all brave and efficient officers, were transferred to the same corps, they being incapacitated from serving in the field from wounds received in battle.

Captain Benjamin F. Fisher, Company H, who was detailed on Signal duty with the Army of the Potomac, left the headquarters of the same, then near Fairfax Court House, on the 17th of June, to report to General Pleasanton, commanding the cavalry near Aldie. The General was directed to furnish him with an escort, to make a reconnaissance to the Blue Ridge, to ascertain the location of Lee's forces, but while *en-route* for Aldie he was captured by a band of Moseby's men, and sent to Libby Prison. After being in this loathsome den for several months, Colonel Ross, of Pennsylvania, also a prisoner, organized a working party to dig themselves out. After many days of anxious labor, they completed a tunnel, some fifty feet long, from the cellar of the prison, under an open lot to the yard of an adjoining building. The work was completed on the 9th of February, and the prisoners emerged from the yard in squads of two and three, and thence made their escape from the insurgent Capital. The exodus was commenced about nine o'clock in the evening, and continued until three o'clock the next morning.

Captain Fisher and a companion came out about ten o'clock, and proceeding northward, crossed the Chickahominy at Meadow Bridge, above Mechanicsville, and got several miles beyond the river before daylight. Through the day they concealed themselves in a heavy thicket, and at dark resumed their journey, and traveled all night, avoiding the roads, and again concealing themselves in the woods and thickets during the day. When near White House, a violent snow-storm set in, and compelled them to lie for two days and a night in a laurel thicket. Being surrounded now by insurgent scouts, who were searching every woods and swamp for them, their progress was slow and very cautious, lest they should be tracked; and, on the night of the 18th, they encountered a party of the enemy, who pursued and fired upon them. The captain's companion was captured, but he succeeded in making his escape; and, after twelve days and nights of exposure and privation, reached, in safety, Williamsburg, where he and others were rescued by the cavalry sent out by General Butler. The captain resumed his place on the staff of the army under General Meade, and was subsequently promoted Colonel, and Chief Signal Officer, U. S. A.

While the Third lay here, twenty-one patriotic young men of Bucks county arrived in camp, to enlist in the regiment, they having paid their own expenses from home, and brought with them, as a present to the boys, a large supply of delicacies, sent by their good neighbors.

On the 16th of December, Governor Curtin sent Colonel R. B. Roberts, of his staff, to present to each of the regiments of the brigade a new flag, the old ones being so torn and damaged by the enemy's balls that it was necessary to carry them with the covers on, except in battle. The presentation took place in the afternoon, with appropriate ceremonies. The following resignations and promotions took place in the regiment while we lay here:

Lieutenant Strickland Yardley, Regimental Quartermaster, resigned, he having been promoted Captain and Assistant Quartermaster, United States Volunteers.

Quartermaster-Sergeant Levi S. Boyer was promoted Lieutenant and Quartermaster.

Assistant Surgeons Samuel L. Orr and George J. Rice, resigned.

Doctors Stanton A. Welch, of Wayne county, and John P. Birchfield, of Centre county, were appointed Assistant Surgeons.

Captain Hugh Harkins, Company G, and Lieutenant George M. Rohne, Company B, resigned.

Second Lieutenant Amos W. Seitzinger, Company A, promoted First Lieutenant.

First Sergeant Daniel Setley, Company A, promoted Second Lieutenant.

First Sergeant Warren G. Moore, Company B, promoted Captain.

Second Lieutenant Henry W. Sutton, Company C, promoted Captain.

Sergeant Zeaman Jones, Company C, promoted Second Lieutenant.

Second Lieutenant Albert Briner, Company D, promoted First Lieutenant.

Sergeant George B. Davis, Company D, promoted Second Lieutenant.

First Lieutenant Albert P. Moulton, Company F, promoted Captain.

Second Lieutenant Henry S. Moulton, Company F, promoted First Lieutenant.

Sergeant Benjamin D. Hemming, Company F, promoted Second Lieutenant.

First Lieutenant John Stanton, Company G, promoted Captain.

Second Lieutenant Francis E. Harrison, Company G, promoted First Lieutenant.

First Lieutenant David Wonderly, Company K, promoted Captain.

Second Lieutenant Thomas C. Spackman, Company K, promoted First Lieutenant.

Sergeant John M. James, Company K, promoted Second Lieutenant.

Lieutenant David W. Donaghy, Company K, was forced to resign on account of his declining health.

Sergeant Aaron W. Buckman, Company C, discharged to receive promotion in the United States colored troops.

Private Morgan Kupp, Company D, was discharged to receive the appointment of Lieutenant and Quartermaster of the One Hundred and Sixty-seventh Pennsylvania Volunteers.

CHAPTER XVI.

1863-64 — Move to Martinsburg — New Creek — After Rosser — Back to Martinsburg — After Gilmore — To Vanclevesville — Harpers Ferry — To Grafton — Webster — Fence Rails — Accident to Major Briner — Arrival of Sickel — To Parkersburg — Down the Ohio and Up the Kanawha — Brownstown.

THE Second Brigade remained here in discharge of the various duties pertaining to the department, without anything of importance occuring until January, 1864. On the 4th of that month, Colonel Sickel received orders to detach the Third, Major Briner, and the Fourth, Lieutenant-Colonel T. F. B. Tapper, the whole under command of Colonel Woolworth, of the Fourth, to West Virginia. Soon after midnight of the next day they left camp, marched into Washington, were loaded into box-cars, and proceeded by the Baltimore and Ohio railroad to Martinsburg, where they arrived on the morning of the 7th. On their route the cars were pushed forward at their utmost speed. The 6th and 7th being the coldest days of the winter, the men suffered terribly from the sharp winter blasts as they were hauled through the gaps and ravines of this mountainous district.

At Martinsburg they found General Averill's cavalry. His command had just returned from a raid upon Salem, an important point on the Virginia and Tennessee railroad, where they destroyed a great quantity of commissary stores which the enemy had collected. On their return they were pursued by a heavy force of insurgents. It was thought that the enemy designed pushing forward to the Baltimore and Ohio railroad, and hence the speedy forwarding of the Reserve regiments to the rescue. Such not proving to be the case, there was no active work for them, and, until the

28th of January, they were engaged in picketing the roads in the vicinity.

On that day the detachment took transportation on cars westward, and, after narrowly escaping being precipitated down a precipice by the cars running off the track, they halted at New Creek, a station in a wild, mountainous district, about one hundred miles west from Martinsburg. Here they reported to Colonel Mulligan,* the commander of the post. They encamped on a flat on the north branch of the Potomac. Soon after dark on the 31st, in the midst of a violent storm, they were ordered to report at the commander's headquarters, with two days' cooked rations. News had been received that the enemy, under General Rosser, who was sent over into West Virginia from the valley, by General Early, had captured a train of wagons moving from New Creek to Petersburg, in Hardy county, a point some forty miles south, an extreme out-post, garrisoned by a small Union force. Under the command of Colonel Mulligan, the Third and Fourth, accompanied by several small squads of cavalry and infantry, commenced the night pursuit. They were marched and counter-marched for six successive days and nights without shelter, over muddy and rocky roads, compelled to ford swollen mountain streams, scour the sides of mountains, penetrate gaps on either side of the narrow valley through which they marched, for the double purpose of finding the enemy and guarding against surprise.

Within five miles of Moorefield, they formed a junction with Averill's cavalry, which had marched from Martinsburg, through Winchester and Romney. The enemy moved with rapidity, and succeeded in escaping with 270 prisoners, 93 six-mule wagons, heavily laden,† and 1,200 cattle and 500

---

* Colonel James A. Mulligan, who defended Lexington, Mo., in 1861. Subsequently promoted a Brigadier-General, and killed near Martinsburg, Va., July 24th, 1864.

† Greeley's American Conflict, II Vol., p. 599.

sheep, stolen from the people of Hardy and Hampshire counties. Completely exhausted from constant marching, want of sleep and exposure, the command returned on the evening of Februrary 26th to their tents, left standing on the banks of the upper Potomac.

On the 10th of February, the Third Reserve was sent east by railroad to Martinsburg, and the Fourth followed two or three days later. On the night of February 11th, a force of insurgent brigands, under the command of the "chivalrous" Harry Gilmore, of Baltimore, threw a passenger train off the track eight miles east of Martinsburg, and robbed the male passengers of their watches, pocket-books and overcoats, and the ladies of their ear-rings, furs and shawls, etc.

Early on the morning of the 12th, Colonel R. S. Rogers, who had command of the post, put the Third Reserve, Eighteenth Connecticut, One Hundred and Twenty-third Ohio and two batteries in motion towards Winchester. Several regiments of cavalry preceded the infantry and artillery. Winchester was reached in the afternoon, but the brigands had fled, after presenting to their lady friends a rich supply of ladies' outer clothing. On the following day Colonel Rogers returned to Martinsburg with his command.

On the 24th of February, the Third marched from Martinsburg to Vanclevesville, five miles east of Martinsburg, on the Baltimore and Ohio railroad; and the Fourth to Kearneysville, nine miles east, on the same road. From these two points the regiments performed picket duty on the railroad, and one company of the Third garrisoned the Block House near the bridge, relieving a detachment of the One Hundred and Sixteenth Ohio Volunteers. On the 7th of March, Colonel Rogers was relieved of the command of the Third Brigade by Colonel Woolworth. It consisted at this time of the Third and Fourth Reserves, Eighteenth

Connecticut, Thirty-fourth Massachusetts, One Hundred and Twenty-third and One Hundred and Sixteenth Ohio, and Battery B, Fifth United States Artillery. Lieutenant George B. Davis, Company D, was appointed Assistant Aid-de-Camp to the Colonel. Privates Adam Schanck, Company G, and Roland G. Scarlet, Company D, were detailed as clerks; and Charles Boyer, Company D, as Orderly at Brigade Headquarters. Private John R. Yeich, Company A, was detailed as Clerk at Brigade Provost Marshal.

On the 29th of March, the Third was moved by rail to Harpers Ferry, whither the Fourth had preceded it two days. The detachment performed picket duty while here, from the Potomac to the Shenandoah rivers, the line forming one side of a triangle. All baggage that could possibly be dispensed with was here stored. Each man was ordered to have a blanket, an overcoat and an extra pair of shoes, two hundred rounds of ammunition, and five days' short rations in his haversack. Thus deprived of many camp comforts, and having received additional burdens, the Reserves were, on the 3d of April, again sent westward, across the Alleghenies to Grafton, two hundred miles from Harpers Ferry; and thence, five miles on the South Branch road leading to Parkersburg, to Webster. Several loyal Virginia regiments had preceded the Reserves to this point, and two batteries followed. Averill's cavalry went into camp several miles further north. Wagons, ambulances and pontoon bridges were collected at Webster. The design of the expedition, which was to start from this point, was to advance upon the Virginia and Tennessee railroad, by marching through Barbour and Randolph counties, and thence directly south through the mountainous district, striking it near the line of Botetourt and Roanoke counties. The continuous rains, however, made the roads impassable; in addition to this, the enemy, having some knowledge of the design and route, had dug down the mountain road in several narrow passes, and felled trees over other portions. It was therefore concluded to abandon the enterprise.

While here an order was issued by General E. O. C. Ord * ("Old Alphabet"), forbidding the burning of fence-rails. The boys, who declared they had lived upon fence-rails for two years, and that the integrity of the Constitution and the perpetuation of the Union depended upon fence-rails, looked upon this order as striking an insidious blow at the cause they fought for. However, as there was plenty of fine standing timber near by, and many of them were expert axmen, they strove to avert the impending calamity by getting up chopping matches; at which the monarchs of the forests were hewed down in an incredible short time. These trunks, split up, made excellent fire-wood, but soon an order was issued forbidding the cutting of more trees until the tops were burnt up. The boys, misunderstanding the spirit of this order, as they sometimes were apt to, immediately set fire to the tops, and they were soon burnt up. Then another order came, threatening to cut off the supply of firewood entirely. This put a grave aspect upon the matter, and seemed to confirm their fearful suspicion. A committee was at once appointed, composed of an equal number of

---

*General Ord was a native of Cumberland, Md., where he was born in 1818, and graduated at West Point in 1839. He served in the Seminole War in 1839-42 and was in the coast survey in 1845-46. Previous to the outbreak of the Rebellion he was engaged for several years in service in California and the Territories. On September 14th, 1861, he was made brigadier-general of volunteers, and commanded a brigade in the Pennsylvania Reserves under General M'Call. He was promoted to a major-generalship in May, 1862, and was placed in command of Corinth, and afterwards of the Second Division of the District of Western Tennesee. At the siege of Vicksburg h e commanded the Thirteenth Corps, and in the operations before Richmond, from July 21st to September 30th, 1864, the Eighteenth Corps. From January to June he was in command of the Department of Virginia, and took part in the siege of Petersburg and the capture of Lee. General Ord was twice wounded at the battle of Hatchie, October 5th, 1862, and in the capture of Fort Harrison. Since the close of the war General Ord has commanded the Departments of California, the Platte and Texas, and in 1866 was made brigadier-general in the regular army. In January, 1881, he was placed on the retired list, and since then has lived most of the time with his son-in-law, General Trevino, formerly the Mexican minister of war. While on his way home from Vera Cruz he was taken with yellow fever, and upon arriving at Havana, was removed to the shore, where he died, July 22d, 1883.

acting assistant corporals and brevet cooks, to investigate the loyalty or sanity of the General, but, before submitting their elaborate report, a ration of whiskey was issued to the men, which seemed to throw new light upon the subject, and the General was at once pronounced "sane," and all difficulties were amicably settled.

While here, the headquarters tent took fire, and Major William Briner so severely injured his right hand in extinguishing it, that he was sent to the hospital in Grafton. He parted from the regiment with much regret, and was succeeded in the command by Captain Jacob Lenhart.

General Grant's comprehensive plan of campaign against Richmond embraced a coöperative movement up the Shenandoah, under General Sigel, aiming at the insurgent resources in the vicinity of Staunton and Lynchburg; and, up the Kanawha, by General George Crook, aiming at Dublin and the lead mines near Wytheville, on the Virginia and Tennessee railroad, cutting the main artery which furnished supplies to Lee's army. Colonel Sickel, who had remained in command of the defences of Alexandria, was ordered, on the 8th of April, by General Grant, to forward the Seventh and the Eighth Reserves to the Army of the Potomac, for service with the balance of the division under General Crawford, and to report in person for duty to General Crook. The force that had been collected about Webster was divided, and sent east and west. Several Virginia regiments were transported to Martinsburg, to join the command of General Sigel.

On the morning of the 22d of April, Colonel Sickel and staff arrived in camp, he receiving a hearty welcome from the officers and men. The next day he moved, with his command, by rail, westward to Parkersburg, at the confluence of the Ohio and Little Kanawha rivers. Here they were transferred to steamboats, and went down the Ohio to the mouth of the Great Kanawha, thence up that river to

Brownstown, ten miles above Charlestown.* This was the only instance during their term of service that the regiments of the Reserve Corps were permanently separated. Heretofore, through all their campaigns and battles, they had marched and fought side by side, and although Sickel was given an important command, it was with regret he separated from the grand old division.

---

* General Wise, in 1861, raised at this place, by conscription, a brigade of 2,500 infantry, 700 cavalry, and three batteries of artillery.—*The Lost Cause, page* 169.

Early in February, General E. P. Scammon, commanding at Charlestown, was surprised and captured, with the steamboat "Levi," on the Kanawha, by Lieutenant Verdigan, of Colonel Ferguson's insurgent guerrillas. Verdigan, with ten men, captured the General, four other officers, and twenty-five privates, besides the steamboat and her crew; throwing overboard the captured arms as fast as he could seize them, so as to preclude the danger of a rescue. Scammon and his two aids were sent prisoners to Richmond; the residue paroled.

CHAPTER XVII.

1864 — GENERAL CROOK'S EXPEDITION — ITS STRENGTH — SICKEL COMMANDS THE THIRD BRIGADE — HIS STAFF — THE MARCH — EX-PRESIDENT HAYES — GREAT FALLS — COTTON MOUNTAIN — FAYETTE COURT HOUSE — AVERILL DETACHED — WILD AND RUGGED COUNTRY — THE MOUNTAINEERS — RALEIGH COURT HOUSE — ROSECRANS' TRAIN — THE MOUNTAINS FIRED — SKIRMISH AT PRINCETON COURT HOUSE — INSURGENTS' WORKS — SKIRMISH — WOOLF CREEK — SKIRMISH — CAPTAIN HARMER KILLED — VERY THOUGHTFUL — SHANNON'S BRIDGE — BATTLE OF CLOYD MOUNTAIN — POSTING THE TROOPS — POSITION OF THE ENEMY — CLIMBING THE MOUNTAIN — WOOLWORTH KILLED AND LENHART WOUNDED — SICKEL LAYS LOW AND FLANKS — SWINGING FROM BUSH TO BUSH — STORMING THE WORKS — VICTORY — ON TO DUBLIN — THE WOUNDED AND TROPHIES — THE LOSSES — TELEGRAPHING TO THE INSURGENTS — BRECKENRIDGE DECEIVED — DESTRUCTION OF DEPOTS — TEARING UP THE RAILROAD — BATTLE OF NEW RIVER BRIDGE — DEFEAT OF M'CAUSLAND — DESTRUCTION OF THE BRIDGE.

GENERAL CROOK had command of the troops concentrating in the Kanawha Valley. The expedition, including those joining at Fayette Court House, consisted of twelve regiments of infantry, three batteries, two thousand cavalry under General Averill, a train of one hundred and fifty wagons, and fifty ambulances. He spent but four days in organizing his fragmentary commands, reducing baggage, sending off the sick, and getting in order his supply and ammunition train. Immediately after landing at Brownstown, on the 26th of April, General Crook placed Colonel Sickel in command of the Third Brigade, composed of the Third Reserves, Captain Jacob Lenhart; the Fourth Reserves, Colonel R. H. Woolworth; the Eleventh West Virginia, Colonel Daniel Frost; and the Fifteenth West Virginia, Colonel M. M'Caslin. On assuming command, the Colonel announced the following named officers as composing his staff:

First Lieutenant Harry S. Jones, Third Reserves, Assistant Adjutant-General.
First Lieutenant C. W. Kirby, Eleventh West Virginia, Inspector-General.
First Lieutenant Theodore P. Mills, Fourth Reserves, Ordnance Officer.
First Lieutenant E. F. Brothers, Fourth Reserves, Assistant Quartermaster.
First Lieutenant L. S. Boyer, Third Reserves, Commissary of Subsistence.
First Lieutenant J. H. M'Laughlin, Eleventh West Virginia, Aid-de-Camp.
Surgeon William H. Davis, Fourth Reserves, Medical Director.
At the same time, Privates William Clark, Thomas Synnamon and Isaac G. Buck were detailed as orderlies at headquarters, and Samuel L. Harrison, Clark Bishop and Henry Barr were detailed to the brigade commissary.
On Saturday morning, April 30th, at five o'clock, Crook's command * started from Camp Piatt,† opposite Brownstown, and marched up the narrow Kanawha Valley. Fording Catcham, Cabin, and other swollen tributaries of the Kanawha, after a fatiguing march of fourteen miles they bivouacked on the banks of Paint creek. The next morning they started early, moving up the road to the Great Falls, near the confluence of Gauley and New rivers (forming the Kanawha), where they arrived about four o'clock in the afternoon. On the

---

*Ex-President Rutherford B. Hayes, a lawyer of Cincinnati, entered the army as Major of the Twenty-Third Ohio Volunteers, which regiment was commanded by Colonel W. S. Rosecrans, subsequently a distinguished general of the war. The regiment entered West Virginia in July, 1861, participated in the many campaigns and expeditions in that rugged country, in the battles of South Mountain and Antietam, and returned to West Virginia in October, 1862. Lieutenant-Colonel Hayes, who was severely wounded at South Mountain, and had refused the commission of Colonel of the Seventy-ninth Ohio Volunteers, was promoted Colonel of his own regiment, the Twenty-third Ohio, and detached to command the brigade. His command formed part of this expedition. Subsequently, with Crook's division, he joined Sheridan in the Shenandoah Valley, and was promoted a brigadier-general and brevet major-general, for his conduct in the brilliant victories that attended that remarkable campaign.

† Named in honor of Brigadier-General Abraham S. Piatt.

morning of the 2d of May, they faced to the south and crossed the Cotton Mountain. The morning was bright, beautiful and quite warm, and many of the men, as they toiled up the steep, rough way, became exhausted, and threw away their overcoats and blankets. At noon dark clouds arose, succeeded by a cold, chilly rain, and by the time they reached the folorn village of Fayette Court House they were greeted with a driving snow-storm. The men, divested of overcoats and blankets, wet to the skin, and shivering with the cold, presented a pitiable sight. Fayette Court House was the extreme out-post held by the Union forces. The brigade of infantry and battery on duty here were added to General Crook's command. Here General Crook detached General Averill, with his 2,000 cavalry, from the main column, and sent him by way of Logan Court House to strike the salt works at Saltville, to which point there was a branch railroad from the Virginia and Tennesse road. To deceive the enemy as to the route intended to be taken, the Fifth West Virginia, under command of Colonel A. A. Tomlinson, with Lieutenant Blazer's scouts, were sent on the Lewisburg road. This feint succeeded admirably in drawing off General M'Causland's Brigade in that direction.

On the 3d, the infantry, artillery, wagon-train and ambulances moved from Fayette Court House, and marched seventeen miles, bivouacking on Keeton's farm. On account of the proximity of the enemy, no calls were sounded. The country through which they passed was sparsely inhabited by a hardy set of tall, raw-boned, Union-loving mountaineers, who depended mainly on hunting for a living. Their log cabins, plastered with mud, were surrounded by a few panels of worm-fence, and a horse, a cow or two, several hogs and a few chickens constituted their worldly wealth. It would have been supposed they and their rugged mountains would have been spared the hardships of war, but the Confederacy never acknowledged the independence of West Virginia, and claimed them as her own. Wherever found they were conscripted into the service. Of those who went voluntarily, nine-tenths followed the old flag. "*Montani semper liberi*," "Mountaineers always free," is the fitly-chosen motto of their State. The next day the Third Regiment took the advance, throwing out Companies A and B as skirmishers. About eleven o'clock they passed through Raleigh Court House, and, near four in the afternoon, bivouacked on Peak Hill. The march was through a continuous woods, and over White Stake and Piney creeks, two large and deep streams. The next morning at five o'clock they were again in line, and, crossing a deep creek, they commenced the ascent of Great Flat-Top Mountain. These wild and rugged mountains were continually intersected by deep and dark ravines and gorges, winding in irregular directions far off on either side of the rough road the army followed. They were, in fact, a succession of high mountains and deep ravines, covered with a dense growth of scrub-oak and pine trees, completely shutting out the view at a short distance. An enemy acquainted with the country had all the advantages of attack and defence, and it afforded every inducement for an enterprising foe to annoy an army on its march.

Some two years previous, a brigade of General Rosecrans' army was conducting a large wagon-train over this same road, and, upon arriving at one of the approaches, an insurgent cavalry force suddenly emerged therefrom, and turned the whole train off the road up the ravine, and with their small force held in check those sent to recapture it. Pushing the enemy slowly back, the pursuers suddenly came upon an insurgent battery, which the train had passed, posted in a narrow gorge, and, before artillery could be brought up to dislodge it, the battery, train and all had disappeared in the, to them, well-known windings of the mountains.

General Crook, to guard against such enterprises by the enemy, who were known to be lurking in the mountains, deployed videttes to the right and left of the advance guard, with orders to fire the distant heights. The scrub-oak has a large, thick leaf, that does not fall until late in the spring, when the new leaf starts. Thus the fire spread with great rapidity, and sometimes the heights for miles would be wrapped in the rolling flames and smoke, presenting a grand and sublime sight. The General had, also, another object in firing the woods. When his column moved over the tops of lofty mountains, they could be seen for many miles, and he wished to conceal from the enemy his real strength and line of march, which the smoke effectually did. Large fires in these mountains were not so uncommon as to awaken any suspicion as to the origin.

The Third, having led the advance the preceding day, dropped to the rear, to work its way up to the head of the column day by day. It, therefore, was acting as wagon-guard, and, by the time the long line of many miles had passed the firing point, the fire had swept across the line of march. The road was lined with the trunks of dead chestnut trees, which burned with great fury. Occasionally a flaming limb or top of a tree would fall across the road, terrifying the horses. It was by no means a pleasant duty to guard wagons loaded with ammunition while passing through such an ordeal as this. The men were all aware that there was great danger of an explosion taking place at any moment, from the sparks that might find their way among the ammunition-boxes. Soldiers, although they may be perfectly willing to face death upon the field, have no liking whatever to being killed, except "according to army regulations," when they know that it is all right. Many trees were found felled across the road, that indicated the presence of the enemy and delayed the advance of the head of the column. The day was excessively warm, and the march slow and tiresome, and sometimes almost suffocating. Wearied and exhausted with struggling for nineteen hours through the smoke and heat, over the steep mountain-sides, marching twenty-two miles, the men stretched their wearied limbs upon the ground to sleep.

At four A.M., on the 6th, they were again under way, fording the Blue Stone river, and passing through a rough, mountainous country. The advance had a lively skirmish with the Sixtieth Virginia, at Princeton Court House, in Mercer county. Such was the celerity of our movement that they were taken almost by surprise. They left their tents standing, and dropped their tools in the trench of the formidable fort they were erecting, and traveled with celerity southward. This little affair gave new life to the men, and the sight of their works called forth prolonged cheers. The army encamped, that night, around the town. The next morning they left Princeton, at half-past four, Companies A and B, of the Third, being deployed in the advance as skirmishers. Firing continued, more or less, all day, the enemy being driven from one ravine to another, but they fell back too fast to make it particularly interesting. Firing at long range is very uncertain and unsatisfactory in its results, and although the "Johnies" doubtlessly thought they were disputing the ground with us inch by inch, the boys got tired of the sport, and contented themselves with driving them, at the point of the bayonet, about a mile off. This silence, however, was productive of happy results, as they got a few capital shots, and sent the recipients of their favors to the "happy hunting-ground."

It was supposed the enemy would make a stand at Rocky Gap, and Colonel Sickel sent the Fourth Reserves to flank it, while the Third ate dinner. When they advanced, however, no resistance was received, and the army passed through unmolested. The march, though exciting, was very severe, the day being warm, and they crossing Black Oak and East River Mountains, and fording Brush and Woolf creeks. The men and officers displayed great courage in crossing the last named stream, the water being deep and turbulent, it occupying five hours for the regiment to get over. That night they bivouacked on its banks. The next day the Third and Fourth were detailed as wagon guard. A brigade, with a battery of artillery, marched through Parisburg, the county seat of Giles county, to Snidow's Falls, and then turning to the right, moved southward; while the main column, passing near the town, moved directly south. While ascending Brushy Mountain, the train was fired upon by a band of guerrillas. A portion of the Third immediately charged up the mountains, and a smart skirmish ensued, in which a number of insurgents were killed, wounded, and taken prisoners. Among the killed was Captain William W. Harmer, a notorious bush-whacker. One of the prisoners informed Colonel Sickel he had "drawn a bead" on him, when he passed by his place of concealment, and would "liked to have brought him," but was afraid of alarming those in the rear. The Colonel was much pleased with the frankness of the fellow, but much more so with his thoughtfulness about creating an alarm. They passed through Poplar Hill, and bivouacked about nine o'clock near Shannon's bridge, after a fatiguing march of thirty miles.

The Battle of Cloyd Mountain, May 9th, 1864.

On the morning of the 9th, the command marched through the gap at Shannon's bridge that opens up to the northwest slope of Walker's, or Cloyd Mountain. The First Brigade was deployed to the right of the road that led directly over the mountain, and advanced up its side. The Second Brigade, Colonel Carr B. White, of the Twelfth Ohio, was sent to the extreme left. The Third Reserves and Eleventh West Virginia, under Colonel Daniel Frost, filed off the mountain road to the left, marched down a densely wooded ravine for a half a mile, and connecting with the Second Brigade, climbed directly to the summit of the mountain. General Crook dismounted, and climbed the heights with them. When the summit was gained, the enemy was discovered posted in apparently an unapproachable position, on a bold ridge running along the foot of a higher mountain. His artillery was posted so as to command the mountain road, rake the narrow openings on either side, and the bridge that spanned the Little Walker, a deep stream that flowed at the mountain's base. The insurgent infantry extended on either side of the batteries, across the open space, until their right and left were lost in the woods on either side of the road. In this open space the enemy were strongly posted, behind a long breast-work of heavy logs, with an abatis in front.

While this was transpiring, Colonel Sickel, with the Fourth Reserves and Fifteenth West Virginia, was moving directly up the mountain road, within range of the enemy's fire. General Crook, from his commanding outlook, formed his plan of battle, and issued orders for the advance. White's Brigade crept secretly along the east side of the mountain, to operate upon the enemy's right. The First Brigade moved steadily forward. The Third Reserves and Eleventh West Virginia rejoined the Third Brigade; and Sickel moved down the (first) mountain, and formed in the edge of the woods, immediately in the enemy's front, under a constant fire from their artillery. As soon as the Second Brigade had fairly engaged the enemy, the First and Third Brigades were ordered to charge. Steadily the men commenced climbing the heights, grasping brush after brush until the summit was reached, which occupied a half hour, during which they were exposed to the deliberate fire of the enemy, which they did not return.

Here the Third Reserve, which was on the left of the Fourth, emerged from the woods to the open ground, when they encountered a terrible fire of grape and canister, sweeping through their ranks, instantly killing Colonel Woolworth, and severely wounding Captain Lenhart, the commanders of the two regiments. But onward the gallant men pressed, and five times their color-bearers were shot down. They were not yet within musket range of the enemy; and Colonel Sickel, seeing the deadly fire they were exposed to, laid down the Virginia regiments and advanced them on their bellies, and obliqued the Reserves to the left, gaining the protection of a hill on the right of the enemy's artillery. Plunging through the deep stream of the ravine, they commenced the ascent of the steep heights. No braver men ever smiled at death than those resolute Reserves that climbed up Cloyd's Mountain that noon, swinging themselves by the bushes from rock to rock, under a withering fire of musketry. Many a strong man was forced to relax his grasp, to be precipitated upon the rocks beneath; but, with iron sinews, heeding not the hail that was poured upon them, they steadily arose, higher and higher, until the summit was reached, when, with a wild cheer, they rushed right over the breast-works. The First Brigade was also gallantly engaged, further to the right; and the Second, after suffering heavy loss, broke in upon the enemy's right. The rout of the foe, both in front and on his right, was simultaneous and complete.

The enfilading fire that was poured into the insurgents on the right, and the fire from the front, as they fled, panic-stricken and in disorder, told with effect. Immediately upon taking the works, the regiments were re-formed; and after detailing a guard over the prisoners, they pushed on with vigor after the flying foe; and Colonel Oley, at the head of four hundred cavalry, that moved up the mountain road, annoyed their rear. Near Dublin, they encountered six hundred cavalry, whom General Morgan* had dispatched from Wytheville to the support of the enemy. A sharp engagement immediately followed, in which our advance drove them from their position, and pushed them through Dublin, which town, with its depot and immense stores, fell into our hands, the enemy retreating westward on Wytheville.

---

* Brigadier-General John Morgan, of guerrilla notoriety, who made the celebrated raid into Indiana and Ohio. Was surprised and killed at Greenville, East Tennessee, by General Gillen, September 3d, 1864.

The battle took place about four miles northeast of Dublin, towards which place the Third, now under the command of Captain Robert Johnson,* advanced about half way, when they were ordered back by General Crook, to take charge of the battle-field. Here the regiment was divided into squads, under the command of officers, to collect the wounded and the arms, and bury the dead. Two hundred and twenty-six of the enemy were buried upon the field. Two hundred and seventy-eight of their wounded were found upon the field, and two hundred and thirty prisoners were taken. Among the wounded was the insurgent commander, General Jenkins,† who died a few days after the battle. Among the spoils collected by the Third was two twelve-pounder brass Napoleon guns, three hundred and fifty-four stand of small arms—all of which were sent to the division—and five caissons and over four hundred muskets, which were burnt for want of transportation. The total loss of the enemy was two hundred and twenty-six killed, five hundred and eighty-five wounded,‡ and three hundred and seventeen prisoners. One hundred and seven of our men were buried upon the field, and our missing and wounded amounted to five hundred and twenty. In the Third, Captain Jacob Lenhart, Jr., First Lieutenant J. B. Bartholomew, Second Lieutenants George B. Davis and Benjamin D. Hemmig, were among the wounded.§ Chaplain Pomeroy buried the remains of Colonel Woolworth, who fell, mortally wounded, at the head of his regiment, together with six soldiers of the

---

* A native of Holmesburg, Pa. At the breaking out of the war he carried on the gas-fitting business, and was connected with a military company in Petersburg, Va. When the state seceded, his company was ordered out for service in the army of the Confederacy. Sacrificing the fruits of years of labor, at great peril of life, he escaped North, and, returning to his native village, was chosen First Lieutenant of the "De Silver Grays," Company E.

† During Lee's invasion of Pennsylvania, Brigadier-General Jenkins, with a brigade of cavalry, marched unopposed in Chambersburg, on the 17th of June, 1863. He took all the horses, cattle and stores he could find, destroyed the railroad, and carried off into slavery some fifty negroes. He was wounded at Gettysburg.

‡ Greeley's American Conflict, II Vol., page 600.

§ For the loss of Third, see Appendix A.

Third and Fourth, underneath a locust tree, near by the stream over which the regiments charged.* Owing to the lack of transportation, about two hundred of the most seriously wounded were left in the large brick mansion of James Cloyd, on the battle-field. Supplies were left with them, and medical attendance provided for. Such of these as belonged to us were subsequently made prisoners and paroled by the enemy. At dark, the ambulances were loaded with the wounded; and, with the Third, and a detachment of the Fourth, moved towards Dublin. They reached the bivouac of the Fourth, now under the command of Lieutenant-Colonel Thomas F. B. Tapper, about midnight, where they lay until morning.

As before stated, Crook's expedition was intended to coöperate with Sigel's, which moved up the Shenandoah Valley, on the 1st of May, ten thousand strong. When Crook's troops entered Dublin, they found the telegraph operator had decamped, leaving his instruments intact. Men were immediately found who could operate them, and Crook put himself into communication with the insurgents at Lynchburg. Telegraphing, in the name of General Jenkins, a glorious victory over the Yankees, and the death of Crook, the insurgents were completely deceived, and, in the excitement over the good news, their operator did not notice a strange hand that was working the instrument at Dublin, and from them Crook learned of the capture, in the valley, of his supply train that was to meet him eight miles north of Lynchburg, and such other information as to leave no doubt in his mind that General Sigel would certainly be defeated.* Before breaking off communication with them, he telegraphed that the Yankees had turned and defeated them, and were marching on Dublin with an overwhelming force, and that Averill had defeated Jones at Wytheville.

---

* Colonel Woolworth's remains were subsequently brought to Philadelphia.

* General Sigel was defeated and routed near New Market, on the 15th, by a superior force of the enemy under General Breckinridge.

This was done to relieve Sigel. Breckinridge, completely deceived by the skillful wording of the message, immediately detached all the troops he could spare, and dispatched them to repel the expected advance of General Crook. He, consequently, was not able to follow up the subsequent defeat of Sigel.

General Crook at once saw the projected coöperation with Sigel was at an end, and had no other course left to pursue but to march on his base. At Dublin there was found stored immense quantities of bacon, corn, and shoes with wooden soles. The negroes, who everywhere proved our friends, and who were the great source of our information throughout the South, were allowed to take what they wanted of these articles, and, after loading our wagons, the rest, with a great amount of military equipments of different kinds, new army wagons and artillery carriages, with the warehouses and depots, were totally destroyed.

The next morning, the 10th, General Crook was taken sick, and turned over the command of the army to Colonel Sickel. The destruction of the railroad was commenced; the boys piling up the ties, and placing the rails across, set fire to them. This warped and twisted the rails, and rendered them unfit for use until re-rolled. The work commenced at a point one mile west of Dublin, and was continued eastward to New river bridge, a distance of over six miles being destroyed. When within a short distance of the river, the command moved on a cross-road through the woods, and along a lane towards the railroad bridge, when the enemy's skirmishers were met. Colonel Sickel immediately deployed our lines, and a sharp engagement ensued. Our artillery, which was not used in the battle of Cloyd Mountain, was now brought into play, and silenced the enemy's guns. The insurgents, who were under the command of General M'Causland,* were finally driven from their position and

---

* The same who captured defenseless Chambersburg, June 30th, 1864, and burnt two-thirds of it, because the citizens could not instantly pay a ransom of $500,000.

across the New river bridge. The Third Reserve and the Fifteenth West Virginia were now ordered forward, to drive the enemy's sharp-shooters from the east side of the river, and to fire the bridge. This immense structure was a covered trestle-work, fully a mile and a half long, and burnt for a long while before it was totally destroyed. Colonel Sickel received a painful wound in the left leg. First Lieutenant F. E. Harrison was also wounded.* After the destruction of the bridge, the command was marched to Pepper's Ferry, some three miles above, and the infantry was crossed in flat-boats. The artillery and wagons, and the ambulances loaded with the wounded, were driven across the deep and rapid stream at a ford about a mile above. Several men and teams were lost in this perilous crossing. The army bivouacked here for the night, during which it rained hard, making the roads very heavy.

---

* For the loss in the Third see Appendix A.

CHAPTER XVIII.

AVERILL'S FIGHT AT WYTHEVILLE—ATTACKING THE REAR GUARD—THE RETURN MARCH—BLACKSBURG—LA RUE'S SKIRMISH—NINETEENTH VIRGINIA CAVALRY—UNION COURT HOUSE—CROSSING THE GREENBRIER—HARD MARCHES—POOR FORAGING—MEADOW BLUFF—SUFFERING OF THE WOUNDED—LEWISBURG—THE RESERVES' THREE YEARS EXPIRE—THE BATTALION—ITS OFFICERS—FAREWELL TO COMRADES—FACES HOMEWARD—CROSS THE SEWELL—REACH CAMP PIATT—BY STEAMER TO PITTSBURG—BY RAIL TO PHILADELPHIA—THE BAND—THE WELCOME.

THE same day of the fight at New river bridge, General Averill struck Wytheville, a town of some eighteen hundred inhabitants, where he was met by a formidable cavalry force, under General Morgan, who had been dispatched by General Jones,* from Saltville. A stubborn fight ensued, in which Averill held his own; but was unable to accomplish the object for which he was sent—the destruction of the salt-works near there. General Crook, the same day, received information of the fight, but General Averill had no knowledge of Crook's whereabouts.

The next morning, for the purpose of getting well clear of the enemy, a portion of the command was sent in pursuit of them, which overtook and attacked their rear guard about ten o'clock, and drove them for some distance. The main body was put in motion early, and marched in rain during the entire day, reaching Blacksburg in the afternoon. Companies C, H and I, of the Third, were sent on picket. Captain La Rue, commanding I, learning that some guerrillas were in close proximity to his post, deployed his company as skirmishers, and advanced up the mountains to drive them off. A smart little skirmish ensued, during which

---

* General W. E. Jones was shot through the head, at Piedmont, near Staunton, June 5th, 1864, in an engagement with the troops under General Hunter.

two of his men were captured. It was instantly determined to recover them, and, pushing onward with renewed energy and spirit, it was at last accomplished. Two of his men were slightly wounded. They killed two, and wounded several, and captured nine good horses, which were turned over to the quartermaster's department. At Blacksburg, comfortable quarters were found for the wounded in the large brick academy building.

During the 12th, it rained hard all day, but they continued their march, moving through Newport, over Walker Mountain, and across Sinking creek, through a wild and rugged country, to the summit of Salt Pond Mountain, where they bivouacked. The enemy opposed their advance at several points. About noon they came suddenly upon the encampment of the Nineteenth Virginia Cavalry; but they left in such a hurry they forgot to take their baggage with them, which, with their camp equipage, was destroyed. The march was very hard and the men much fatigued. Owing to the impassable nature of the roads, and the worn-out and almost starved condition of the animals, it was found necessary to destroy part of the loads, and, in some instances, the wagons. The next day they took up their line of march again, the enemy still showing themselves in the front. About noon a smart engagement took place, in which we captured a train of fifteen wagons and a piece of artillery. This day and the preceding, they had been fording streams that flowed into the Ohio, the Potomac and the James rivers.

On the 14th, the Third acted as wagon guard, and commenced moving at noon, crossing Big Stony creek, Peter's and Wiseman's mountains, and bivouacked about dark. The next day the Fourth was added to the wagon guard, and marching early, they passed through Salt Sulphur and near Sweet Sulphur Springs, and reached Union, the county seat of Monroe county, about two o'clock in the afternoon, and bivouacked beyond the town. On the 16th, they left camp at seven o'clock, and marching thirteen miles, bivouacked near Anderson's Ferry, on the Greenbrier river, where they lay until the morning of the 18th. The stream was very turbulent and much swollen. The ambulances, wagons and artillery were taken across in a single flat-boat, and the infantry forded breast deep. The march was only four miles. The reason for these alternate long and short marches was, that the expedition was entirely destitute of provisions, and forced to forage on the barren and poverty-stricken country for subsistence for both man and beast. For this purpose they were forced to halt, to collect corn, and grind it at the mills they passed, a great part of which work was done at night. The poor young cattle collected in the mountains furnished their rations of meat, which was eaten without salt. This day General Averill, with his cavalry, joined the main column.

On the 19th the command marched at five o'clock, crossed the Little Sewell Mountain, and passed through the Blue Sulphur Springs, and, making fifteen miles, halted at Meadow Bluff,* in the southeastern extremity of Fayette county, after twenty days' continuous marching. The distance marched during this time was two hundred and fifty-five miles. Half of this time some portion of the army was skirmishing with the enemy. Every night great precaution had to be taken to avoid surprise. From the long marches over the flinty mountains, all their shoes were worn out, and at least one-third of them were entirely destitute of soles.

---

*After being discomforted by General Rosecrans at Carnifax Ferry, in September, 1861, Brigadier-General John B. Floyd, ex-Governor of Virginia, and ex-Secretary of War under Buchanan; and Brigadier-General Henry A. Wise, ex-Governor of Virginia and victor of John Brown, hastily retreated, with loss of much of their equipage and baggage, to Sewell's Mountain. The two Ex's being more of politicians than soldiers, had at heart the good of themselves more than the Confederacy, and became envious of each others bright fame. Neither would acknowledge the other as his superior in command, and both reported direct to Richmond. Floyd encamped at Meadow Bluff on one side of the mountain, and Wise on the other side, calling his camp "Defiance." Soon after General R. E. Lee, who had been appointed to succeed General Garnett, who had been defeated and killed at Carrick's Ford, and had himself been repulsed by General Reynolds at Cheat Mountain, arrived and took the chief command.

There they received their mail, the first since they had left Brownstown.

The sufferings of the wounded—riding for ten consecutive days over horrible roads, fording deep streams that frequently entered the ambulance beds, and over rugged mountains—cannot be described. From Meadow Bluff, the wounded were sent to the Kanawha river, loaded on boats, and from thence taken to Gallipolis, on the Ohio river.

On the 22d, the Third marched with Colonel Sickel's Brigade to Millville, near Lewisburg, in Greenbrier county. This place was settled by old Virginia families, and was strongly secession in its proclivities. While here, the Third's and Fourth's term of service expired, and they received orders to return to Pennsylvania, to be mustered out. The recruits that had been received into the regiments since their organization, whose term of service had not yet expired, and the men who had re-enlisted as veterans, were formed into a battalion of five companies. Colonel Sickel detailed from the Third, Captain Albert P. Moulton, First Lieutenants John H. Crothers and Amos W. Seitzinger, Second Lieutenants George B. Davis and William M'Carty; and from the Fourth, Captain Abel T. Sweet, First Lieutenant James W. Blundin, and Second Lieutenant W. H. Derrickson, to officer them. Captains Sweet, Moulton, Seitzinger, Blundin and Davis commanded the companies. The battalion was commanded by Captain Sweet, and Captain Blundin acted as Adjutant and Captain Davis as Quartermaster. It participated in all the engagements from Meadow Bluff to Staunton, and thence to Lynchburg, being principally employed as skirmishers. They were the first to break the lines of the enemy at Lynchburg, and were upon the point of entering the town when they were ordered to retire. It was, on the 4th of July following, consolidated with the Fifty-fourth Pennsylvania, Colonel Jacob M. Campbell. Captain Moulton, who remained with it, was subsequently promoted to the colonelcy.

THE THIRD RESERVE. 255

Bidding farewell to their comrades and the gallant Eleventh and Fifteenth West Virginia, on the 30th of May, the two regiments faced homeward.* Marching from Millville to Meadow Bluff, thence across the Big Sewell Mountains, eastward of New river, to Gauley's bridge and down the north bank of the Kanawha, they reached Camp Piatt, from which the expedition started on the 30th of April. On the 4th of June they embarked upon the steamer Jonas Powell and proceeded down the Kanawha to the Ohio, and thence to Pittsburg. At all the towns they passed, at Pittsburg and thence through the length of old Pennsylvania, they received a welcome and hearty greeting from the patriotic people. The brass band of the Reserve returned the greeting in the same soul-stirring strains as reverberated amid the hills and mountains of West Virginia.

This band has a peculiar and honorable history. Captain W. A. Pennypacker, of the Fourth, originated it while the detachment was on duty at Alexandria. The members were officers and privates of the two regiments. After leaving Washington, in all their wanderings, and buffetings, this musical organization was still preserved. Bands and

---

*After General Crook arrived at Meadow Bluff, he sent his wagons, under an escort of Averill's cavalry, to Gauley's bridge—his base—for supplies, and forwarded to Washington his official report of the expedition, and nearly five hundred prisoners. He then pushed over the mountains, with the whole of his command, into the Shenandoah Valley, and joined General Hunter, whom Grant had sent to relieve General Sigel at Staunton, June 8th. Hunter, being forced to retreat from Lynchburg, marched west on the railroad to Salem, and thence, via New Castle Court House, to Meadow Bluff, where he arrived June 25th. Thence, the whole command was moved by Kanawha, Ohio, Parkersburg and Grafton, to Harpers Ferry. Crook, left in command, pushed out to Winchester, and was overwhelmed by General Early, fighting there July 23d and at Martinsburg on the 25th. General Sheridan soon after assumed command in the valley. At the battle of Opequan Creek, September 19th, Crook gained enviable distinction for his skill and bravery. He also took part in the battle of Cedar Creek, October 18th and 19th. He and General Kelly were taken prisoners at Cumberland, Md., February 21st, 1865. Being soon after exchanged, he commanded with distinction a division of cavalry, under Sheridan, at the capture of Lee's army. The General at this time was about forty years of age, medium height, light complexion and hair, and keen brown eyes. His countenance was of a thoughtful cast, and his manners reserved, but he was a sincere and warm-hearted gentleman. He was a graduate of West Point Military Academy, and an officer of the regular army. Since the war he has gained a high reputation as an Indian fighter.

drum corps are usually in the rear when there is danger, or fighting to be done. In this case instruments were simply sent to the rear, and Captain Pennypacker and his fellow musicians were always found in their places when the enemy was to be met. Helping to overcome the foe, they were the men to sound forth the pæans of victory when the field was won.

On Wednesday evening, June 8th, the detachment arrived at the West Philadelphia depot, where they were met by a large concourse of citizens. The procession being formed, they were escorted through the principal streets of the city to the American Mechanics Hall, where a sumptuous collation was spread for the veterans and their friends. After partaking of the good things before them, and the interchange of friendly greetings with the delegations of citizens, General Sickel ordered the baggage and government property placed under an officer and guard within the Hall, and furloughed the boys until ten o'clock the next day, when they dispersed to their happy homes. Reassembling, they marched to Camp Cadwallader, near Ridge avenue and beyond Girard College, where they remained until the 17th, when the Third was mustered out of service.

And thus closed the glorious career of the Third Reserve, and now, one by one, they are being laid beneath the sod, and soon the bodies of all will form part and parcel of the land they loved so well.

APPENDICES.

APPENDIX A.

KILLED, WOUNDED AND MISSING.

RANK.	NAME.	CO.	RANK.	NAME.	CO.
	Mechanicsville.			*Wounded.*	
	Wounded.		Private...	Peter F. Holland........	A.
Sergeant..	Samuel Flemming......	E.	"	Wm. M'Donough........	A.
Private...	Henry Otten...............	A.	"	Harrison Harbach.......	A.
"	Daniel Wissinger........	H.	"	Augustus Rhein.........	A.
	Missing.		"	Frederick Saylor........	A.
"	Harry K. Hoff.............	E.	"	Daniel Shafer.............	A.
"	Adam Schank............	G.	"	Henry A. Harner........	A.
	Gaines' Mill.		"	John Hauk...............	B.
	Killed.		"	James Ryan...............	C.
1st Serg't.	Thomas P. Goheen......	C.	"	Henry Barr...............	D.
Sergeant..	Charles Fredericks......	A.	"	Peter Cunningham.....	D.
"	Edward L. Lennon......	C.	"	Jere. C. Hunsberger....	D.
Corporal..	Gabriel S. Brown.........	B.	"	Geo. A. Rawdenbush...	D.
Private...	Daniel S. Dickins........	B.	"	John Schiefley............	D.
"	Geo. P. Eushiro...........	B.	"	Jeremiah Boone..........	D.
"	Charles Robinson........	C.	"	James L. Hobson........	D.
"	Jacob Mellen...............	D.	"	John Lynn..................	E.
"	John Seidere...............	F.	"	William J. Nield.........	E.
"	John H. Killion...........	F.	"	Frederick B. Scott.......	E.
"	Henry Harsta.............	F.	"	John Brown...............	F.
"	Adam Keiser...............	H.	"	Allen Christinan.........	F.
"	Jacob L. Stouffer.........	H.	"	Joseph Conner............	F.
"	C. Miltenberger...........	I.	"	Daniel Filbert.............	F.
"	Henry E. Phillips.........	K.	"	Edward Killpatrick.....	F.
	Wounded.		"	Andrew J Adrian........	H.
1st Serg't.	Jacob V. Shilling........	D.	"	Geo. W. Reiter............	H.
Sergeant..	Michael Walters..........	A.	"	John Shively..............	H.
Corporal..	George Mosser............	A.	"	William G. Knight......	I.
"	William K. Leaman....	D.	"	Joshua Nickerson.......	K.
"	Harrison Lutz.............	F.	"	*Henry E. Phillips......	K.
"	Irvine C. Wright..........	I.		*Wounded and Missing.*	
Private...	Levi Richards.............	A.	Corporal..	John Hetzel................	B.
"	Francis Kocker...........	A.	Private...	William J. Hand.........	B.
			"	Joshua R. Thomas......	B.

* Mortally.

APPENDIX A.

RANK.	NAME.	CO.	RANK.	NAME.	CO.
	Wounded and Missing.			*Killed.*	
Private	James Fleming	C.	Private	Thomas Fennemore	I.
"	Matthew Mills	C.	"	James Reading	I.
"	Henry A. Lorah	D.		*Wounded.*	
"	Geo. W. Crapp	G.	Captain	Joseph Thomas	H.
"	James Duddy	G.	"	H. Clay Beatty	I.
"	Michael Hickey	G.	"	William Brian	K.
"	Mark M'Grath	G.	2d Lieut.	Joseph B. Roberts	C.
"	*John K. Smith	G.	1st Serg't.	Jacob H. Unrugh	G.
"	Theo. C. Peters	H.	Sergeant.	Samuel J. Griffee	C.
"	Wayne F. Weider	H.	"	George Rahn	G.
"	Nathan Harkness	I.	"	*Isaac E. Lewis	H.
"	John F. Bender	K.	Corporal.	Amos W. Seitzinger	A.
"	Wesley Schroyer	K.	"	Daniel P. Burkit	C.
	Missing.		"	T. Watson Bewly	C.
1st Lieut.	Geo. C. Davenport	B.	"	William Dennison	K.
"	John C. Bland	C.	Private	Henry Kenler	A.
"	Robert Kelly	C.	"	William Stiffenburg	A.
"	James M'Carn	C.	"	Wm. G. Bortree	B.
"	John W. Fletcher	E.	"	Nicholas Dunborn	B.
"	Charles W. Stout	E.	"	Edward Machan	B.
Private	John Andy	F.	"	Porter C. Johnson	B.
"	Joseph Bellas	F.	"	Thomas Adams	C.
"	Edward Clater	F.	"	William J. Fennell	C.
"	Cyrus Reed	F.	"	William Haines	C.
"	Hugh Sweeny	F.	"	Joseph London	C.
"	Adam Weber	F.	"	Joseph Stout	C.
"	James Leeson	H.	"	David C. Epphimer	D.
"	Milton Reed	H.	"	H. H. Hemming	D.
"	John Trumbower	H.	"	John Johnson	E.
"	Edward C. Jacoby	I.	"	S. S. Shaner	E.
"	Samuel M. Adair	K.	"	Samuel Yonker	E.
	Glendale.		"	William Abrams	G.
	Killed.		"	Elisha A. Carr	G.
1st Serg't.	Joel Chester	I.	"	Charles M'Devitt	G.
Sergeant.	Francis D. Nagle	A.	"	Henry Praul	G.
"	John A. Price	D.	"	Frederick H. Wurst	G.
Corporal.	Jacob Thomas	E.	"	B. Longenbucher	H.
"	Harvey Alabach	H.	"	B. O. Ruter	H.
Private	Nicholas Ribble	A.	"	Joseph Bradon	I.
"	Oliver L. Bath	B.	"	Edward Hellings	I.
"	Joseph Hammer	C.	"	Wm. H. Nelson	I.
"	William Hillborn	C.	"	Thomas E. Swan	K.
"	David Bechtel	D.		*Wounded and Missing.*	
"	Joseph Rorke	D.	1st Lieut.	Jacob Lehman	A.
"	Cyrus Schwartz	D.	2d Lieut.	Francis E. Harrison	G.

* Mortally.

APPENDIX A.

RANK.	NAME.	CO.	RANK.	NAME.	CO.
	Wounded and Missing.			*Killed.*	
Private...	Levi B. Rhoads............	A.	Private...	A. J. Roberts.............	H.
"	Hugh M'Gettigan........	A.	"	William Smith............	I.
"	Charles Weber.............	A.		*Wounded.*	
"	Benjamin Bennet.........	B.	Sergeant..	William F. Roberts.....	C.
"	*William Cogswell......	B.	"	William H. Parker......	D.
"	Sydney Cornell...........	B.	"	*Isaac E. Lewis...........	H.
"	*Thomas Firth............	B.	Corporal..	John Martz.................	B.
"	Uriah Nunemacher.....	F.	Private...	William Stiffenburg.....	A.
"	Christian Stumsfelts....	I.	"	Abraham Perry...........	A.
	Missing.		"	William Lamb.............	D.
1st Lieut..	David W. Donaghy......		"	Samuel M'Chalicker....	D.
Sergeant..	John H. Crothers.........	C.	"	Samuel Yonker............	D.
Private...	Samuel Derr.................	A.	"	John Murphy..............	G.
"	William Degroat..........	A.	"	John A. Pearley..........	G.
"	James A. Fix................	A.	"	Dennis Sullivan...........	G.
"	Henry C. Keehn...........	A.	"	Alfred W. Hong..........	G.
"	Patrick Murphy...........	A.	"	Jeremiah Snable..........	H.
"	William Warner...........	A.	"	Augustus Neiffer..........	H.
"	C. W. Hubbard.............	B.	"	Joseph Kerns...............	H.
"	I. Kennedy...................	B.	"	Charles Carlin.............	I.
"	Eugene B. Mitchell......	B.	"	Charles M. Ryon.........	I.
"	Richard Bambrick.......	E.	"	Frank R. Wofter..........	I.
"	David R. Bennet..........	E.		*Wounded and Missing.*	
"	Robert Chambers.........	E.	Corporal..	Charles Grovat............	I.
"	John M'Bride...............	E.	"	George S. Silbert.........	I.
"	Charles H. Rich...........	E.	Private...	Frederick Garst...........	A.
"	William W. Solly.........	E.	"	Albert Flanagan..........	C.
"	Richard Wright............	E.	"	Amos Eckley...............	E.
"	Peter Rusk...................	F.		*Missing.*	
"	William Walters...........	F.	Sergeant..	George Rahn...............	G.
"	Alexander Park............	G.	"	Edward Young............	K.
"	Albert Harkens............	I.	Corporal..	Richard Wilson............	G.
"	Manuel La Rue............	I.	Private...	Daniel Greaff...............	A.
"	Ebenezer Wilson..........	I.	"	Samuel B. Frey...........	A.
"	John B. Beaumont.......	K.	"	William P. Holland.....	A.
"	Wesley Schroyer..........	K.	"	Abraham Lewis...........	C.
"	Thomas Wilson............	K.	"	William Ashton..........	E.
	Second Bull Run.		"	Samuel Bisbin.............	G.
	Killed.		"	John M'Millen.............	G.
Captain...	H. Clay Beatty.............	I.	"	Lewis Margerum..........	G.
Corporal..	Charles Carley.............	G.	"	William Dougherty.....	H.
Private...	John Babb....................	D.	"	Mahlon Geathers.........	I.
"	Frederick Switzer.........	E.	"	James W. Clayton.......	K.
"	Henry Burkhart...........	F.	"	Thomas Williams........	K.
"	Andrew Huff................	H.	"	Thomas White.............	K.

* Mortally.

APPENDIX A.

RANK.	NAME.	CO.	RANK.	NAME.	CO.
	Antietam.			*Wounded.*	
	Killed.		Private...	John K. Yeakel............	H.
Captain...	Florentine H. **Staub**....	D.	"	John Trumbower..........	H.
1st Serg't.	John Blaker.................	E.	"	George W. Ritter..........	H.
Sergeant..	Hobart Nicholson.........	B.	"	J. Newholt..................	H.
Corporal..	Jesse R. Dickens...........	B.	"	John Schaeffer.............	I.
"	Richard Wilson............	G.			
"	William Brittain...........	K.		**Fredericksburg.**	
"	Henry Otten................	A.		*Killed.*	
Private...	Frederick Hendley.......	D.	1st Lieut..	Jacob V. Shilling..........	D.
"	Luther Kreuson............	E.	1st Serg't.	James Schrader............	D.
"	James **Leese**...............	F.	"	Ephraim Case..............	H.
"	Henry Jones................	F.	Corporal..	John G. Bland..............	D.
"	Peter Rusk..................	F.	"	Henry Setler................	D.
"	James Bingham............	G.	"	Lewis D. M'Farland......	F.
"	Peter Dunbar...............	G.	"	Wm. W. Smith.............	I.
"	Lewis Brown................	H.	Private...	David English..............	A.
"	Jacob B. Crater............	H.	"	Andrew Jackson..........	A.
"	Joseph Rudolph...........	K.	"	Alex. H. Stewart...........	B.
			"	Arichibald S. Little........	B.
	Wounded.		"	Robert Dillon...............	C.
Captain...	Geo. C. Davenport........	B.	"	Thomas Dillon..............	C.
1st Lieut..	Fred. G. Nicholson........	B.	"	George W. Wiggins........	C.
Corporal..	Benj. F. Crosedale........	C.	"	Jacob Bechtel...............	D.
"	Edward Toon...............	G.	"	Charles E. Wright.........	D.
"	Nathan Hauch..............	H.	"	Jacob A. Johnson..........	E.
"	Israel Long..................	H.	"	Jacob Smith.................	E.
Private...	James D. Ash...............	A.	"	Joseph L. Toy...............	E.
"	John Rork....................	A.	"	Henry Acker................	F.
"	Joseph **Bachon**...........	B.	"	James Duddy................	G.
"	Daniel **Garman**..........	B.	"	Frank Sellers................	H.
"	Jacob **Johnson**...........	B.	"	John T. Scott................	I.
"	John Marsh..................	B.	"	Benjamin Clark.............	I.
"	Henry S. Potter............	B.	"	Henry T. Shock............	I.
"	*Alfred Williams.........	B.	"	Lemuel Mitchell............	K.
"	Obediah Achey.............	D.			
"	Josiah Coller................	D.		*Wounded.*	
"	Peter B. Keehn.............	D.	1st Lieut..	Michael Watlers............	A.
"	James **Boulton**...........	E.	1st Serg't.	Jackson Hutchinson...	I.
"	D. M. **Wilson**..............	E.	Sergeant.	Daniel Murphy.............	F.
"	William Jones...............	F.	"	John Smith	G.
"	Levan Lehr..................	F.	Corporal..	Flarian Harbach............	A.
"	John Silbeman..............	F.	"	William Henry.............	F.
"	George W. Crapp..........	G.	"	Richard Evans..............	G.
"	James Murray...............	G.	"	Levi Frey	H.
"	Thomas Haran.............	G.	"	Israel Long..................	H.
"	Emanuel English..........	H.	"	Augustus Neiffer...........	H.

* Mortally.

APPENDIX A.

RANK.	NAME.	CO.	RANK.	NAME.	CO.
	Wounded.			*Wounded and Missing.*	
Corporal..	Thomas C. Leet	I.	Private...	Daniel Garman	B.
Private...	John Brodhurst	A.	"	Richard Dickens	B.
"	John Bedencup	A.	"	Adam Graham	C.
"	Jacob S. Kunsman	A.	"	Abraham Lewis	C.
"	Francis Kocher	A.	"	Bartlett Smith	C.
"	Peter M'Quaid	A.	"	John Scheifley	D.
"	William Peters	A.	"	Heber M'Cord	D.
"	Levi B. Rhoades	A.	"	John M'Bride	E.
"	Freeling Brundage	B.	"	David Scott	E.
"	John Campbell	B.	Musician.	John P. Douth	F.
"	Michael Mitchell	B.	Private....	Henry Ecknold	F.
"	William J. Fennell	C.	"	Levi Schneer	F.
"	Charles Hitchcock	C.	"	Thomas Kochel	F.
"	James M'Carn	C.	"	John Silbeman	F.
"	Samuel Walton	C.	"	John Wentzel	F.
"	William Carlin	D.	"	Samuel Cowell	G.
"	William Ellis	D.	"	Barnard Crilley	G.
"	Emanuel Good	D.	"	Alfred Bishop	G.
"	Solomon S. Shaner	D.	"	Thomas Mitchell	G.
"	Andrew M. Shepherd..	D.	"	Stewart M'Donald	G.
"	Richard Bambrick	E.	"	Alexander Park	G.
"	Nelson Shemaley	E.	"	David Piffer	G.
"	Charles Dewees	E.	"	Wm. H. Walters	G.
"	Theo. Killpatrick	F.	"	Allen L. Garwood	I.
"	John Devlin	G.	"	Samuel M. Adair	K.
"	Henry Dager	G.	"	Wm. M'Donald	K.
"	Christian B. Guiger	G.	"	Geo. W. Morgan	K.
"	R. J. B. Mitchell	G.	"	Valentine W. Spink	K.
"	John Wilson	G.	"	David Stackhouse	K.
"	John S. Small	H.	"	Joseph Watson	K.
"	Milton Scheetz	H.		*Missing.*	
"	Abram Ladshaw	H.			
"	Owen M. Straun	H.	Corporal..	Harrison Lutz	F.
"	Daniel Milloy	H.	Private....	John W. Fletcher	E.
"	Michael Uile	H.	"	Lynford Williams	E.
"	George W. Reiter	H.	"	Allen Walters	F.
"	Abraham States	H.	Musician.	Calvin Reedy	F.
	Wounded and Missing.			**Cloyd's Mountain.**	
Captain...	William Brian	K.		*Killed.*	
Sergeant..	Daniel P. Burkit	C.	Corporal..	Israel Long	H.
Corporal..	Abraham B. Yocum	D.	Private....	James B. Old	A.
"	Richard Evans	G.	"	Jason B. Pidcock	E.
"	James Brooke	K.		*Wounded.*	
Private....	Wm. P. Holland	A.			
"	Charles Schroth	A.	Captain...	Jacob Lenhart, Jr.	A.
"	Henry S. Smith	A.	1st Lieut.	J. B. Bartholomew	H.
"	Enoch Shade	A.	2d Lieut..	George B. Davis	D.

APPENDIX A.

RANK.	NAME.	CO.	RANK.	NAME.	CO.
	Wounded.			*Wounded.*	
2d Lieut..	B. D. Hemming	F.	Private....	*James Thomas	I.
Sergeant..	T. Watson Bewly	C.	"	John Collins	K.
"	Jesse Keller	H.		*Wounded and Prisoners.*	
Corporal..	John Martz	B.			
"	William Carlin	D.	Sergeant..	George W. Vaux	H.
"	H. H. Hemming	D.	Private....	John H. Babb	A.
Private....	Andrew Fegely	A.	"	John O'Niel	A.
"	Albert S. Henershotz	A.	"	Jere. C. Hunsberger	D.
"	Henry G. Milans	A.	"	R. J. B. Mitchell	G.
"	John Yohu	A.	"	†William H. Nelson	I.
"	Charles Schaneberger	A.			
"	Joseph Hillborn	C.		**New River Bridge.**	
"	Daniel Stevenson	C.		*Killed.*	
"	Charles H. Barber	D.	Private....	Robert Caldwell	G.
"	Levi Bernheisel	F.		*Wounded.*	
"	Uriah Nunemacker	F.			
"	Washington Long	H.	Colonel....	Horatio G. Sickel	
"	Milton Reed	H.	1st Lieut..	Frank E. Harrison	G.
"	Hugh Mackie	I.	Private....	George F. Reinboth	K.
"	S. V. Richardson	I.	"	Samuel H. Simm	K.

* Died at Washington, June 3d, 1864.
† Died in Andersonville Prison, September 21st, 1864; grave 9,434.

APPENDIX B.

FIELD AND STAFF OFFICERS OF THE THIRD RESERVE.

NAME.	RANK.	DATE OF MUSTER.	RESIDENCE.	REMARKS.
Horatio G. Sickel	Colonel	May 27, '61	Philadelphia	Promoted from Captain Co. K, to Colonel, June 21, 1861. Wounded at New River Bridge, May 10, 1864. Mustered out with regiment, June 17, 1864.
William S. Thompson	Lt.-Colonel	May 29, '61	Bucks	Killed in naval action, April 19, 1865. Resigned July 9, 1862.
*John Clark	Lt.-Colonel	May 31, '61	Philadelphia	Promoted from Captain Co. E, to Lieutenant-Colonel, July 10, 1862. Mustered out with regiment, June 17, 1864.
Richard H. Woolworth	Major	June 1, '61	Philadelphia	Promoted to Lieutenant-Colonel 4th Reserves, June 1, 1862; to Colonel, Dec. 24, 1862. Killed at Cloyd's Mountain, May 9, 1864.
William Briner	Major	June 7, '61	Berks	Promoted from Captain Company D, to Major, July 10, 1862. Mustered out with regiment, June 17, 1864.
†Albert H. Jamison	Adjutant	June 11, '61	Berks	Appointed Adjutant, June 24, 1861. Discharged on Surgeon's certificate, Sept. 30, 1862.
Harry S. Jones	Adjutant	July 28, '61	Philadelphia	Promoted from Sergeant-Major to 2d Lieutenant Company F, July 29, 1862; to Adjutant, Oct. 1, 1862. Mustered out with regiment, June 17, 1864.
‡Franklin S. Bickley	Quarterm'r	June 7, '61	Berks	Appointed Quartermaster, June 22, 1861. Discharged on Surgeon's certificate, Nov. 13, 1861.

* Died at Holmesburg, Pa., June, 1872. † Died of consumption, 1865. ‡ Died at Reading, Pa., 1872.

FIELD AND STAFF OFFICERS.

NAME.	RANK.	DATE OF MUSTER.	RESIDENCE.	REMARKS.
Strickland Yardley	Quarterm'r	June 10, '61	Bucks	Appointed Quartermaster, April 11, 1863. Promoted Assistant Quartermaster, U. S. Vols., Aug. 10, 1863.
Levi S. Boyer	Quarterm'r	July 28, '61	Berks	Promoted to Quartermaster Sergeant, Oct. 1, 1861; to Regimental Quartermaster, Sept. 1, 1863. Mustered out with regiment, June 17, 1864.
James Collins	Surgeon	June 21, '61	Philadelphia	Appointed Surgeon, June 21, 1861. Transferred to U. S. Vols., as Assistant Surgeon, April 14, 1864.
*George L. Pancoast	Assist. Surg.	June 6, '61	Philadelphia	Appointed Assistant Surgeon, June 21, 1861. Promoted Surgeon U. S. Vols., Oct. 20, 1861.
Henry S. Colston	Assist. Surg.	Oct. 24, '61	Dauphin	Promoted to Surgeon 81st Regiment, Pa. Vols., Aug. 19, 1862.
Samuel S. Orr	Assist. Surg.	July 13, '62	Philadelphia	Resigned, March 13, 1863.
George J. Rice	Assist. Surg.	Aug. 2, '62	Bucks	Resigned, Jan. 17, 1863.
Stanton A. Welch	Assist. Surg.	Jan. 28, '63	Wayne	Mustered out with regiment, June 17, 1864.
John P. Birchfield	Assist. Surg.	May 14, '63	Centre	Left, at muster out, in charge of Veterans from 3d and 4th Regiments Reserves.
William H. Leake	Chaplain	June 5, '61	Wayne	Promoted from Private Co. B. to Chaplain, Aug. 1, 1861. Resigned, February 28, 1862.
George H. Frear	Chaplain	April 8, '62	Philadelphia	Resigned, July 9, 1862.
John J. Pomeroy	Chaplain	Sept. 10, '62	Franklin	Mustered out with regiment, June 17, 1864.

NON-COMMISSIONED STAFF.

NAME.	RANK.	DATE OF MUSTER.	RESIDENCE.	REMARKS.
William P. Smith	Serg. Major	May 27, '61		Promoted to Sergeant-Major, March 1, 1863. Mustered out with regiment, June 17, 1864.

* Died at Washington, August, 1865.

Name	Rank	Date	County	Remarks
George M. Rhone	Serg. Major	July 17, '61	Wayne	Promoted to Sergeant-Major, August 1, 1862; to 2d Lieutenant Co. B, March 1, 1863.
Irvine C. Wright	Q. M. Serg.	May 29, '61		Promoted to Commissary Sergeant, Nov. 1, 1862; to Quartermaster Sergeant, March 13, 1864. Mustered out with regiment, June 17, 1864.
Albert Briner	Q. M. Serg.	July 28, '61		Discharged on Surgeon's Certificate, Sept. 30, 1861.
D. C. Eppeheimer	Com. Serg.	June 7, '61		Promoted to Commissary Sergeant, March 1, 1864. Mustered out with company, June 17, 1864.
Duval Doran	Com. Serg.	May 29, '61		Promoted to Commissary Sergeant, June 1, 1861. Discharged on Surgeon's Certificate, Oct. 22, 1862.
Lemuel Mitchell	Hos. Stew'd.	May 27, '61	Bucks	Transferred as Private to Co. K, Sept. 30, 1861.
Frank Niblo	Hos. Stew'd.	Sept. 4, '61		Mustered out Sept. 6, 1864. Expiration of term.
Charles K. Bechtel	Pr. Music'n.	July 21, '61		Promoted to Principal Musician, Sept. 1, 1862. Mustered out with regiment, June 17, 1864.
M. L. Huntzberger	Pr. Music'n.	June 11, '61		Promoted to Principal Musician, July 1st, 1863. Mustered out with regiment, June 17, 1864.

REGIMENTAL BAND.

John Adams, Amos Barton, David Kliminan, Jacob Kliminan, Albert Osmond, George Smith, Henry Smith,	Enlisted for the Band, and mustered out Aug. 4, 1862.	
Herman L. Strong, Robert Warwick, Marshal Darling, Swazy Gordon,	Enlisted for the Band, and mustered out Aug. 4, 1862.	
Christian Kliminan, William Walters, William Whitely.	Transferred to Band. Returned to company Aug. 4, 1862.	

COMPANY A, RECRUITED AT READING, BERKS COUNTY.

NAME.	RANK.	DATE OF MUSTER.	REMARKS.
Jacob Lenhart, Jr.	Captain	June 7, '61	Rank from May 4, 1861. Wounded at Cloyd's Mountain, May 9, 1864. Mustered out with company, June 17, 1864.
Jacob Lehman	1st Lieutenant	June 7, '61	Discharged by order of War Dep't, Aug. 19, 1862.
Michael Walters	"	July 28, '61	Promoted 2d Lieutenant, Aug. 1, 1862; to 1st Lieutenant, October 1st 1862. Discharged for disability, Sept. 15, 1863. Now in Veteran Reserve Corps.
Amos N. Seitzinger	"	June 7, '61	Promoted to 2d Lieutenant, Sept. 26, 1862; to 1st Lieutenant, Oct. 26, 1863. Mustered out with company, June 17, 1864.
Jeremiah A. Clouse	2d Lieutenant	June 7, '61	Rank from June 13, 1861. Resigned, Feb. 17, 1862.
Sebastian Eckle	"	June 7, '61	Promoted, Feb. 29, 1862. Resigned, July 18, 1862.
Daniel Setley	"	June 7, '61	Promoted 1st Sergeant, Nov. 1, 1862; to 2d Lieutenant, Sept. 16, 1863. Mustered out with company, June 17, 1864.
John S. Painter	1st Sergeant	June 18, '61	Promoted to 1st Sergeant, Nov. 1, 1863. Mustered out with company, June 17, 1864.
Jacob C. Esterly	"	June 7, '61	Discharged on Surgeon's Certificate, Oct., 1862.
George Mosser	"	June 7, '61	Promoted to Sergeant, Nov. 1, 1862. Mustered out with company, June 17, 1864.
Lewis Griffith	"	June 7, '61	Promoted to Sergeant, Nov. 1, 1864. Mustered out with company, June 17, 1864.
Henry K. Mull	"	June 7, '61	Promoted to Sergeant, Nov. 1, 1862. Mustered out with company, June 17, 1864.
Charles Fredericks	"	June 7, '61	Discharged on Surgeon's certificate, Dec. 31, 1862.
John Witich	"	June 7, '61	Discharged on Surgeon's certificate, June 14, 1862.
Richard Yeager	"	July 9, '61	Transferred to 3d Brigade, 2d Div., Dep't West Vs., June 6; to 54th Regiment, Pa. Vols., July 4, 1864.

Name	Rank	Date	Remarks
Francis D. Nagle	1st Sergeant	June 7, '61	Killed at White Oak Swamp, June 30, 1862.
Henry Kenler	Corporal	June 18, '61	Promoted to Corporal, July 1, 1862. Mustered out with company, June 17, 1864.
Peter Hartenstein	"	June 7, '61	Promoted to Corporal, March 1, 1863. Mustered out with company, June 17, 1864.
William J. Smith	"	June 7, '61	Promoted to Corporal, Nov. 1, 1862. Mustered out with company, June 17, 1864.
Henry W. Esser	"	June 7, '61	Promoted to Corporal, Nov. 1, 1862. Mustered out with company, June 17, 1864.
Flarian Harbach	"	June 7, '61	Discharged on Surgeon's certificate, Feb. 28, 1863.
Henry J. Richards	"	June 7, '61	Mustered out with company, June 17, 1864.
John D. Hertzog	Musician	June 7, '61	Mustered out as Private, with company, June 17, 1864.
Angstadt, Jacob D	Private	June 7, '61	Mustered out with company, June 17, 1864.
Ash, James D	"	June 18, '61	Discharged on Surgeon's certificate—date unknown.
Bedencup, John	"	June 7, '61	Mustered out with company, June 17, 1864.
Boone, Richard	"	June 7, '61	Mustered out with company, June 17, 1864.
Broadhurst, John	"	June 7, '61	Mustered out with company, June 17, 1864.
Brady, Benjamin	"	Sept. 23, '62	Discharged on Surgeon's certificate, Aug. 24, 1863.
Bowman, Henry	"	June 7, '61	Transferred to 54th Regiment, Pa. Vols., July 4, 1864. Veteran.
Rabb, John H	"	June 7, '61	Wounded and prisoner at Cloyd Mountain, West Va., May 9, 1864. Mustered out, May 30, 1865.
Calvert, James	"	June 18, '61	Deserted; date unknown.
Derr, Samuel	"	June 18, '61	Mustered out with company, June 17, 1864.
Degroat, William	"	Feb. 19, '62	Transferred to 3d Brigade, 2d Div., Dep't West Va., June 6, and to 54th Regiment, Pa. Vols., July 4, 1864.
English, David	"	July 20, '61	Killed at Fredericksburg, Dec. 13, 1862.
Fegely, Andrew	"	June 7, '61	Mustered out with company, June 17, 1864.
Frey, Samuel B	"	June 7, '61	Mustered out with company, June 17, 1864.
Fix, James A	"	June 7, '61	Discharged on Surgeon's certificate, Feb. 23, 1863.
Frey, Allen M	"	Feb. 1, '64	Transferred to 3d Brigade, 2d Div., Dep't West Va., June 6, and to 54th Regiment, Pa. Vols., July 4, 1864.

(13)

COMPANY A—Continued.

NAME.	RANK.	DATE OF MUSTER.	REMARKS.
Graeff, Daniel	Private	June 7, '61	Mustered out with company, June 17, 1864.
Goodman, David J	"	June 7, '61	Mustered out with company, June 17, 1864.
Gauster, Jacob	"	June 7, '61	Discharged on Surgeon's certificate, Feb. 13, 1863.
Good, Joseph	"	July 18, '61	Discharged on Surgeon's certificate, Feb. 28, 1863.
Garst, Frederick	"	July 28, '61	Discharged on Surgeon's certificate—date unknown.
Greth, Albert S	"	June 7, '61	Transferred to 54th Regiment, Pa. Vols., July 4, '64. Veteran.
Harner, Henry A	"	June 7, '61	Mustered out with company, June 17, 1864.
Hodern, George	"	June 7, '61	Mustered out with company, June 17, 1864.
Hodern, John	"	June 7, '61	Mustered out with company, June 17, 1864.
Hart, Lewis	"	July 28, '61	Discharged on Surgeon's certificate, Oct. 17, 1861.
Holland, Peter F	"	June 7, '61	Discharged on Surgeon's certificate, Oct. 29, 1862.
Haws, Marks D	"	July 18, '61	Transferred to 3d Brigade, 2d Div., Dep't W.Va., June 6, and 54th Regiment, Pa. Vols., July 4, 1864.
Harbach, Harrison	"	July 20, '61	Transferred to 3d Brigade, 2d Div., Dep't W.Va., June 6, and 54b Regiment, Pa. Vols., July 4, 1864.
Holland, William P	"	June 7, '61	Transferred to 54th Regiment, Pa. Vols., July 4, 1864. Veteran.
Henershotz, Albert S	"	June 7, '61	Transferred to 54th Regiment, Pa. Vols., July 4, 1864. Veteran.
Harbach, Daniel	"	July 20, '61	Died at Washington, June 7, 1862. Buried in Military Asylum Cemetery.
Jackson, Andrew	"	June 7, '61	Killed at Fredericksburg, Dec. 13, 1862.
Koch, Christian J	"	June 7, '61	Mustered out with company, June 17, 1864.
Koch, John	"	July 7, '61	Mustered out with company, June 17, 1864.
Kocher, Francis	"	June 18, '61	Mustered out with company, June 17, 1864.
Kunsman, Jacob S	"	June 7, '61	Wounded at Fredericksburg, Dec. 13, 1862. Absent, in hospital, at muster out.
Kissinger, Samuel S	"	July 18, '61	Discharged on Surgeon's certificate, Nov. 18, 1862.

(14)

Name	Rank	Date of Enlistment	Remarks
Keehn, Henry C.	Private	July 18, '61	Transferred to 54th Regiment, Pa. Vols., July 4, '64. Veteran.
Kershner, Lewis	"	July 19, '61	Transferred to 3d Brigade, 2d Div., Dep't West Va., June 6, and to 54th Regiment, Pa. Vols., July 4, 1864.
Marquat, Augustus	"	July 18, '61	Discharged on Surgeon's certificate, Oct. 28, 1863.
Milans, Henry G.	"	Sept. 9, '61	Wounded and ordered to report to the Adjutant-General's Office, Washington.
Murphy, Patrick	"	Feb. 11, '62	Transferred to 3d Brigade, 2d Div., Dep't West Va., June 6, and to 54th Regiment, Pa. Vols., July 4, 1864.
M'Donough, William	"	June 18, '61	Wounded at Gaines' Mill, June 27, 1862. Absent, at hospital, at muster out.
M'Quaid, Peter	"	June 18, '61	Mustered out with company, June 17, 1864.
M'Donough, John	"	June 18, '61	Discharged on Surgeon's certificate, June 26, 1863.
M'Gettigan, Hugh	"	July 28, '61	Discharged on Surgeon's certificate, Dec. 7, 1862.
Neebe, Charles	"	July 18, '61	Mustered out with company, June 17, 1864.
O'Niel, John	"	June 17, '61	Wounded and prisoner, at Cloyd Mountain, W. Va., May 9, 1864. Mustered out, Sept. 23, 1864.
Otten, Henry	"	June 17, '61	Died at Smoketown Hospital, Md., Oct. 12, 1862, of wounds received at Antietam, Sept. 17, 1862. Buried in Antietam National Cemetery, grave No. 232, lot C, section 26.
Old, James B.	"	July 18, '61	Killed at Cloyd Mountain, May 9, 1864. Veteran.
Peters William	"	June 7, '61	Mustered out with company, June 17, 1864.
Perry, Abraham	"	Feb. 17, '62	Discharged on Surgeon's certificate, Nov. 4, 1864.
Richards, Levi	"	July 28, '61	Mustered out with company, June 17, 1864.
Rhein, Augustus	"	June 7, '61	Mustered out with company, June 17, 1864.
Rhoades, Levi B.	"	June 7, '61	Mustered out with company, June 17, 1864.
Rork, John	"	June 18, '61	Mustered out with company, June 17, 1864.
Rupp, Ludwig	"	June 18, '61	Mustered out with company, June 17, 1864.
Richards, Emanuel	"	June 7, '61	Discharged on Surgeon's certificate, Jan. 16, 1863.
Ribble, Nicholas	"	July 18, '61	Killed at the battle of Glendale, June 30, 1862.
Schroth, Charles	"	June 7, '61	Mustered out with company, June 17, 1864.
Sellers, Ephraim Z.	"	June 7, '61	Mustered out with company, June 17, 1864.

COMPANY A—Continued.

NAME.	RANK.	DATE OF MUSTER.	REMARKS.
Smith, Henry S.	Private	June 7, '61	Mustered out with company, June 17, 1864.
Stiffenburg, William	"	June 7, '61	Mustered out with company, June 17, 1864.
Stawiler, Albert S.	"	June 7, '6...	Discharged on Surgeon's certificate, June 2, 1862.
Schofield, James A.	"	June 7, '61	Discharged on Surgeon's certificate, Feb. 9, 1863.
Saylor, Frederick	"	July 20, '61	Transferred to 54th Regiment, Pa. Vols. Veteran.
Sallada, James	"	Sept. 23, '62	Transferred to 3d Brigade, 2d Div., Dep't West Va., June 6, and to 54th Regiment, Pa. Vols, July 4, 1864.
Schaneberger, Charles	"	July 20, '61	Transferred to 3d Brigade, 2d Div., Dep't West Va., June 6, 1864, and to 54th Regiment, Pa. Vols., July 4, 1864.
Shade, Enoch	"	July 24, '61	Transferred to 3d Brigade, 2d Div., Dep't West Va., June 6, and to 54th Regiment, Pa. Vols, July 6, 1864.
Shafer, Daniel	"	June 7, '61	Deserted, Sept. 5, 1862.
Warner, William	"	June 7, '61	Mustered out with company, June 17, 1864.
Weber, Charles	"	June 7, '61	Mustered out with company, June 17, 1864.
Weidenhamer, A.	"	June 7, '61	Mustered out with company, June 17, 1864.
Youse, Jonas	"	June 7, '61	Mustered out with company, June 17, 1864.
Yeich, John R.	"	June 7, '61	Mustered out with company, June 17, 1864.
Yohn, John M.	"	June 7, '61	Transferred to 54th Regiment, Pa. Vols, July 4, 1864. Veteran.

COMPANY B, RECRUITED IN WAYNE COUNTY.

NAME.	RANK.	DATE OF MUSTER.	REMARKS.
William D. Curtis	Captain	June 5, '61	Rank from May 13, 1861. Resigned, July 16, 1862.
George C. Davenport	"	June 5, '61	Rank as 1st Lieutenant, from May 13, 1861; to Captain, Aug. 19, 1862. Transferred to Veteran Reserve Corps, Aug. 5, 1863.

Name	Rank	Date	Remarks
Warren G. Moore	Captain	June 5, '61	Promoted to 1st Sergeant, Aug. 19, 1862; to Captain, Aug. 5, 1863. Mustered out with company, June 17, 1864.
F. Gilbert Nicholson	1st Lieutenant	June 5, '61	Promoted to 1st Sergeant, Aug. 16, 1862; to 1st Lieutenant, Nov. 19, 1862. Mustered out with company, June 17, 1864.
J. M. Buckingham	2d Lieutenant	June 5, '61	Rank from May 13, 1861. Resigned, Nov. 14, 1861.
Lyman W. Hamlin	"	June 5, '61	Promoted 2d Lieutenant, Nov. 16, 1861. Discharged on Surgeon's certificate, Nov. 11, 1862.
George M. Rohne	"	July 17 '61	Promoted to Sergeant-Major, Aug. 1, 1862; to 2d Lieutenant, March 1, 1863. Dismissed, Nov. 13, 1863.
Dudley K. Watrous	1st Sergeant	June 5, '61	Promoted to Sergeant, Aug. 1, 1862; to 1st Sergeant, Nov. 1, 1862. Mustered out with company, June 17, 1864.
Lester T. Adams	Sergeant	June 5, '61	Promoted to Sergeant, Aug. 1, 1862. Mustered out with company, June 17, 1864.
John Hetzel	"	June 5, '61	Promoted to Corporal, July 22, 1861; to Sergeant, Jan. 5, 1863. Mustered out with company, June 17, 1864.
Adolphus Monnis	"	June 28, '61	Promoted to Corporal, Aug. 1, 1862; to Sergeant, Nov. 1, 1863. Mustered out with company, June 17, 1864.
Florence B. Hamlin	"	June 5, '61	Discharged on Surgeon's certificate, Sept. 1, 1861.
James W. Carrier	"	June 5, '61	Discharged on Surgeon's certificate, July 25, 1862.
William Biesecker	"	June 5, '61	Discharged on Surgeon's certificate, Aug. 1, 1862.
Henry C. Tripp	"	July 22, '61	Promoted to Corporal, Nov. 16, 1861; to Sergeant, Jan. 18, 1862. Transferred to 54th Regiment, Pa. Vols., July 4, 1864.
Hobart Nicholson	"	June 5, '61	Promoted to Sergeant, Nov. 16, 1861. Killed at Antietam, Sept. 17, 1862; buried at Antietam National Cemetery, grave —.
Charles H. Loper	Corporal	June 5, '61	Promoted to Corporal, July 22, 1861. Transferred to Veteran Reserve Corps, July 30, 1863.

COMPANY B—Continued.

NAME.	RANK.	DATE OF MUSTER.	REMARKS.
George W. Martin	Corporal	June 28, '61	Promoted to Corporal, Jan. 5, 1863. Mustered out with company, June 17, 1864.
Michael Cobb	"	June 5, '61	Promoted to Corporal, Jan. 5, 1863. Mustered out with company, June 17, 1864.
John Martz	"	June 13, '61	Promoted to Corporal, Aug. 1, 1862. Transferred to 54th Regiment, Pa. Vols., July 4, 1864. Veteran.
Russell P. Abbey	"	Sept. 19, '61	Promoted to Corporal, Nov. 1, 1863. Transferred to 54th Regiment, Pa. Vols., July 4, 1864. Veteran.
Gabriel S. Brown	"	June 5, '61	Killed at Gaines' Mill, June 27, 1862.
Jesse R. Dickens	"	June 5, '61	Killed at Antietam, Sept. 17, 1862.
William Green	Musician	June 5, '61	Appointed Musician, Jan. 29, 1862. Transferred to Veteran Reserve Corps, July 30, 1863.
William L. Money	Private	Oct. 5, '61	Discharged on Surgeon's certificate, Oct. 16, 1862.
Ames, Warner J.	"	June 5, '61	Discharged on Surgeon's certificate, Feb. 19, 1862.
Akers, William F.	"	June 5, '61	Discharged on Surgeon's certificate, Sept. 16, 1862.
Andrews, Daniel	"	June 13, '61	Discharged on Surgeon's certificate, Feb. 10, 1862.
Bschon, Joseph	"	June 5, '61	Mustered out with company, June 17, 1864.
Barbrite, William H	"	June 28, '61	Mustered out with company, June 17, 1864.
Bortree, William G	"	June 5, '61	Mustered out with company, June 17, 1864.
Burbank, John W	"	June 5, '61	Discharged on Surgeon's certificate, Jan. 18, 1862.
Bronson, Eli	"	June 5, '61	Discharged on Surgeon's certificate, Aug. 23, 1862.
Bishop, David	"	June 13, '61	Discharged on Surgeon's certificate, Nov. 20, 1862.
Bennet, Benjamin	"	July 29, '61	Discharged on Surgeon's certificate, Oct. 14, 1862.
Brundage, Freeling	"	July 29, '61	Transferred to the Veteran Reserve Corps, July 30, 1863.
Buckingham, J. M.	"	Mar. 30, '64	Transferred to 54th Regiment, Pa. Vols., July 4, 1864.
Brownson, Justus	"	Mar. 30, '64	Transferred to 54th Regiment Pa. Vols., July 4, 1864.

(18)

Name	Rank	Date of muster	Remarks
Brooks, Andrew	Private	Oct. 5, '61	Transferred to 54th Regiment Pa. Vols., July 4, 1864. Veteran.
Buallesoa, Job	"	June 5, '61	Absent at muster out.
Bath, Oliver L	"	July 9, '61	Killed at Glendale, June 30, 1862.
Bidwell, Hiram	"	June 13, '61	Died, Oct. 20, 1862.
Briscoe, John	"	June 5, '61	Deserted, July 29, 1861.
Cornell, Sidney	"	Aug. 10, '61	Discharged on Surgeon's certificate, Dec. 26, 1862.
Cartright, Emily D	"	Mar. 30, '64	Transferred to 54th Regiment, Pa. Vols., July 4, 1864.
Campbell, John	"	July 9, '61	Transferred to 54th Regiment, Pa. Vols., July 4, 1864. Veteran.
Cogswell, William	"	July 17, '61	Died, Aug. 12, 1862.
Campfield, Geo. N	"	June 13, '61	Deserted, Dec. 29, 1862.
Duborn, Nicholas	"	June 5, '61	Discharged on Surgeon's certificate, Jan. 31, 1862.
Dickens, Richard	"	July 17, '61	Transferred to 54th Regiment, Pa. Vols., July 4, 1864.
Donelson, James	"	Sept. 13, '61	Transferred to 54th Regiment, Pa. Vols., July 4, 1864.
Dickins, Daniel S	"	June 5, '61	Killed at Gaines' Mill, June 27, 1862.
Bushiro, Geo. P	"	June 5, '61	Killed at Gaines' Mill, June 27, 1862.
Frisbie, Geo. S	"	Sept. 19, '61	Discharged on Surgeon's certificate, March 6, 1862.
Frisbie, James P	"	March 30, '64	Transferred to 54th Regiment, Pa. Vols., July 4, 1864.
Firth, Thomas	"	June 13, '61	Died, July 26, 1862, of wounds received at Glendale, June 30, 1862. Buried at Cypress Hill Cemetery, Long Island.
Gorman, Daniel	"	June 5, '61	Mustered out with company, June 17, 1864.
Gibbs, Alfred	"	March 30, '64	Transferred to 54th Regiment, Pa. Vols., July 4, 1864.
Gillet, Oliver	"	June 5, '61	Died at Washington, May 21, 1862. Buried in Military Asylum Cemetery.
Handenberger, J. B	"	June 28, '61	Promoted to Sergeant, Jan. 5, 1863; resigned Jan. 18, 1863. Mustered out with company, June 17, '64.
Hauk, John	"	June 5, '61	Transferred to Veteran Reserve Corps, July 30, 1863.
Hinds, Henry	"	June 5, '61	Mustered out with company, June 17, 1864.
Hubbard, C. W	"	June 13 '61	Mustered out with company, June 17, 1864.
Hubler, Robert	"	June 5, '61	Discharged on Surgeon's certificate, April 6, 1862.
Howe, Edward	"	March 30, '64	Transferred to 54th Regiment, Pa. Vols., July 4, 1864.
Howe, James H	"	March 30, '64	Transferred to 54th Regiment, Pa. Vols., July 4, 1864.
Hoover, Joseph F	"	July 29, '61	Transferred to 54th Regiment, Pa. Vols., July 4, 1864.

COMPANY B—Continued.

NAME.	RANK.	DATE OF MUSTER.	REMARKS.
Hand, William J.	Private	Aug. 10, '61	Mustered out, Aug. 18, 1864.
Jones, Robert D.	"	June 5, '61	Mustered out with company, June 17, 1864.
Johnson, Jacob	"	June 28, '61	Discharged on Surgeon's certificate, Nov. 25, 1862.
Johnson, Porter C.	"	July 19, '61	Discharged on Surgeon's certificate, Sept. 25, 1862.
Kennedy, John S.	"	June 5, '61	Died, July, 1862.
Leake, William H.	"	June 5, '61	Promoted to Chaplain of the Regiment, Aug. 1, 1861.
London, Joseph	"	July 20, '61	Transferred to 54th Regiment, Pa. Vols., July 4, 1864. Veteran.
Little, Archibald S.	"	June 28, '61	Died, December 19, 1862, at Richmond, Va., of wounds received at Fredericksb'g, Dec. 13, 1862.
Marsh, John	"	June 5, '61	Absent, sick, at muster-out.
Marshall, Edwin A.	"	June 5, '61	Mustered out with company, June 17, 1864.
Mitchell, Charles E.	"	June 5, '61	Mustered out with company, June 17, 1864.
Moore, William G.	"	June 13, '61	Mustered out with company, June 17, 1864.
Moyer, Anthony	"	June 5, '61	Mustered out with company, June 17, 1864.
Mitchell, Eugene B.	"	June 5, '61	Discharged on Surgeon's Certificate, Dec. 29, 1862.
Mitchell, Michael	"	June 5, '61	Discharged on Surgeon's certificate, Feb. 3, 1862.
Machan, Edward	"	July 29, '61	Discharged on Surgeon's certificate—date unknown.
Miller, Quinters	"	July 29, '61	Transferred to 54th Regiment, Pa. Vols., July 4, 1864.
Mitchell, Davis	"	Oct. 1, '62	Transferred to 54th Regiment, Pa.Vols., July 4, 1864.
Marshall, Frederick	"	June 5, '61	Died, October 12, 1862.
Miller, David	"	Feb. 3, '64	Not on muster-out roll.
Perry, James P.	"	June 5, '61	Discharged on Surgeon's certificate, Jan. 17, 1862.
Peet, Daniel N.	"	June 5, '61	Discharged on Surgeon's certificate, May 25, 1862.
Potter, Henry S.	"	Aug. 10, '61	Discharged on Surgeon's certificate, Dec. 22, 1862.
Pinkerton, John	"	June 5, '61	Transferred to 54th Regiment, Pa. Vols., July 4, 1864. Veteran.
Peet, Daniel N.	"	March 30, '64	Wounded and missing, at Cloyd Mountain, W. Va., May 9, 1864.

Name	Rank	Date	Notes
Pillard, Emil	Private	June 28, '61	Deserted, July 25, 1861.
Riley, James E	"	July 29, '61	Transferred to Veteran Reserve Corps, Nov. 1, 1863.
Riley, John	"	Feb. 4, '64	Transferred to 54th Regiment, Pa. Vols., July 4, 1864.
Sheppard, M. L	"	June 5, '61	Discharged on Surgeon's certificate, Feb. 3, 1863.
Swingle, William	"	March 30, '64	Transferred to 54th Regiment, Pa. Vols., July 4, 1864.
Swingle, Sharp L	"	Oct. 25, '61	Transferred to 54th Regiment, Pa. Vols., July 4, 1864.
Stewart, Archibald H	"	July 20, '61	Killed at Fredericksburg, Dec. 13, 1862.
Simmonson, Ass	"	June 5, '61	Wounded and missing at Cloyd Mountain, W. Va., May 9, 1864. Veteran.
Thomas, Joshua R	"	April 4, '62	Transferred to Veteran Reserve Corps, July 1, 1863.
Townsend, Edward	"	Sept. 19, '61	Mustered out, Sept. 30, 1864.
Walter, Albert	"	June 5 '61	Mustered out with company, June 17, 1864.
Wortman, Henry	"	June 28, '61	Mustered out with company, June 17, 1864.
Warner, George	"	July 17, '61	Transferred to 4th Reserves—date unknown.
Wagner, Joseph G	"	March 31, '64	Transferred to 54th Regiment, Pa. Vols., July 4, 1864.
Woodruff, Selden A	"	July 16, '61	Transferred to 54th Regiment, Pa. Vols., July 4, 1864.
Watrouse, Friend	"	Aug. 10, '61	Transferred to 54th Regiment, Pa. Vols., July 4, 1864.
Wright, Albert A	"	June 13, '62	Transferred to 54th Regiment, Pa. Vols., July 4, 1864.
White, Henry	"	July 16, '61	Died at Washington, Sept. 23, 1861. Buried in Military Asylum Cemetery.
Williams, Alfred	"	July 29, '61	Died, Sept. 26, 1862, of wounds received at Antietam, Sept. 17, 1862. Buried in Antietam National Cemetery, Grave No. —.
Whipple, Stephen F	"	July 9, '61	Deserted, Nov. 1, 1862.
Wright, Eugene H	"	June 13, '61	Discharged on Surgeon's Certificate, Oct. 25, 1862.
Young, Elliott	"	Aug. 10, '61	Mustered out, Aug. 18, 1864.
Young, George	"	Aug. 10, '61	Mustered out, Aug. 18, 1864.

COMPANY C, RECRUITED IN BUCKS COUNTY.

NAME.	RANK.	DATE OF MUSTER.	REMARKS.
David V. Feaster	Captain	June 10, '61	Rank from April 26, 1861. Discharged on Surgeon's certificate, Oct. 12, 1862.
Harry W. Sutton	"	June 10, '61	Promoted to Corporal, Aug. 21, 1861; to 2d Lieutenant, Oct. 1, 1862; to Captain, May 1, 1863. Mustered out with company, June 17, 1864.
Strick'd Yardley	1st Lieutenant	June 10, '61	Rank from April 26, 1861. Appointed Regimental Quartermaster, June 21, 1861. Promoted to Captain and Assistant-Quartermaster, U.S. Vols., Aug. 10, 1863.
John H. Crothers	"		Promoted from 1st Sergeant to 1st Lieutenant, Oct. 1, 1862. Mustered out with company, June 17, 1864.
Joseph B. Roberts	2d Lieutenant	June 10, '61	Rank from April 26, 1861. Discharged, Sept. 23, 1862, for wounds received at Charles City Cross Roads, Va., June 30, 1862.
Zeaman Jones	"	June 10, '61	Promoted from Corporal to Sergeant, date unknown; to 2d Lieutenant, May 1, 1863. Mustered out with company, June 17, 1864.
Daniel P. Burkit	1st Sergeant	June 10, '61	Promoted from Corporal to Sergeant. Mustered out with company, June 17, 1864.
T. Watson Bewly	Sergeant	June 10, '61	Promoted from Corporal to Sergeant, Sept. 1, 1863. Mustered out with company, June 17, 1864.
Thomas Adams	"	June 10, '61	Promoted from Corporal to Sergeant, Sept. 1, 1864. Mustered out with company, June 17, 1864.
Perry H. Vanhorn	"	June 10, '61	Promoted from Corporal to Sergeant, Oct. 1, 1863. Mustered out with company, June 17, 1864.
Aaron W. Buckman	"	June 10, '61	Discharged, to receive a commission in the U. S. colored troops, Aug 19, 1863.
William F. Roberts	"	June 10, '61	Discharged, Nov. 22, 1862, for wounds at Bull Run.

(22)

Name	Rank	Date	Remarks
Samuel J. Griffee	Sergeant	June 10, '61	Discharged, Nov. 18, 1862, for wounds received at Charles City Cross Roads, Va.
James E. M'Masters	"	June 10, '61	Discharged on Surgeon's certificate, May 11, 1863.
Thomas P. Goheen	"	June 10, '61	Killed at Gaines' Mill, June 27, 1862.
Edward I. Lennon	"	June 10, '61	Killed at Gaines' Mill, June 27, 1862.
Martin V. Taylor	Corporal	June 10, '61	Promoted to Corporal, Jan. 15, 1863. Mustered out with company, June 17, 1864.
Charles Y. Clark	"	June 10, '61	Promoted to Corporal, Jan 21, 1864. Mustered out with company, June 17, 1864.
Benjamin F. Crosedale	"	June 10, '61	Discharged, May 20, 1863, for wounds at Antietam.
William Gray	"	June 10, '61	Discharged on Surgeon's certificate, Sept. 10, 1863.
John D. Blaker	"	June 10, '61	Discharged on Surgeon's certificate, Dec. 24, 1862.
Matthew Mills	"	June 10, '61	Killed accidentally at Wood's Mills, Va., June 6, 1864. Veteran.
Allen, William	Private	July 17, '61	Discharged on Surgeon's certificate, Dec. 1, 1862.
Blaker, Edward H	"	June 10, '61	Mustered out with company, June 17, 1864.
Barker, Francis	"	July 13, '61	Discharged on Surgeon's certificate, Sept. 10, 1862.
Black, Edward	"	July 11, '61	Discharged on Surgeon's certificate, July 29, 1862.
Bodine, John R	"	July 13, '61	Discharged on Surgeon's certificate, April 2, 1862.
Bennett, William	"	Feb. 17, '62	Discharged on Surgeon's Certificate, Oct. 16, 1862.
Brown, James L	"	June 10, '61	Transferred to 54th Regiment, Pa. Vols., July 4, 1864. Veteran.
Bennett, Henry	"	June 10, '61	Mustered out, Feb. 8, 1865.
Caffee, William	"	June 10, '61	Discharged on Surgeon's certificate, Oct 16, 1862.
Corbet, Matthew	"	June 10, '61	Discharged on Surgeon's certificate, Feb. 6, 1863.
Craver, Philip	"	June 10, '61	Discharged on Surgeon's certificate, July 25, 1862.
Cooper, Owen	"	June 10, '61	Transferred to Battery C, 5th U. S. Artillery, Oct. 19, 1862.
Carver, John W	"	June 10, '61	Deserted, Dec. 11, 1862; returned, Jan 25, 1864. Transferred to 54th Regiment, Pa. Vols., July 4, 1864.
Caffee, Joseph K	"	July 8, '61	Died at Mill Creek, Va., Sept. 19, 1862.
Dillon, Andrew J	"	July 20, '61	Mustered out, Sept. 4, 1864.
Doan, Howard	"	June 10, '61	Transferred to 54th Regiment, Pa. Vols., July 4, 1864. Veteran.

COMPANY C—Continued.

NAME.	RANK.	DATE OF MUSTER.	REMARKS.
Ditmars, Isaac	Private	July 9, '61	Transferred to 54th Regiment, Pa. Vols, July 4, 1864.
Dillon, Thomas	"	Aug. 26, '62	Killed at Fredericksburg, Dec. 13, 1862.
Dillon, Robert	"	Aug. 25, '62	Killed at Fredericksburg, Dec. 13, 1862.
Eizenbrey, Edwin	"	July 18, '61	Transferred to 54th Regiment, Pa. Vols, July 4, 1864. Veteran.
Fitzpatrick, Joseph	"	June 10, '61	Mustered out with company, June 17, 1864.
Flanagan, Albert	"	June 10, '61	Discharged on Surgeon's certificate, Dec. 23, 1862.
Fennell, William J	"	June 10, '61	Transferred to 54th Regiment, Pa. Vols., July 4, 1864. Veteran.
Fetherby, George W	"	July 17, '61	Transferred to 54th Regiment, Pa. Vols, July 4, 1864.
Fleming, James	"	June 10, '61	Transferred to 54th Regiment, Pa. Vols., July 4, 1864. Veteran.
Fifer, Richard	"	June 10, '61	Transferred to 54th Regiment, Pa. Vols, July 4, 1864. Veteran.
Gordon, Swayze	"	June 17, '61	Mustered out with company, June 17, 1864.
Grady, George	"	June 10, '61	Discharged, March 17, 1863, for wounds received at Charles City Cross Roads, Va.
Graham, Adam	"	June 10, '61	Transferred to 54th Regiment, Pa. Vols, July 4, 1864.
Harris, William H	"	June 10, '61	Mustered out with company, June 17, 1864.
Hibbs, Algernon	"	June 10, '61	Mustered out with company, June 17, 1864.
Helly, Jonathan T	"	Jan. 27, '62	Discharged on Surgeon's certificate, July 25, 1863.
Hough, Calvin	"	June 10, '61	Transferred to Battery C, 5th U. S. Artillery, Oct. 19, 1862.
Hillborn, Joseph	"	June 10, '61	Transferred to 54th Regiment, Pa. Vols, July 4, 1864. Veteran.
Harrison, Charles	"	Oct. 4, '62	Transferred to 54th Regiment, Pa. Vols., July 4, 1864.
Hough, George W	"	June 10, '61	Transferred to 54th Regiment, Pa. Vols., July 4, 1864.
Hillborn, William	"	June 10, '61	Killed at White Oak Swamp, Va.
Hammer, Joseph	"	July 21, '61	Killed at White Oak Swamp, June 30, 1862.

Name	Rank	Date	Remarks
Hitchcock, Charles	Private	June 10, '61	Deserted—date unknown.
Johnson, Lyman	"	June 10, '61	Mustered out with company, June 17, 1864.
Kinsey, Jonathan	"	June 10, '61	Mustered out with company, June 17, 1864.
Kelly, Robert	"	July 21, '61	Transferred to 54th Regiment, Pa. Vols., July 4, 1864.
Longshare, William G	"	June 10, '61	Mustered out with company, June 17, 1864.
Long, Henry	"	June 10, '61	Discharged on Surgeon's certificate, May 21, 1862.
London, Joseph	"	July 17, '61	Discharged, Jan. 12, 1863, from wounds received at Glendale, Va., June 30, 1862.
Lugar, James M	"	June 10, '61	Discharged on Surgeon's certificate, Jan. 21, 1862.
Lewis, Abraham	"	June 10, '61	Transferred to 54th Regiment, Pa. Vols., July 4, 1864. Veteran.
Large, Joseph H	"	July 29, '61	Mustered out, Aug. 20, 1864.
Morris, George W	"	June 10, '61	Mustered out with company, June 17, 1864.
Mitchell, Jeremiah	"	June 10, '61	Deserted, April 13, 1862.
Mershon William	"	June 10, '61	Deserted, Dec. 13, 1862.
M'Connell, John	"	June 10, '61	Mustered out with company, June 17, 1864.
M'Carn, Barnard	"	June 10, '61	Mustered out with company, June 17, 1864.
M'Carn, James	"	June 10, '61	Discharged on Surgeon's certificate, Feb 14, 1863.
Phillips, Banner T	"	June 10, '61	Mustered out with company, June 17, 1864.
Reeder, Henry P	"	June 10, '61	Transferred to 54th Regiment, Pa. Vols., July 4, 1864.
Ryan, James	"	June 10, '61	Transferred to 55th Regiment, Pa. Vols., July 4, 1864.
Rose, John L	"	June 10, '61	Transferred to 54th Regiment, Pa. Vols., July 4, 1864.
Roberts, George W	"	Aug. 12, '62	Transferred to 54th Regiment, Pa. Vols., July 4, 1864.
Rose, James	"	June 10, '61	Died at Camp Pierpont, Va., Feb. 22, 1862.
Robinson, Charles	"	July 13, '61	Killed at Gaines' Mill, June 27, 1862.
Runk, Charles	"	June 10, '61	Deserted, Nov. 2, 1862, from Battery C, 5th U. S. Artillery.
Swartz, Larne	"	June 10, '61	Discharged on Surgeon's certificate—date unknown.
Smith, Bartlett	"	July 21, '61	Transferred to 54th Regiment, Pa. Vols., July 4, 1864.
Smith, John	"	Sept. 22, '62	Transferred to 54th Regiment, Pa. Vols., July 4, 1864.
Stevenson, Daniel	"	July 11, '61	Transferred to 54th Regiment, Pa. Vols., July 4, 1864.
Stone, Thomas	"	June 10, '61	Transferred to Battery C, 5th U. S. Art., Oct. 19, 1862.
Stout, Joseph	"	July 8, '61	Transferred to 54th Regiment, Pa. Vols., July 4, 1864.
Southwick, John	"	July 18, '61	Transferred to Battery C, 5th U. S. Art., Oct. 19, 1862

COMPANY C—Continued.

NAME.	RANK.	DATE OF MUSTER.	REMARKS.
Steifle, John	Private	June 10, '61	Killed, March 26, 1864, near Kearneysville, Va. Veteran. Buried at Winchester, Va.—Grave No.—, Lot—, Section 26.
Stewart, Henry	"		Deserted, October 1, 1861.
Thornton, Charles	"	June 18, '61	Mustered out with company, June 17, 1864.
Tapp, John S.	"	June 10, '61	Mustered out with company, June 17, 1864.
Trimmer, Elwood	"	June 10, '61	Transferred to 54th Regiment, Pa.Vols, July 4, 1864.
Vanhorn, Joseph	"	July 17, '61	Transferred to 54th Regiment, Pa.Vols, July 4, 1864.
Walton, Samuel	"	June 10, '61	Mustered out with company, June 17, 1864
Wiggins, Charles	"	June 10, '61	Mustered out with company, June 17, 1864.
Woolman, Lewis N.	"	June 10, '61	Mustered out with company, June 17, 1864.
Wall, Anthony J.	"	July 29, '61	Transferred to 54th Regiment, Pa.Vols, July 4, 1864.
Wynkoop, S. W.	"	Oct. 4, '62	Transferred to 54th Regiment, Pa.Vols, July 4, 1864.
Wells, Charles	"	July 21, '61	Transferred to Battery C, 5th U.S. Art., Oct. 19, 1862.
Williamson, Levi	"	July 17, '61	Transferred to Veteran Reserve Corps, July 29, 1863.
Wittee, Peter W.	"	July 20, '61	Died at Camp Pierpont, Va., Nov. 26, 1862.
Wiggins, George W.	"	July 29, '61	Killed at Fredericksburg, Va., Dec. 13, 1862.
White, George W.	"	July 11, '61	Deserted, October 1, 1861.
Young, Absolam B.	"	June 10, '61	Mustered out with company, June 17, 1864.
Young, Wesley S.	"	June 10, '61	Transferred to 54th Regiment, Pa.Vols, July 4, 1864. Veteran.

COMPANY D. RECRUITED IN BERKS COUNTY.

William Briner	Captain	June 7, '61	Rank, from May 1, 1861; to Major, Aug. 1, 1862.
Florentine H. Straub	"	June 7, '61	Promoted to 2d Lieutenant, May 1, 1861; to 1st Lieutenant, Nov. 19, 1861; to Captain, Aug. 1, 1862. Killed at Antietam, Sept. 17, 1862.

Name	Rank	Date	Remarks
Andrew J. Stetson	Captain	June 7, '61	Promoted 2d Lieutenant, Nov. 19, 1861; to 1st Lieutenant, Aug. 1, 1862; to Captain, Oct. 1, 1862. Mustered out with company, June 17, 1864.
Franklin S. Bickley	1st Lieutenant	June 7, '61	Rank, from June 4, 1861. Resigned, Nov. 13, 1861.
Jacob V. Shilling	"	June 7, '61	Promoted to 1st Sergeant, Jan. 7, 1862; to 2d Lieutenant, Aug. 1, 1862; to 1st Lieutenant, Oct. 1, 1862. Killed at Fredericksburg, Va., Dec. 13, 1862.
Albert Briner	"	June 7, '61	Promoted to 1st Sergeant, Aug. 1, 1862; to 2d Lieutenant, Oct. 1, 1862; to 1st Lieutenant, Dec. 14, 1862. Mustered out with company, June 17, 1864.
George B. Davis	2d Lieutenant	June 7, '61	Promoted to Sergeant, August 1, 1862; to 2d Lieutenant, March 6, 1863. Mustered out with company, June 17, 1864.
Abraham B. Yocum	1st Sergeant	June 7, '61	Promoted to Corporal, Nov. 20, 1861; to Sergeant, Jan. 1, 1863; to 1st Sergeant, May 1, 1863. Mustered out with company, June 17, 1864.
James Schrader	"	June 11, '61	Promoted to Sergeant, March 1, 1862; to 1st Sergeant, Oct. 1, 1862. Killed at Fredericksburg, Dec. 13, 1862.
David Hollenback	"	June 7, '61	Promoted to 1st Sergeant, Nov. 20, 1861. Deserted, Jan. 7, 1862.
William K. Leaman	Sergeant	June 7, '61	Promoted to Corporal, Nov. 20, 1861; to Sergeant, January 1, 1863. Mustered out with company, June 17, 1864.
Franklin Trussel	"	June 7, '61	Promoted to Corporal, August 1, 1862; to Sergeant, January 1, 1863. Mustered out with company, June 17, 1864.
Levi Boyer	"	June 7, '61	Promoted to Quartermaster-Sergeant, Sept. 30, 1861.
William H. Parker	"	July 21, '61	Promoted to Corporal, March 20, 1863; to Sergeant, January, 1863. Transferred to 54th Regiment, Pa. Vols., July 4, 1864.
Francis Eisenbeis	"	July 18, '61	Promoted to Corporal, Aug. 1, 1862; to Sergeant, May 1, 1863. Transferred to 54th Regiment, Pa. Vols., July 4, 1864.

COMPANY D—Continued.

NAME.	RANK.	DATE OF MUSTER.	REMARKS.
John A. Price	Sergeant	June 7, '61	Promoted to Sergeant, Nov. 19, 1861. Killed at Glendale, June 30, 1862.
John W. Smith	"	June 7, '61	Promoted to Sergeant, Aug. 1, 1862. Deserted, Dec. 19, 1862.
H. H. Hemming	Corporal	July 18, '61	Promoted to Corporal, Jan. 1, 1863. Mustered out with company, June 17, 1864.
Nelson G. Sheeder	"	June 11, '61	Promoted to Corporal, Jan. 1, 1863. Mustered out with company, June 17, 1864.
Lewis F. Henderson	"	June 11, '61	Promoted to Corporal, Jan. 1, 1863. Mustered out with company, June 17, 1864.
William Carlin	"	June 7, '61	Promoted to Corporal, Jan. 1, 1863. Mustered out with company, June 17, 1864.
William S. Lamb	"	June 7, '61	Promoted to Corporal, Jan. 1, 1863. Mustered out with company, June 17, 1864.
Peter B. Keehn	"	June 11, '61	Promoted to Corporal, Jan. 1, 1863. Mustered out with company, June 17, 1864.
Adam F. Waid	"	July 13, '61	Promoted to Corporal, Jan. 1, 1863. Transferred to 54th Regiment, Pa. Vols., July 4, 1864.
Ephream Strohecker	"	June 7, '61	Died at Washington, March 19, 1862.
John G. Bland	"	June 7, '61	Promoted to Corporal, Nov. 20, 1861. Killed at Fredericksburg, Dec. 13, 1862.
Henry Setley	"	July 9, '61	Promoted to Corporal, March 1, 1862. Killed at Fredericksburg, Dec. 13, 1862.
John S. Keever	Musician	June 7, '61	Mustered out with company, June 17, 1864.
Charles K. Bechtel	"	July 21, '61	Promoted to Principal Musician, Sept. 1, 1862.
M. L. Huntzberger	"	June 11, '61	Promoted to Principal Musician, July 1, 1863.
Achey, Obediah	Private	June 7, '61	Died at Van Clevesville, W. Va., March 25, 1864.
Allen, Edward	"	July 28, '61	Transferred from Company I. Deserted, Apr. 14, 1862.

Name	Rank	Date of Muster	Remarks
Barr, Henry	Private	June 7, '61	Mustered out with company, June 17, 1864.
Bishop, Clark	"	June 7, '61	Mustered out with company, June 17, 1864.
Boone, Jeremiah	"	June 7, '61	Mustered out with company, June 17, 1864.
Boone, Thomas D	"	June 11, '61	Transferred to U. S. Signal Corps, August 29, 1861. Mustered out with company, June 17, 1864.
Boyer, Charles	"	June 7, '61	Mustered out with company, June 17, 1864.
Billing, Philip	"	June 6, '61	Discharged on Surgeon's certificate, Dec. 10, 1862.
Bobst, Samuel	"	June 7, '61	Discharged on Surgeon's certificate, Jan. 29, 1862.
Broom, William	"	Sept. 19, '62	Discharged on Surgeon's certificate, Feb. 1, 1863.
Barber, Charles H	"	July 13, '61	Transferred to 54th Regiment, Pa. Vols., July 4, 1864. Veteran.
Becker, John H	"	July 12, '61	Transferred to 54th Regiment, Pa.Vols, July 4, 1864.
Boyer, Washington L	"	June 7, '61	Transferred to 54th Regiment, Pa.Vols, July 4, 1864.
Briner, Jefferson	"	July 12, '61	Transferred to 54th Regiment, Ps.Vols., July 4, 1864.
Babb, John	"	June 7, '61	Killed at second Bull Run, Aug. 30, 1862.
Bechtel, David	"	July 18, '61	Wounded and missing, at Glendale, June 30, 1862.
Bechtel, Jacob	"	July 18, '61	Wounded and missing at Fredericksburg, Vª, Dec. 13, 1862.
Boyer, John H	"	June 7, '61	Mustered out with company, June 17, 1864.
Cunningham, Peter	"	June 7, '61	Mustered out with company, June 17, 1864.
Coller, Josiah	"	June 7, '61	Discharged on Surgeon's certificate, March 25, 1863.
Caldwell, James	"	June 7, '61	Deserted, April 14, 1862.
Daviee, Samuel	"	June 7, '61	Mustered out with company, June 17, 1864.
De Parson, De Lozier	"	Sept. 30, '62	Discharged on Surgeon's certificate, March 1, 1863.
Dehart, Peter	"	July 13, '61	Transferred to 54th Regiment, Pa. Vols, July 4, 1864.
Dengler, Henry	"	Sept. 30, '62	Transferred to 54th Regiment, Pa. Vols, July 4, 1864.
Doty, James	"	June 7, '61	Deserted, Dec. 9, 1862.
Epphimer, David C	"	Sept. 30, '62	Promoted to Commissary Sergeant, March 1, 1864.
Ellis, William	"	June 7, '61	Transferred to 54th Regiment, Pa.Vols, July 4, 1864.
Ellis, Franklin	"	Sept. 30, '62	Deserted, Dec. 10, 1862.
Focht, Josiah	"	June 7, '61	Discharged on Surgeon's certificate, Nov. 27, 1862.
Frill, Edward	"	June 11, '61	Deserted, Oct. 30, 1862.
Fisher, David	"	Sept. 30, '62	Mustered out, June 23, 1865.
Geiger, Henry	"	June 11, '61	Mustered out with company, June 17, 1864.

COMPANY D—Continued.

NAME.	RANK.	DATE OF MUSTER.	REMARKS.
Good, William S............	Private........	June 11, '61.........	Mustered out with company, June 17, 1864.
Gearhart, Reuben G.........	"	June 11, '61.........	Discharged on Surgeon's certificate, Feb., 1862.
Good, Emanuel..............	"	Sept. 19, '62........	Discharged on Surgeon's certificate, July 25, 1863.
Good, Henry S..............	"	July 18, '61.........	Transferred to 54th Regiment, Pa. Vols., July 4, 1864. Veteran.
Grath, William.............	"	Aug. 26, '62.........	Transferred to 54th Regiment, Pa.Vols., July 4, 1864.
Geiger, Alexander..........	"	July 13, '61.........	Killed at Bull Run, Aug. 30, 1862.
Harner, Alfred.............	"	June 11, '61.........	Mustered out with company, June 17, 1864.
Harrison, Samuel L.........	"	June 11, '61.........	Mustered out with company, June 17, 1864.
Hoffman, Henry.............	"	June 7, '61..........	Mustered out with company, June 17, 1864
Hobson, James L............	"	June 11, '61.........	Discharged on Surgeon's certificate, Nov. 24, 1862.
Hendley, Frederick.........	"	June 11, '61.........	Killed at Antietam, Sept. 17, 1862.
Hunsberger, Jeremiah C.....	"	July 13, '61.........	Wounded and prisoner, at Cloyd Mountain, W. Va., May 9, 1864.
Helmer, Albert D...........	"	July 12, '61.........	Deserted, March 2, 1864.
Kupp, Morgan...............	"	June 7, '61..........	Promoted to Quartermaster 167th Regiment, Pa. Vols., Dec. 11, 1862.
Kelchner, William..........	"	Aug. 30, '62.........	Transferred to 54th Regiment, Pa. Vols, July 4, 1864.
Kellar, Adam F.............	"	June 11, '61.........	Deserted, July 25, 1861.
Long, James................	"	June 7, '61..........	Mustered out with company, June 17, 1864.
Lorah, Henry A.............	"	June 7, '61..........	Mustered out with company, June 17, 1864.
Lowrey, Patrick............	"	June 7, '61..........	Mustered out with company, June 17, 1864.
Lorah, Alexander...........	"	July 20, '61.........	Mustered out, Aug. 12, 1864.
Levan, David...............	"	Sept. 8, '62.........	Deserted, Dec. 10, 1862.
Lichtenfelt, Henry.........	"	June 11, '61.........	Deserted, July 25, 1861.
Mann, Samuel...............	"	June 7, '61..........	Deserted, Dec. 10, 1862. Returned, April 1, 1863. Mustered out with company, June 17, 1864.
Miles, Nathaniel...........	"	June 7, '61..........	Mustered out with company, June 17, 1864.
Miller, William............	"	June 7, '61..........	Discharged on Surgeon's certificate, May 18, 1862.

Name	Rank	Date	Remarks
Mellen, Jacob	Private	June 7, '61	Killed at Gaines' Mill, June 27, 1862.
Moohn, Isaac	"	Sept. 30, '62	Deserted, Dec. 9, 1862.
M'Chalicker, Samuel	"	July 13, '61	Discharged, Nov. 27, 1862, for wounds received at Bull Run, Aug. 30, 1862.
M'Cord, Heber	"	July 18, '61	Transferred to 54th Regiment, Pa. Vols., July 4, 1864.
Raudenbush, G. A.	"	June 7, '61	Mustered out with company, June 17, 1864.
Rank, William	"	June 7, '61	Died at Fairfax Seminary Hospital, Va., Sept. 24, 1862.
Rorke, Joseph	"	July 13, '61	Wounded and missing in action at New Market Cross Roads, June 30, 1862.
Sagee, William S.	"	June 7, '61	Mustered out with company, June 17, 1864.
Sayboldt, Augustus	"	June 7, '61	Promoted from Corporal to Sergeant, Nov. 19, 1861. Resigned, Oct. 1, 1862. Mustered out with company, June 17, 1864.
Scarlet, Roland G.	"	June 7, '61	Mustered out with company, June 17, 1864.
Shaner, Solomon S.	"	June 7, '61	Mustered out with company, June 17, 1864.
Slichter, Joseph	"	June 7, '61	Mustered out with company, June 17, 1864.
Schiefley, John	"	June 7, '61	Discharged, June 22, 1863, for wounds received at Fredericksburg, Dec. 13, 1862.
Steeve, Richard	"	June 7, '61	Discharged on Surgeon's certificate, April 10, 1862.
Shaffer, Harrison	"	Aug. 25, '62	Transferred to 54th Regiment, Pa. Vols, July 4, 1864.
Simmons, Henry J	"	Aug. 30, '62	Transferred to 54th Regiment, Pa. Vols, July 4, 1864.
Shepherd, A. M.	"	July 18, '61	Transferred to 54th Regiment, Pa. Vols, July 4, 1864.
Schwartz, Cyrus	"	June 7, '61	Wounded and missing in action at Glendale, June 30, 1862.
Setley, George	"	June 11, '61	Died at Stafford Court House, Va., Nov. 24, 1862.
Shaffer, George	"	Sept. 9, '62	Deserted, Dec. 14, 1862.
Thomas, James P.	"	Sept. 1, '62	Transferred to 54th Regiment, Pa. Vols., July 4, 1864.
Walker, Benjamin F.	"	June 7, '61	Mustered out with company, June 17, 1864.
Waun, Henry	"	June 7, '61	Mustered out with company, June 17, 1864.
Weigner, George O.	"	June 7, '61	Mustered out with company, June 17, 1864.
Wright, Charles E.	"	June 6, '61	Wounded and missing at, Fredericksburg, Dec. 13, 1862.
Wilkins, Charles	"	July 18, '61	Deserted, Dec. 14, 1862.
Yoder, Samuel	"	June 7, '61	Discharged, Nov. 28, 1862, for wounds received at second Bull Run, August 29, 1862.

COMPANY E, RECRUITED IN PHILADELPHIA.

NAME.	RANK.	DATE OF MUSTER.	REMARKS.
John Clark	Captain	May 31, '61	Rank from May 24, 1861. Promoted to Lieutenant-Colonel, July 10, 1862.
Robert Johnson	"	May 31, '61	Promoted from 1st Lieutenant to Captain, Aug. 1, 1862. Mustered out with company, June 17, 1864.
Thomas H. Bradford	1st Lieutenant	May 31, '61	Promoted to Sergeant, Aug. 1, 1861; to 1st Lieutenant, Aug. 1, 1862. Mustered out with company, June 17, 1864.
George H. Lindsey	2d Lieutenant	May 31, '61	Rank from May 24, 1861. Resigned July 19, 1862.
Edwin A Glenn	"	May 31, '61	Promoted to Sergeant, Aug. 1, 1861; to 2d Lieutenant, Aug. 1, 1862. Mustered out with company, June 17, 1864.
Alfred B. Day	1st Sergeant	May 31, '61	Promoted to Sergeant, Aug. 1, 1862; to 1st Sergeant, Oct. 1, 1862. Mustered out with company, June 17, 1864.
John Blaker	"	May 31, '61	Died of wounds received at Antietam, Sept. 17, 1862.
Dennis C. Duggan	Sergeant	May 31, '61	Promoted to Sergeant, Aug. 1, 1862. Mustered out with company, June 17, 1864.
Jesse Wells	"	May 31, '61	Promoted to Sergeant, Oct. 1, 1862. Mustered out with company, June 17, 1864.
J. Y. Martindale	"	May 31, '61	Promoted to Sergeant, Nov. 1, 1862. Mustered out with company, June 17, 1864.
Charles W. Stout	"	May 31, '61	Prisoner at Gaines' Mill, June 27, 1862. Promoted to Sergeant, March 1, 1863. Mustered out with company, June 17, 1864.
John B. Clift	"	May 31, '61	Discharged on Surgeon's certificate, July 11, 1862.
Samuel Flemming	"	May 31, '61	Discharged, Nov. 12, 1862, for wounds received at Mechanicsville, June 26, 1862.
Harry S. Jones	"	May 31, '61	Promoted to Sergeant-Major, July 1, 1861; to 2d Lieutenant, Company F, July 29, 1862.

(32)

Name	Rank	Date	Remarks
George Wells	Corporal	May 31, '61	Promoted to Corporal, Aug. 2, 1862. Mustered out with company, June 17, 1864.
John R. Wagner	"	May 31, '61	Promoted to Corporal, Oct. 1, 1862. Mustered out with company, June 17, 1864.
James P. Brown	"	May 31, '61	Promoted to Corporal, Nov. 1, 1862. Mustered out with company, June 17, 1864.
Edward Tustin	"	May 31, '61	Promoted to Corporal, March 1, 1863. Mustered out with company, June 17, 1864.
Edward J. Haines	"	May 31, '61	Promoted to Corporal, March 1, 1863. Mustered out with company, June 17, 1864.
Lynford Finlayson	"	May 31, '61	Discharged on Surgeon's certificate, Feb. 18, 1863.
George T. Mills	"	May 31, '61	Discharged on Surgeon's certificate, Feb. 20, 1863.
Samuel Cartledge	"	May 31, '61	Transferred to Signal Corps, July 18, 1861. Discharged at expiration of term.
Henry B. Weed	"	July 9, '61	Transferred to 54th Regiment, Pa. Vols., July 4, 1864.
Alfred Haines	"	May 31, '61	Transferred to 54th Regiment, Pa. Vols., July 4, 1864. Veteran.
Jacob Thomas	"	May 31, '61	Killed at White Oak Swamp, June 30, 1862.
George Morgan	Musician	May 31, '61	Mustered out with company, June 17, 1864.
John Stack	"	May 31, '61	Mustered out with company, June 17, 1864.
Achuff, Isaac	Private	May 31, '61	Transferred to 54th Regiment, Pa. Vols., July 4, 1864. Veteran.
Atkinson, William H	"	May 31, '61	Transferred to 54th Regiment, Pa. Vols., July 4, 1864. Veteran.
Ackley, Benjamin	"	July 16, '61	Transferred to 54th Regiment, Pa. Vols., July 4, 1864.
Artman, Owen	"	July 17, '61	Transferred to 54th Regiment, Pa. Vols., July 4, 1864.
Ashton, William	"	May '31, 61	Transferred to 54th Regiment, Pa. Vols., July 4, 1864.
Booth, Walter	"	May 31, '61	Mustered out with company, June 17, 1864.
Bambrick, Richard	"	May 31, '61	Wounded at Fredericksburg. Mustered out with company, June 17, 1864.
Bennett, David R	"	May 31, '61	Prisoner at Charles City Cross Roads. Mustered out with company, June 17, 1864.
Boileau, Tustin	"	May 31, '61	Mustered out with company, June 17, 1864.

COMPANY E—Continued.

NAME.	RANK.	DATE OF MUSTER.	REMARKS.
Boulton, James.............	Private........	May 31, '61........	Wounded at Antietam. Discharged on Surgeon's certificate, January 18, 1863.
Bartlow, Warren............	"	May 31, '61........	Transferred to 54th Regiment, Pa. Vols., July 4, 1864. Veteran.
Benger, William H.........	"	July 22, '61.......	Transferred to 54th Regiment, Pa. Vols, July 4, 1864.
Boyd, James.................	"	Sept. 10, '62.......	Transferred to 54th Regiment, Pa. Vols, July 4, 1864.
Brophy, James...............	"	May 31, '62........	Deserted, June 5, 1861. Released on writ of *habeas corpus*. Minor.
Chambers, Robert...........	"	May 31, '61........	Mustered out with company, June 17, 1864.
Clark, William...............	"	May 31, '61........	Mustered out with company, June 17, 1864.
Clinton, John.................	"	May 31, '61........	Mustered out with company, June 17, 1864.
Crippe, William..............	"	May 31, '61........	Mustered out with company, June 17, 1864.
Clark, Robert................	"	July 18, '61........	Transferred to 54th Regiment, Pa. Vols., July 4, 1864.
Cochran, Matthew...........	"	July 21, '61........	Transferred to 54th Regiment, Pa. Vols., July 4, 1864.
Carman, William............	"	March 16, '61......	Transferred to 54th Regiment, Pa. Vols, July 4, 1864.
Dewees, Charles.............	"	May 31, '61........	Wounded at Fredericksburg. Mustered out with company, June 17, 1864.
Dugan, Michael..............	"	May 31, '61........	Mustered out with company, June 17, 1864.
Drexler, Frederick...........	"	May 31, '61........	Discharged on Surgeon's certificate, Sept. 21, 1862.
Downing, William............	"	Sept. 11, '62.......	Transferred to 54th Regiment, Pa.Vols., July, 4, 1864.
Eckley, Amos.................	"	May 31, '61........	Mustered out with company, July 17, 1864.
Eckley, John T...............	"	May 31, '61........	Discharged on Surgeon's certificate, Jan. 20, 1863.
Eckley, Joseph...............	"	May 31, '61........	Discharged on Surgeon's certificate, May 11, 1863.
Egee, George H..............	"	May 31, '61........	Deserted, Dec. 12, 1862.
Fullerton, John...............	"	May 31, '61........	Mustered out with company, June 17, 1864.
Fletcher, John W............	"	May 31, '61........	Absent at muster-out.
Fletcher, George W.........	"	May 31, '61........	Deserted, Dec. 12, 1862.
Hoff, Henry K...............	"	May 31, '61........	Mustered out with company, June 17, 1864.
Johnson, John................	"	July 15, '61........	Discharged on Surgeon's certificate, Dec. 23, 1862.

Name	Rank	Date of muster in	Remarks
Johnson, Jacob A	Private	July 22, '61	Killed at Fredericksburg, Dec. 13, 1862.
Kreuson, Luther	"	May 31, '61	Died from wounds received at Antietam, Sept. 17, 1862; buried in National Cemetery at Antietam, grave No. 179, lot B, section 26.
Kennedy, John	"	Jan. 22, '64	Not on muster-out roll.
Kelly, John F	"	Nov. 11, '64	Not on muster-out roll.
Lynn, John	"	May 31, '61	Transferred to 54th Regiment, Pa. Vols., July 4, 1864. Veteran.
Mooney, George W	"	May 31, '61	Mustered out with company, June 17, 1864.
Miller, Frederick C	"	May 31, '61	Mustered out with company, June 17, 1864.
Maybery, Martin	"	Sept. 27, '61	Deserted, Jan. 21, 1862.
M'Bride, John	"	May 31, '61	Mustered out with company, June 17, 1864.
M'Callough, Joseph Jr	"	May 31, '61	Mustered out with company, June 17, 1864.
M'Creedy, Charles	"	May 31, '61	Mustered out with company, June 17, 1864.
Nield, William J	"	May 31, '61	Mustered out with company, June 17, 1864.
Pidcock, Benjamin	"	May 31, '61	Mustered out with company, June 17, 1864.
Pidcock, Jason	"	Aug. 2, '62	Killed at Cloyd Mountain, May 9, 1864.
Ryan, William	"	May 31, '61	Mustered out with company, June 17, 1864.
Rich, Charles H	"	May 31, '61	Mustered out with company, June 17, 1864.
Solly, William W	"	May 31, '61	Prisoner at Mechanicsville, June 26, 1862. Mustered out with company, June 17, 1864.
Saul, Robert B	"	May 31, '61	Discharged on Surgeon's certificate, Feb. 2, 1863.
Scott, David	"	March 1, '62	Transferred to 54th Regiment, Pa. Vols., July 4, 1864.
Shemaley, Nelson	"	July 16, '61	Wounded at Fredericksburg, Dec. 13, 1862. Transferred to 54th Regiment, Pa. Vols., July 4, 1864. Veteran.
Shaw, William F	"	Sept. 9, '62	Transferred to 54th Regiment, Pa. Vols., July 4, 1864.
Smith, Jacob	"	July 16, '61	Killed at Fredericksburg, Dec. 13, 1862.
Scott, Frederick B	"	May 31, '61	Wounded and missing in action at Mechanicsville, June 26, 1862.
Switzer, Frederick	"	July 15, '61	Missing in action at second Bull Run, Aug. 28, 1862.
Seaver, Samuel	"	May 31, '61	Deserted, Jan. 21, 1862.
Travis, James	"	May 31, '61	Mustered out with company, June 17, 1864.
Thompson, William B	"	May 31, '61	Mustered out with company, June 17, 1864.

COMPANY E—Continued.

NAME.	RANK.	DATE OF MUSTER.	REMARKS.
Toy, Joseph H.	Private	May 31, '31	Transferred to 54th Regiment, Pa. Vols., July 4, 1864. Veteran.
Tomlinson, E. L.	"	July 15, '61	Transferred to 54th Regiment, Pa. Vols., July 4, 1864. Veteran.
Taylor, Hallowell	"	Sept. 27, '62	Transferred to 54th Regiment, Pa. Vols., July 4, 1864.
Toy, Joseph L.	"	May 31, '62	Wounded and missing at Fredericksburg, Dec. 13, 1862.
Vanhorn, George	"	May 31, '61	Mustered out with company, June 17, 1864.
Wilson, Robert	"	May 31, '61	Mustered out with company, June 17, 1864.
Wells, Joseph H.	"	May 31, '61	Mustered out with company, June 17, 1864.
Wright, Richard	"	May 31, '61	Mustered out with company, June 17, 1864.
Williams, Lynford	"	May 31, '61	Prisoner at Fredericksburg, Dec. 13, 1862. Mustered out with company, June 17, 1864.
Wilson, David M.	"	May 31, '61	Wounded at Antietam, Sept. 17, 1862. Discharged on Surgeon's Certificate, Dec. 1, 1863.
Ward, Samuel P.	"	July 15, '61	Transferred to 54th Regiment, Pe. Vols., July 4, 1864. Veteran.
Yonker, Samuel	"	May 31, '61	Wounded at Antietam, Sept. 17, 1862. Discharged on Surgeon's certificate, Oct. 1, 1862.

COMPANY F, RECRUITED IN BERKS COUNTY.

NAME.	RANK.	DATE OF MUSTER.	REMARKS.
Washington Bichards	Captain	June 11, '61	Rank from May 15, 1861. Transferred to Veteran Reserve Corps, July 1, 1863. Resigned, Sept. 5, 1863.
Albert P. Moulton	"	June 11, '61	Rank as 1st Lieutenant from June 1, 1861. Promoted Captain, Sept. 15, 1863. Transferred to Company M, 54th Regiment, Pa. Vols., July 4, 1864.

Name	Rank	Date	Remarks
Henry S. Moulton	1st Lieutenant		Promoted to 2d Lieutenant, Oct. 1, 1862; to 1st Lieutenant, Sept. 15, 1863. Mustered out with company, June 17, 1864.
Albert H. Jamison	2d Lieutenant	June 11, '61	Rank from June 1, 1861. Promoted to Adjutant, June 24, 1861.
Edward K. Mull	"	June 11, '61	Promoted 2d Lieutenant, Feb. 26, 1862. Resigned, July 26, 1862.
Benjamin D. Hemming	"	June 11, '61	Promoted 2d Lieutenant, Aug. 20, 1863. Mustered out, Sept. 27, 1864.
Isaac Addis	Sergeant	June 11, '61	Detached to Batery G, 1st Pa. Reserve Vol. Artillery Corps. Discharged, Dec. 4, 1862.
Daniel Murphy	"	June 11, '61	Wounded. Discharged, March 4, 1863.
Leir Hoffmaster	"	June 11, '61	Discharged on Surgeon's certificate, Dec. 9, 1862.
Robert Smith	"	June 20, '61	Transferred to 54th Regiment, Pa. Vols, July 4, 1864. Veteran.
John Vandorn	"	June 11, '61	Transferred to 54th Regiment, Pa. Vols, July 4, 1864. Veteran.
Edward Clater	"	June 11, '61	Prisoner at Gaines' Mill. Transferred to 54th Regiment, Pa. Vols, July 4, 1864. Veteran.
James M. Phillips	"	June 11, '61	Transferred to 54th Regiment, Pa. Vols, July 4, 1864. Veteran.
John M. Biery	"	June 11, '61	Transferred to 54th Regiment, Pa. Vols, July 4, 1864. Veteran.
George Able	Corporal	June 11, '61	Mustered out with company, June 17, 1864.
Levan Lehr	"	June 27, '61	Mustered out with company, June 17, 1864.
Wellington Miller	"	June 11, '61	Mustered out with company, June 17, 1864.
John P. Douth	Musician	June 11, '61	Mustered out with company, June 17, 1864.
Calvin Reedy	"	June 11, '61	Appointed Musician, Oct. 1, 1861. Mustered out with company, June 17, 1864.
Andy, John	Private	June 20, '61	Prisoner at Gaines' Mill. Mustered out, Oct. 27, 1865, to date June 17, 1864.
Adler, Charles	"	July 18, '61	Transferred to 54th Regiment, Pa. Vols, July 4, 1864. Veteran.
Adams, Jesse		June 20, '61	Transferred to 54th Regiment, Pa. Vols, July 4, 1864. Veteran.

COMPANY F—Continued.

NAME.	RANK.	DATE OF MUSTER.	REMARKS.
Acker, Henry	Private	June 20, '61	Killed at Fredericksburg, Dec. 13, 1862.
Brown, John	"	June 11, '61	Wounded at Gaines' Mill, June 27, 1862. Transferred to Veteran Reserve Corps, July 1, 1863.
Bard, John L	"	June 20, '61	Discharged on Surgeon's certificate, Sept. 1, 1862.
Butz, William P	"	June 20, '61	Discharged on Surgeon's certificate, Feb. 6, 1863.
Bowman, Henry	"		Discharged on Surgeon's certificate, May 13, 1863.
Blose, Edward	"	July 21, '61	Transferred to 54th Regiment, Pa. Vols., July 4, 1864. Veteran.
Beechart, Levi	"	July 17, '61	Transferred to 54th Regiment, Pa. Vols., July 4, 1864. Veteran.
Bernheisel, Levi	"	June 11, '61	Transferred to 54th Regiment, Pa. Vols., July 4, 1864. Veteran.
Borman, William	"		Transferred to 54th Regiment, Pa. Vols., July 4, 1864. Veteran.
Boger, Henry	"	June 27, '61	Transferred to Company K, Oct. 2, 1861.
Becker, John A	"	July 18, '61	Died at Mill Creek, Va., Sept. 19, 1862.
Burkhart, Henry	"	June 11, '61	Killed on picket, July 10, 1862.
Bellas, Joseph	"	June 27, '61	Taken prisoner at Gaines' Mill. Deserted, Oct. 12, 1862.
Conner, Joseph	"	June 11, '61	Wounded at Gaines' Mill, June 27, 1862. Mustered out with company, June 17, 1864.
Christman, Allen	"	July 20, '61	Wounded at Gaines' Mill, June 27, 1862. Transferred to 54th Regiment, Pa. Vols., July 4, 1864. Veteran.
Cooper, Jacob	"	June 11, '61	Deserted, July 23, 1861.
Eisenboth, Henry	"	July 20, '61	Discharged by order of War Dep't, Aug. 6, 1862.
Ecknold, Henry	"	June 11, '61	Transferred to 54th Regiment, Pa. Vols., July 4, 1864. Veteran.
Filbert, Daniel	"	June 27, '61	Wounded at Gaines' Mill, June 27, 1862. Discharged, June 20, 1862.

Name	Rank	Date	Remarks
Gilbert, Adam	Private	June 11, '61	Mustered out with company, June 17, 1864.
Gangwer, Andrew	"	June 20, '61	Transferred to 54th Regiment, Pa. Vols., July 4, 1864.
Glennose, James	"	July 20, '61	Transferred to 54th Regiment, Pa. Vols., July 4, 1864.
Hartzel, James	"	June 28, '61	Mustered out with company, June 17, 1864.
Heming, Jacob	"	June 11, '61	Mustered out with company, June 17, 1864.
Haverstick, Rudy	"	June 11, '61	Died at Camp Washington, Easton, Pa., July 10, 1861.
Herbrant, Joseph	"	June 11, '61	Died at Washington, Aug. 24, 1861. Buried in Military Asylum Cemetery.
Harsta, Henry	"	June 11, '61	Killed at Gaines' Mill, June 27, 1862.
Henry, William	"	June 11, '61	Deserted, July 1, 1863.
Hogan, Mark	"		Died at Philadelphia, Oct. 7, 1862.
House, John	"		Deserted, July 9, 1861.
Helbrick, Joseph	"		Deserted, July 9, 1861.
Jones, William	"	June 27, '61	Wounded. Discharged, Feb. 1, 1863.
Jones, Henry	"	June 11, '61	Killed at Antietam, Sept. 17, 1862.
Jennings, Charles	"	July 22, '61	Transferred to 54th Regiment, Pa. Vols., July 4, 1864. Veteran.
Killpatrick, Edward	"	June 11, '61	Wounded at Gaines' Mill, June 27, 1862. Transferred to Veteran Reserve Corps, July 1, 1863.
Killpatrick, Theo	"	June 11, '61	Transferred to 54th Regiment, Pa. Vols., July 4, 1864. Veteran.
Kochel, Thomas	"	June 11, '61	Transferred to 54th Regiment, Pa. Vols., July 4, 1864. Veteran.
Killian, John H.	"	June 20, '61	Killed at Gaines' Mill, June 27, 1862.
Kline, Manassah	"	June 20, '61	Derserted—date unknown.
Kelly, John	"	June 11, '61	Deserted, Oct. 7, 1861.
Labold, Willouby	"	June 20, '61	Mustered out with company, June 17, 1864.
Lippi, Pompelius	"	June 30, '61	Mustered out with company, June 17, 1864.
Lutz, Harrison	Corporal	June 11, '61	Wounded in thigh at Gaines' Mill. Mustered out, Oct. 27, 1865, to date June 17, 1864.
Leese, James	Private	June 20, '61	Killed at Antietam, Sept. 17, 1862. Buried in National Cemetery at Antietam, grave No. 145, lot B, section 26.
Leh, Franklin	"	July 8, '61	Deserted, Dec. 12, 1862.
Miles, Samuel	"	June 11, '61	Mustered out with company, June 17, 1864.

COMPANY F—Continued.

NAME.	RANK.	DATE OF MUSTER.	REMARKS.
Mertz, Eugene	Private	June 28, '61	Transferred to 54th Regiment, Pa. Vols., July 4, 1864. Veteran.
Mier, Adam	"	June 11, '61	Transferred to 54th Regiment, Pa. Vols., July 4, 1864. Veteran.
Mertz, Monroe	"	June 20, '61	Deserted, Dec. 12, 1862.
M'Farland, I. L. D.	"	June 20, '61	Killed at Fredericksburg, Dec. 13, 1862.
Neal, George S.	"	June 11, '61	Transferred to 54th Regiment, Pa. Vols., July 4, 1864. Veteran.
Nunemacher, W.	"	June 20, '61	Transferred to 54th Regiment, Pa. Vols., July 4, 1864. Veteran.
Ruth, Josephus	"	July 18, '61	Discharged on Surgeon's certificate, Dec. 1, 1862.
Rambo, Alexander	"	June 11, '61	Transferred to 54th Regiment, Pa. Vols., July 4, 1864. Veteran.
Rusk, Peter	"	July 18, '61	Killed at Antietam, Sept. 17, 1862.
Ruhle, John	"	June 11, '61	Deserted, July 2, 1861.
Reed, Cyrus	"	July 20, '61	Prisoner at Gaines' Mill. Deserted, Dec. 12, 1862.
Rohrer, Andrew	"	Feb. 26, '62	Not on muster-out roll.
School, John	"	June 11, '61	Mustered out with company, June 17, 1864.
Silbeman, John	"	June 11, '61	Mustered out with company, June 17, 1864.
Schneer, Levi	"	June 11, '61	Transferred to 54th Regiment, Pa. Vols., July 4, 1864. Veteran.
Stotz, William H.	"	June 20, '61	Transferred to 54th Regiment, Pa. Vols., July 4, 1864. Veteran.
Seidere, John	"	June 28, '61	Killed at Gaines' Mill, June 27, 1862.
Stadler, John	"	July 20, '61	Deserted, July, 1861.
Seidere, Joseph	"	July 24, '61	Deserted, Oct. 12, 1862.
Sweeney, Hugh	"	July 15, '61	Prisoner at Gaines' Mill. Deserted, Dec. 12, 1862.
Stallnecker, John H.	"	July 18, '61	Deserted, Dec. 12, 1862.
Tonis, William	"	June 20, '61	Mustered out with company, June 17, 1864.

Name	Rank	Date	Remarks
Tracy, Michael	Private	July 20, '61	Discharged by Sentence of General Court Martial, Oct. 28, 1862.
Trexler, John	"	July 12, '61	Transferred to 54th Regiment, Pa. Vols., July 4, 1864. Veteran.
Tice, Lewis B	"	June 11, '61	Deserted, July 1, 1861.
Trapold, Jacob	"	June 11, '61	Deserted, July 28, 1861.
Walters, William	"	June 11, '61	Discharged on Surgeon's certificate, Sept. 1, 1862.
Weber, Adam	"	June 27, '61	Prisoner at Gaines' Mill. Transferred to 54th Regiment, Pa. Vols, July 4, 1864. Veteran.
Wentzel, John	"	July 12, '61	Transferred to 54th Regiment, Pa. Vols., July 4, 1864.
Wild, Edward	"	July 20, '61	Deserted, Aug. 9, 1861.
Whiteneck, Jacob	"	June 11, '61	Deserted, Aug. 25, 1862.
Zetze, Adolph	"	June 11, '61	Transferred to 54th Regiment, Pa. Vols., July 4, 1864. Veteran.

COMPANY G, RECRUITED IN PHILADELPHIA.

Name	Rank	Date	Remarks
R. H. Woolworth	Captain	June 1, '61	Promoted to Major, June 21, 1861.
Hugh Harkins	"	June 1, '61	Rank as 1st Lieutenant from June ——. Promoted to Captain, June 27, 1861. Discharged, July 22, 1863.
John Stanton	"	June 1, '61	Rank as 2d Lieutenant from June ——. Promoted 1st Lieutenant, June 27, 1861; to Captain, Jan. 6, 1864. Mustered out with company, June 17, 1864.
Francis E. Harrison	1st Lieutenant	July 10, '61	Promoted to 2d Lieutenant, Dec. 13, 1861; to 1st Lieutenant, Jan. 6, 1864. Mustered out with company, June 17, 1864.
John Connolly	2d Lieutenant	June 1, '61	Promoted to 2d Lieutenant, June 27, 1861. Died at Camp Pierpont, Va., Dec. 2, 1861.
George W. Unrugh	1st Sergeant	June 1, '61	Promoted to 1st Sergeant, Dec. 1, 1862. Mustered out with company, June 17, 1864.
Jacob H. Unrugh	"	June 1, '61	Promoted to 1st Sergeant, April 1, 1862. Discharged, Nov. 29, 1862, for wounds received at Glendale, June 30, 1862.
James Rider	Sergeant	June 1, '61	Mustered out with company, June 17, 1864.

(41)

COMPANY G—Continued.

NAME.	RANK.	DATE OF MUSTER.	REMARKS.
Benjamin D. Bowles	Sergeant	June 1, '61	Promoted to Corporal, Dec. 1, 1862; to Sergeant, Jan. 1, 1863. Mustered out with company, June, 17, 1864.
William Moore	"	June 1, '61	Promoted to Sergeant, July 1, 1863. Mustered out with company, June 17, 1864.
D. Schenerman	"	June 1, '61	Promoted to Sergeant, July 1, 1863. Mustered out with company, June 17, 1864.
John Smith	"	June 1, '61	Promoted to Corporal, April 1, 1862; to Sergeant, July 29, 1862. Wounded and taken prisoner at Gaines' Mill. Wounded at Fredericksb'g. Transferred to Veteran Reserve Corps, July 1, 1863.
William Ratcliff	"	June 1, '61	Deserted, July 31, 1861.
Richard Evans	Corporal	June 1, '61	Promoted to Corporal, Aug. 1, 1862. Wounded and prisoner at Fredericksburg. Mustered out with company, June 17, 1864.
William H. Heckroth	"	June 1, '61	Promoted to Corporal, Dec. 1, 1862. Mustered out with company, June 17, 1864.
Thomas Haran	"	June 1, '61	Promoted to Corporal, Dec. 29, 1863. Mustered out with company, June 17, 1864.
Thomas Stoop	"	June 1, '61	Promoted to Corporal, May 1, 1864. Mustered out with company, June 17, 1864.
Edward Toon	"	June 1, '61	Promoted to Corporal, Nov. 27, 1861. Discharged, April 6, 1863, for wounds received at Antietam, Sept. 17, 1862.
Charles A. Doster	"	June 1, '61	Promoted to Corporal, Nov. 27, 1861. Discharged on Surgeon's certificate, Jan. 5, 1863.
Michael Hickey	"	June 1, '61	Promoted to Corporal, Dec. 1, 1862. Wounded and prisoner at Gaines' Mill. Transferred to Veteran Reserve Corps, July 1, 1863.

(42)

Name	Rank	Date	Remarks
Charles Carley	Corporal	June 1, '61	Promoted to Corporal, April 1, 1862. Killed at second Bull Run.
Alexander Park	"	June 1, '61	Promoted to Corporal, July 1, 1863. Wounded and prisoner at Gaines' Mill. Wounded and prisoner at Fredericksburg. Died of Wounds at New Creek, W. Va., May 16, 1864.
Richard Wilson	"	June 1, '61	Killed at Antietam, Sept. 16, 1862. Buried in Antietam National Cemetery, grave No. 144, lot B, section 26.
Tennis Ploid	"	June 1, '61	Deserted, July 31, 1861.
Israel Crocket	Musician	June 1, '61	Deserted, July 30, 1861.
Joseph R. Crumulland	"	June 1, '61	Deserted, June 23, 1861.
Abrams, William	Private	July 17, '61	Wounded in the foot at Glendale. Transferred to Veteran Reserve Corps, July 1, 1863.
Brown, Jeremiah	"	June 1, '61	Mustered out with company, June 17, 1864.
Bott, Joseph	"	June 1, '61	Mustered out with company, June 17, 1864.
Bishop, Alfred	"	June 1, '61	Wounded and prisoner at Fredericksburg. Mustered out with company, June 17, 1864.
Boisbrun, George	"	June 1, '61	Mustered out with company, June 17, 1864.
Bisbing, Samuel	"	June 1, '61	Returned to company from Engineer Corps, June 8, 1864. Mustered out with company, June 17, 1864.
Bisbing, Manuel	"	June 1, '61	Discharged on Surgeon's certificate, Dec. 13, 1862.
Bingham, James	"	June 1, '61	Killed at Antietam, Sept. 17, 1862. Buried in Antietam National Cemetery, grave No. 143, lot B, section 26.
Beglir, John C.	"	July 17, '61	Deserted, July 24, 1861.
Broadnax, Joseph	"	Sept. 4, '6'	Deserted, Jan. 30, 1864. Veteran.
Broadnax, Jeremiah	"	Sept. 4, '6'	Deserted, Dec. 1, 1862.
Crapp, George W	"	June 1, '61	Wounded and prisoner at Gaines' Mill. Mustered out with company, June 17, 1864.
Cowell, Samuel	"	June 1, '61	Wounded and prisoner at Fredericksburg. Transferred to Veteran Reserve Corps. Returned, June 8, 1864. Mustered out with company, June 17, 1864.

COMPANY G—Continued.

NAME.	RANK.	DATE OF MUSTER.	REMARKS.
Crilley, Barnard	Private	June 1, '61	Wounded and prisoner at Fredericksburg. Transferred to Veteran Reserve Corps, July 1, 1863. Returned, April 5, 1864. Mustered out with company, June 17, 1864.
Carr, Elisha A.	"	June 1, '61	Discharged, Oct. 10, 1862, for wounds in the thigh and eye, received at Glendale, June 30, 1862.
Catterson, David H.	"	April 9, '62	Died, Aug. 9, 1862.
Caldwell, Robert	"	Sept. 3, '62	Killed at New Bridge, W. Va., May 10, 1864.
Dodd, William	"	June 1, '61	Mustered out with company, June 17, 1864.
Deal, Charles	"	June 1, '61	Mustered out with company, June 17, 1864.
Duckworth, Samuel	"	June 1, '61	Discharged on Surgeon's certificate, June 10, 1862.
Devlin, John	"	July 14, '61	Wounded at Fredericksburg. Transferred to 54th Regiment, Pa. Vols., July 4, 1864. Veteran.
Dager, Henry	"	Aug. 27, '62	Wounded at Fredericksburg. Transferred to Veteran Reserve Corps, July 1, 1863.
Dunbar, Peter	"	June 1, '61	Killed at Antietam, Sept. 17, 1862.
Duddy, James	"	June 1, '61	Wounded and prisoner at Mechanicsville, June 26, 1862. Died, Dec. 14, 1862, of wounds received at Fredericksburg, Dec. 13, 1862.
Dutton, Thomas	"	June 1, '61	Deserted, July 30, 1861.
Filmore, Richard	"	June 1, '61	Deserted, June 12, 1861.
Guiger, Christopher B.	"	June 1, '61	Discharged, April 3, 1863, for wounds received in the foot at Fredericksburg.
Heckroth, Henry W.	"	June 1, '61	Mustered out with company, June 17, 1864.
Howie, John	"	June 1, '61	Mustered out with company, June 17, 1864.
Hartley, Charles	"	July 10, '61	Mustered out with company, June 17, 1864.
Hacket, Charles	"	June 1, '61	Discharged on Surgeon's certificate, Aug. 14, 1862.
Hong, Alfred W.	"	July 14, '61	Discharged, Jan. 27, 1863, for wounds received at Bull Run, Aug. 29, 1863.

Name	Rank	Date	Remarks
Henreatty, John	Private	Oct. 4, '62	Deserted, December 1, 1862.
Jones, Jacob	"	June 1, '61	Mustered out with company, June 17, 1864.
Jobbins, Thomas	"	June 1, '61	Died at Grafton, W. Va., April 27, 1864.
Kennedy, George W	"	Sept. 15, '62	Discharged on Surgeon's certificate, Feb. 2, 1863.
Killan, Mark	"	April 1, '62	Transferred to Veteran Reserve Corps, July 1, 1863.
Kreer, Joseph	"	June 1, '61	Transferred to Gunboat Service, Feb. 15, 1862.
Kelley, John	"	July 14, '61	Transferred to 54th Regiment, Pa. Vols., July 4, 1864.
Lutz, Conrad	"	Sept. 2, '62	Discharged on Surgeon's certificate, Feb. 2, 1863.
Long, Robert	"	July 24, '61	Transferred to 54th Regiment, Pa. Vols., July 4, 1864.
Murter, Robert J	"	June 1, '61	Mustered out with company, June 17, 1864.
Margerum, Lewis	"	June 1, '61	Mustered out with company, June 17, 1864.
Murphy, John	"	June 1, '61	Discharged, Dec. 30, 1862, for wounds received at Bull Run, Aug. 30, 1862.
Murray, James	"	June 1, '61	Discharged, Feb. 6, 1863, for wounds received at Antietam, Sept. 17, 1862.
Maguire, John	"	July 10, '61	Discharged on Surgeon's certificate, Feb. 4, 1862.
Mitchell, Thomas	"	Sept. 3, '62	Transferred to 54th Regiment, Pa. Vols., July 4, 1864.
Martz, Adam	"	July 16, '61	Died at Camp Pierpont, Va., Nov. 30, 1861.
Mitchell, R. J. B.	"	Sept. 8, '62	Wounded and prisoner at Cloyd Mountain, W. Va., May 9, 1864.
M'Millen, John	"	June 1, '61	Mustered out with company, June 17, 1864.
M'Grath, Mark	"	June 1, '61	Transferred to Veteran Reserve Corps, July 1, 1863. Returned, April 5, 1864. Mustered out with company, June 17, 1864.
M'Devitt, Charles	"	July 14, '61	Discharged, Oct. 31, 1862, for wounds received at Glendale, June 30, 1862.
M'Gittigan, Hugh	"	June 1, '61	Transferred to company A, July 29, 1861.
M'Donald, Stewart	"	Sept. 3, '62	Transferred to 54th Regiment, Pa. Vols., July 4, 1864.
M'Cloud, David	"	June 1, '61	Died at Camp Pierpont, Va., Dec. 4, 1861.
Noble, George	"	Sept. 16, '62	Transferred to 54th Regiment, Pa. Vols., July 4, 1864.
Newcamp, John	"	June 1, '61	Transferred to 54th Regiment, Pa. Vols., July 4, 1864. Veteran.
Ogden, Edward	"	June 1, '61	Deserted, July 24, 1861.
Porter, James	"	June 1, '61	Mu- ered out with company, June 17, 1864.
Praul, Henry	"	June 1, '61	Discharged—date unknown.

COMPANY G—Continued.

NAME.	RANK.	DATE OF MUSTER.	REMARKS.
Piffer, David	Private	June 1, '61	Mustered out with company, June 17, 1864.
Presgrave, John	"	June 1, '61	Mustered out with company, June 17, 1864.
Pearley, John A	"	June 1, '61	Discharged, Nov. 8, 1862, for wounds received at Bull Run, Aug. 30, 1862.
Rahn, George	"	June 1, '61	Mustered out with company, June 17, 1864.
Schank, Adam	"	June 1, '61	Mustered out with company, June 17, 1864.
Stone, Thomas	"	June 1, '61	Mustered out with company, June 17, 1864.
Sullivan, Dennis	"	June 1, '61	Mustered out with company, June 17, 1864.
Sample, William M	"	June 1, '61	Transferred to 54th Regiment, Pa. Vols., July 4, 1864.
Swift, Joseph	"	Sept. 2, '62	Killed accidentally, at Grafton, W. Va., Apr. 16, 1864.
Smith, John K	"	June 1, '61	Died, July 11, 1862, at Richmond, Va., of wounds received at Gaines' Mills, June 27, 1862.
Smith, Peter	"	July 8, '61	Deserted, June 5, 1862.
Trumbower, W. H	"	June 1, '61	Mustered out with company, June 17, 1864.
Trumbower, S. Z	"	June 1, '61	Discharged on Surgeon's certificate, Dec. 31, 1861.
Ubil, William B	"	Aug. 26, '61	Died at Sharpsburg, Md., Oct. 12, 1862.
Wallace, John	"	June 1, '61	Mustered out with company, June 17, 1864.
Winton, Hamilton	"	June 1, '61	Mustered out with company, June 17, 1864.
Wurst, Frederick H	"	June 1, '61	Mustered out with company, June 17, 1864.
Walters, William H	"	June 1, '61	Mustered out with company, June 17, 1864.
Wilson, John	"	June 1, '61	Transferred to Veteran Reserve Corps.
Wells, Frederick	"	June 1, '61	Deserted, July 31, 1861.

COMPANY H, RECRUITED IN BUCKS COUNTY.

NAME.	RANK.	DATE OF MUSTER.	REMARKS.
Joseph Thomas	Captain	June 18, '61	Resigned, July 6, 1862.
Benjamin F. Fisher	"	June 18, '61	Detached to Signal Corps, Aug. 27, 1861. Promoted Captain, July 7, 1862. Appointed Chief Signal Officer and Colonel U. S. A.

Name	Rank	Date	Remarks
J. B. Bartholomew	1st Lieutenant	June 18, '61	Promoted from 1st Sergeant to 2d Lieutenant, Jan. 1, 1862; to 1st Lieutenant, July 7, 1862. Mustered out with company, June 17, 1864.
Nelson Applebach	2d Lieutenant	June 18, '61	Resigned on account of physical disability, Dec. 9, 1861.
William M'Carty	"	June 18, '61	Promoted from 1st Sergeant to 2d Lieutenant, July 7, 1862. Detached, May 30, 1864, to command 61st, Company Veterans, Third Brigade, Second Division, Dep't West Virginia.
Andrew J. Adrian	1st Sergeant	June 18, '61	Mustered out with company, June 17, 1864.
Ephraim Case	"	June 18, '61	Killed at Antietam, Sept. 17, 1862.
J. H. F. A. Christern	Sergeant	June 18, '61	Mustered out with company, June 17, 1864.
Jesse Keller	"	June 28, '61	Mustered out with company, June 17, 1864.
Isaac E. Lewis	"	June 18, '61	Died of wounds at Alexandria, Sept. 24, 1862. Grave No. 1,598.
George W. Vaux	"	June 18, '61	Wounded and prisoner at Cloyd Mountain, W. Va., May 9, 1864.
Hugh O. Connell	Corporal	June 29, '61	Mustered out with company, June 17, 1864.
Augustus Neiffer	"	June 29, '61	Mustered out with company, June 17, 1864.
Marshall Darling	"	June 18, '61	Mustered out with company, June 17, 1864.
Daniel Frankenfield	"	June 18, '61	Discharged and re-enlisted in Battery C, 5th U. S. Art., Nov. 29, 1862.
Nathan Hauch	"	June 29, '61	Discharged on Surgeon's certificate, Jan. 20, 1863.
Rozell M. Gaylord	"	June 22, '61	Transferred to Veteran Reserve Corps.
Jackson Bachman	"	June 18, '61	Died at Fortress Monroe, Sept. 21, 1862.
Israel Long	"	June 29, '61	Died of wounds received at Cloyd Mountain, May 9, 1864.
Harvey Alabach	"	June 18, '61	Killed at Glendale, June 30, 1862.
Levi Frey	"	June 29, '61	Deserted, Feb. 6, 1863.
C. Kluman	Musician	June 18, '61	Mustered out with company, June 17, 1864.
William Burnes	"	June 29, '61	Transferred to Company I, July 1, 1861.
Albright, John	Private	June 18, '61	Discharged. Re-enlisted in Battery C, 5th U. S. Artillery, Nov. 24, 1862.
Brey, Adam S	"	June 18, '61	Absent, sick, at muster out.
Beidlingmoyer, C	"	July 15, '61	Absent, sick, at muster out.

(47)

COMPANY H—Continued.

NAME.	RANK.	DATE OF MUSTER.	REMARKS.
Boone, Allen	Private	July 8, '61	Discharged on Surgeon's certificate, Nov. 21, 1862.
Burnes, Lewis	"	April 10, '62	Discharged on Surgeon's certificate, Feb. 24, 1863
Bushnell, Samuel A	"	July 29, '61	Transferred to 54th Regiment, Pa. Vols., July 4, 1864. Veteran.
Barth, Frederick R	"	June 18, '61	Transferred to 54th Regiment, Pa. Vols., July 4, 1861. Veteran.
Brown, Lewis	"	June 18, '61	Killed at Antietam, Sept. 17, 1862.
Beidleman, Theodore	"	July 21, '61	Deserted, Aug. 12, 1861.
Bushnell, Samuel A	"	June 27, '61	Deserted, March 22, 1864; returned, April 8, 1864; mustered out with company, June 17, 1864.
Crib, William	"	July 29, '61	Discharged on Surgeon's Certificate, Oct. 16, 1862.
Crater, Jacob B	"	June 18, '61	Killed at Antietam, Sept. 17, 1862.
Dougherty, William	"	June 29, '61	Absent, sick, at muster out.
English, Emanuel	"	July 20, '61	Discharged on Surgeon's certificate, Jan. 21, 1863.
Evans William D	"	Sept. 1, '61	Mustered out, Sept. 4, 1864—expiration of term.
Flinn, Peter	"	June 18, '61	Mustered out with company, June 17, 1864.
Fill, John	"	June 29, '61	Transferred to 54th Regiment, Pa. Vols., July 4, 1864.
Foll, John G	"	June 18, '61	Deserted, Sept. 24, 1862.
Gearheart, A. C	"	June 18, '61	Mustered out with company, June 17, 1864.
Greenwood, Lewis	"	Sept. 2, '62	Transferred to 54th Regiment, Pa. Vols., July 4, 1864.
Gerbron, Joseph	"	Sept. 2, '62	Transferred to 54th Regiment, Pa. Vols., July 4, 1864.
Gerlach, Charles	"	June 15, '61	Deserted, May 26, 1863.
Huff, Frederick	"	June 18, '61	Mustered out with company, June 17, 1864.
Huver, James	"	July 20, '61	Mustered out with company, June 17, 1864.
Houseworth, Josiah	"	July 20, '61	Mustered out with company, June 17, 1864.
Hertle, Michael	"	June 18, '61	Absent, sick, at muster out.
Hendricks, Hil'y O	"	June 18, '61	Discharged on Surgeon's certificate, Nov. 20, 1863.
Hager, John S	"	Oct. 10, '62	Transferred to 54th Regiment, Pa. Vols., July 4, 1864.
Huff, Andrew	"	June 29, '61	Killed at Bull Run, Aug. 30, 1862.

(48)

Name	Rank	Date of muster into service	Remarks
Jones, James	Private	July 9, '61	Discharged on Surgeon's certificate, Dec. 2, 1862. Re-enlisted March 31, 1864. Transferred to 54th Regiment, Pa. Vols., July 4, 1864.
Keeler, Joshua	"	June 18, '61	Mustered out with company, June 17, 1864.
Kerns, Joseph	"	Aug. 6, '62	Transferred to 54th Regiment, Pa. Vols., July 4, 1864.
Keiser, Jesse	"	June 29, '61	Died at Alexandria, Va., Jan. 13, 1862.
Keiser, Adam	"	June 29, '61	Killed at Gaines' Mill, June 27, 1862.
Ladshaw, Abram	"	June 29, '61	Mustered out with company, June 17, 1864.
Lambenstine, John	"	June 18, '61	Mustered out with company, June 17, 1864.
Long, Washington	"	Oct. 28, '62	Transferred to 54th Regiment, Pa.Vols., July 4, 1864.
Longenbucher, G.	"	June 18, '61	Died at Harrisburg, Pa., Jan. 28, 1862.
Milloy, Daniel	"	Sept. 15, '62	Discharged on Surgeon's certificate, Sept. 9, 1863.
Martin, John	"	Sept. 3, '62	Transferred to 54th Regiment, Pa. Vols., July 4, 1864.
Miller, Jeremiah	"	July 9, '61	Deserted, Dec. 11, 1862.
Miller, William	"	June 18, '61	Deserted, Dec. 22, 1862.
Uhl, John W.	"	Sept. 18, '62	Discharged on Surgeon's certificate, Jan. 18, 1863.
Peters, Theodore C.	"	June 18, '61	Discharged on Surgeon's certificate, Feb. 11, 1863.
Pennypacker, J.	"	Sept. 27, '62	Transferred to 54th Regiment, Pa. Vols., July 4, 1864.
Reed, James A.	"	June 29, '61	Mustered out with company, June 17, 1864.
Reiter, Benjamin	"	June 18, '61	Mustered out with company, June 17, 1864.
Reiter, George W.	"	June 29, '61	Transferred to 54th Regiment, Pa. Vols., July 4, 1864. Veteran.
Reed, Milton	"	March 27, '62	Transferred to 54th Regiment, Pa. Vols., July 4, 1864.
Roberts, A. J.	"	June 18, '61	Killed at Bull Run, Aug. 29, 1862.
Reiter, George W.	"	July 29, '61	Deserted, Dec. 29, 1863.
Rebman, George	"	Aug. 30, '62	Not on muster-out roll.
Scheetz, Milton	"	June 18, '61	Mustered out with company, June 17, 1864.
Small, John S.	"	June 29, '61	Mustered out with company, June 17, 1864.
Seifert, Charles G.	"	June 18, '61	Mustered out with company, June 17, 1864.
Shively, John	"	July 16, '61	Discharged on Surgeon's certificate—date unknown.
Straum, Owen M.	"	Sept. 8, '62	Transferred to Veteran Reserve Corps, July 29, 1863.
Shilb, Frederick	"	June 18, '61	Transferred to 54th Regiment, Pa. Vols., July 4, 1864.
Snable, Jeremiah	"	July 20, '61	Transferred to 54th Regiment, Pa. Vols., July 4, 1864. Veteran.

COMPANY H—Continued.

NAME.	RANK.	DATE OF MUSTER.	REMARKS.
Small, John	Private.	June 29, '61	Transferred to Western Gunboat Service, Feb. 28, 1862.
Schaarschmidt, E.	"	June 29, '61	Deserted, Dec. 17, 1862.
Stouffer, Jacob I.	"	June 18, '61	Missing in action at Gaines' Mill, June 27, 1862.
Sellers, Frank	"	June 18, '61	Killed at Fredericksburg, Dec. 13, 1862.
Thomas, George	"	June 18, '61	Died at Washington, Aug. 24, 1861. Buried in Military Asylum Cemetery.
Trumbower, John	"	June 18, '61	Transferred to 54th Regiment, Pa. Vols., July 4, 1864.
Trumbower, John	"	July 29, '61	Deserted, March 22, 1864.
Walp, Charles J.	"	June 29, '61	Mustered out with company, June 17, 1864.
Wenkoldt, J. F.	"	June 29, '61	Mustered out with company, June 17, 1864.
Wile, Michael	"	July 9, '61	Mustered out with company, June 17, 1864.
Willuner, Jesse	"	June 29, '61	Mustered out with company, June 17, 1864.
Weider, Wayne F.	"	June 18, '61	Discharged on Surgeon's certificate, Mar. 5, 1863.
Wissinger, Christian	"	June 18, '61	Discharged on Surgeon's certificate, Feb. 11, 1863.
Wissinger, Daniel	"	June 13, '61	Discharged on Surgeon's certificate, May 25, 1863.
Warner, Stephen	"	July 20, '61	Transferred to 54th Regiment, Pa. Vols., July 4, 1864. Veteran.
Worthington, George	"	June 18, '61	Transferred to Signal Corps, Aug. 27, 1861.
Warner, Stephen	"	July 29, '61	Deserted, Mar. 22, 1864.
Yeakel, John K.	"	Aug. 17, '62	Transferred to Veteran Reserve Corps, July 29, 1863.
Yolter, Martin	"	June 29, '61	Transferred to 54th Regiment, Pa. Vols., July 4, 1864.
Yeakel, Samuel K.	"	Aug. 28, '62	Transferred to 54th Regiment, Pa. Vols., July 4, 1864.
Zainer, Levi	"	June 29, '61	Discharged on Surgeon's certificate, Apr. 27, 1862.
Zimmerman, Lewis	"	June 18, '61	Transferred to 54th Regiment, Pa. Vols., July 4, 1864. Veteran.
Zimmerman, Lewis	"	July 29, '61	Deserted, Mar. 22, 1864.

COMPANY I, RECRUITED IN BUCKS COUNTY.

Name	Rank	Date	Remarks
H. Clay Beatty	Captain	May 29, '61	Killed at Bull Run, Aug. 30, 1862.
Samuel J. LaRue	"	May 29, '61	Promoted from 1st Lieutenant to Captain, Oct. 1, 1862. Mustered out with company, June 17, 1864.
Samuel Beatty	1st Lieutenant	May 29, '61	Promoted from 2d to 1st Lieutenant, Oct. 1, 1862. Mustered out with company, June 17, 1864.
J. Hutchinson	2d Lieutenant	May 29, '61	Promoted to Corporal, Oct. 1, 1861; to 1st Sergeant, Nov. 1, 1861; to 2d Lieutenant, Oct. 1, 1862. Mustered out with company, June 17, 1864.
Samuel P. Banes	1st Sergeant	May 29, '61	Promoted from Corporal to Sergeant, Oct. 1, 1862; to 1st Sergeant, Mar. 7, 1863. Mustered out with company, June 17, 1864.
Joel Chester	"	May 29, '61	Killed at Glendale, June 30, 1862.
Joseph M. Read	Sergeant	May 29, '61	Wounded at Antietam. Not on muster-out roll.
Edward Richards	"	May 29, '61	Promoted from Corporal to Sergeant, Oct. 1, 1862. Mustered out with company, June 17, 1864.
Albert Gardner	"	May 29, '61	Discharged on Surgeon's certificate, Oct. 14, 1862.
Thomas C. Leet	"	July 17, '61	Transferred to 54th Regiment, Pa. Vols, July 4, 1864.
John Ferris	"	May 29, '61	Transferred to 54th Regiment, Pa. Vols, July 4, 1864. Veteran.
Irvine C. Wright	"	May 29, '61	Promoted to Commissary Sergeant, Nov. 1, 1862.
Robert Booz	"	May 29, '61	Died, June 18, 1862.
Howard Reeder	"	May 29, '61	Deserted, Aug. 30, 1862.
Lewis Holt	Corporal	May 29, '61	Promoted to Corporal, Oct. 1, 1862. Mustered out with company, June 17, 1864.
Simon C. Moorhead	"	May 29, '61	Promoted to Corporal, Oct. 1, 1862. Mustered out with company, June 17, 1864.
Nathan Harkness	"	May 29, '61	Promoted to Corporal, Oct. 1, 1862. Mustered out with company, June 17, 1864.
William H. Cooper	"	May 29, '61	Promoted to Corporal, Mar. 1, 1863. Mustered out with company, June 17, 1864.
William L. Allen	"	May 29, '61	Promoted to Corporal, July 1, 1863. Mustered out with company, June 17, 1864.
Lewis W. Gilkeson	"	May 29, '61	Discharged on Surgeon's certificate, Dec. 24, 1861.

COMPANY I—Continued.

NAME.	RANK.	DATE OF MUSTER.	REMARKS.
George S. Silbert	Corporal	Sept. 5, '62	Discharged on Surgeon's certificate, Jan. 2, 1863.
Charles Grovat	"	May 29, '61	Discharged, Feb. 10, 1863, for wounds received at Bull Run, Aug. 30, 1862.
Jacob Coombs	"	May 29, '61	Transferred to Regimental Band, Oct. 1, 1861. Died—date unknown.
William W. Smith	"	Sept. 25, '62	Killed at Fredericksburg, Dec. 13, 1862.
William Whitely	Musician	May 29, '61	Mustered out with company, June 17, 1864.
William Burns	"	July 29, '61	Discharged, July 21, 1862.
James K. P. Barry	"	Dec. 10, '61	Transferred to 54th Regiment, Pa. Vols., July 4, 1864.
Arrison, Jonathan	Private	May 29, '61	Mustered out with company, June 17, 1864.
Anderson, William B.	"	May 29, '61	Mustered out with company, June 17, 1864.
Akers, William A.	"	May 29, '61	Discharged on Surgeon's certificate, April 9, 1862.
Andrews, Samuel	"	July 17, '61	Discharged on Surgeon's certificate, Oct. 10, 1862.
Allen, Charles S.	"	July 20, '61	Mustered out, July 26, 1864—expiration of term.
Allen, Edward	"	May 29, '61	Transferred to Company D, Oct. 1, 1861.
Booz, Charles	"	May 29, '61	Mustered out with company, June 17, 1864.
Brelsford, William	"	Sept. 25, '61	Not on muster-out roll.
Bushnell, Samuel A.	"	May 29, '61	Transferred to Company C, July 1, 1861.
Banes, Roadman	"	May 29, '61	Transferred to Signal Corps, April 7, 1864. Discharged—date unknown. Re-enlisted.
Bradon, Joseph	"	Sept. 25, '61	Transferred to 54th Regiment, Pa. Vols., July 4, 1864.
Burgion, John	"	Sept. 3, '62	Transferred to 54th Regiment, Pa. Vols., July 4, 1864.
Benfer, John L.	"	Sept. 3, '62	Transferred to 54th Regiment, Pa. Vols., July 4, 1864.
Clark, William	"	May 29, '61	Discharged on Surgeon's certificate, Jan. 10, 1862.
Carlin, Charles	"	May 29, '61	Discharged on Surgeon's certificate—date unknown.
Carr, Thomas	"	Aug. 30, '62	Transferred to Veteran Reserve Corps, July 29, 1863.
Coppel, Joseph	"	July 17, '61	Transferred to 54th Regiment, Pa.Vols., July 4, 1864.
Cummings, William	"	May 29, '61	Died at Philadelphia, Feb. 19, 1863.
Clark, Benjamin	"	May 29, '61	Killed at Fredericksburg, Dec. 13, 1862.

Name	Rank	Date	Remarks
Curran, Daniel	Private	May 29, '61	Deserted, June 10, 1863.
Donkel, John	"	July 20, '61	Discharged by sentence of General Court Martial for desertion, Feb. 6, 1862.
Dorran, Duval	"	May 29, '61	Promoted to Commissary Sergeant, June 1, 1861.
Douglass, John M	"	May 29, '61	Deserted, Aug. 30, 1862.
Erich, John	"	May 29, '61	Mustered out with company, June 17, 1864.
Fennemore, Thomas	"	July 17, '61	Killed at Glendale, June 30, 1862.
Force, George W	"	Aug. 13, '62	Died, Dec. 12, 1863.
Geathers, Mahlon	"	July 17, '61	Transferred to 54th Regiment, Pa. Vols., July 4, 1864.
Garwood, Allen L	"	Aug. 13, '62	Transferred to 54th Regiment, Pa. Vols., July 4, 1864.
Gibson, Tolbert	"	Sept. 25, '61	Deserted, Oct. 1, 1861.
Geary, Charles	"	Sept. 5, '62	Deserted—date unknown.
Guy, Robert E	"	July 21, '61	Deserted—date unknown.
Gosline, Richard	"	Sept. 13, '61	Not on muster-out roll.
Hunter, John	"	May 29, '61	Mustered out with company, June 17, 1864.
Hellings, Edward	"	May 29, '61	Discharged, Dec. 17, 1862, for wounds received at Glendale, June 30, 1862.
Hall, Williams	"	Sept. 25, '61	Discharged on Surgeon's certificate, Oct. 11, 1862.
Harkens, Albert	"	May 29, '61	Discharged on Surgeon's certificate, Feb. 4, 1863.
Highland, Eugene	"	Sept. 25, '61	Transferred to 54th Regiment, Pa. Vols., July 4, 1864.
Howell, F. B	"	March 20, '62	Transferred to 54th Regiment, Pa. Vols., July 4, 1864.
Hare, John	"	Feb. 23, '64	Transferred to 54th Regiment, Pa. Vols., July 4, 1864.
Jacoby, Edward C	"	May 29, '61	Mustered out with company, June 17, 1864.
Johnson, Charles	"	May 29, '61	Deserted, Dec. 11, 1862. Returned, May 5, 1863. Mustered out, Aug. 23, 1864, to date June 17, 1864.
Jolly, James M	"	Sept. 5, '61	Transferred to 54th Regiment, Pa. Vols., July 4, 1864. Veteran.
Johnson, David P	"	May 29, '61	Transferred to 54th Regiment, Pa. Vols., July 4, 1864. Veteran.
Knight, William G	"	July 17, '61	Discharged—date unknown.
Kennedy, George E	"	May 29, '61	Deserted, April 13, 1862.
Landreth, Edward	"	May 29, '61	Mustered out with company, June 17, 1864.
Leeti, Samuel H	"	May 29, '61	Transferred to 54th Regiment, Pa. Vols., July 4, 1864. Veteran.

COMPANY I—Continued.

NAME.	RANK.	DATE OF MUSTER.	REMARKS.
Lashels, John L.	Private	Sept. 25, '61	Transferred to 54th Regiment, Pa. Vols., July 4, 1864.
La Rue, Manuel	"	July 22, '61	Deserted—date unknown.
Leeson, James	"	May 29, '61	Deserted—date unknown.
Mackie, Hugh	"	May 29, '61	Mustered out with company, June 17, 1864.
Moorehead, T. J	"	May 29, '61	Transferred to Western Gun-boat service.
Miles, Thomas	"	July 22, '61	Discharged on Surgeon's certificate, Oct. 14, 1862.
Mooney, E. W.	"	May 29, '61	Discharged on Surgeon's certificate, March, 1863.
Miltenberger, C.	"	July 22, '61	Killed at Gaines' Mill, June 27, 1862.
Martin, John D.	"	May 29, '61	Deserted—date unknown.
M'Kenna, Michael	"	March 2, '64	Not on muster-out roll.
Nelson, Alexander	"	Sept. 25, '61	Discharged on Surgeon's certificate, Feb. 4, 1863.
Newcamp, John	"	June 1, '61	Transferred to Company G, Oct. 1, 1861.
Nelson, William H.	"	May 29, '61	Wounded and Prisoner at Cloyd Mountain, May 9, 1864. Died at Andersonville, Sept. 21, 1864. Grave 9,434, National Cemetery, Andersonville.
Oesterben, George	"	May 29, '61	Transferred to 54th Regiment, Pa. Vols., July 4, 1864. Veteran.
Ogelby, Isaac	"	Aug. 22, '62	Transferred to 54th Regiment, Pa. Vols., July 4, 1864.
Peters, Caleb	"	July 29, '61	Transferred to 54th Regiment, Pa. Vols., July 4, 1864.
Rue, James W.	"	May 29, '61	Mustered out with company, June 17, 1864.
Roberts, Mahlon	"	May 29, '61	Discharged on Surgeon's certificate, Feb. 4, 1863.
Ryon, Charles M.	"	July 20, '61	Transferred to 54th Regiment, Pa. Vols., July 4, 1864.
Richardson, S. V.	"	July 19, '61	Transferred to 54th Regiment, Pa. Vols., July 4, 1864. Veteran.
Rodamaker, William	"	Sept. 15, '61	Transferred to 54th Regiment, Pa. Vols., July 4, 1864. Veteran.
Reading, James	"	Sept. 25, '61	Died of wounds received at Glendale, June 30, 1862.
Schaeffer, John	"	May 29, '61	Mustered out with company, June 17, 1864.
Stackhouse, William	"	May 29, '61	Mustered out with company, June 17, 1864.

Name	Rank	Date of enlistment	Remarks
Subers, Edward	Private	May 29, '61	Mustered out with company, June 17, 1864.
Stumsfelts, Christian	"	May 29, '61	Discharged, Oct. 6, 1862, for wounds received at Glendale, June 30, 1862.
Smith, Joseph	"	Sept. 5, '61	Transferred to 54th Regiment, Pa. Vols., July 4, 1864.
Synnamon, H.	"	Aug. 29, '61	Transferred to Company B, 54th Regiment, Pa. Vols., July 4, 1864.
Synnamon, Thomas	"	Aug. 29, '61	Transferred to Company B, 54th Regiment, Pa. Vols., July 4, 1864.
States, Abraham	"	Aug. 29, '61	Transferred to 54th Regiment, Pa. Vols., July 4, 1864.
Smith, William	"	May 29, '61	Killed at Bull Run, Aug. 30, 1862.
Scott, John T.	"	July 22, '61	Killed at Fredericksburg, Dec. 13, 1862.
Shock, Henry T.	"	Sept. 5, '62	Killed at Fredericksburg, Dec. 13, 1862.
Severns, Allen	"	Sept. 25, '61	Died at Harrisburg—date unknown.
States, William	"	Sept. 23, '61	Not on muster-out roll.
Torry, William	"	May 29, '61	Discharged on Surgeon's certificate, Dec. 25, 1862.
Tarpy, John	"	Sept. 25, '61	Transferred to 54th Regiment, Pa. Vols., July 4, 1864.
Thomas, James	"	May 29, '61	Died, June 3, 1864, at Washington, D. C., of wounds received at Cloyd Mountain, W. Va., May 9, 1864.
Vansant, William	"	May 29, '61	Mustered out with company, June 17, 1864.
Welch, Michael	"	May 29, '61	Mustered out with company, June 17, 1864.
Wilson, Ebenezer	"	May 29, '61	Mustered out with company, June 17, 1864.
Wofter, Frank R.	"	July 29, '61	Discharged on Surgeon's certificate, Oct. 10, 1862.
Whicher, Henry C.	"	May 29, '61	Discharged on Surgeon's certificate, Feb. 27, 1862.
Wilkie, Samuel	"	May 29, '61	Discharged on Surgeon's certificate, Feb. 4, 1863.
Welsh, John	"	Sept. 25, '61	Transferred to 54th Regiment, Pa. Vols., July 4, 1864.
Wright, John	"	Sept. 16, '62	Transferred to 54th Regiment, Pa. Vols., July 4, 1864.
Ward, James	"	May 29, '61	Deserted, Dec. 4, 1862.
Wilson, Henry	"	March 11, '64	Not on muster-out roll.
Wright, Robert E.	"	July 29, '61	Deserted—date unknown.

COMPANY K, RECRUITED IN PHILADELPHIA.

NAME.	RANK.	DATE OF MUSTER.	REMARKS.
Horatio G. Sickel	Captain	May 27, '61	Promoted to Colonel, June 21, 1861.
William Brian	"	May 29, '61	Appointed Captain, July 5, 1861. Discharged for wounds received at Fredericksburg, Feb. 15, 1863. Appointed Captain V. R. C., Sept. 15, 1863.
David Wonderly	"	May 27, '61	Promoted to 1st Lieutenant, Feb. 1, 1863; to Captain, Sept. 16, 1863. Discharged on Surgeon's certificate, May 23, 1864.
David W. Donaghy	1st Lieutenant	May 27, '61	Discharged on Surgeon's certificate, Jan. 27, 1863.
Thomas C. Spackman	"	July 11, '61	Promoted to Corporal, Mar. 1, 1862; to Sergeant, July 31, 1862; to 1st Sergeant, Aug. 1, 1862; to 2d Lieutenant, Feb. 1, 1863; to 1st Lieutenant, Sept. 16, 1863. Mustered out with company, June 17, 1864.
John M. James	2d Lieutenant	May 27, '61	Promoted to Sergeant, Mar. 1, 1862; to 1st Sergeant, Mar. 1, 1863; to 2d Lieutenant, Sept. 16, 1863. Mustered out with company, June 17, 1864.
William Krause	1st Sergeant	May 27, '61	Promoted to Corporal, Aug. 19, 1862; to Sergeant, Dec. 10, 1862; to 1st Sergeant, Nov. 1, 1863. Killed, accidentally, June 7, 1864.
Randolph Williamson	Sergeant	May 27, '61	Promoted to Corporal, March 1, 1862; to Sergeant, December 11, 1862. Mustered out with company, June 17, 1864.
Gabriel L. Todd	"	May 27, '61	Promoted to Corporal, Aug. 1, 1862; to Sergeant, March 1, 1863. Mustered out with company, June 17, 1864.
Edward Wood	"	May 27, '61	Promoted to Corporal, Oct. 17, 1862; 1st Sergeant, July 1, 1863. Mustered out with company, June 17, 1864.

Name	Rank	Date	Remarks
Robert D. D. Brian	Sergeant	March 1, '62	Promoted to Corporal, Oct. 17, 1862; 1st Sergeant, Dec. 26, 1863. Transferred to 54th Regiment, Pa. Vols., July 4, 1864.
William P. Smith	"	May 27, '61	Promoted to Sergeant, Feb. 28, 1863; to Sergeant-Major, March 1, 1863.
William H. Brian	"	July 29, '61	Promoted to Corporal, March 1, 1862; to Sergeant, Dec. 10, 1862. Deserted, May 25, 1863.
Thomas Kane	Corporal	May 27, '61	Promoted to Corporal, Dec. 10, 1862. Mustered out with company, June 17, 1864.
James Brooke	"	May 27, '61	Promoted to Corporal, Dec. 10, 1862. Mustered out with company, June 17, 1864.
Charles Morgan	"	May 27, '61	Promoted to Corporal, Dec. 10, 1862. Mustered out with company, June 17, 1864.
Wm. H. Lewis	"	May 27, '61	Promoted to Corporal, Feb. 8, 1862. Transferred to Battery C, 5th U. S. Artillery, Dec. 9, 1862.
Charles Brook	"	May 27, '61	Discharged on Surgeon's certificate, Dec. 11, 1861.
William Dennison	"	May 27, '61	Promoted to Corporal, Aug. 6, 1861. Discharged Dec. 7, 1862, for wounds received in action.
William Hazlett	"	July 18, '61	Promoted to Corporal, Dec. 1, 1861. Discharged on Surgeon's certificate, Nov. 2, 1862.
Owen Jones	"	May 27, '61	Promoted to Corporal, March 1, 1862. Discharged on Surgeon's certificate, Dec. 2, 1862.
George M. Sailor	Private	May 27, '61	Promoted to Corporal, Dec. 1, 1861. Discharged on Surgeon's certificate, Feb. 10, 1862.
Matthew Jordon	"	May 27, '61	Promoted to Corporal, Dec. 10, 1862. Transferred to 54th Regiment, Pa. Vols, July 4, 1864. Veteran.
William Brittain	"	May 27, '61	Promoted to Corporal, Feb. 8, 1862. Killed at Antietam, Sept. 17, 1862.
Francis Conner	Musician	May 27, '61	Mustered out with company, June 17, 1864.
Aldworth, John	Private	May 27, '61	Mustered out with company, June 17, 1864.
Adair, Samuel M.	"	July 13, '61	Transferred to 54th Regiment, Pa. Vols, July 4, 1864.
Adams, Joseph	"	May 27, '61	Deserted, Dec. 4, 1862.
Boger, Henry D.	"	June 27, '61	Mustered out with company, June 17, 1864.
Bryant, Joseph	"	May 27, '61	Transferred to Veteran Reserve Corps, Dec. 2, 1863.

COMPANY K—Continued.

NAME.	RANK.	DATE OF MUSTER.	REMARKS.
Brown, Stephen	Private	May 27, '61	Mustered out with company, June 17, 1864.
Bender, John F	"	May 27, '61	Discharged on Surgeon's certificate, Feb. 26, 1863.
Bechtel, John	"	May 27, '61	Discharged on Surgeon's certificate, July 26, 1862.
Brockway, John	"	May 27, '61	Transferred to 54th Regiment, Pa. Vols., July 4, 1864. Veteran.
Black, James	"	July 16, '61	Transferred to Veteran Reserve Corps, July 29, 1863.
Buck, Isaac G	"	July 9, '61	Transferred to 54th Regiment, Pa. Vols., July 4, 1864.
Bows, Dennis	"	July 17, '61	Transferred to 54th Regiment, Pa. Vols., July 4, 1864.
Bressler, John	"	July 11, '61	Transferred to 54th Regiment, Pa. Vols., July 4, 1864. Veteran.
Barr, Joseph	"	May 27, '61	Died, Nov. 26, 1862
Beck, Augustus	"	July 17, '61	Deserted, Aug. 1, 1862.
Beaumont, John B	"	May 27, '61	Deserted, Aug. 22, 1862.
Clayton, James W	"	May 27, '61	Mustered out with company, June 17, 1864.
Clayton, Henry M	"	May 27, '61	Mustered out with company, June 17, 1864.
Collins, John	"	May 27, '61	Mustered out with company, June 17, 1864.
Carr, Edwin A	"	May 27, '61	Mustered out with company, June 17, 1864.
Conway, William	"	Sept. 4, '62	Transferred to 54th Regiment, Pa. Vols., July 4, 1864. Veteran.
Carpenter, John B	"	July 16, '61	Deserted, Aug. 25, 1861.
Callahan, Hugh	"	May 27, '61	Deserted, June 20, 1861.
Devitt, Henry B	"	May 27, '61	Promoted to Corporal, July 1, 1861; to Sergeant, Dec. 1, 1861—reduced. Discharged on Surgeon's Certificate, Aug. 7, 1863.
De Baufre, William	"	July 29, '61	Discharged on Surgeon's certificate, April 12, 1862.
Eckard, George W	"	May 27, '61	Mustered out with company, June 17, 1864.
Evins, Christopher	"	May 27, '61	Mustered out with company, June 17, 1864.
Fisher, Albert D	"	May 27, '61	Mustered out with company, June 17, 1864.
Frazier, Alexander	"	May 27, '61	Deserted, Aug. 22, 1862.

Name	Rank	Date	Remarks
Ferguson, David	Private	July 16, '61	Deserted, July 19, 1861.
Gosler, Isaiah S.	"	May 27, '61	Deserted, June 10, 1863.
Haynes, William H.	"	May 27, '61	Mustered out with company, June 17, 1864.
Helfricht, George I.	"	May 27, '61	Absent, sick, at muster-out.
Hopper, Jacob	"	May 27, '61	Discharged on Surgeon's certificate, Feb. 27, 1863.
Humison, Hiram	"	July 17, '61	Discharged on Surgeon's certificate, Dec. 25, 1861.
Handerhill, Daniel	"	July 17, '61	Deserted, July 26, 1861.
Hanold, Charles	"	May 27, '61	Deserted, Dec. 12, 1862.
Jones, David	"	May 27, '61	Mustered out with company, June 17, 1864.
Jaquett, Joseph	"	May 27, '61	Mustered out with company, June 17, 1864.
Loag, James	"	Sept. 6, '62	Transferred to 54th Regiment, Pa. Vols., July 4, 1864.
Leonard, Thomas	"	May 27, '61	Killed by gun-shot while in discharge of duty, Apr. 2, 1862.
Lenay, John	"	May 27, '61	Deserted, Sept. 16, 1862; arrested, Oct. 8, 1863; deserted again, July 6, 1864.
Lantz, Jacob	"	May 27, '61	Discharged on Surgeon's certificate—date unknown.
Morgan, George W.	"	May 27, '61	Mustered out with company, June 17, 1864.
Mitchell, Lemuel	"	May 27, '61	Missing in action at Fredericksburg, Dec. 13, 1862.
Mooney, Hugh	"	May 27, '61	Deserted, Aug. 25, 1861.
M'Donald, William	"	May 27, '61	Mustered out with company, June 17, 1864.
Nickerson, Joshua	"	May 27, '61	Discharged for wounds received in action.
Neid, John	"	Sept. 4, '62	Transferred to 54th Regiment, Pa. Vols., July 4, 1864.
Painter, William	"	May 27, '61	Discharged on Surgeon's certificate, June 29, 1863.
Phillips, Henry E.	"	May 27, '61	Died at Annapolis, Oct. 11, 1862.
Quick, Abraham J.	"	May 27, '61	Discharged on Surgeon's certificate, Sept. 26, 1862.
Reinboth, George F.	"	May 27, '61	Mustered out with company, June 17, 1864.
Ramler, Leonard	"	May 27, '61	Mustered out with company, June 17, 1864.
Rudolph, Joseph	"	May 27, '61	Killed at Antietam, Sept. 17, 1862.
Sim, Samuel H.	"	May 27, '61	Mustered out with company, June 17, 1864.
Swan, Thomas E.	"	May 27, '61	Mustered out with company, June 17, 1864.
Snyder, Benjamin K.	"	May 27, '61	Reduced from Sergeant. Deserted, Aug. 22, 1862; arrested, Nov. 13, 1863.
Sample, Thomas	"		Discharged on Surgeon's certificate, May 24, 1862.
Schroyer, Wesley	"	July 11, '61	Discharged on Surgeon's certificate, July 25, 1862.
Shaw, W. H. H.	"	May 27, '61	Discharged on Surgeon's certificate, July 28, 1862.

COMPANY K—Continued.

NAME.	RANK.	DATE OF MUSTER.	REMARKS.
Stackhouse, David	Private	May 27, '61	Transferred to 54th Regiment, Pa. Vols, July 4, 1864. Veteran.
Shaw, William H	"	May 27, '61	Transferred to 54th Regiment, Pa. Vols., July 4, 1864. Veteran.
Stern, Valentine	"	July 13, '61	Transferred to 54th Regiment, Pa. Vols., July 4, 1864. Veteran.
Spink, Valentine W	"	Sept. 10, '61	Transferred to 54th Regiment, Pa. Vols., July 4, 1864. Veteran.
Stillman, Thomas	"	May 27, '61	Deserted, Aug. 1, 1862; arrested, Dec. 5, 1863; deserted again, Jan. 6, 1864.
Todd, James A	"	May 27, '61	Mustered out with company, June 17, 1864.
Thomas, George	"	May 27, '61	Discharged on Surgeon's certificate, Dec. 14, 1861.
Ungerbuchler, W	"	May 27, '61	Transferred to Veteran Reserve Corps, Feb. 11, 1864.
Vanhorn, John	"	May 27, '61	Mustered out with company, June 17, 1864.
Watson, Joseph	"	May 27, '61	Mustered out with company, June 17, 1864.
Wilson, Thomas	"	May 27, '61	Mustered out with company, June 17, 1864.
Williams Thomas	"	May 27, '61	Transferred to Veteran Reserve Corps, Oct. 26, 1863.
Wright, Enos L	"	July 29, '61	Discharged on Surgeon's certificate, Nov. 26, 1862.
Wine, George	"	May 27, '61	Discharged on Surgeon's certificate, Oct. 21, 1862.
Wondesland, Peter	"	May 27, '61	Discharged on Surgeon's certificate—date unknown.
White, Thomas	"	July 9, '61	Transferred to 54th Regiment, Pa. Vols., July 4, 1864.
Wright, George	"	July 29, '61	Missing in action at Glendale, June 30, 1862.
Young, Edward	"	May 27, '61	Mustered out with company, June 17, 1864.

UNASSIGNED MEN.

NAME.	RANK.	DATE OF MUSTER.	REMARKS.
Durr, John	Private	March 10, '64	Not on muster-out roll.
Foy, Joseph H	"	Nov. 6, '63	Not on muster-out roll.
White, Thomas S	"	March 10, '64	Not on muster-out roll.

INDEX.

A.

Anderson, G. B., General, 91, 92.
Anderson, Robert, Lieutenant-Colonel, 160, 184.
Alexander, Samuel, Assistant Surgeon, 51.
Amsden's Battery, 207.
Applebach, Nelson, Lieutenant, 26, 57.
Applebachville Guards, 26.
Archer, General, 208, 213, 214.
Averill, William Woods, General, 64, 136, 139, 231, 232, 238, 240, 248, 251, 253.
Ayres, Ira, Jr., Colonel, 96*.
Alabama 10th Regiment, 107.
Alabama 14th Regiment, 112.

B.

Baird, Edward C., Captain and Assistant Adjutant-General, 41, 222, 225.
Baker, Edward D., General, 48.
Bamford, Thomas H., Lieutenant, 134.
Banks, Nathaniel P., General, 72, 80, 142, 143, 146, 147, 167, 180.
Bardwell, George H., Major, 216*.
Barksdale, William, General, 203, 216.
Barlow, Francis C., General, 187.
Barnard, John G., General, 77*.
Barr, Henry, 239.
Barr, Joseph R., 52.
Barnes, General, 192.

Barry, W. F., General, 77*.
Barth, Frederick R., Sergeant, 136.
Bartholomew, J. B., Lieutenant, 57, 134, 247.
Bates, Samuel P., Professor, 36, 103, 104, 107, 108.
Battery A, 33, 42.
" B, 33, 42, 46.
" C, 33.
" D, 33.
" E, 33.
" F, 33.
" G, 33, 42.
" H, 33.
Battle of Allen's Farm, 97.
" Antietam, 180.
" Bull Run, First, 28.
" Bull Run, Second, 147.
" Chantilly, 165.
" Cloyd Mountain, 244.
" Drainesville, 53.
" Fair Oaks, 77, 80.
" Fredericksburg, 203, 205.
" Gaines' Mill, 87.
" Glendale, 101.
" Malvern Hill, 119.
" Mechanicsville, 80.
" New River Bridge, 249.
" Princeton, 243.
" Savage Station, 98.
" South Mountain, 173.
" Yorktown, 76.
Bayard, George D., General, 42, 47, 51, 60, 70, 72, 211.
Beauregard, P. T. G., General, 19, 28, 46, 63.

INDEX.

Beatty, Estruries, Captain, 42, 60, 71, 110, 116.
Beatty, H. Clay, Captain, 27, 111. 163, 194.
Beatty, Samuel, Lieutenant, 25, 27, 194.
Bender, John F., Sergeant, 136.
Biddle, Chapman, Colonel, 196.
Biddle, Charles J., Colonel, 41, 42. 47, 199.
Biddle, Henry J., Captain and Assistant Adjutant-General, 20, 105, 110.
Bickley, Franklin S., Quartermaster, 26, 27, 49.
Birchfield, John P., Assistant Surgeon, 229.
Birney, David Bell, General, 166. 210, 211.
Bishop, Clark, 239.
Blazer, Lieutenant, 240.
Blenker, Louis, General, 50.
Blundin, James N., Captain, 254.
Boger, Henry D., 67.
Bolinger, H. C., General, 177, 225.
Bonham, General, 51.
Boyer, Charles, 234.
Boyer, Levi S., Quartermaster, 229, 239.
Branch, L. O'B., General, 81, 188.
Breckinridge, John C., General, 249.
Brian, William, Captain, 27, 111, 132, 217, 227.
Briner, Albert, Quartermaster-Sergeant, 194, 227, 229.
Briner, William, Major, 23, 26, 42, 134, 144, 231, 236.
Brooke, James, Sergeant, 227.
Brooks, W. T. H., General, 224.
Brothers, E. F, 239.
Brown, John, 54*, 253*.
Buch, Isaac G., 225.
Buchanan, R. C., 162.

Buchanan, Frank, Commodore, 141.
Buck, Isaac G. 239.
Buckman, Aaron N., Sergeant, 230.
Buckingham, J. M., Lieutenant, 26, 49.
Bucktails, 33, 41, 45, 47, 53, 54, 55, 71, 72, 81, 82, 85, 103, 156, 176, 181, 189, 197, 205, 206.
Buffington, Adjutant, 60.
Buford, John, General, 146.
Burnside, Ambrose E., General, 139, 143, 175, 180, 188, 198, 199, 204, 209, 212, 213, 216, 217, 218, 220, 222, 224.
Butler, Benjamin F., General, 36, 228.
Butterfield, Daniel, General, 169.

C.

Carper, Philip, 51.
Cadwallader, Jacob A., 137.
Caldwell, General, 187.
Cameron, Simon, Hon., 36, 50.
Camp Washington, Pa., 21.
Camp Curtin, Pa., 29.
Camp Piatt, 239.
Camp Pierpont, Va., 45, 50, 64.
Camp Cadwallader, 256.
Camp Hawkhurst, Va., 65.
Camp Tenally, 34, 42.
Campbell, Charles T., Colonel, 42, 47, 60.
Campbell, Jacob Miller, Colonel, 254.
Carondelet, Gun-boat, 62.
Carrier, James W., 67.
Charley Reb., 201.
Childs, James H., Colonel, 82, 102.
Christein, John H. F. A., Sergeant, 136.
Cincinnati Society, 36, 38.
Clark, C. Y., Corporal, 227.

INDEX. 3

Clark, John, Lieutenant-Colonel, 26, 52, 133, 164, 177, 181, 184, 201.
Clark, Robert, Corporal, 136.
Clark, William, 239.
Clouse, Jeremiah A., Lieutenant, 26, 62.
Clow, James B., Captain, 41, 42.
Cobb, Howell, General, 124†.
Cobb, T. R. R., General, 92.
Cochrane, John, General, 224.
Coleman, Thomas, 51.
Collis Zouaves, 210.
Collins, James, Surgeon, 27, 122, 128, 132, 194.
Colquitt, General, 182.
Colston, Henry S., Assistant Surgeon, 133.
Confederate Eagle, 68.
Connally, John, Lieutenant, 26, 52.
Connecticut 18th Regiment, 233, 234.
Conrad, Captain, 109.
Comte de Paris, 46, 91.
Cook, Captain, 175.
Cook, P. St. George, General, 88, 90.
Cooper's Battery, 35, 82, 85, 102, 106, 181, 207.
Cooper, James H., Captain, 42, 46, 109, 160.
Coppeé, Henry, Professor, 42.
Cothrans, Captain, 185.
Couch, Darius W., General, 120, 121, 181, 192, 197, 216.
Cox, Daniel D., General, 174, 175.
Crawford, Samuel Wylie, General, 142, 184, 185, 227, 236.
Crook, George, General, 236, 238, 239, 240, 241, 244, 245, 247, 248, 249, 251.
Cross, Augustus, Adjutant, 173.
Crothers, John H., Lieutenant, 194, 254.
Cummings, Robert P., Colonel, 196.

Curtin, Andrew Gregg, War Governor, 20, 27, 32, 36, 55, 172, 195, 224, 228.
Curtis, William D., Captain, 23, 26, 42, 43, 133.
Cuthbertson, Captain, 108†.
Coleman, Charles, 51.
Cutts, Captain, 54.

D.

Dana, Napoleon J. T., General, 186.
Davenport, George C., Captain, 26, 59, 93, 134, 189, 227.
Davis George B., Lieutenant, 92, 190, 196, 229, 234, 247, 254.
Davis, Jefferson, Hon., 18, 28†, 103, 119.
Davis, William H., Surgeon, 239.
Day, Dr., 51.
De Bow's Review, 28.
DeCaradence, T., Lieutenant, 52.
Dehart, Captain, 82.
Dehon, Lieutenant, 219.
DeKorponay, Gabriel, Colonel, 20, 25.
Derrickson, W. H., 254.
DeSilver Greys, 26.
Dietrich, Captain, 102.
District Columbia 1st Volunteers, 225.
Dix, John A., General, 30.
Donaghy, David W., Lieutenant, 27, 52, 230.
Donnelly, Edward, Surgeon, 122, 128.
Doran, Duvall, Commissary Sergeant, 42.
Doubleday, Abner, General, 148, 153, 181, 182, 183, 184, 207, 224.
Duc de Chartres, 46, 91.
Duckworth, Samuel, 67.
Dunn, Captain, 198.
Dunn, Simon, Sergeant, 110.
Duryea, Abram, General, 177.

E.

Early, Jubal A., General, 208, 232.
Easton, Hezekiah, Captain, 42, 82, 83.
Eberhart, Lieutenant, 225.
Eckle, Sebastian, Lieutenant, 62, 133.
Edwards, Captain, 84.
Ellwood, J., Lieutenant, 31.
Ent, Wellington H., Colonel, 53.
Ewell, R. S., General, 88, 94, 121, 142, 147, 148, 165, 182.

F.

Farley, W., Captain, 51.
Farnsworth, E. J., General, 81.
Feaster, David D., Captain, 26, 42, 70, 71, 193.
Ferguson, Colonel, 237*.
Ferrero, Edward, General, 224.
Finnie, J. O., Captain, 21, 23.
Fisher, Benjamin F., Captain, 26, 35, 134, 225, 226, 227, 228.
Floyd, John B., General, 253*.
Forney, John H., General, 54, 55.
Franklin, William Buell, General, 50, 78, 100, 102, 117, 120, 123, 146, 165, 168, 179, 180, 181, 188, 197, 199, 206, 211, 212, 220, 224.
Frear, George H., Chaplain, 62, 133, 194.
Fredericks, James P., Captain, 41.
Fremantle, Colonel, 77†.
Fremont, John C., General, 142.
French, William H., General, 90, 98, 187, 216.
Frost, Daniel, Colonel, 238, 244.
Fuller, A. B., Rev., 205.

G.

Gallagher, Thomas F., Colonel, 41, 82, 177.
Garland, General, 54, 182.

Garnett, General, 253*.
Geary, John White, General, 143.
Georgia 19th Regiment, 215.
Georgia, 44th Regiment, 85.
Germantown Guards, 26.
Gibbons, John, General, 148, 210, 213, 216.
Gillem, Alvan C., General.
Gilmore, Harry, Major, 233.
Glenn, Edwin A., Lieutenant, 134, 225.
Gordon, George H., General, 186.
Gorman, Willis A., General, 186.
Greeley, Horace, Hon., 93.
Green, George S., General, 184, 185.
Gregg, Maxey, General, 112, 208, 213, 214.
Griffin, Charles, General, 84, 85, 165, 167, 192.
Griffith, Lewis, Sergeant, 227.
Grover, Cuvier, General, 153.
Guernsey, A. H., Doctor, 146, 151, 167.
Gilbert, Albert, 62.
Georgia 2d Infantry, 188.
" 20th " 188.
Grant, U. S., General, 236.

H.

Hooker, Joseph, General, 80, 102, 106, 114, 125*, 135, 136, 147, 148, 165, 171, 175, 176, 177, 181, 182, 183, 184, 186, 199, 206, 211, 216, 224, 226.
Hall, Chandler, Captain, 41, 42.
Halleck, Henry W., General, 138, 139, 218.
Hamilton, Captain, 206, 213.
Hamlin, Lyman W., Lieutenant, 49.
Hampton, Captain, 185.
Hampton, Wade, General, 203.
Hancock, Winfield Scott, General, 216.

Hardie, General, 211*.
Harkins, Hugh, Captain, 27, 229.
Harkness, N. S., 136.
Harmer, William N., Captain, 244.
Harrison, Francis C., Lieutenant, 52, 111, 230, 250.
Harrison, Samuel L., 239.
Hart, James, Major, 73.
Hatch, John P., General, 153, 154, 159.
Hartranft John F., General, 188.
Hartsuff, George L., General, 183.
Harvey, Elisha B., Colonel, 41, 82, 83, 103, 109.
Hayes, Rutherford B., General, 169, 239*.
Hayes, George S., Colonel, 41, 82, 105.
Heenan, Dennis, Colonel, 216*.
Henning, Benjamin D., Lieutenant, 136, 229, 247.
Henderson, R. M., Lieutenant Colonel, 156*.
Henry, Patrick, 63*.
Higgins, Jacob, Lieutenant Colonel, 53.
Hill, A. P., General, 83, 88, 97, 103, 109, 112, 120, 146, 188, 190, 192, 212, 214.
Hill, D. H., General, 83, 88, 121, 171, 174, 190, 203, 209.
Holmes, General, 117.
Hood, John B., General, 154, 182.
Hooker, Joseph, General.
Hoover, Joseph F., 225.
Howard, Oliver, O., General, 185.
Howard, Dr., 136.
Huger, General, 80, 89, 97, 98, 103, 120, 121.
Hughling, Joseph, 51.
Humphrey, Andrew Atkinson, General, 216.

E

Hurlbert, William Henry, 78*.
Hunt, Henry J., General, 95, 97.
Hunter, M., 28†.
Hunter, David, General, 255*.
Hutchinson, Edward, 137.
Hutchinson, Jackson, Lieutenant, 194.
Heintzleman, S. P. General, 50, 64, 80, 97, 111†, 114, 120, 123, 139, 147, 150, 151, 153, 156, 158, 159, 161.
Haupe, General, 201.

I.

Illinois Eighth Cavalry, 81.
Irvin, Edwin A., Captain, 81.

J.

Jackson, Conrad Faeger, General, 41, 53, 55, 82, 102, 106, 144, 154, 199, 205, 210, 219.
Jackson, Thomas Jonathan, General, 72, 80, 84, 88, 97, 102, 120, 121, 139, 143, 146, 147, 148, 149, 150, 151, 153, 159, 165, 166, 168, 172, 180, 182, 190, 206, 209, 214, 215, 216, 217, 218.
James, John M., Lieutenant, 196, 230.
Jamieson, Albert H., Adjutant, 26, 27, 56, 194.
Jenkins, General, 180, 247, 248.
Johnston, Joseph E., General, 28, 63, 80.
Johnson, Robert, Captain, 26, 134, 225, 247.
Jones, D. R., General, 182, 183, 188.
Jones, Harry S., Adjutant, 194, 222, 225, 239.
Jones, Owen, Major, 52.
Jones, W. E., General, 182, 251.
Jones, Zeaman, Lieutenant, 229.

INDEX.

Judson, J. A., Captain, 154.

K.

Kane, Thomas Leiper, General, 53, 54, 72.
Kearney, Philip, General, 102, 110, 114, 124, 148, 153, 166, 211.
Kelley, Benj. F., General, 255*.
Kelley, William D., Hon., 36.
Kennerheim, Captain, 102.
Kern, Mark, Captain, 42, 52, 82, 82, 102, 106.
Kentucky 1st Rifles, 54, **55**.
Keyes, Erasmus D., General, 64, 78*, **95**, 120, 123, 126.
Kimball, Captain, 23.
King, **James** B., Surgeon, **41**.
King, Corporal, 110.
King, John H., General, **72, 142,** 143, **148, 151, 153, 156, 158,** 168.
Kingsberry, Chas., Captain, 41, **91**.
Kirby, C. W., Lieutenant, 239.
Kirk, James Thompson, Colonel, 82, 102.
Knapp, Captain, 185.
Kuhn, **J.** Hamilton, Captain, 41.
Kupp, Morgan, 230.

L.

Lamborne, Charles B., Lieutenant, 41.
Lane, General, 208, 213, 214.
La Rue, Samuel J., Lieutenant, 27, 136, 194, 251.
Lawton, General, 182, 190.
Leak, William H., Chaplain, **27,** 33, 62.
Lee, Robert E., General, 80, 83, 84, 94, 97, 103, 112, 113, 114, **115, 121,** 124, 127, 142, 144, 146, 157, 163‡, 165, 167, 168, **171,** 172, 180, 181, 190, 191, **193**, 203, 206, 212, 217, 226, 236.

Lehman, Jacob, Lieutenant, 26, 45, 111, **132, 133.**
Lenhart, **Jacob, Jr.**, Captain, 23, 26, 222, **236, 238, 245**, 247.
Lennon, Edward L., Sergeant, 79.
Leonard, Thomas, 67.
Lincoln, Abraham, **President,** 17, 18, 19, 30, 50, 63, **132,** 193, **195**, 223.
Lindsey, George H., Lieutenant, 26, 133.
Longstreet, James, General, 83, 88, **97,** 103, 109, 112, 114, 115, **120, 146, 148, 149,** 150, 151, **152, 153, 154, 159,** 167, 168, 169, **174, 175, 178,** 180, 190, 206, **217.**
Loper, Charles H., **Corporal,** 136.
Lowman, **W. G.**, Surgeon, 41.

M.

Maconkey, Eldridge, Lieutenant, 42.
Magilton, Colonel, 82, 172.
Magruder, J. B., 76†, 80, 89, 94*, 97, 98, 112, 114, 120, 121, 127.
Maine 23d Regiment, 225.
Mann, William B., Colonel, 20, **21,** 24, 41.
Mansfield, Joseph K. F., **General,** 36, 181, 184, **185.**
March, Robert G., Colonel, 20, 22, 25, 41.
Marsh, Surgeon, 114.
Martin, Lieutenant-Colonel, 55.
Martz, Adam, 52.
Massachusetts 1st Regiment, 177.
Massachusetts 16th Regiment, 106, **205.**
Massachusetts 34th Regiment, 234.
Masters, James E., Corporal, 79.
Maxwell, H. D., Paymaster, 27.
Maxwell, Judge, 36.
Mayo, Colonel, 110.

Meade, George Gordon, General, 41, 47, 49, 52, 55, 74, 82, 85, 88, 89, 98, 102, 107, 109, 111, 115, 130, 144, 147, 157, 161, 162, 163, 172, 177, 181, 182, 183, 184, 186, 188, 189, 196, 208, 209, 210, 211, 212, 213, 214, 215*, 219, 221, 222, 224, 226, 228.
Meade's Colored Man, 86.
Mealey, Timothy, Captain, 23.
Meagher, Thomas F., General, 90, 91, 120, 122, 187.
Mechanic Infantry, 26.
Michigan 4th Regiment, 84, 89.
Michigan 17th Regiment, 175.
Miles, Dixon S., Colonel, 179.
Mills, Theodore P., Lieutenant, 239.
Minnigerode, Reverend Mr., 78*.
Montgomery Guards, 27.
Moore, Warren G., Lieutenant, 229.
Moore's Rebellion Record, 108.
Moorehead, S. C., Corporal, 227.
Morgan, John, General, 246, 251.
Morrell, George W., General, 87, 99, 169.
Morris, George W., 62.
Moseby, Colonel, 225, 227.
Moulton, Albert P., Captain, 26, 225, 229, 254.
Moulton, Henry S., Lieutenant, 134, 194, 229.
Mulholland, A. St. Clair, Lieutenant-Colonel, 216*.
Mull, Edward K., Lieutenant, 133.
Mulligan, James A., General, 232.
M'Call, George Archibald, General, 24, 25, 32, 33, 34, 35, 36, 37, 40, 42, 47, 48, 49, 52, 53, 55, 71, 73, 83, 84, 85, 95, 98, 99, 100, 102, 103, 107, 108, 110, 111, 114, 115, 116, 123, 137.

M'Calmont, John S., Colonel, 41, 49, 53, 55.
M'Candless, William, General, 81, 82, 104, 154, 159, 210, 218, 225, 226.
M'Carty, William, Lieutenant, 134, 227, 254.
M'Caslin, M., Colonel, 238.
M'Causland, General, 240, 249.
M'Clellan, George B., General, 33, 35, 36, 46, 48, 50, 53, 63, 64, 75, 76, 79, 80, 89, 94, 96, 111, 113, 114, 115, 121, 123, 127, 130, 132, 138, 139, 140, 142, 144, 168, 171, 172, 177, 179, 189, 191, 193, 196, 198.
M'Donough, Captain, 221.
M'Dowell, Irwin, General, 28, 50, 64, 67, 68, 72, 78, 80, 142, 144, 146, 147, 148, 150, 151, 152, 153, 156, 157, 158, 159, 160, 169, 171.
M'Intire, Henry M., Lieutenant Colonel, 79, 110.
M'Laughlin, J. H., Lieutenant, 239.
M'Law, General, 174, 179.
M'Master, James E., 135.
M'Murtrie, Theodore, Adjutant, 104.
M'Neal, Hugh W., Colonel, 189.
M'Pherson, Edward H., Captain, 42.
M'Lean, 160.
M'Kean, Lieutenant-Colonel, 82.
M'Rae, Colonel, 182.

N.

New Jersey 4th Regiment, 89, 91.
"   "   1st Cavalry, 73.
Newton, John, General, 224.
New York, 61st Regiment, 187.
"   "   51st   "   188.
"   "   64th   "   187.

INDEX.

New York 79th Regiment, 175.
" " 153d " 225.
New York World, 146, 151.
Nicholson, Gilbert F., **Lieutenant,** 134, 189, 225.
Niblo, **Frank M., Hospital Sergeant,** 42.
North Carolina 1st Regiment, 84.
" " 19th " 92.
" " 7th " 213.
" " 18th " 213.

O.

Ohio 12th Regiment, 244.
" 116th " 233, 234.
" 123d " 233, 234.
Oley, Colonel, 246.
Ontario Guards, 21, 27.
Ord, E. O. C., **General,** 41, 47, 53, 54, 72, 79*, 235.
Ord, Placides, Captain, 41.
Orr, Samuel S., Assistant Surgeon, 134, 229.

P.

Painter, W., Captain, 41.
Pancoast, George L., Assistant Surgeon, 27.
Patrick, General, 153.
Peck, John J., General, 222.
Pelham, Major, 207*.
Pender, General, 208*.
Pendelton, General, 192.
Pennypacker, N. A., **Captain,** 255, 256.
Pennsylvania 4th **Cavalry,** 82, 88, 102, 110.
Pennsylvania 6th Cavalry, 88.
" 28th Regiment, 143.
" 51st " 188.
" 54th " 254.
" 81st " 133.
" 114th " 210.
" 118th " 133, 192.

Pennsylvania 121st Infantry, 196, 199, 224.
Pennsylvania 142d Regiment, 196, 225.
Pennsylvania 167th **Regiment,** 230.
Phillips, Alfred, 46.
Piatt, Abraham S., General, **165,** 167.
Pickett, General, 91.
Pierpont, Francis H., Governor, 46.
Piper, Doctor, 187.
Pleasanton, Alfred, General, 136, 173, 174, 181, 188, 222, 227.
Pollard's *Lost Cause,* 64, 85, 180.
Pomeroy, John J., **Chaplain, 194,** 218, 247.
Pomeroy, John M., **Paymaster,** 49, 59, 73, 136, 200.
Pope, John, General, 138, 139, 142, 143, 145, 146, 147, 148, 149, 150, 151, 152, 153, 155*, 157, 158, 163, 165, 167, 168, 169, 171.
Porter, Fitz John, General, 50, 77, 80, 85, 87, 88, 89, 95*, 99, 100†, 102, 115, 117, 119, **120,** 121, 123, 124, 127, 147, 150, 151, 152, 153, 156, 158, 160, 161, 162, 165, **168, 169, 170,** 180, 192, 198.
Potomac Lodge, 43.
Prevost, Colonel, 192.
Pryor, Roger A., General, 112.

R.

Randall, Captain, 102, 107, 109, 111.
Ransom, General, 154, 161, 162, 177, 180, 181, 183, 205, 207.
Reed, Thomas B., Surgeon, 69.
Reno, **Jesse L.,** General, 146, 147, 148, 150, 153, 156, 158, 159, 164, 166, 174, 175, 176.

Reserve 1st Cavalry, 42, 47, 49, 51.
" 1st Artillery, 42, 47, 49.
" 1st Rifles, 41.
" 1st Infantry, 154.
" 2d " 83, 104, 105, 144, 154, 156, 176, 206, 214, 215.
Reserve 3d Infantry, 26, 238, 243, 244, 248, 250, 254.
Reserve 4th Infantry, 102, 108, 209, 214, 233, 238, 243, 244, 245, 248, 254.
Reserve 5th Infantry, 81, 84, 104, 105, 106.
Reserve 6th Infantry, 144, 206.
" 7th " 83, 102, 103, 107, 214, 215, 236.
Reserve 8th Infantry, 31, 104, 105, 106, 147, 209, 214, 236.
Reserve 9th Infantry, 104, 106, 206.
" 10th " 104, 106, 205.
" 11th " 89, 91.
" 12th " 104, 105.
Reynolds, John Fulton, General, 41, 47, 49, 55, 73, 75, 78, 79, 82, 85, 88, 91, 98, 102, 137, 138, 144, 150, 153, 154, 156, 158, 159, 160, 161, 162, 163, 196, 206, 207, 211, 224, 226.
Rice, George J., Assistant Surgeon, 134, 229.
Richards, Washington, Captain, 23, 26, 42, 56, 59, 60, 196, 227.
Richardson, Israel B., General, 77, 187, 188.
Richmond Examiner, 86.
Richmond Enquirer, 180*.
Ricketts, W. Wallace, Colonel, 41.
Ricketts, James B., General, 143, 148, 149, 151, 152, 156, 158, 159, 160, 167, 181, 182, 184.
Ringwalt, Samuel, Captain, 41, 59.
Ripley, R. S., General, 124†, 182.

Roberts, Joseph B., Lieutenant, 26, 52, 59, 111, 132, 194.
Roberts, R. Biddle, Colonel, 41, 82, 102, 186, 228.
Rodman, Isaac P., General, 175, 188.
Rogers, John, Commodore, 120.
Rogers, R. S., Colonel, 233.
Rohne, George M., Lieutenant, 222, 225, 229.
Rosecrans, W. S., General, 241.
Ross, Colonel, 227.
Rosser, General, 232.
Roster of the Third Reserve, Appendix B.
Ruffin, Edmund, Honorable, 135.
Rodine, James, 62.
Rose, James, 62.

S.

Salem Independents, 26.
Scammon, Eliakim P., General, 146, 237*.
Scarlet, Roland G., 234.
Schank, Adam, 234.
Scheetz, Henry A., Lieutenant, 26, 42, 60, 110.
Schenck, Robert C., General, 152.
Schooler, Miss, 201.
Second Reading Artillery, 26.
Secrest, Lieutenant-Colonel, 54.
Sedgwick, John, General, 136, 185, 186.
Seifert, Frederick B., 46.
Seitzenger, Amos N., Lieutenant, 134, 229, 254.
Setley, Daniel, Lieutenant, 229.
Seward, William H., Honorable, 50, 72.
Seymour, Truman, General, 79, 85, 95, 98, 102, 105, 106, 111, 118, 130, 132, 133, 144, 154, 161, 162, 163, 176, 181, 182, 183, 184, 186, 187, 199.

Sharp, A. Brady, Lieutenant, 41.
Shelmire, John H., Colonel, 73.
Sheridan, Philip H., General, 225*.
Sherman, William Tecumseh, 86.
Shields, General, 72.
Shilling, Jacob V., Lieutenant, 134, 194, 217.
Sickle, Horatio Gages, General, 21, 23, 26, 27, 29, 33, 35, 41, 42, 43, 69, 77, 81, 82, 83, 89, 103, 108, 118, 120, 122, 130, 133, 135, 144, 147, 155, 164, 172, 194, 199, 209, 210, 218, 222, 224, 225, 226, 231, 236, 238, 243, 244, 245, 249, 250, 254, 255*.
Sigel, Franz, General, 143, 145, 146, 150, 152, 153, 156, 199, 236, 248, 249.
Simmons, Seneca G., Colonel, 37, 41, 81, 82, 91, 104, 105, 111.
Simpson, James H., Colonel, 89.
Simpson, Captain, 205, 206, 207.
Sinclair, William, General, 199, 218.
Salm Salm, Felix, Colonel Prince, 72.
Slough, John P., General, 225.
Slocum, H. W., General, 89.
Smead, Captain, 82.
Smith, John, Captain, 73.
Smith, H. H., Surgeon-General, 36.
Smith, P. I., Captain, 21, 23.
Smith, William F., General, 40, 45, 47, 50, 224.
South Carolina 6th Regiment, 54, 55.
Spackman, Thomas C., Lieutenant, 230.
Spear, Henry S., Lieutenant, 41.
Stanton, David, Surgeon, 51.
Stanton, John, Capt., 26, 136, 230.
Stark, General, 182.

Staub, Florentine H., Captain, 26, 49, 134, 189, 194.
Stetson, Andrew Jackson, Captain, 49, 79, 134, 194.
Stephens, Isaac J., General, 166.
Steward, Samuel S., Lieutenant, 41.
Stocker, Anthony E., Surgeon, 41, 42.
Stone, Roy, Colonel, 81, 82, 103.
Stone, Thomas C., 62.
Stoneman, George, General, 126, 211.
Stout, Charles W., Sergeant, 227.
Strong, H. L., 42.
Stuart, J. E. B., General, 54, 94, 143, 146, 173, 180, 192, 193.
Sturges, General, 175.
Sumner, Edwin V., General, 64, 78*, 97, 102, 120, 123, 165, 168, 181, 185, 186, 187, 188, 192, 199, 203, 206, 220, 224.
Sutton, Harry W., Captain, 194, 229.
Swearenger, Adjutant, 147.
Sweet, Abel T., Captain, 254.
Synnamon, Thomas, 239.
Sykes, George, General, 88, 99, 163, 169.
Sydney, W. B., 79.

T.

Taggart, John H., Colonel, 41, 53, 54, 82, 83, 85, 102, 104, 106.
Taliaferro, General, 208, 213, 214.
Talley, General, 210.
Tapper, Thomas F. B., Colonel, 108, 231, 248.
Taylor, George W., General, 146.
Taylor, J. H., Colonel, 54, 224.
Taylor, Doctor, 206.
Tatnall, Commodore, 141*.
Thomas, Joseph, Captain, 26, 111, 133, 213.

Thomas, Lorenzo, Adjutant-General, 36, 208.
Thompson, William S., Lieutenant-Colonel, 23, 26, 27, 42, 43, 45, 69, 77, 110, 130, 133.
Tillapaugh, James M., Captain, 41.
Toombs, Robert, General, 188.
Tomlinson, A. A., Colonel, 240.
Trego, Howard, Doctor, 136.
Trego, William, Doctor, 136.
Tressel, Franklin, Corporal, 136.
Trimble, J. R., General, 122*, 146.
Trimer, Elwood, 79.
Tripp, Henry C., Sergeant, 42, 227.
Towers, 160.

U.
Uncle Ben, 61.
Union Rifles, 26.
United States 1st Cavalry, 88.
" 5th " 88.
" Battery B, 5th Artillery, 234.
Upjohn, Charles, 215.
Unruh, George W., Sergeant, 136.

V.
Van Renssellear, Colonel, 237*.
Verdigan, Lieutenant, 237*.
Virginia 7th Regiment, 104.
" 9th " 103.
" 11th " 54.
" 14th " 91.
" 15th " 250.
" 16th " 241.
" 17th " 104, 129, 178.
" 18th Cavalry, 136.
" 19th " 252.
" 47th " 110, 201.
" 60th " 243.

W.
Walker, Colonel, 207.
Walker, W. H. J., General, 172, 179.

Warren, Fitz Henry, General, 117.
Walters, Michael, Lieutenant, 134, 217, 227.
Weighter, Frank, 67.
Walters, Miss Marietta, 60.
Ward, General, 211.
Washington Guards, 26.
Washington, Mary, 73.
Watmough, William H., Captain, 41.
Welch, Stanton A., Assistant Surgeon, 229.
West Virginia 5th Regiment, 240, 245.
West Virginia 11th Regiment, 238, 244.
West Virginia 15th Regiment, 238, 245, 255.
White, Carr B., Colonel, 244.
Whiting, George C., 42.
Whitings, General, 121.
Whittee, Peter W., 52.
Wilcox, O. B., General, 113, 175.
Williams, General, 184, 185, 192.
Winder, C. S., General, 143.
Wise, Henry A., General, 114, 237*.
Woodward, E. M., Captain, 21, 23, 26, 82.
Woodward, G. A., Captain, 21, 23, 26.
Woolworth, Rich'd H., Colonel, 26, 27, 209, 231, 233, 238, 245, 247.
Wonderly David, Captain, 27, 35, 230.
Worstall, George, 137.
Woodberry, Colonel, 84.

Y.
Yardley, Strickland, Quartermaster, 26, 49, 194, 229.
Yeich, John R., 136, 234.
Young, Mr., 25.

www.ingramcontent.com/pod-product-compliance
Lightning Source LLC
Chambersburg PA
CBHW030005240426
43672CB00007B/836